COLLEGE SUCCESS

Roberta Moore
Barbara A. Baker
Arnold H. Packer

Prentice Hall, Upper Saddle River, New Jersey 07458

Library of Congress Cataloging-in-Publication Date
Moore, Roberta
    College success / Roberta Moore, Barbara A. Baker, Arnold Packer.
      p. cm.
    Includes index.
    ISBN 0-13-527391-9
    1. College student orientation.   2. Study skills.   I. Baker,
Barbara A.   II. Packer, Arnold H.   III. Title.
LB2343.3.M65   1997
378.1'98--dc20   96-22936
                                                               CIP

Acquisitions editor: *Todd Rossell*
Editorial production supervision: *Barbara Marttine Cappuccio*
Director of manufacturing and production: *Bruce Johnson*
Managing editor: *Mary Carnis*
Manufacturing buyer: *Ed O'Dougherty*
Marketing manager: *Frank Mortimer, Jr.*
Editorial assistant: *Jennifer Collins*
Interior design: *Amy Rosen*
Creative director: *Marianne Frasco*
Formatter: *Stephen Hartner*
Cover design: *Ruta K. Fiorino*
Cover illustration: *David Cutler/Stock Illustration Source*
Director, Image Resource Center: *Lori Morris-Nantz*
Photo resource supervisor: *Melinda Lee Reo*
Image permission supervisor: *Kay Delloso*
Photo researcher: *Sherry Cohen*

 ©1997 by Prentice-Hall, Inc.
Simon & Schuster / A Viacom Company
Upper Saddle River, New Jersey 07458

All rights reserved. No part of this book may be
reproduced, in any form or by any means,
without permission in writing from the publisher.

Printed in the United States of America

10 9 8 7 6 5 4 3 2 1

ISBN 0-13-527391-9

Prentice-Hall International (UK) Limited, *London*
Prentice-Hall of Australia Pty. Limited, *Sydney*
Prentice-Hall Canada Inc., *Toronto*
Prentice-Hall Hispanoamericana, S.A., *Mexico*
Prentice-Hall of India Private Limited, *New Delhi*
Prentice-Hall of Japan, Inc., *Tokyo*
Simon & Schuster Asia Pte. Ltd., *Singapore*
Editora Prentice-Hall do Brasil, Ltda., *Rio de Janeiro*

CONTENTS

PART ONE 1
COLLEGE SUCCESS STRATEGIES

ONE: A SUCCESSFUL START 3

You're in Charge 3
Building Your Self-Esteem 4
Practicing Positive Thinking 5
Understanding Your Learning Styles 7

Challenges and Adjustments 11
Diversity: What Does It Mean? 11
Appreciating and Learning from Diversity 14

Your Educational Goals 15
Ten Goal-Setting Guidelines 16
Your Major 19
Preparing Yourself for Work—SCANS 20
Making the System Work for You 22
Campus Resources and Support Services 24

TWO: TAKING CONTROL OF YOUR TIME 31

Time Management: A System of Control 32
Some Basic Techniques for Getting Organized 32
Make Plans 32
Make Time Projections 32
Prioritize 33
Develop a System 33

Developing a Time Management System 34
Setting Up Schedules 35
Making Out a Schedule for the Term 38
Planning Weekly and Daily Activities 39
Maintaining a To Do List 41

Coping with Procrastination 42
What Really Causes Procrastination 43
Ten Anti-Procrastination Strategies 44

Balancing Acts 45
Family Responsibilities 46
Plan Stress Reduction 46

PART TWO 53
DEVELOPING YOUR STUDY SKILLS

THREE: APPLYING STUDY AND RESEARCH SKILLS TO MASTERY 55

Preparing for Study Sessions 56
A Space Where You Can Study 56
A Space That Works 56
The Importance of Being Rested 59
A Clear Head for Productive Studying 59
Goals for Your Study Session 60

Study Techniques 60
Recite 61
Get a Study Partner 61
Form a Study Group 61
Study According to How You Will Be Tested 62

Developing Your Research Skills 63
Get to Know the Library 63
Plan Your Research 67
Gather the Information 69

FOUR: LEARNING IN THE CLASSROOM 76

A Positive Attitude for Learning 77
Get Rid of Negative Thoughts 77
Connect to Learning 77

Guidelines for Establishing Good Classroom Habits 79
Be Rested 79
Get a Good Seat 79

iii

Don't Sit with Friends   79
  Bring Relevant Materials   80
  Review Notes and Texts   80
  Set Aside Your Assumptions   80
  Attend Class Regularly   80
Active Listening Strategies   81
  Look at the Instructor   82
  Decide to Pay Attention   82
  Listen for Key Ideas and Important Phrases   83
  Pay Attention to Outlines, Formulas, and Data on the Board   83
Take Notes   83
  Listen Critically   84
  Listen to the Very End   84
Class Participation   85
  Ask Questions   85
  Talk to Your Instructor   85
  Talk to Other Students   85
After-Class Review   86
  Review Your Class Notes   86
  Summarize   86
  Coordinate Class Notes with Textbook Notes   86

FIVE: LEARNING THROUGH READING   92

The Case for Active Reading   93
  Active Reading Improves Performance   94
  The Payoff from Active Reading   94
Active Reading Techniques   95
  Know Your Purpose   95
  Preview the Material   96
  Connect New Material to Your Prior Knowledge   97
  Pose Questions and Then Read to Find Answers   97
  Visualize   98
  Use Graphics to Aid Understanding   98
  Reread   101
  Talk It Out   103
  Underline and Highlight   104
  Take Notes   104
  Read Beyond Your Textbook   105
  Pay Attention to Word Hurdles   106
  Chase Away Mental Blocks   106
  Additional Techniques for Specific Subject Matter   106

SIX: WRITING YOUR WAY TO THE TOP   112

Messages That Make Their Point   113
  A Clear Message   113
  A Concise Message   116
  A Considerate Message   116
  Grammar Review   118
A Method for Good Writing   119
  Plan Your Attack   119
  Take a Stab at It (First Draft)   121
  Make It Better (Second Draft...)   122
  Make It Perfect (Final Draft)   122
Specific Writing Assignments   123
  The Journal Entry   124
  The Essay   124
  The Report   125
  The Research Paper   126
Electronic Help for Writers   126
  Word Processing and Desktop Publishing Programs   127
  Electronic Storage   127
  Formatting Capabilities   127

SEVEN: PREPARING FOR AND TAKING TESTS   133

Preparing for Tests   134
Strategies to Help You Win   134
  Schedule Study Time   135
  Develop a Study Plan   135
  Apply Sound Study Techniques   137
Improving Your Memory   138
  Examine Your Attitudes   139
  How Memory Works   139
  Memorization Techniques   141
Test-Taking Strategies   142
  The Day of the Test   142
  Answering Objective Test Questions   143
  Answering Subjective Test Questions   144
  Other Kinds of Tests   145

Handling Test Anxiety 147
Appraising Your Performance 147

PART THREE 153
DEVELOPING YOUR PERSONAL SKILLS

EIGHT: USING CRITICAL THINKING SKILLS 155

Why Critical Thinking Skills Are Important 156
What Is Critical Thinking? 156
  Critical Thinking in Decision Making 157
  Critical Thinking in Problem Solving 157
Critical Thinking Techniques 158
  Question 158
  Interpret 159
  Analyze 160
  Conceptualize 160
  Compare and Contrast 160
  List Advantages and Disadvantages 161
  Synthesize 161
Creative Thinking Techniques 162
  Brainstorm 163
  Discover New Perceptions About Old Ideas 164
  Trust Your Instincts 165
Using Creative Thinking to Solve Problems 165
  Identify the Problem 165
  Narrow the Problem 166
  Develop Alternatives 166
  Weigh/Evaluate Alternatives 167
  Solve the Problem 167

NINE: RELATIONSHIPS 173

Personal Relationships 174
  Nurturing Good Relationships 174
  Handling Relationship Conflicts 174
  Working at Relationships 175
  Assertiveness 177
  Conflict Resolution 179
  Negotiation Skills 179
  Responsibility in Relationships 180

Relationships with Instructors 180
  Getting to Know Your Instructors 181
  Resolving Problems 182
  Accepting Criticism 183
  Dealing with Sexual Harassment 184
Other Relationships on Campus 185
  Valuing Diversity 186
  Communication Skills: A Key to Good Relationships 186
  Leadership Skills: A Key to Good Relationships 187

TEN: TAKING CARE OF YOURSELF 194

Stress and Your Health 195
  Recognizing the Signs of Stress 195
  Reactions to Stress 195
  Handling Stress—Coping Mechanisms 196
Nutrition and Fitness 200
  Healthy Eating 200
  Exercise and Fitness 202
  Body Image 203
A Healthy Lifestyle 204
  Quit Smoking 204
  Avoiding Problems with Alcohol 206
  Avoiding Other Harmful Drugs 206
  Dealing with Drug Abuse 207
  A Safe Sex Life 208

ELEVEN: MANAGING YOUR FINANCIAL RESOURCES 213

Financing Your Education 214
  Employment 214
  Federal and State Loans and Grants 214
  Scholarships and Other Sources 215
Budgeting 216
  Identify Your Spending Habits 216
  Developing a Budget 218
Maintaining Your Financial Health 219
  Deal with Deficits 220
  Use Credit Wisely 220
  Beware of Cash Machines 221
  Pay Bills on Time 221

CONTENTS v

Use Financial Services 222
Read the Fine Print 222
Solve Financial Problems 222

PART FOUR 227
LOOKING TOWARD THE FUTURE

TWELVE: PREPARING FOR YOUR CAREER 229

Resources for Career Planning 230
College Courses 230
Career Planning Center 230
Student Counselors/Advisors 231
Assessment Instruments 231
Online Resources 232

Keeping Your Eye on the Job Market 233
Selecting a Major 233
Preparing for Your Career Outside of the Classroom 234
Requirements for Completing Your Major 235

Developing a Career Plan 236
Goals 236
Activities 236
Timelines 237

Building a Personal Portfolio in College 237
Transcripts 237
Character References 238

Getting Ready for the Job Search 239

INDEX 247

PREFACE

"Any success worth pursuing is a journey, a process, an adventure. And any journey undertaken intelligently requires preparation." This quote comes from a book called *True Success*, written by a professor of philosophy, Tom Morris. It is an interesting way to think about success, because it helps you see its concrete qualities: A journey requires a plan, a process is carried out in stages, and an adventure is a positive experience only if you can meet the challenges of the unexpected.

This text is an important item to have with you as you progress on your journey to success. In fact, taking this course and using the information in this text *can be the most important thing you will do in your college career.* Why? Because this is your opportunity to learn new skills that will help you become a better student and improve your chances of success in the workplace. You can improve your ability to study effectively, increase your personal effectiveness, and have more control over your future. The text offers many useful ideas and strategies, along with tools you can use for personalizing them to suit your individual needs. Read on to find out exactly what this book can help you do.

Improve Study Skills

You will examine the study skills you use now and find out how and why they do or do not work well for you. You will learn new strategies and skills that will help you achieve success as a student.

- Through developing a profile of your *personal learning style*, you will find out how it has helped or hindered your educational performance in the past. You will learn how you can adapt your learning style to different courses and methods used by your instructors and, thus, improve your ability to do well in all of your courses.
- You will learn new ways to use the tools of learning—texts, notes, classroom participation, study time, and test preparation time—to make your classroom and study time pay higher dividends.
- You will learn new strategies that will make you a better listener, reader, and writer.
- You will learn techniques for preparing for tests: how to predict what will be covered on tests; strategies for studying for tests; and techniques for improving your ability to remember what you learn and be confidently prepared on the day of an important examination. You will also learn strategies for taking different kinds of tests and find out what to look for on a test to increase your chances of answering questions quickly and accurately.

Improve Personal Qualities and Skills

Most people who are successful in their careers believe that personal qualities are as important—if not more important—than technical knowledge and skills. But there is no point in arguing which is more important, because they both are. Aiming high in terms of self-development is a decision you have already made or you would not be here. The chapters that cover personal development skills in this text can help you in many ways.

vii

- Recognize the critical thinking skills you use every day and learn to harness the power of the thinking process to analyze information, solve problems, and make better decisions about your coursework, career goals, and personal life.
- Get more control over your life by learning to use time management tools to create a personalized system that prioritizes your activities and helps you balance school, study, work, family, and other responsibilities.
- Create a plan for managing your health and well being. By looking at your lifestyle as a whole and the personal habits that affect how you handle stress, how you keep yourself fit and energetic, and how you may need to change some personal habits that work against you, you will have a basis for making necessary changes that will make you a happier and healthier person.
- Gain insights into dealing with personal relationships and get a better understanding of positive ways to handle conflicts and interact with people to get what you want. You will learn strategies for dealing with instructors, as well as developing relationships with people with whom you share interests and with people whose backgrounds and life experiences are different from your own.
- Learn strategies for financing your education and handling your personal finances so that money is not a source of stress in your life, but a tool to help you achieve your goals and work toward financial security.

Prepare for Success in the Workplace

One of the advantages of college is that it prepares you for "the real world"—a world in which you are expected to perform competently and to take responsibility for "getting the job done." Throughout this text you will encounter the acronym, SCANS. It stands for Secretary's Commission on Achieving Necessary Skills. Teachers and students alike need to believe that what they are teaching and learning truly matters. And what matters most today, both inside and outside of the classroom, is the ability to perform according to standards that will ensure workplace success. The SCANS commission talked to business owners, public employers, managers, union officials, and to workers on the line and at their desks. The message they received was the same across the country and in every kind of job: good jobs depend on people who can put knowledge to work. Workers must be creative and responsible problem solvers and have the skills and attitudes on which employers can build.

Each chapter in this text relates what you are learning to *workplace know-how* identified by SCANS research. The specific skills and competencies are outlined in detail in Chapter 1, and you will find related information and applications in each chapter of the book (see the chart on page xii). The goal of SCANS can be summarized as follows: Workplace know-how = high workplace performance = success for both the employee and the employer.

How to Use This Book

College Success is divided into four parts. Part I, College Success Strategies, has two chapters that are important to getting started. Chapter 1 focuses on coming to terms with your self image and attitudes about learning. It also contains some thoughts about adjusting to the role of a student and guidelines to help you think through your short-term and long-term goals. Chapter 2 has important information on organizing yourself and developing a time management system that works for you. Part II, Developing Your Study Skills, covers a range of skills that are critical to your success as a student: studying and research, classroom learning, reading, writing, and taking tests. Part III, Developing Your Personal Skills, focuses on areas that are critical to school, work, and life in general. Chapters in this part cover using critical thinking skills, handling relationships, taking care of your health and well being, and managing your personal finances. Part IV, Looking Toward the Future, presents ideas about what you should be doing while in college to ensure your readiness to go after and achieve your career goals.

You may read all or parts of these chapters, depending on what is assigned by your instructor and what you feel is important to you. Whether you use all of the information now or come back to some of it at a later date, there is much here that will help you throughout your college career. You may want to start off by reading on your own Chapter 5, the chapter that covers strategies for active reading and getting the most out of your textbooks, so that you can begin right away to apply good reading strategies to this book.

Each chapter has many features that will aid your learning and provide interesting and enjoyable ways to apply the information. Here are some suggestions on how to use these tools.

Journal College Success has "guided" journal entries where you are asked to stop and make notes or write about some specific topic in the text. For your convenience, space to write is provided in the book. If you are a more prolific writer, you may want to keep a separate notebook journal. The ideas and information in your journal will be useful to you as you plan goals and develop your personal success strategies.

Self-Assessments These little "self-tests" provide an opportunity for you to analyze yourself in a specific area. They offer guidance on future directions, depending on the results of your "test." You will find the Self-Assessments fun to do and also fun to share with classmates, friends, or a partner at home. It can be very enlightening to find out how the perceptions of someone who knows you differ from your perceptions of yourself.

Review and Recall These questions may be used as a self-testing tool. As you answer the questions, make notes in the margin on things you want to go back and review in the chapter. You can also use them again when preparing for tests and quizzes.

Apply Critical Thinking When you read Chapter 8 on critical thinking, you will gain insight into the strategies you are practicing as you do these activities. They are" thinking exercises," giving you a chance to practice solving problems, analyzing and interpreting information, and using other thinking skills that will help you sharpen your ability to reason and make good judgments.

SCANS Applications

These applications are designed to help you acquire the basic skills, workplace competencies, and personal qualities outlined by the SCANS commission. As you approach these applications, review the SCANS list in Chapter 1 and refer to the SCANS chart to refresh your memory.

School to Work Applications These applications help you develop specific workplace competencies by doing activities related to this course. You will be able to see how the SCANS skills are transferable from one situation to another. For instance, while working with your classmates on a project you can practice one of the key SCANS workplace competencies: working successfully as a member of a team.

Workplace Applications These applications are based on actual situations you might encounter on a job. Some of them you will do alone; others you will do as a group project. Again, you are getting valuable experience in thinking through situations and performing tasks that are based on research of what employers want.

Personal Progress Applications These applications show you how information in the text can be applied toward developing the SCANS personal qualities of responsibilities, self-esteem, sociability, self-management, and integrity/honesty. They also give you strategies for using and applying what you learn in each chapter on an ongoing basis.

College Success takes into account that individual needs are unique. It does not try to come up with "one size fits all" formulas and prescriptions. You may or may not accept certain theories, ideas, values, or advice that are presented. All of these are here for you to evaluate and adapt to your personal needs and abilities. The more you can personalize the strategies, the greater the benefit you will get from them over the long term. And, when you finish this course, keep this book and the materials you develop at hand. It is likely that you will need to "brush up" on some of the information and skills as you face new and different challenges each year of your college career.

Supplements

Instructor's Manual A complete package of resource material, including syllabus, course outline, and scheduling guidelines; course teaching tips; material for supplementing classroom lectures and activities, including class exercises, discussions, and/or demonstrations, homework suggestions, and resources; transparency masters; and keys and teaching suggestions coordinated to the end-of-chapter applications.

Power Point Software For classroom presentation.

NCS Testing Program A career assessment inventory that compares individual occupational interests and personality preferences with hundreds of careers.

Acknowledgments

We would like to thank the instructors who assisted us with reviews of the text during its development: Barbara L. Cheek, Pierce College, Washington; Elizabeth Davidson, Passaic County College, New Jersey; and Thomas S. Tyson, SUNY at Stony Brook, New York. Acknowledgment is also given to the instructors who contributed information and expert advice: Susan Chin, DeVry Institute of Technology, Georgia; Kevin Dohrenwend, Middlesex County College, New Jersey; Scott Drakalich, Essex County College, New Jersey; Richard Glazer, Westchester Community College, New York; Carol Lindquist, Manhattan Community College, New York; and Earl Wilke, Pennsylvania Institute of Technology, Pennsylvania.

We are also grateful to the professionals at Prentice Hall for their expertise, guidance, and support: Editors, Elizabeth Sugg and Todd Rossell; Production Editor, Barbara Cappuccio; Creative Director, Marianne Frasco; Marketing Manager, Frank Mortimer. Jr.; and Editorial Assistant, Jennifer Collins.

We extend special thanks and acknowledgment to Jeff King, Professor, College Success course, The Art Institute of Dallas, for his assistance with and material contributions to the *College Success* text and instructor's manual.

Roberta Moore
Barbara A. Baker

TO THE INSTRUCTOR

SCANS Applying Scans

In the Spring of 1990, then Secretary of Labor, Elizabeth Dole, created the Secretary's Commission on Achieving Necessary Skills or SCANS. Many of the members came from industry—typically vice presidents for human resources. Representatives from labor, teaching, and government also served along with two eminent cognitive scientists. William Brock, a former Secretary of Labor and U.S. Senator, served as chair.

The Commission's goal was defined by the title of their first publication, *What Work Requires of Schools*. As you will see in this book, the Commission's response—its definition of *workplace know-how*—was five competencies built on a three-part foundation. Students, so equipped, will be able to efficiently allocate resources such as time, money, and space. They will know how to acquire, evaluate, organize and maintain information, including using computers for these purposes. They will be comfortable with technology of different sorts, and be adept at working with others in a variety of roles, including teacher and negotiator. Finally, they will understand "systems" of various kinds, including the one the college uses. In addition, students will know how to read, write, compute and problem solve and will be responsible, honest, ethical, and possess other personal qualities.

The chart that follows correlates SCANS competencies to the content objectives in each chapter of *College Success*. You can use this chart as a guideline, keeping in mind that many of the SCANS skills and competencies apply almost across-the-board. The inclusion of SCANS adds a critical feature to your instructional program. It allows students to connect learning to the skills and competencies they will use throughout their working lives.

Arnold H. Packer

CHAPTER	SCANS COMPETENCY	CONTENT OBJECTIVES

CHAPTER 1
A SUCCESSFUL START
	INTERPERSONAL
	  Participates as Team Member
	  Exercises Leadership
	  Works with Cultural Diversity
	INFORMATION
	  Acquires and Evaluates
	  Organizes and Maintains
	SYSTEMS
	  Understands Systems
	THINKING SKILLS
	  Knowing How to Learn
		Assess attitudes and evaluate past experiences.
		Develop techniques for positive thinking.
		Understand learning styles and adapt to different instructional methods.
		Set goals and make plans for achievement.
		Acquire and use information about support systems and resources on campus.

CHAPTER 2
TAKING CONTROL OF YOUR TIME
	RESOURCES
	  Allocates Time
	  Allocates Human Resources
	INFORMATION
	  Interprets and Communicates
	INTERPERSONAL
	  Negotiates
	  Exercises Leadership
	SYSTEMS
	  Monitors/Corrects Performance
	  Improves/Designs Systems
	PERSONAL QUALITIES
	  Displays Responsibility
		Understand the purpose of time management.
		Use organizational techniques to plan, make time projections, and prioritize.
		Develop a time management system: develop short- and long-term schedules; keep To-Do lists; use time management tools, such as calendars and written schedules.
		Recognize and correct procrastination.
		Work with others to share responsibilities.
		Develop techniques for stress management.

CHAPTER 3
APPLYING STUDY AND RESEARCH SKILLS TO MASTERY
	SYSTEMS
	  Understands Systems
	INFORMATION
	  Acquires and Evaluates
	INTERPERSONAL
	  Participates as Team Member
	  Teaches Others New Skills
	THINKING SKILLS
	  Knowing How to Learn
		Design work/study area.
		Plan study sessions.
		Practice sound study techniques.
		Practice sound research techniques.
		Study as a member of a group.

CHAPTER 4
LEARNING IN THE CLASSROOM
	BASIC SKILLS
	  Reading, Writing
	  Arithmetic/Mathematics
	  Listening, Speaking
	THINKING SKILLS
	  Knowing How to Learn
	INFORMATION
	  Acquires and Evaluates
	  Organizes and Maintains
	  Interprets and Communicates
		Develop a positive attitude toward learning.
		Practice good classroom habits.
		Use active listening strategies.
		Participate in class.
		Develop techniques for class/text notes review.

CHAPTER	SCANS COMPETENCY	CONTENT OBJECTIVES

CHAPTER 5
LEARNING THROUGH READING
	BASIC SKILLS
	  Reading
	THINKING SKILLS
	  Visualizes
	INFORMATION
	  Acquires and Evaluates
	  Organizes and Maintains
	  Interprets and Communicates
		Understand the concept of active reading.
		Use active reading techniques.
		Develop strategies for handling specific subject areas.

CHAPTER 6
WRITING YOUR WAY TO THE TOP
	BASIC SKILLS
	  Writing
	THINKING SKILLS
	  Thinks Creatively
	INFORMATION
	  Interprets and Communicates
	  Uses Computers to Process
		Understand the basics of good writing.
		Utilize good writing methods.
		Develop skills for specific writing tasks.
		Use electronic processing for writing.

CHAPTER 7
PREPARING FOR AND TAKING TESTS
	THINKING SKILLS
	  Decision Making
	  Problem Solving
	  Seeing Things in Mind's Eye
	  Knowing How to Learn
	  Reasoning
	PERSONAL QUALITIES
	  Responsibility
	  Self-Management
	  Integrity/Honesty
	INFORMATION
	  Interprets and Communicates
	TECHNOLOGY
	  Selects Technology
	INTERPERSONAL
	  Participates as Team Member
	  Teaches Others
	  Selects Technology
		Use study skills to prepare for tests.
		Practice test study techniques.
		Create personalized learning aids.
		Understand how memory works.
		Practice memory improvement techniques.
		Learn strategies for answering different kinds of test questions.
		Learn techniques for handling test anxiety.
		Work with classmates to develop study tools.
		Explore the use of technology in testing.

CHAPTER 8
USING CRITICAL THINKING SKILLS
	THINKING SKILLS
	  Creative Thinking
	  Decision Making
	  Problem Solving
	  Reasoning
	INTERPERSONAL
	  Participates as Team Member
	  Teaches Others
	INFORMATION
	  Acquires and Evaluates
		Understand the concept of critical thinking.
		Use critical thinking techniques.
		Use creative thinking techniques.
		Use creative thinking to solve problems.
		Use critical thinking skills to plan a group project.
		Use critical thinking skills to solve problems with a group.
		Acquire information to make decisions.

CHAPTER	SCANS COMPETENCY	CONTENT OBJECTIVES

CHAPTER 9 RELATIONSHIPS	PERSONAL QUALITIES
	  Self-Esteem
	  Sociability
	INTERPERSONAL
	  Participates as Team Member
	  Exercises Leadership
	  Negotiates
	  Works with Cultural Diversity
	SYSTEMS
	  Understands Systems
	BASIC SKILLS
	  Speaking, Listening
		Analyze personal relationships.
		Handle relationship conflicts.
		Practice techniques for assertiveness, conflict resolution, and negotiation.
		Develop strategies for positive relationships with instructors.
		Understand the campus system for formal conflict resolution.
		Develop relationships with classmates.
		Appreciate cultural diversity.
		Understand the need for communication and leadership skills.

CHAPTER 10 TAKING CARE OF YOURSELF	THINKING SKILLS
	  Decision Making
	  Problem Solving
	PERSONAL QUALITIES
	  Responsibility
	  Self-Esteem
	  Self-Management
	  Integrity/Honesty
	SYSTEMS
	  Monitors/Corrects Perform.
	INTERPERSONAL
	  Participates as Team Member
		Understand stress reactions and potential consequences.
		Develop strategies for coping with stress.
		Develop strategies for maintaining health and fitness.
		Recognize the importance of a healthy lifestyle.
		Recognize health issues and safe practices regarding smoking, drugs, alcohol and sexuality.

CHAPTER 11 MANAGING YOUR FINANCIAL RESOURCES	THINKING SKILLS
	  Decision Making
	  Problem Solving
	PERSONAL QUALITIES
	  Responsibility
	  Self-Management
	RESOURCES
	  Allocates Money
	INFORMATION
	  Organizes and Maintains
		Identify resources for financing education.
		Develop a long-term plan for financing education.
		Identify spending habits and develop strategies for budgeting funds.
		Develop and maintain a budget.
		Use strategies for solving financial problems.

CHAPTER 12 PREPARING FOR YOUR CAREER	PERSONAL QUALITIES
	  Responsibility
	  Self-Management
	INFORMATION
	  Acquires and Evaluates
	  Organizes and Maintains
		Use resources to develop career plans.
		Acquire information about the job market.
		Identify career goals and relate them to educational programs.
		Develop a long-term career plan.

PART ONE

College Success Strategies

CHAPTER 1
A Successful Start

CHAPTER 2
Taking Control of Your Time

A Successful Start

CHAPTER OUTLINE

You're In Charge
  Building Your Self-Esteem
  Practicing Positive Thinking
  Understanding Your Learning Styles

Challenges and Adjustments
  Diversity: What Does It Mean?
  Appreciating and Learning from Diversity

Your Educational Goals
  Ten Goal-Setting Guidelines
  Your Major
  Preparing Yourself for Work—SCANS
  Making the System Work for You
  Campus Resources and Support Services

The elevator to success is out of order. You'll have to use the stairs one step at a time.
—Joe Girard

If you were to ask ten people to tell you the meaning of the word "success," chances are you would get ten different answers. What is your definition of success? Jot down an answer in the Journal section on the following page.

While people define success in different ways, successful people do share some important characteristics in common. Some of these include: having a positive image of themselves, being aware of their strengths and weaknesses, knowing what they want, having a plan and setting realistic goals to achieve it, being able to adjust to challenges and changes, and knowing how to find and utilize resources and support as needed. This chapter presents some strategies that will help you develop or enhance these traits in yourself. Some of them you will be able to accept and use immediately; others you may need to adapt to your personal style and way of thinking; still others you may discard entirely or come back to at a later date when you have the need.

As you go through this chapter, keep your definition of success in mind and consider how you can best use the "success strategies" suggested here.

You're in Charge

You are at the beginning of your "career" as a student and there is no doubt in your mind that you will succeed. Right? Are you nodding affirmatively? Are you hesitating? Are you experiencing doubts? If so, why?

Most successful people will tell you that you can achieve whatever you want in life. You just have to believe in yourself and never give up on your dreams. Your response to this may be, "Easier said than done." For where does that solid base of belief come from? Why do some people seem to find a clear path to their goals, while others struggle to overcome the problems and obstacles that life puts in the way? Much of the answer to these questions lies in your attitude toward yourself. Everyone faces challenges and problems. It is how you deal with them that makes the difference between success and failure.

If you are a positive, self-confident person, you will have an easier time coming up with solutions that keep you moving forward. You will not be stalled and defeated by self-doubt and recrimination. On the other hand, if you have negative attitudes toward yourself, you will perceive problems as a pattern in your life and doubt your ability to overcome them. How would you categorize yourself? Are you a positive thinker or a negative thinker? Do you have self-confidence or do you doubt yourself? Have your past experiences made you feel good about yourself, or do you look back at your past with regret and self-recrimination? How you view yourself, your learning abilities, and the challenges you face as a student will greatly influence your ability to succeed.

I define success as _____

_____

_____

_____

I am a (positive/negative) thinker because _____

_____

_____

_____

Building Your Self-Esteem

Your attitudes about yourself and your ability to succeed reflect your level of **self-esteem**—your confidence and satisfaction in yourself. Levels of self-esteem fluctuate as we encounter different situations and events in life. Everyone has experienced feelings of success at some points and feelings of failure at other times. If you generally have a high level of self-esteem, you are able to focus on your successes and work toward your strengths, instead of dwelling on your failures and worrying about your areas of weakness. People who have high self-esteem measure themselves against their own standards and experiences. They are able to accept criticism and setbacks without losing their motivation. That is because they are aware of their own strengths and weaknesses, and recognize that life is about the process of coming to terms with these two aspects of themselves.

Self-esteem is tied to feelings of value or worthiness to yourself and to others. For example, you may have low self-esteem because you are unhappy with the way

> **QUOTE**
> The best-laid plans and strategies are useless unless you expect to win. And you must know you are going to win before you start.
> —Ivanla Vanzant

your body looks or because you feel that you are not as smart as other people. These feelings may or may not be supported by other people's feelings or attitudes toward you.

Practicing Positive Thinking

At times when your self-esteem is low, you may find it difficult to shift your mind toward thinking positively no matter how hard you try. You will tend to focus on your failures which, in turn, creates anxiety and fear. Sometimes others are all too willing to assist in this regard. Parents and teachers can often be harsh in their judgments without being aware of the long-term impact of their negative feedback. Some people also suffer from being their own worst critics. Being a perfectionist can translate into never quite being satisfied with yourself or what you have achieved.

When things go wrong, it is natural to look for explanations. This can be done in a positive way that builds you up and helps you do better next time, or it can be done in a negative way that weakens you and makes you feel helpless. To the extent that you can control your responses to events and make them positive, you will be able to increase your level of self-esteem.

Negative thinking is often reflected in the negative messages that you send to yourself. These negative messages trigger not only actions that are not in your best interest, but feelings that consume your energy and smother your optimism.

Dr. David Burns, a leading authority and teacher in the field of psychiatry, describes much of the negative thinking that leads to poor self-esteem as **distorted thinking**. Dr. Burns says, "When you feel upset, the thoughts that make you feel bad are often illogical and distorted, even though these thoughts may seem as real as the skin on your hand! In other words, when you feel lousy, you are nearly always fooling yourself about something, even though you aren't aware of this. It's as though you are wearing a strong pair of eyeglasses that distort your view of the world, or looking into the trick mirrors at the amusement park that make you look too fat, too short, or too skinny."

Review the chart in Figure 1-1 and ask yourself, "Do I engage in distorted thinking when things go wrong?" Check off each item that applies to you. If you aren't sure, practice tuning in to your **inner voice**—the voice inside your head that talks to you all the time. As you go through the day and confront different thoughts about your problems, listen to what you are saying to yourself. When you hear yourself thinking you can't do something or find yourself remembering a past failure, stop and try to turn your thinking around. Be especially aware of messages that include the words "I always," "I never," "I won't be able to," "I can't," "I should." These words may be triggering negative messages that have been programmed into your mind since your childhood.

Suppose your advisor suggests that taking a couple of accounting courses will help round out your business program. You hear yourself saying, "I've always done poorly in math. I won't be able to pass an accounting course." What should you do? First, think about how this attitude is going to affect your approach to these courses? Will you go in with high expectations of yourself or will you meet with a self-fulfilling prophesy of low expectations? Then, think about what you can do to change your attitude. Should you enroll in a basic math course before taking accounting? Can you fit additional study time into your schedule? Can you get help from a friend or relative who excels in math? How about a tutor? All of these are positive steps you can take that will change your negative mindset toward math.

> **TEN QUALITIES OF PEOPLE WITH HIGH SELF-ESTEEM**
>
> 1. They are focused on the future and not overly preoccupied by past mistakes or failures.
> 2. They accept disappointments and setbacks and continue moving forward with their lives.
> 3. They experience a range of emotions and are able to express them appropriately.
> 4. They are aware of their strengths and weaknesses, and are able to use their strengths to help others and seek out help in their areas of weakness.
> 5. They respect other people and accept differences without being judgmental or overtly negative toward others.
> 6. They have self-confidence without being arrogant, self-absorbed, or braggadocios.
> 7. They are able to accept compliments and criticism gracefully.
> 8. They have a sense of humor about themselves.
> 9. They feel comfortable being alone.
> 10. They are able to think and act independently and express opinions without fear of what others will think.

DISTORTED THINKING

☐ 1. **All-or-nothing thinking:** You look at things in absolute, black-and white categories.

☐ 2. **Overgeneralization:** You view a negative event as a never-ending pattern of defeat.

☐ 3. **Mental filter:** You dwell on the negatives and ignore the positives.

☐ 4. **Discounting the positives:** You insist that your accomplishments or positive qualities don't count.

☐ 5. **Jumping to conclusions:** You conclude things are bad without any definite evidence.

☐   (a) **Mind reading:** You assume that people are reacting negatively to you.

☐   (b) **Fortune-telling:** You predict that things will turn out badly.

☐ 6. **Magnification or minimization:** You blow things way out of proportion or you shrink their importance.

☐ 7. **Emotional reasoning:** You reason from how you feel: "I feel like an idiot, so I must be one."

☐ 8. **"Should" statements:** You criticize yourself or other people with "shoulds," "shouldn'ts," "musts," "oughts," and "have-tos."

☐ 9. **Labeling:** Instead of saying, "I made a mistake," you tell yourself, "I'm a jerk" or "a loser."

☐ 10. **Blame:** You blame yourself for something you weren't entirely responsible for, or you blame other people and overlook ways that you contribute to a problem.

Source: David D. Burns, M.D., *Ten Days To Self-Esteem*, Quill William Morrow. New York, 1993. Reprinted with permission.

FIGURE 1-1 Distorted Thinking

When Positive and Negative Thoughts Battle For Your Attention, Which One Usually Wins?

Reprogramming Practice

Make a list of the courses in which you did well in the past and those in which you did not do well. Then list what you think the reasons were for your "good" and "bad" performance. How many of your reasons can be attributed to either positive or negative feedback from yourself and others?

_____

_____

_____

_____

_____

Over the course of the next week, complete the Reprogramming Practice Log in Figure 1-2. Get together with a group to discuss the log.

Understanding Your Learning Styles

The feedback you have received throughout your years of schooling has had an impact on your self-esteem as a student. You probably take for granted that you are "good" in some courses and "bad" in others. When asked what courses you like, you are likely to respond by naming the courses in which you get the best grades. It is also likely that you will select a major based on what you perceive as your strengths and weaknesses in different subject areas. But have you ever tried to discover why you have these strengths in some areas and weaknesses in others? Are you better in math and science or English and social science? Do you learn more in courses that have small-group discussion than in courses that require a lot of reading? Do you prefer art classes, lab classes, or anything that is "hands on" over courses that are taught mainly through lecture methods? What kinds of tests do you prefer? How do you feel most comfortable expressing your ideas? Your answers to all of these questions are clues to your preferred **learning style**.

Psychologists and educators have written extensively on the subject of individual learning styles. The results of their research have led to the development of theories about how individuals learn, how teachers should teach, and how subject matter should be presented.

People learn by processing information on a sensory level. The major **sensory activities** for learning are: reading, listening, talking, visualizing, writing, and hands-on (touching). This is called **Kinesthetic** learning or learning-by-doing. As a student you have little to say about teachers' methods and course content. You will have no choice but to adapt to all of these methods of processing information in the various courses you will take. Understanding your own preferred learning style can help you improve your performance in different types of courses.

It is important to note that there is no "right" learning style. Individuals have different "preferred" or "strong" learning style preferences that are developed through early educational experiences. They are a combination of innate qualities and learned responses. People who become good readers at an early age tend to prefer this learning style. In the past, this was true of the majority of people because most information was print-based. Today, young people who are accustomed to television, videos, and computers often prefer visualizing and listening learning styles.

CHAPTER 1   A Successful Start

PROGRAMMING PRACTICE LOG

Negative Thoughts (Write exactly what you say to yourself)	**Distorted Thinking** (Indicate the type of distorted thinking this is)	**Positive Thoughts** (Substitute other thoughts that are more positive and realistic)

Source: David D. Burns, M.D., *Ten Days To Self-Esteem*, Quill William Morrow. New York, 1993. Reprinted with permission.

FIGURE 1-2 Reprogramming Practice Log

Being aware of your preferred learning style can help you focus on why learning comes easily to you in some types of courses and is harder in others. You may discover that you tend to "tune out" information that does not come to you in one of your preferred styles. In courses that do not reach you through your preferred learning style, you can look for alternate methods of learning to compensate for what you may be missing. For example, if you are a listener rather than a reader, working with a study group in courses that require heavy reading may assist you in processing written information.

Learning Styles

Take this self-assessment to find which sensory activities you prefer.

Circle One

READING

1. I like to read	Yes	No
2. I read for fun	Yes	No
3. I often read the daily newspaper	Yes	No
4. I like doing research at the library	Yes	No

LISTENING

5. I like to listen to the radio	Yes	No
6. I like to play tapes and cassettes	Yes	No
7. I think that I am a good listener	Yes	No
8. I nearly always listen attentively in class	Yes	No

TALKING

9. I like to talk on the phone	Yes	No
10. I like to talk in small groups	Yes	No
11. I like to tell jokes	Yes	No
12. I enjoy giving talks	Yes	No

VISUALIZING

13. I like to daydream	Yes	No
14. I sometimes picture the future	Yes	No
15. I am good at describing movies I have seen	Yes	No
16. I can look at plans and visualize a finished product	Yes	No

WRITING

17. I often make lists	Yes	No
18. I often or always take notes in class	Yes	No
19. I like to write letters	Yes	No
20. I keep a diary	Yes	No

KINESTHETIC

21. I like to work with my hands	Yes	No
22. I often make things from scratch	Yes	No
23. I can do things easily, if someone shows me	Yes	No
24. I prefer playing to watching sports	Yes	No

> Review the items for which you circled "Yes." This information will help you recognize your areas of strength. Use it to match your preferences to learning activities and to strengthen other styles of learning. If you had at least three "Yes" items circled within each group, your learning styles are flexible. You should be able to adapt to a variety of situations.
>
> If you checked three or more "No" items in any group, think about how you can work on these areas. Look at each group of items carefully and list five "No" items that you want to work on. Write down the item and plan an activity that will strengthen you in this area. For example, if you need to work on writing, you can broaden your ability to learn through writing by increasing the amount of writing you do. Try taking notes while you are reading your assignments, as well as in class, keeping a diary or journal, and writing letters. Create activities that make you write. The more you write, the easier it will become.

You can also use the self-assessment information to choose learning strategies that best fit your current learning preferences. For example, if you are strong in visualization, seek out videos, CD-ROM media, films, and pictorial printed matter to supplement your lecture and textbook materials. If you have strong listening and talking preferences, look for courses that offer small-group discussion sessions or seek out study groups to supplement your classroom learning.

Understanding various learning styles also helps you recognize and appreciate the differences in how your instructors teach. For example, you may be frustrated with the way a certain instructor always relies on lectures to convey information and stresses the memorization of facts for testing. You may prefer another teacher who avoids lectures altogether and acts more as a facilitator, posing questions and encouraging student discussion. Both teachers are teaching according to *their* preferred learning style. You can't change how your instructors teach their courses, but you can change your response to their methods. By recognizing that they are using a style that is more comfortable for them, your attitude toward your own comfort level will be more positive. Remember, your goal in college is to learn as much as you can; a positive attitude about your classes and the ability to adapt to your instructors will help you attain that goal.

Here are some strategies for you to use to convert what you have to learn into your preferred style when it is not already being presented in that manner:

- Ask the instructor to translate. If your teacher lectures and you're a reading learner, taking extensive notes to read later will help you. If you're a kinesthetic learner, ask your teacher to explain the concepts you're having trouble with in a way a "hands-on" learner would understand them. That doesn't mean the teacher has to create an experiment for you to do. It only means hearing the concepts explained using analogies and metaphors that relate to the sense of touch or personal engagement.
- Find other sources that already have the information in the format matching your preferred style. Go to the library and find textbooks by different authors. Some of those authors present information in a style more compatible with yours, and their explanations will work for you more naturally.
- Find a classmate with the same preferred style and study together. Insights one of you gets from the material will probably be explained to the other in naturally accessible terms.
- Translate to your preferred style. If your preference is visual, draw diagrams and maps of the information—this will help you see connections you may be missing. If you prefer auditory learning, talk through the difficult section of the material (in the text or from your notes) out loud. Work with other auditory learners, if possible, by using the technique of asking questions based

on topic headings and key terms. If you are a kinesthetic learner, break the material down into small bits, put each bit of information on a note card, then stand up in front of a table and lay the note cards out, rearranging them in different ways until you find the layout that feels most comfortable. This will activate your kinesthetic sense of information input.

- Become more proficient in your non-preferred styles. In each class in which the teacher is using a style other than your preference, take it as an opportunity to translate to your style. Eventually the translation process will start to be automatic and your understanding of the information will happen naturally, even though it is being presented in a different style.

Challenges and Adjustments

In the past, college campuses were a place where you could find an almost completely homogeneous population. The majority of students were **traditional students**—young adults between the ages of 18 and 25 just out of high school. This created a "collegiate" atmosphere on campus. Students shared similar backgrounds, experiences, and goals. On college campuses today, anywhere from 25 to 50 percent of students are classified as **nontraditional students**. This category includes "older" adults, members of minority groups, foreign students from other countries, people with disabilities, and possibly others.

Diversity: What Does It Mean?

Diversity is the popular way to describe the changes in population demographics that are being felt not only on campuses, but throughout our society wherever large groups of people come together. Many communities where people live throughout the United States are segregated along racial, economic, and ethnic lines. At the same time the population as a whole is becoming increasingly diverse. Consequently, people live separately and become accustomed to interacting with people like themselves who share the same background, values, and cultural norms. When they leave home, they are confronted with differences. Differences become magnified because people are not accustomed to them.

There are two important sides of the diversity issue for you to consider. First, where do you fit—what groups do you belong to, and how does this affect how comfortable you feel in the role of student—your level of motivation, your expectations, and the challenges you face? Second, from your vantage point, both as a unique individual and as a member of a group, how do you respond to the diversity surrounding you?

Our society, especially the mass media, loves to categorize people as members of a particular group. This is helpful for the purposes of discussion but, in fact, everyone belongs to many groups and changes group identity according to the situation or issue at hand. The following discussion focuses on some challenges you may face as a member of different groups, and presents some ideas that you may find helpful when facing these challenges.

Traditional Students. If you have taken the traditional route to college, which is to begin right after completing high school, you may find that your biggest adjustment is being completely on your own for the first time. If you are living in a campus residence or in a place of your own, you have to adjust to taking complete responsibility for all of your needs. If you have roommates, you will probably have to adapt to the habits of a stranger (or several strangers). While it may be liberating not to have parents or family members "in the way," you may also miss the companionship and support they provided. You will have to schedule time for meals, laundry, shopping, and other chores in between classes and study or on weekends. You will also have to learn to balance the freedom to socialize whenever you choose with the discipline needed to spend the necessary time studying, attending classes, and doing other types of course work. If you are on campus, however, you are among the fortunate students who are captive to an educational setting that is designed to facilitate you in achieving your educational goals.

Commuting Students.
If you are a commuter student, as are the majority of college students in the United States, you will have to make many of the same adjustments as the on-campus student. If you are lucky enough to have your own place or share with other students, your life will be very similar to an on-campus existence. If you are like many commuter students, however, you are still living at home with parents and possibly siblings, or you may have a family of your own. In this case, you will need to enlist their support in helping you set up a place of your own where you can study undisturbed. They may need to cut back on their demands for your time and you may need to learn to say "no" more often.

If you are like most commuter students, you may have lots of friends who are not in school. They may have more time than you for social and leisure activities. Don't assume that people in your life will all support you in your efforts to do well in school. Friends who are not in school may feel threatened by your ambition or envious of your ability to pursue goals that they may feel are beyond their reach financially, academically, or for some other reason. You may need to resist their efforts to distract you from your goals. Setting strict schedules for yourself and sticking firmly to your plans will send the message that you are not going to be steered off course.

First-Generation Students.
American colleges and universities are becoming more conscious of students who are the first in their families to attend college. There is general agreement that the number of people in this category is growing, and that they face some unique challenges. If you are a first-generation college student, some of the special challenges you may face include:

- A feeling of disconnection between life as it is in the present and as it will be in the future; a sense of leaving the past behind and, possibly with it, parents, siblings, and friends who do not share the same life goals.
- A lack of a designated time or place to study at home and lack of support for these needs, which can range from indifference to actual criticism or anger.
- A sense of alienation from your community and commonly shared cultural experiences as new interests and tastes take hold, based on exposure to a broader range of cultural experiences.
- Attending college on a part-time basis and having significant job and family responsibilities as compared to other students.
- Feeling less well prepared for academic demands and the bureaucratic environment of higher education than classmates who come from college educated families.

Any one or all of these feelings can lead to ambivalence toward your commitment to completing your degree. When difficulties arise, first-generation students are less likely to have the resources and support needed to overcome them. Consequently, the drop-out rate among this group is high.

In interviews with first-generation college students, experts found out that the more such students reach out to campus support services, the more likely they are to complete their college education successfully. Some recommendations that ease the transition for first-generation as well as other students include:

- Enroll in courses that are offered to improve basic academic and study skills.
- Seek out support from peers by getting to know classmates, joining study groups, and participating in extracurricular activities whenever time allows.
- Don't be intimidated by the physical dimensions of the campus. Take time to explore what it has to offer and become familiar with study areas, lounges, eating places, and other places where students meet.
- Seek out supportive academic department offices, advising services, and other opportunities to interact with faculty members.
- Seek out institutionally sanctioned networking groups, such as minority student affiliations, religious groups, sports, and other activities that offer opportunities to interact with your peers.

Adult Students. With the growing population of adult students—people 25 and older—colleges are looking at ways to help these students feel more comfortable on campus. Many adult students are people who have had some college education in the past and are returning to complete a higher education degree. Others are starting college for the first time, taking courses related to their work, or getting new training to improve their marketability in their chosen career. As an older adult, you may find it difficult to adapt to the role of student. Learning new things and facing new challenges can be an uncomfortable experience in contrast to a familiar job or duties in the home. You may have held jobs with authority over others and may have experience in training others. Now it is necessary to adjust to being in the subordinate role of "the learner." If you are going back to school because you have been displaced from your job, you may be particularly vulnerable to feelings of inadequacy. Looking at younger people who are just starting out may bring up feelings of regret that you did not pursue higher education earlier. A feeling of being behind in the game and worry about having to compete with the younger generation can detract from the positive feelings you should have about this new direction in your life.

In addition to the challenges mentioned above, adult students are the most likely of all populations to be juggling conflicting responsibilities such as jobs, families, and financial problems and are, therefore, more susceptible to the stress involved in trying to make changes in their lives. Adults as well as other students, can ease their transition into the educational setting by following some of the guidelines below:

- Involve family members, especially those who are dependent on you, in the decision to enroll in school. Ask them to identify what they can do to help you carve out the time you need to devote to this new undertaking.
- Sort out your priorities and come to terms with what you can and cannot do while you are enrolled in school. Eliminate activities from your life, if necessary.
- Select a program of study that is related to your interests and experience. You are less likely to become discouraged if you stay in territory that is at least somewhat familiar.
- Look for courses that emphasize critical and analytical thinking. These courses are likely to be more satisfying than those geared toward rote learning.

Minority-Group Students. Minority-group students are, of course, a diverse group within themselves. The largest minority groups are African-American, Hispanic, and Asian. On some campuses, however, these groups may actually comprise a majority of students. Some of the challenges students from minority groups may experience include the following:

- Feeling alienated from the majority population because of a lack of prior exposure to people from different backgrounds. Minority-group students

often gravitate toward "self-segregation" by living in separate residences, participating in separate social and campus activities, and avoiding interaction with people outside of their group.
- Feeling resentment and anger toward the school administration due to a perception that the composition of the faculty and the content of the curriculum does not adequately reflect the backgrounds, interests, and contributions of minorities in American society.
- Minority students are more likely than other groups to be first-generation students, experiencing the challenges listed in the preceding section.

As a minority-group student you will, of course, be a member of some of the other groups already mentioned. The suggestions given for these groups and the section below will work well in helping to ease your transition into student life.

Appreciating and Learning from Diversity

> I always knew that deep down in every human heart, there is mercy and generosity. No one is born hating another person because of the color of his skin, or his background, or his religion. People must learn to hate, and if they can learn to hate, they can be taught to love, for love comes more naturally to the human heart than its opposite. Even in the grimmest times in prison, when my comrades and I were pushed to our limits, I would see a glimmer of humanity in one of the guards, perhaps just for a second, but it was enough to reassure me and keep me going. Man's goodness is a flame that can be hidden but never extinguished.
>
> —Nelson Mandela,
> President of South Africa

All students can use their college experience as an education in open-mindedness toward and understanding of people of different backgrounds. This is a major advantage of getting a higher education. You can begin this process by first examining your own attitudes about yourself and others. If you find that you have negative attitudes and preconceptions, work at setting them aside. Minorities have every right to expect members of the majority population to put aside their prejudices and biases and treat them as individuals. Members of minority groups must do likewise. It is the responsibility of every individual to work toward harmony and understanding among the diverse population that comprises America. Some positive attitudes that can assist in this process include:

- Expect fair treatment from instructors, administrators, and peers. Look at each person you encounter as an individual. Challenge those who are unfair, but don't assume that everyone is the same.
- Confront problems and challenges in dealing with others in a constructive, problem-solving mode, not in an angry, provocative mode. Put aside the "us vs. them" mentality that pervades social and political discourse in our society. Look for common ground and mutually beneficial ways of working out differences.
- Don't segregate yourself. Be open to social relationships with people of all backgrounds. Use this opportunity to learn as much as you can about yourself and others. This attitude will be of great benefit in the workplace and wherever else in the world your future takes you.

"Remember and help America remember that the fellowship of human beings is more important than the fellowships of race and class and gender in a democratic society." This quote comes from *The Measure of Our Success*, a book by Marian Wright Edelman, Executive Director of the Children's Defense Fund. Write a couple of paragraphs describing your reactions to this statement. Do you agree with it completely or partially or not at all? Explain why. Describe what, in your life experience, makes you feel that you can or cannot live your life according to this "lesson."

PART ONE   College Success Strategies

_____

_____

_____

Your Educational Goals

In general terms, education is a goal unto itself. The knowledge you acquire in academic courses, such as literature, history, and social science, helps you understand the world and the society you live in. Taking basic courses like English, math, and science help you function well in everyday life. While education for education's sake is important, today, more than ever before in our nation's history, higher education is perceived as preparation for work. Whether you are planning to get a two-year degree, four-year degree, or are enrolling to take some courses without getting a degree, you are probably thinking about your career plans and goals as you select your courses and decide on a major.

It is important that you set long-term and short-term goals for your education. Your short-term goals will take you from term to term and keep you on course to finish within the timeframe you have set for yourself. Most students attending what are called two-year and four-year colleges do not actually graduate within those timeframes. The time it takes you to graduate is up to you. Setting a specific, long-term goal for graduation is important. Hard work is always more tolerable when you can "see the light at the end of the tunnel."

Self-Audit For Goal Setting

For each statement, circle NA for "Nearly Always," S for "Sometimes" or R for "Rarely" as it applies to you.

1. When I set a goal I write it down.	NA	S	R
2. I describe my goal in specific, measurable terms.	NA	S	R
3. I often visualize my goals.	NA	S	R
4. My goals are achievable.	NA	S	R
5. I set realistic deadlines for achieving my goals.	NA	S	R
6. I break large goals into manageable units.	NA	S	R
7. I look for the potential problems that may keep me from reaching my goals.	NA	S	R
8. I take action to remove or minimize those potential problems.	NA	S	R
9. I review progress toward my goals on a regular basis.	NA	S	R
10. I know the personal rewards of reaching my goals.	NA	S	R

Assess your responses by counting the number of times you responded "Nearly Always," then multiply by 3. Multiply the number of times you answered "Sometimes" by 2, and "Rarely" by 1. Add these up for a final score.

Nearly Always	_____	(Number of Responses) x 3 = _____
Sometimes	_____	(Number of Responses) x 2 = _____
Rarely	_____	(Number of Responses) x 1 = _____
Total =		_____

If your total score was between 24 and 30, then you are doing an excellent job of setting goals. A score of 18 to 24 indicates that you are well on your way to achieving effective goal setting. Concentrate on the statements to which you answered "Sometimes" or "Rarely." A score below 18 means there are several areas in which you can improve your goal setting. Read the guidelines below to become a better goal setter.

Ten Goal-Setting Guidelines

Goals are the points on your road map where you can apply your talents and energies. Without them, your life is governed by whim or emergency. Effective goals will provide you with the internal control to make things happen the way you want them to.

Here are some concrete ideas to help you develop concrete, meaningful goals.

1. **Write down your goals**. Many of us daydream about what we would like to accomplish, but not many of us pick up a pen and actually commit our desires to paper. Once you do, the dream becomes more concrete. Your dream is given a sense of reality. Writing down your goals is the first step on the road to achieving them.
2. **Put goals in specific, measurable terms.** A goal needs to be measurable so you can evaluate your progress.
3. **Visualize your goals.** Picture yourself reaching your goal. Picture the result the moment you achieve your goal, and your feelings about it.
4. **Set achievable goals.** Goals need to challenge your skills and abilities, without discouraging your effort and performance. As competence, success, and confidence grow, you may then decide to reach for higher goals.
5. **Set realistic deadlines.** Goals need a schedule. You are more likely to take action when you set a realistic timeframe for accomplishing your goals. Schedule enough time to reach your goal, but not so much time that you lose interest in it.
6. **Break down goals into manageable steps.** Sometimes a goal can seem overwhelming because of its size or scope. But if it is divided into smaller components, it becomes easier to manage and is more attainable.
7. **Analyze your goals for potential problems.** As you establish a goal, consider the steps you must take to accomplish it and what might come up to prevent you from reaching it. If you consider what could go wrong early on, then you can take action to resolve or minimize problems before they occur. Critical thinking helps you cover all the angles and stay on the path toward achieving your goal.
8. **Eliminate or minimize potential problems.** Identify the action required to remove the cause of a problem or try to minimize a problem's consequences.
9. **Review your progress regularly.** A periodic review of your goals will help ensure that they continue to be realistic, timely, and relevant.

10. **Establish goals that will be rewarding.** We stay motivated to work toward our goals when we know the rewards. Identify at least one meaningful reward for each goal. The goals you set will provide direction for your life; they focus your activities.

Source: Susan B. Wilson, *Goal Setting*. AMACOM Books, a division of the American Management Association. New York, 1994. Reprinted with permission.

Use the goal-setting worksheet in Figure 1-3 to write down your goals. If you have your own computer, it would be a good idea to duplicate this form electronically, so that you can easily adapt it to suit your needs and keep it up to date.

GOAL SETTING WORKSHEET

Time Period From _____ **To** _____

GOAL #1: _____

Steps	**Deadline**	**Measure of Achievement**
a.	a.	a.
b.	b.	b.
c.	c.	c.

Progress Notes: _____

GOAL #2: _____

Steps	**Deadline**	**Measure of Achievement**
a.	a.	a.
b.	b.	b.
c.	c.	c.

FIGURE 1-3 Goal-Setting Worksheet

CHAPTER 1   A Successful Start

FIGURE 1-3 Goal-Setting Worksheet *(continued)*

Progress Notes: _____
_____
_____

GOAL #3: _____
_____
_____

Steps	Deadline	Measure of Achievement
a. _____	a. _____	a. _____
b. _____	b. _____	b. _____
c. _____	c. _____	c. _____

Progress Notes: _____
_____
_____

GOAL #4: _____
_____
_____

Steps	Deadline	Measure of Achievement
a. _____	a. _____	a. _____
b. _____	b. _____	b. _____
c. _____	c. _____	c. _____

Progress Notes: _____
_____
_____

Your Major

A **major** is a field of study. The good news is that you are allowed to select whatever field of study you wish. The bad news is that this often is an extremely difficult decision to make. If you have never worked in a particular field, how do you know you will like it? How do you know you will be successful in it? If you are thinking of changing fields, how big a risk are you taking? When facing this decision, you might find it helpful to examine your aptitudes, interests, and needs objectively.

Your **aptitudes** are determined by your innate abilities or natural talents. For example, some people's aptitudes are more suited to fields that require conceptual thinking and analysis, while others' are suited to manual operations or technical skills. You are probably aware of your aptitudes, based on your performance in previous educational programs, jobs, or other aspects of your life. It is presumed that you will be more successful if you pursue a field in which your natural aptitudes are explored to their highest potential. However, you can be just as successful in other areas—you will probably just have to work harder. If you are unsure about what your aptitudes are, you can take an aptitude test. The placement office on your campus may offer such tests. If not, they can help you find out where you can be tested.

For most people, aptitudes and **interests** coincide. This is because we tend to gravitate toward things we do well or the things we find easy to do. Often though, young people are encouraged by adults, sometimes even pressured, to pursue something they have an aptitude for. For instance, students who excel in science are often persuaded to think about careers in the medical field. As adults, these same people may find that they are not interested in work that requires them to be responsible for the health and well being of others. On the other side, many people want to pursue an interest, but are afraid because they feel they have no talent for it. We are all familiar with the would-be musician who is tone deaf. If you have interests that don't seem to match your aptitudes, make sure that you are not looking at the field too narrowly. Maybe the tone-deaf musician has an aptitude for design, promotion, or sales—talents the music industry needs plenty of. Visit the library or the campus career center and make sure you are aware of all the different types of work you can do in the field that interests you. There are very few, if any, career areas that do not need people with a variety of aptitudes.

Think of your **needs** as the framework in which you will make decisions about everything you do in your life. Your needs are the things that bring you intrinsic happiness and self-esteem; they are based on your values. Needs motivate you on both a conscious and subconscious level. They also change over time as you experience changes in your life. Changing needs bring about changes in values and goals. At times you may have experienced anger toward yourself when you found that a decision you made was not making you happy. There is a tendency to look back and feel you made a "wrong" decision. Upon reflection on what is going on in your life and in the world around you, you will probably find that your need for change is a natural response to life's events. This will help you get on with your life and not waste time beating up on yourself.

Right now, as you are setting goals for your future, consider all the things that are influencing your decision. In order to pursue what you need, you may find it necessary to go against some prevailing attitudes and assumptions, as well as advice and consent of others. Remember two things: one, it is your life and two, there are few decisions in life that are irrevocable.

One of the most important problems in being an entrepreneur is the problem of happiness after success. Many people might say, "Hey, Baby, give me the success, and I'll worry about the happiness afterwards." Unfortunately, it doesn't happen that way. Unless you consider happiness before you consider success, then the manner in which you achieve your success will be something that will destroy you at some later date. Many people, in their rise to success, are so busy running to the top, stepping on their competitors, stepping on their enemies, and saddest of all, stepping on their friends and loved ones, that when they get to the top, they look around and discover that they are extremely lonely and unhappy. They'll ask me, "Where did I go wrong?" My answer has always been, "Probably at the beginning."

—Berry Gordy,
Founder of Motown Industries

CHANGE IS A CONSTANT

Our needs also change as a response to the outside world and how society defines its values at different periods of time. People who are middle-aged today have already experienced at least three major shifts in society's thinking about needs. In the 60s and 70s, the Age of Aquarius prevailed. College students rejected materialism and pursued goals of inner peace, love, and equality. This was followed by the 80s—the Age of Acquisition—the flower children became YUPPIES and decided that money and status were pretty important after all. College students went to business school in droves and the dream job was to be a Wall Street investment broker or a corporate fast tracker. The 90s—the Age of Information—has brought a retreat from the complexities of life and a longing among Baby Boomers for family, community, and security. It is predicted that the 2000s—the Age of Technology—will foster increasing needs for security, safety, and stability.

CHAPTER 1   A Successful Start

Preparing Yourself for Work—SCANS

If you read the introduction to this text, you know that the U.S. Department of Labor's Secretary's Commission on Achieving Necessary Skills (SCANS) identified a set of skills and competencies needed for success in the workplace. The idea is to make education relevant to work by connecting the things you learn in the educational setting to the things you do at work. As you select your major and consider jobs in your chosen field, you can use this text to connect what you are learning to what you will be doing or what you are currently doing at work. Completing the activities will help you make sure your studies and the skills you are learning will prepare you to be a competent employee. The important thing about SCANS is that the skills and competencies apply across the board to all kinds of jobs in every field.

SCANS — The Foundation Skills

Basic Skills

Reading—Locates, understands, and interprets written information in prose and documents—including manuals, graphs, and schedules—to perform tasks; learns from text by determining the main idea or essential message; identifies relevant details, facts, and specifications; infers or locates the meaning of unknown or technical vocabulary; and judges the accuracy, appropriateness, style, and plausibility of reports, proposals, or theories of writers.

Writing—Communicates thoughts, ideas, information, and messages in writing; records information completely and accurately; composes and creates documents such as letters, directions, manuals, reports, proposals, graphs, and flow charts with the language, style, organization, and format appropriate to the subject matter, purpose, and audience; includes, where appropriate, supporting documentation, and attends to level of detail; checks, edits, and revises for correct information, appropriate emphasis, form, grammar, spelling, and punctuation.

Arithmetic—Performs basic computation; uses basic numerical concepts such as whole numbers and percentages in practical situations; makes reasonable estimates of arithmetic results without a calculator and uses tables, graphs, diagrams, and charts to obtain or convey quantitative information.

Mathematics—Approaches practical problems by choosing appropriately from a variety of mathematical techniques; uses quantitative data to construct logical explanations for real world situations; expresses mathematical ideas and concepts orally and in writing; and understands the role of chance in the occurrence and prediction of events.

Listening—Receives, attends to, interprets, and responds to verbal messages and other cues such as body language in ways that are appropriate to the purpose—for example, to comprehend, learn, critically evaluate, appreciate, or support the speaker.

Speaking—Organizes ideas and communicates oral messages appropriate to listeners and situations; participates in conversation, discussion, and group presentation; selects an appropriate medium for conveying a message; uses verbal language and other cues such as body language in a way appropriate in style, tone, and level of complexity to the audience and the occasion; speaks clearly and communicates a message; understands and responds to listener feedback; and asks questions when needed.

Thinking Skills

Creative Thinking—Generates new ideas by making nonlinear or unusual connections, changing or reshaping goals, and imagining new possibilities; uses imagination freely, combining ideas or information in new ways, making connections between seemingly unrelated ideas, and reshaping goals in ways that reveal new possibilities.

Decision Making—Specifies goals and constraints, generates alternatives, considers risks, and evaluates and chooses best alternatives.

Problem Solving—Recognizes that a problem exists (i.e., that there is a

FIGURE 1-4 Foundation Skills

discrepancy between what is and what should be); identifies possible reasons for the discrepancy, and devises and implements a plan of action to resolve it; evaluates and monitors progress, revising the plan as indicated by findings.

Mental Visualization—Sees things in the mind's eye by organizing and processing symbols, pictures, graphs, objects, or other information—for example, sees a building from a blueprint, a system's operation from schematics, the flow of work activities from narrative descriptions, or the taste of food from reading a recipe.

Knowing How to Learn—Recognizes and can use learning techniques to apply and adapt existing and new knowledge and skills in both familiar and changing situations; is aware of learning tools such as personal learning styles (visual, aural, etc.), formal learning strategies (notetaking or clustering items that share some characteristics), and informal learning strategies (awareness of unidentified false assumptions that may lead to faulty conclusions).

Reasoning—Discovers a rule or principle underlying the relationship between two or more objects and applies it in solving a problem—for example, uses logic to draw conclusions from available information, extracts rules or principles from a set of objects or a written text, or applies rules and principles to a new situation (or determines which conclusions are correct when given a set of facts and conclusions).

Personal Qualities

Responsibility—Exerts a high level of effort and perseverance toward goal attainment; works hard to become excellent at doing tasks by setting high standards, paying attention to details, working well even when assigned an unpleasant task, and displaying a high level of concentration; displays high standard of attendance, punctuality, enthusiasm, vitality, and optimism in approaching and completing tasks.

Self-Esteem—Believes in own self-worth and maintains a positive view of self. demonstrates knowledge of own skills and abilities, is aware of one's impression on others, and knows own emotional capacity and needs and how to address them.

Sociability—Demonstrates understanding, friendliness,, adaptability, empathy, and politeness in new and ongoing group settings; asserts self in familiar and unfamiliar social situations; relates well to others; responds appropriately as the situation requires; and takes an interest in what others say and do.

Self-Management—Accurately assesses own knowledge, skills, and abilities; sets well-defined and realistic personal goals; monitors progress toward goal attainments and motivates self through goal achievement; exhibits self-control and responds to feedback unemotionally and nondefensively.

Integrity/Honesty—Recognizes when being faced with making a decision or exhibiting behavior that may break with commonly held personal or societal values; understands the effects of violating these beliefs and codes on an organization, oneself, and others; and chooses an ethical course of action.

FIGURE 1-4 Foundation Skills *(continued)*

Workplace Competencies

Resources

Manages Time—Selects relevant, goal-related activities, ranks them in order of importance, allocates time to activities, and understands, prepares, and follows schedules.

Manages Money—Uses or prepares budgets, including making cost and revenue forecasts; keeps detailed records to track budget performance; and makes appropriate adjustments.

Manages Material and Facility Resources—Acquires, stores, and distributes materials, supplies, parts, equipment, space, or final products in order to make the best use of them.

Manages Human Resources—Assesses knowledge and skills, distributes work accordingly, evaluates performance, and provides feedback.

Interpersonal

Participates as a Member of a Team—Works cooperatively with others and contributes to group efforts with ideas, suggestions, and effort.

Teaches Others—Helps others learn needed knowledge and skills.

SCANS

FIGURE 1-5 Workplace Competencies

CHAPTER 1   A Successful Start   21

FIGURE 1-5 Workplace Competencies *(continued)*

Serves Clients/Customers—Works and communicates with clients and customers to satisfy their expectations.

Exercises Leadership—Communicates thoughts, feelings, and ideas to justify a position, encourage, persuade, convince, or otherwise motivate an individual or group, including responsibly challenging existing procedures, policies, or authority.

Negotiates to Arrive at a Decision—Works towards an agreement that may involve exchanging specific resources or resolving divergent interests.

Works with Cultural Diversity—Works well with men and women and with people from a variety of ethnic, social, or educational backgrounds.

Information

Acquires and Evaluates Information—Identifies a need for data, obtains the data from existing sources or creates them, and evaluates their relevance and accuracy.

Organizes and Maintains Information—Organizes, processes, and maintains written or computerized records and other forms of information in a systematic fashion.

Uses Computers to Process Information—Employs computers to acquire, organize, analyze, and communicate information.

Systems

Understands Systems—Knows how social, organizational, and technological systems work and operates effectively within them.

Monitors and Corrects Performance—Distinguishes trends, predicts impacts of actions on system operations, diagnoses deviations in the functioning of a system/organization, and takes necessary action to correct performance.

Improves and Designs Systems—Makes suggestions to modify existing systems in order to improve the quality of products or services and develops new or alternative systems.

Technology

Selects Technology—Judges which sets of procedures, tools, or machines, including computers and their programs, will produce the desired results

Applies Technology to Tasks—Understands the overall intents and the proper procedures for setting up and operating machines, including computers and their programming systems.

Maintains and Troubleshoots Technology—Prevents, identifies, or solves problems in machines, computers, and other technologies.

Making the System Work for You

Colleges are usually referred to as educational *institutions*. Like any other institution, a college is a **system** composed of many parts that work together to produce a product—college graduates. Once you enter the system that is your college, you are responsible for understanding its rules, regulations, procedures, and requirements. Many schools offer freshman orientation sessions to all students to explain registration procedures, academic requirements, campus logistics, and other vital information. Other institutions expect students to read the catalog and figure things out on their own. Part of the maturity of going to college is learning to take responsibility for yourself.

To make the most of your college experience you need to understand thoroughly how the system operates. You need to know what it offers you and what it requires of you. As already mentioned, the college catalog is a basic tool for acquiring this knowledge. Get to know your catalog thoroughly. It contains vital information that you need to understand about the system you are now a part of. Refer to the catalog often, ask questions of advisors, instructors, counselors, and fellow students. Then, question the advice you get. Make sure it makes sense to you and that it is well-founded information. For example, if you are not sure whether or not a course is a requirement for graduation, don't simply take another student's word for it. Find out for sure before deciding you can skip it—the last thing you want is to find out in your last term that you need it to graduate. This happens to many students who are not careful enough in planning their programs each term.

The following section covers some of the basic aspects of the educational system that you should understand and explore as necessary.

Student Status and Credits.

Student status is determined by whether or not you are working toward fulfilling the requirements for a degree and by the number of credits you are taking. **Matriculated** students are students enrolled in degree programs. Nonmatriculated students are enrolled in courses, but are not working toward a degree. At most schools, in order to be considered a full-time student, you must be taking at least 12 credits. Anything less than that is considered part-time status.

If you are a matriculated student, at the beginning of each term you will need to assess where you are in regard to meeting the requirements for graduation. Read the college catalog, talk with an advisor, and make sure you are taking the courses and number of credits you need to graduate. If you attend a school that refers to credits as credit hours, make sure you don't confuse credit hours with contact hours. **Credit hours** refers to the number of credits a course counts toward completion of your degree. **Contact hours** are the number of hours a course meets each week.

Sometimes you can get a **waiver** of a required course. A waiver means that you have official permission to graduate without having taken a course that is normally required for graduation. Usually this is done through an agreement with your advisor for specific reasons that only he or she may approve. Make sure that any such agreement is officially processed and recorded.

Grading Systems.

Make sure you understand your school's system for grading and computing your **grade point average (GPA)**. Although grading systems vary, the majority of colleges use the letter grading system, with grade points assigned to each letter: A = 4 points; B = 3 points; C = 2 points; D = 1 point; F (Failure), I (Incomplete), W (Approved Withdrawal) all equal 0 points. Some schools assign fractional points for plus (+) and minus (-) grades.

Make sure you understand the rules for withdrawing from courses. In most institutions, an F grade accompanies a late withdrawal from a course. An incomplete grade in a course means that you will complete outstanding work and will be given a final grade once the work is complete. This can occur if you are ill during a term, miss turning in an important project, or are unable to take a final exam. If you take an incomplete grade, make sure you have a clear understanding with the instructor about what you need to do and when you need to do it in order to earn a final grade in the course.

The GPA is calculated according to the number of credit hours each course represents. Grade points are determined by multiplying credit hours by grade points. A grade of B (3 points) in a 3 hour course would contribute 9 grade points. The grade points earned for all courses are divided by the total number of hours to determine the GPA.

While you should strive to do well in all of your courses, keep in mind that grades received in courses in your major may carry more weight with potential employers than grades in other courses. However, also bear in mind that the job market might not be good in your field when you graduate or, for some other reason, you may decide to pursue employment in some other field. In that case, you don't know which of your grades will be perceived as carrying the most weight.

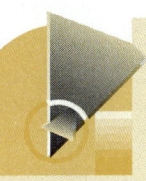

TYPICAL CAMPUS SERVICES

LIBRARIES
- Books on General and Specialized Topics
- Periodicals and Newspapers
- Reference Books
- Electronically Stored (CD-ROM) Information
- On-line Computer Research Services
- Interlibrary Loan Services
- Librarians and Information Services Staff

COUNSELING SERVICES
- Academic Advisors
- Career Counseling
- Financial Counseling
- Disabled Student Counseling
- Foreign Student Counseling
- Professional Psychological Counseling
- Substance Abuse Counseling

HEALTH SERVICES
- Emergency Medical Care
- Physical Examinations
- Medical Treatment
- Medical Referrals
- Information on Health-Related Issues
- Nutrition/Fitness Programs

STUDENT SERVICES/SUPPORT
- Housing
- Tutoring
- Childcare Center
- Childcare Network

CAREER PLANNING
- Career Aptitude Testing
- Internships/Cooperative Education Programs
- Career Resource Center
- Career Fairs/Recruitment Activities
- Job Placement for Graduates
- Alumni Mentoring Services

CLUBS AND ORGANIZATIONS
- Academic Clubs
- Organized Sports Teams
- Fraternities/Sororities
- Theater Club
- Minority Student Clubs
- Women's Organizations

CHAPTER 1   A Successful Start

Most schools have a procedure that allows students to appeal a grade beyond the instructor of the course, if the student feels the grade was unfairly or mistakenly received. Make sure you understand your school's procedure for this situation.

Most schools also have programs that acknowledge academic excellence. Find out what special honors, societies, or other awards are available for students with high academic achievement.

Transfer Courses. If you plan to transfer to another college or university in the future, you need to make sure that the courses you are taking are transferable. Courses that are **electives**, that is, your option to take or not, at your current school may be requirements at the school to which you plan to transfer. Get a catalog from the school you plan to attend, and check all the requirements to make sure you will have the hours and the courses you need to transfer.

Finances. Finances are one of the main causes of students not being able to complete their education. If you are lucky enough to have private financing of your education, make sure that you budget your money wisely and use it only for its designated purpose. If you are borrowing money, make sure that you can live with the accumulation of debt as time goes by. Also be aware that your **academic standing**—the number of credit hours you accumulate and your grade point average—can have an effect on your eligibility for financial aid. You should also be aware that most schools reserve the right to withhold transcripts and other records that may be requested by you or by a potential employer, if there is a failure to meet the conditions of a financial aid agreement.

Often students begin to feel overwhelmed by the financial burden of completing their education. Fear of a slow job market after graduation or having to postpone other goals, such as marriage and a family, can lead to a decision to quit. One way to avoid this fear is to face it from the start. The fact is, that completing your education is likely to get you a better paying job than you will have if you stop in the middle. Come to terms with the total cost of your education and develop a plan for financing it. Chapter 10 has more information on handling the financial aspects of your education.

Campus Resources and Support Services

Whatever your background or current situation, you can feel good about the fact that you are becoming a part of an institution whose sole function is to serve your needs. Without you, the institution would not exist. They want you. They want you to stay, they want you to finish, and they want you to be successful. Your tuition dollars pay for many things more than the classrooms, laboratories, libraries, and instructor's salaries. Learn about all of the resources and services offered on your campus and take advantage of them. If there are services that you feel you need that don't exist, form a group and lobby for them.

Write down some notes on your plans for following up on each of the topics discussed in this chapter.

Increasing your self-esteem:

Identifying and adjusting to your individual learning style:

_____
_____
_____

Adjusting to being a student:

_____
_____
_____

Appreciating and learning from diversity:

_____
_____
_____

Setting educational goals:

_____
_____
_____

Utilizing campus resources and services:

_____
_____
_____

Review and Recall

1. Five characteristics of people who have high self-esteem are:

    a. _____

    b. _____

    c. _____

    d. _____

    e. _____

CHAPTER 1   A Successful Start

2. To "reprogram" your inner voice means _____

_____

_____

This can improve your self-esteem because _____

_____

3. The six types of learning styles are:

   a. _____

   b. _____

   c. _____

   d. _____

   e. _____

   f. _____

4. What is the difference between a traditional student and a nontraditional student?

_____

_____

_____

5. List at least two student "groups" of which you are a member and list several of the ideas presented in this chapter that you feel will be most helpful to you in handling the challenges you face as a member of these groups.

_____

_____

_____

_____

6. List the ten goal-setting guidelines given in this chapter.

   a. _____

   b. _____

   c. _____

   d. _____

e. _____

f. _____

g. _____

h. _____

i. _____

j. _____

7. Define the following words:

   Aptitudes: _____
   _____

   Interests: _____
   _____

   Needs: _____
   _____

8. Explain the importance of the SCANS foundation skills and workplace competencies and their relationship to your college education.

   _____
   _____
   _____
   _____

9. Define the following terms:

   Matriculated Student: _____
   _____

   Waiver: _____
   _____

   Academic Standing: _____
   _____

   Electives: _____
   _____

CHAPTER 1   A Successful Start   27

10. What is the difference between course contact hours and course credit hours?

Apply Critical Thinking

Write a short description of the community you live in, the environment in which you work (if you are currently employed), and the school you are attending in terms of their diversity. Explain how these situations are alike and how they are different. What are the advantages and disadvantages of these situations as you perceive them.

SCANS School to Work Applications

INFORMATION: *Acquires and Evaluates Information*

1. Go to the library and research information on how child rearing practices of parents can affect self-esteem. Look for current articles as well as books with information on this subject. Read the articles and make notes about your findings. Write an entry in your journal describing how your childhood experiences affected your self-esteem positively and negatively.
2. Make a list of the resource centers and services listed in your catalog. Visit the site of each one to gather information. Pick up any written literature they have available; ask questions of staff members. Make notes about location, hours, and services offered and organize them for your future reference. Evaluate the available services and highlight the ones that you feel will be most useful to you.

INFORMATION: *Organizes and Maintains Information*

3. Write down your long-term goal for completing your education and then list the short-term goals you need to accomplish in order to achieve it. Then, draw a timeline, beginning with the start of the current term and continuing through the month and year in which you intend to get your degree. Fill in your short-term goals with dates along the timeline. Organize the file and update it each semester.

SYSTEMS: *Understands Systems*

4. Review your college catalog and talk with appropriate people on campus to find out the rules and procedures governing the aspects of the system discussed in this chapter. Make notes or highlight this information in the catalog. Extend this activity to include other information crucial to your success at operating within your institution's system.

INTERPERSONAL: *Participates as a Member of a Team*

5. Make a list of your aptitudes, interests, and needs. Your list can be as long or as short as you like. What relationships do you see among them? Where do they diverge? Discuss your conclusions with a group of classmates or a partner in your class, and exchange ideas about how you can use this information to solidify your plans for the future.

SCANS Workplace Application

We commonly talk about school and the workplace as two different places with two different functions. In fact, educational institutions are workplaces and they function in many ways like any other service business. As a service business, an educational institution must continually assess the quality of its goods and services to make sure they are meeting customer needs.

Suppose, instead of being a student, you were a consultant hired by the administration to assess the quality of the existing systems in your school. Based on the experiences you have had with important parts of the system—the application process, enrollment, registration, selection of courses, and others—write a short report to the administration summarizing the positive and negative qualities of these functions. What kinds of problems did you encounter? Did you experience frustrations, delays, red tape? How were you treated by staff members with whom you interacted? What worked well, maybe even better than you had expected? What are your recommendations for quality improvement? Be specific about your recommendations and their benefits to the organization.

Personal Progress Application

SCANS

THINKING SKILLS: *THINKS CREATIVELY, MAKES DECISIONS, SOLVES PROBLEMS, VISUALIZES, KNOWS HOW TO LEARN, AND REASONS*

Knowing how to learn is essential in today's workplace. Employers identify this trait as one of the most important attributes they look for when hiring employees. Rapidly advancing technology means employees today must be able to learn the new skills and concepts required by each new technological improvement on their jobs. That means employers find themselves more and more in the role of educators. They want good learners because good learners save them time and money in training expenses.

Knowing your preferred learning style and possessing strategies to tap into that power make you a better learner. The important thing to remember is that no one ever exclusively uses only one learning style; we all use aspects of every style throughout each day. Your *preferred* style or combination of styles, however, is the one with which you're most comfortable.

Below is another learning style assessment tool. It will identify you as preferring a *visual*, *auditory*, or *kinesthetic* ("hands-on" and/or "internal feeling") approach. Use a scale of one to five in marking your answers: five means you completely agree, one means you completely disagree.

Discovering Your Personal Learning Style

1. ___ Talking on the phone is one way I spend a significant amount of leisure time.
2. ___ I possess a well-defined concept of how I want to live my life.
3. ___ I trust my gut instincts to know how I feel about somebody.
4. ___ Soaking in a nice, hot bath is a favorite way to release tension and stress for me.
5. ___ Just staying home and wearing comfortable clothes is one way I really enjoy spending my time.
6. ___ People who know me would call me a good listener.
7. ___ I have a nicely decorated, color-coordinated bedroom.
8. ___ My judgment of people is based more on their appearance and their clothing than on the way they talk or the way they respond physically to me.
9. ___ If the radio or stereo is playing, I'm often singing or humming along.
10. ___ If a movie has great special effects, scenery, or costumes, I'll go see it.
11. ___ I make sure I look good before I leave my home.
12. ___ The decoration of a room and the art on the walls are some of the first things I notice when entering a room.
13. ___ The music I really enjoy is the music that helps me relax.
14. ___ I'm attracted to books with colorful, handsome covers.
15. ___ I'm a doodler and a fidgeter when I talk on the phone.
16. ___ It's often the case that I have a difficult time unwinding and that I continue to feel tense after a stressful day.
17. ___ I like to watch people at the shopping mall.
18. ___ My first impressions of people are based more on how they use their voices than on how they look or act.

19. ___ I like movies with plots that slowly unwind and have a relaxed pace more than noisy, action movies with lots of special effects.
20. ___ I can create clear, vivid pictures in my imagination.
21. ___ I like to take frequent stretch breaks, get out of my seat, and move around while I'm working on something.
22. ___ I spend a lot of time listening to the radio or my tapes or CDs.
23. ___ A lively, stimulating conversation is one of the ways I most enjoy spending my time.
24. ___ When engaged in activities that don't take a lot of concentration, like driving or showering, I often talk to myself or sing or hum.
25. ___ When eating alone, I usually watch TV or read.
26. ___ I like talk radio programs.
27. ___ I feel comfortable giving a hug to someone whom I've just met.
28. ___ I'd rather hear a story read by a good reader than read the book.
29. ___ Loud noises and voices bother me when I'm trying to study.
30. ___ A good shoulder and neck message relaxes me more than just about anything.

Total for Questions 2, 7, 8, 10, 11, 12, 14, 17, 20, and 25 = _____ V

Total for Questions 1, 6, 9, 18, 22, 23, 24, 26, 28, and 29 = _____ A

Total for Questions 3, 4, 5, 13, 15, 16, 19, 21, 27, and 30 = _____ K

The "V" total is your visual score, the "A" total is your auditory score, and the "K" total is your kinesthetic score.

In very general terms, here's what your scores mean:

If you have a high visual score, you prefer to learn things by seeing them, by looking at diagrams and pictures, by taking in information through your sense of sight. If you have a high auditory score, you like to learn by hearing explanations, by talking things through, by listening to the material being presented. If you scored high in the kinesthetic category, you like "hands on" learning, to learn by doing and by going on field trips, to learn using your sense of touch, and by realizing you understand something because it just "feels right."

Analyze Your Instructors' Styles

Make your own evaluation of each of your instructors' teaching styles. Teachers who mostly lecture are presenting information in an auditory style; teachers who use a lot of overheads and films or slides, who write on the board a lot, and who pass out numerous handouts are visual presenters; and teachers who move around the room a great deal, who frequently use props and objects to make their points, and who often have the class do in-class exercises and drills are kinesthetic presenters. For each of these kinds of teachers, use the information and strategies presented in this chapter to make the translations.

Teachers who use a balanced style of presentation, making sure to explain things in different styles throughout their presentations, are special teachers. Sign up for their classes! Find out who these teachers are by asking students who have taken the class before you.

In the columns below, list each course, teaching style, and the method you intend to use to translate to your preferred style, if applicable. Keep in mind that because of past experiences, your preferred learning styles may vary, depending on the type of course.

COURSE	TEACHING STYLE	TRANSLATION METHOD(S)
_____	_____	_____
_____	_____	_____
_____	_____	_____
_____	_____	_____
_____	_____	_____

TWO

TAKING CONTROL OF YOUR TIME

CHAPTER OUTLINE

Time Management: A System of Control

Some Basic Techniques for Organizing Yourself
  Make Plans
  Make Time Projections
  Prioritize
  Develop a System

Developing a Time Management System
  Setting Up Schedules
  Making Out a Schedule for the Term
  Planning Weekly and Daily Activities
  Maintaining a To Do List

Coping with Procrastination
  What Really Causes Procrastination?
  Ten Anti-Procrastination Strategies

Balancing Acts
  Family Responsibilities
  Plan Stress Reduction

Aside from velcro, time is the most mysterious substance in the universe.
—Dave Barry

Think of all the roles you play in life—student, worker, friend, parent, sibling, spouse, volunteer, housekeeper, gardener, driver—pick the labels or add others that apply to you. Is it any wonder that you often feel overwhelmed by tasks and frustrated because there isn't enough time to get everything done? Yet, somehow, you must find a way to make the tasks fit the time, for they are the only things you can hope to control. But using your time effectively is always easier in theory than in practice.

Being able to prioritize your commitments, responsibilities, and personal needs so that you can do everything you want and need to do is the essential challenge of time management. This chapter will help you develop some effective habits and systems for planning ahead, organizing yourself, and taking control of your time.

You will get the most out of these ideas if you are willing to look critically at yourself and your habits and make a commitment to necessary changes. At the same time, you will need to recognize that there are certain things that you cannot or do not want to change. Developing a system that plays to your strengths and works around your weaknesses is a good way to approach the challenge of taking control of your time. Your goal is to feel that you have a reasonable amount of control over your daily life and a method for achieving your goals with as little stress as possible.

Time Management: A System of Control

A time management system is really a system for becoming organized—for planning and structuring your time so that you feel less time pressure than do disorganized people. People who are "organized" are comfortable using organizational tools, such as appointment books and planning calendars. However, even organized people become pressured when they try to fit too many things into too short a period of time. The person who schedules three important appointments in one afternoon is not going to feel any less pressured because the times and places are written neatly into an appointment book.

It is not enough to acquire and use the tools of time management, such as calendars, daily planners, and "To Do" lists. Equally important is making a commitment to continually assess your priorities, to make plans and follow through on them, and to evaluate your situation regularly, so that the goals you set are realistic and attainable.

Some Basic Techniques for Getting Organized

People who are exceptionally well organized can generally be described as people the rest of us love to hate and also envy. How do they do it? Aren't they secretly unhappy with their rigid "everything in it's place" lifestyle? Don't they actually long to oversleep, rush around getting dressed, and then have to search frantically for their keys before flying out the door? While it is true that being too rigidly organized can create a level of stress all it's own, it is also true that people who are organized feel less time pressure than do disorganized people. The key is *control*. To the extent that you can plan your own schedule, discipline yourself to abide by your plans, and follow some kind of system for getting things done on time, you will not only *feel* in control of your life, you will actually *be* in control. And having control is one of the best stress reducers you can find.

Make Plans

To plan is to identify what you need to do and when you need to do it. Making a list is one good way to plan. Writing down all the things you feel you must do within a given period of time clears away the feeling that commitments are closing in on you. If you put into words and look at everything you think you must get done in the next week or the next month, the first thing you will probably find is that the world won't fall apart if you don't do them all.

Make Time Projections

In order to know how many things you can get done in a given period of time, you need to have an idea of how long each one will take. This sounds simple, but it is actually not easy to calculate how much time it will take to prepare a major term paper, for instance, or how much time you will need to spend in the computer lab to master the use of a software program. Nevertheless, you need to assign an amount of time that you are willing to devote, or that you feel you have to devote, to various tasks and activities. Some of these time commitments need to be calculated incrementally, that is, in small manageable steps. So, instead of thinking "it will take me a month to prepare a term paper," think "I will spend at least three hours per week for the next four weeks on my physical science term paper."

> Most of us think of ourselves as standing wearily and helplessly at the center of a circle bristling with tasks, burdens, problems, annoyances, and responsibilities which are rushing in upon us. At every moment we have a dozen different things to do, a dozen problems to solve, a dozen strains to endure. We see ourselves as overdriven, overburdened, overtired.
>
> This is a common mental picture—and it is totally false. No one of us, however crowded his life, has such an existence.
>
> What is the true picture of your life? Imagine that there is an hourglass on your desk. Connecting the bowl at the top with the bowl at the bottom is a tube so thin that only one grain of sand can pass through it at a time. That is the true picture of your life, even on a super-busy day. The crowded hours come to you always one moment at a time. That is the only way they can come. The day may bring many tasks, many problems and strains, but invariable they come in single file.
>
> You want to gain emotional poise? Remember the hourglass, the grains of sand dropping one by one.
>
> —*James Gordon Gilkey, Author*

Prioritize

To **prioritize** means to establish in your mind the relative importance of the all the things you have to get done, along with the things you don't have to do, but would like to do. The reason most people feel disorganized and frustrated that there isn't enough time in the day is because there really isn't enough time in the day. Life is complicated and often we just can't do everything we wish to do, promised to do, and have been trying to do, and still get done what we absolutely *need* to do. Accept it. Put your life in perspective and decide what is most important at this particular time. Then make a list of the things you are willing to give up or suspend temporarily. Will you have more time if you put a club membership on hold? Stop singing in the church choir for a while? Spend less time with your family or your friends? Give up your evening basketball game? Maybe instead of giving up some activities you will decide to cut back the amount of time you spend on them. Whatever you decide, stick to it and don't let others persuade you otherwise.

Develop a System

After you have thought through what you need to do and the relative importance of your commitments, you will need a system for making sure that you follow through on your plans. This system must be one that is comfortable for you. In the course of reading this chapter you will be presented with a variety of planning strategies and time management systems. Some of them require a time commitment unto themselves and a willingness to review the details of your life on a continuing basis. If your psyche just doesn't respond favorably to any kind of stringent routine, then you will need to adapt these ideas to what you can handle. The last thing you want is to be frustrated and annoyed by your own time management system. The right type of system and your positive attitude toward it will be a major help to you in achieving your goals. Remember, the key is control.

How Well Organized Are You?

If you can answer "Yes" to at least ten of the following questions, you are a pretty organized and time conscious person. If the majority of your answers are "No," you will be surprised at how much a time management system can improve your life.

		YES	NO
1.	I always wear a watch.	☐	☐
2.	I usually save all my errands and do them at one time.	☐	☐
3.	I make lists of things I need to do.	☐	☐
4.	I usually carry an appointment book around with me.	☐	☐
5.	I leave home at exactly the same time every morning.	☐	☐
6.	I prefer to have my meals at regular times.	☐	☐
7.	I like to arrive a little early for appointments.	☐	☐
8.	I plan vacations and other leisure activities well in advance.	☐	☐
9.	I try to get the same number of hours of sleep every night.	☐	☐
10.	I always try to leave extra time to get to an airport or train station, so I won't have to worry about missing a flight or a train.	☐	☐
11.	I am usually able to find enough time in the week to do all the things I consider to be important.	☐	☐
12.	I feel that I am able to spend quality time with my family and friends.	☐	☐

13. I feel most comfortable with my life when I am able to follow a daily routine. ☐ ☐
14. I don't feel much stress from the effort it takes to do all the things I need to get done. ☐ ☐
15. I don't often have to juggle my plans around, and when I do, it's for a good reason. ☐ ☐

Developing a Time Management System

Having made the decision to further your education, you are left pretty much to your own devices to impose the structure and discipline you need to do well in your classes and balance school with the rest of your life. Most people find this easier to do on the job in a situation where other people are actually controlling much of their time. The motivation to not miss a meeting or a deadline, or to avoid upsetting the boss by showing up late for an appointment, is strong incentive to stick to a schedule. Once we get outside of an imposed structure, we immediately want to "breathe free" and some, if not all, of our self-discipline starts to evaporate.

To develop an effective time management system, you need to acquire some basic tools. Calendars, appointment books, and schedules are excellent tools. Computerized schedules and software programs are also useful if you have a personal computer. Using time management tools to schedule your activities and filling in time blocks with all the important things you have to do can be a satisfying task unto itself. The act of thinking things through and creating a plan of action will, in fact, increase your level of organization and efficient use of your time, even if you just carry the schedule around in your head. But, to get the most out of time management tools, you must use them on a regular basis and make them a part of your life.

What kind of time management system do you currently use? Make a list of all the things that you currently do to schedule and control your time. Rate your current system on a scale of 1 to 10, with 1 being not in control and 10 being completely in control of your time. What needs to change in order for you to raise your level of control over your time?

Figure 2-1 on page 36 is a tool you can use to analyze your current time management status. Write down your daily plans for the next two days in the "Estimated Use of Time" column. At the end of each day, fill in the "Actual Use of Time" column. At the bottom, write down your observations about the discrepancies between what you planned and what actually happened. Note in particular any patterns you see in what is causing you to lose control over your daily schedule. You may want to duplicate this form or set it up on your computer and use it as a time management assessment tool for an extended period of time.

Setting Up Schedules

Once you are registered for a term, a good part of your schedule is already set up. You then have to plan your study time, family, social, and other commitments around the times you have no choice but to attend class.

Setting Up Your Class Schedule. Here are some things to keep in mind:

- If you are a full-time student, try to schedule classes with blocks of time in between. When you take several classes in succession or try, you are apt to suffer from "information overload." Time between classes gives you the chance to review your notes, make plans for completing assignments, and reflect on what you learned in class. You are also likely to have more physical energy and feel less need for "down time" if you are not sitting in classes for extended periods of time.
- When considering the number of classes to take, keep in mind that experts recommend devoting at least two hours of study and preparation out of class for every hour in class. So, if you take a full course load of 12 hours, you need to schedule an additional 24 hours weekly for study, preparation, and completion of assignments.
- If you are working part time or full time, or if you have heavy family responsibilities, a part-time class load will enable you to have more control over all the important things you need to do and still do well in your studies.
- When selecting courses to take each term, consider the level of difficulty you anticipate with each course. Try to take a mix of difficult and easy courses, based on what you know about your own aptitudes (and what you hear about instructors). Also try to balance courses you find boring with those in which you have a high level of interest.

SUPPORT SYSTEMS

When setting up your class schedule, you may need to consult with others and enlist their support. For instance, will your boss let you leave a half hour early on certain days so that you won't be late for an evening class? Do your child-care arrangements need to be changed so that you are not worried and feeling hassled about being home or picking up your children at a certain hour? Will your spouse or another significant person in your life be depending on you for social activity? Is that person willing to accept that you must temporarily give up doing some things without making you feel torn between a personal commitment and your studies?

Seek out those who can help you. Beware of those who can harm your efforts by making you feel guilty or selfish because you have decided to pursue a personal goal that they may see as excluding them.

CHAPTER 2   Taking Control of Your Time

FIGURE 2-1 Time Management Assessment

DATE _____

ESTIMATED USE OF TIME		ACTUAL USE OF TIME	
6:00 _____	1:00 _____	6:00 _____	1:00 _____
6:30 _____	1:30 _____	6:30 _____	1:30 _____
7:00 _____	2:00 _____	7:00 _____	2:00 _____
7:30 _____	2:30 _____	7:30 _____	2:30 _____
8:00 _____	3:00 _____	8:00 _____	3:00 _____
8:30 _____	3:30 _____	8:30 _____	3:30 _____
9:00 _____	4:00 _____	9:00 _____	4:00 _____
9:30 _____	4:30 _____	9:00 _____	4:00 _____
10:00 _____	5:00 _____	10:00 _____	5:00 _____
10:30 _____	5:30 _____	10:30 _____	5:30 _____
11:00 _____	6:00 _____	11:00 _____	6:00 _____
11:30 _____	6:30 _____	11:30 _____	6:30 _____
12:00 _____	7:00 _____	12:00 _____	7:00 _____
12:30 _____	7:30 _____	12:30 _____	7:30 _____

OBSERVATIONS:
_____
_____
_____

- Are you a morning, afternoon, or night person? Try to schedule classes, especially the ones you expect to be difficult, during the period of day when you usually feel most alert and least distracted by other things in your life.

Scheduling Other Activities. After you have determined how much class time and study/preparation time you need to set aside each week, make a list of the other activities in your life and prioritize it. Start by identifying the things that you absolutely cannot eliminate. Such a list might include:

- Sleeping/relaxing
- Shopping for necessities
- Spending time with family/children
- Commuting
- Preparing/eating meals
- Working
- Physical activity/exercise

Things you want to consider eliminating or cutting back on might include:

- Working
- Socializing with friends/family
- Hobbies
- Religious activities
- Clubs/organizations
- Community/volunteer work
- Physical activity/exercise

Prioritize Your Life

Make a list of all of the important activities and responsibilities (excluding your studies) in your life that must remain the same despite your decision to get a college degree. Arrange the list in order of priority—from most important to least important. Now add attending classes and studying to the list and then prioritize it once again. Is there anything at the bottom of the list that can be eliminated? Does the list look manageable? If not, what can you do to make the number of activities fit the time you have available? Be creative in your thinking and planning.

Important Activities _____

_____

_____

_____

_____

_____

_____

_____

CHAPTER 2   Taking Control of Your Time

Prioritized Activities _____

_____
_____
_____
_____
_____
_____
_____

Making Out a Schedule for the Term

Within the first week or two of the beginning of a term, you should have a pretty good idea of what major events you need to plan for ahead of time. Consider making out a master schedule or having some kind of "master plan" to follow as you go along. Such a plan will help you sleep better at night because you will know where you stand with things that are coming up. You want to prevent falling into a "crisis" approach where you find yourself staying up all night to study for an exam or read an entire book, or trying to write a research paper in one day.

A useful tool for long-term planning is a large desk calendar. Try to find one that has a section in the front for monthly planning (see Figure 2-2). Use this section for developing a framework for your monthly, weekly, and daily planning. As soon as you know them, fill in the dates for mid-terms, finals, major projects or paper due dates, and whatever else takes advance preparation and work. Identify timeframes for studying for mid-terms and finals. See Figure 2-2 and use it as a model to create your own. This can easily be translated to a computerized system.

> QUOTE
> The trouble with the future is that it usually arrives before we're ready for it.
> —Arnold H. Glasow

MONDAY	TUESDAY	WEDNESDAY	THURSDAY	FRIDAY	SATURDAY	SUNDAY
1	2 Eve: work	3	4 Eve: work	5 Holiday	6 Complete reading for Eng. paper	7 →
8 Spring Break	9 → Eve: work	10 →	11 → Eve: work	12 →	13 Write 1st draft	14 →
15	16 Eve: work	17	18 Inventory at store / work all day	19 Mom's B'day	20 Write final draft	21 →
22	23 Eve: work	24 English Paper due	25 Eve: work	26	27	28
29	30 Begin planning for Finals Eve: work					

Month of _April_

FIGURE 2-2 Filled-in Monthly Planner

PART ONE College Success Strategies

Planning Weekly and Daily Activities

If you don't already have the habit of keeping a weekly and daily schedule, now is a good time to try to develop it. Trying to keep things in your head or writing lists on scraps of paper will not work for long. A weekly planner like the one in Figure 2-3 can be used to make note of important events and develop an overview of what your week looks like. A daily schedule can also be kept (see Figure 2-4). You may want to make up a notebook size daily planner, buy a small pocket-size appointment book, or print out your daily schedule from your computer.

```
                          WEEKLY PLANNER
WEEK BEGINNING _____
MONDAY _____     THURSDAY _____
AM _____     AM _____
_____      _____
_____      _____
Noon _____     Noon _____
_____      _____
_____      _____
_____      _____
PM _____     PM _____
_____      _____
_____      _____
_____      _____
TUESDAY _____     FRIDAY _____
AM _____     AM _____
_____      _____
_____      _____
Noon _____     Noon _____
_____      _____
_____      _____
_____      _____
PM _____     PM _____
_____      _____
_____      _____
_____      _____
WEDNESDAY _____     SATURDAY _____  SUNDAY _____
AM _____     AM _____  _____
_____      _____   _____
_____      _____   _____
Noon _____     Noon _____  _____
_____      _____   _____
_____      _____   _____
_____      _____   _____
PM _____     PM _____  _____
_____      _____   _____
_____      _____   _____
_____      _____   _____
```

FIGURE 2-3 Weekly Planner

FIGURE 2-4 Daily Planner

Daily Planner

Date: _____

6:00	4:00
6:30	4:30
7:00	5:00
7:30	5:30
8:00	6:00
8:30	6:30
9:00	7:00
9:30	7:30
10:00	8:00
10:30	8:30
11:00	9:00
11:30	9:30
12:00	10:00
12:30	10:30
1:00	11:00
1:30	11:30
2:00	12:00
2:30	12:30
3:00	1:00
3:30	1:30

As mentioned earlier, just the act of writing things down forces you to stop and think about what you are trying to do. You have to calculate how much time to allow for things, and you can easily recognize if you are trying to cram too many activities into an afternoon, a day, or a week. This gives you a chance to make decisions about priorities ahead of time so that you are truly focusing on what's important as opposed to responding to whatever is upon you. Later, the blueprint of your plan will be imprinted on your mind, even if you don't have the discipline to carry your calendar around, refer to it daily, and keep it up-to-the-minute. You will see the benefit from sitting down once a week and planning a weekly/daily schedule. If you can further develop the habit of following your planned schedule and referring to it before making any plans, you will achieve a higher level of effective time management.

Maintaining a To Do List

An even more detailed tool recommended by time management experts is the "To Do List." This is a list of everything you need to do, usually updated daily. A To Do List will only lead to frustration if you put too many things on it, although some people like to write down things that they know they will do in order to experience the satisfaction of crossing them off.

A To Do List needs to be prioritized, with the lowest priority items being things that it would be nice to get done that day if possible. Label items A for urgent/very important; B for important but not urgent; and C for not urgent or important at the moment. At the end of the day, some of your B and C items may carry over to the next day's list. C items may become B and finally A items if they keep getting moved to the next day. For instance on Monday, "pick up clothes from dry cleaner" may be a C. However, if you need one of the clothing items for a special evening out on Friday night, the trip to the cleaners will become an A by Thursday or Friday. See Figure 2-5 for an example form to use for a To Do List.

The busier you are, the more likely it is that you will have to put things off. This is where having a To Do List can really help you. The very act of having to rewrite an item each time you move it to the next day will motivate you to exam-

FIGURE 2-5   To Do List

ine why you haven't done it. Getting rid of the sinking feeling in your stomach each time you confront an item such as "begin research for paper due in two weeks" may be incentive enough to help you actually get started.

If you decide to keep a To-Do list, it should be regularly updated in the morning or at the end of the day. Morning is probably best, to avoid any late evening stress caused by "not done" items. Thinking about them at night could interfere with a good night's sleep.

Many people avoid making a To-Do list because they believe it will take away some of the spontaneity of their lives. The reverse is actually true. Using a To-Do list helps you get things accomplished. When you have completed your tasks you're better able to enjoy your remaining free time. Also, you can schedule a relaxing activity on your To-Do list as a strategy to give yourself the downtime you need to avoid burnout.

A To-Do list is not a harsh taskmaster to which you pay homage by forcing yourself to accomplish things in a given order with no concern for the fact that you're a human with a real life. It is simply a tool to keep your daily goals in front of you so you don't waste time in unproductive activities when you could be accomplishing something that will advance you toward those achievements you truly value.

Coping with Procrastination

Any discussion of time management would not be complete without an examination of the most well-intentioned person's worst enemy—procrastination. The dictionary (Webster's New Collegiate) defines **procrastination** as "the act of putting off intentionally and habitually the doing of something that should be done." Interestingly, most procrastinators do not feel that they are acting intentionally. On the contrary, they feel that they fully *intend* to do whatever it is, but they simply cannot, will not, or—bottom line—they *do not* do it. Procrastinators usually have good reasons for their procrastination (some would call them excuses): "didn't have time," "didn't feel well," "couldn't figure out what to do," "couldn't find what I needed," "the weather was too bad"—the list is never-ending.

> Time rushes by and yet is frozen. Funny how we get so exact about time at the end of life and at its beginning. She died at 6:08 or 3:46, we say, or the baby was born at 4:02. But in between we slosh through huge swatches of time—weeks, months, years, decades even.
>
> —Helen Prejean, Nun, Author, Dead Man Walking

FIGURE 2-6 Sample Project Planning Form

PROJECTS	ACTION STEPS	Date Due	Completion Date	Done	NOTES
Oral presentation	Select Topic (Read/research)	2/15	2/1	2/5	
	Develop Outline/Research		2/3	2/5	Schedule library time
	Organize Notes		2/5	2/7	Type on 3x5 cards
	Create Visuals		2/7	2/10	Computer?
	Practice		2/13-2/14		Schedule "audience"
English Composition	Write outline	2/17	2/2	2/2	
	Do background reading		2/7-2/8	2/6	
	Revise Outline		2/10	2/12	
	Write first draft		2/10	2/12	
	Edit/proofread		2/12		
	Get someone to read draft		2/12		
	Final draft		2/15		

What Really Causes Procrastination?

Even procrastinators themselves know that the surface reasons for their procrastination are, for the most part, not valid. When procrastination becomes extreme, it is a self-destructive course and yet, people feel that they are powerless to stop it. This perception can become reality if the underlying cause is not uncovered. Experts have identified some of the serious underlying causes of procrastination. Think about them the next time you find yourself struck by this problem.

Fear/Worry. Often procrastination stems from a real or imagined fear or worry that is focused not so much on the thing you are avoiding but its potential consequences. For instance, your procrastination over preparing for an oral presentation could be based on your fear that no matter how well prepared you are, you will be overcome by nerves and forget whatever you prepared to say. Every time you think about working on the speech, you become so worried about doing "a bad job" that you have to put the whole thing out of your mind to calm down. You decide that you will feel calmer about it tomorrow and will be in a much better frame of mind to tackle it. Tomorrow the scenario gets repeated. The best way to relieve your anxiety would be to dig in and prepare so well that you can't possibly do poorly.

Perfectionism. Being a perfectionist is one of the main traits that spawns fear and anxiety. Whose expectations are we afraid of not meeting? Often it is our own harsh judgment of ourselves that creates the problem. We set standards that are too high and then judge ourselves too critically. When you picture yourself speaking before a group, are you thinking about how nervous the other students will be as well, or are you comparing your speaking abilities to the anchorperson on the six o'clock news? A more calming thought is to recall how athletes measure improvements in their performances by tracking and trying to improve

PLANNING LARGE PROJECTS

1. Write down the target date and count the number of weeks you have until the work is due.
2. Divide the projects into logical segments or steps.
3. Arrange the steps in chronological order.
4. Write down every task you can think of that you will need to do to complete each step. Make the list as detailed as possible.
5. Now that you can see how many tasks comprise each major step toward completion, you can assign a timeframe to each step.
6. As you work on each step of the project, add to the list of tasks as necessary. These tasks are what should be written into your weekly/daily planning schedule and your To Do List.
7. As you progress through each step, make sure you keep track of any unfinished tasks, such as tracking down a particular piece of vital information. Try to tie up all loose ends before you begin the last step.

on their own "personal best." Champions have to work on beating themselves in order to become capable of competing against their better opponents. Concentration on improving upon your own past performance, and thinking of specific ways to do so, relieves performance anxiety.

Lack of Motivation. On the surface this would seem to be the reason for all procrastination, and that the obvious answer is for the procrastinator to find a way to "get motivated." There are situations where lack of motivation is an indicator that you have taken a wrong turn. When you seriously do not want to do the things you need to do, you may need to reevaluate your situation. Did you decide to get a degree in Information Systems because everyone says that's where the high paying jobs are going to be, when you really want to be a social worker or a travel agent? If so, when you find yourself shooting hoops or watching television when you should be putting in time at the computer lab, it may be time to reexamine your decision. Setting out to accomplish something difficult when your heart isn't in it, is often the root cause of self-destructive behavior.

> QUOTE
> Why not spend some time in determining what is worthwhile for us, and then go after that?
> —William Ross

Burnout. Often procrastination is due to an inability to concentrate or a feeling of being overwhelmed and indecisive. While everyone experiences these feelings during a particularly stressful day or week, a continuation of these feelings could indicate that you are in a state of burnout. **Burnout** is a serious problem that occurs when you have overextended yourself for too long a period of time. It is especially likely to occur if you are pushing yourself both physically and mentally. By failing to pace yourself, you will "hit the wall," like the long distance runner who runs too fast at the beginning of the race. Overworking yourself for too long without mental and physical relaxation is a sure way to run out of steam. Learning to balance your time and set realistic expectations for yourself will prevent burnout.

Feeling Stymied. Sometimes you put off doing something because you literally don't know how to do it. This may be hard to admit to yourself, so you may make other excuses. When you can't get started on something, consider the possibility that you need help. For example, if you get approval from your favorite instructor for a term paper topic that requires collecting data and creating graphics, you can become stymied if you don't have the necessary skills and tools to do the work and do it well. Does the collection and analysis of the data require the use of a software program that you don't have and cannot afford to buy? Sometimes it is difficult to ask for help and sometimes it is even hard to recognize that you need help. When you feel stymied, ask yourself, "Do I need help?" Do you need information but haven't a clue as to where to go to get it? Have you committed to doing something that is really beyond your level of skills? Being able to own up to personal limitations and seek out support and resources where needed is a skill used everyday by highly successful people.

Ten Anti-Procrastination Strategies

Following are some tips you can use to counteract procrastination:

1. Make To Do Lists and give each item a priority label; set a limit to how many times you are allowed to move an item within a week.
2. Break long projects down into small, manageable steps and set reasonable timeframes for each step.
3. Set a deadline and plan a nice reward for yourself if you meet it.
4. Set aside time to review your progress toward goals and deadlines. Focus on what you have successfully accomplished. Look at how you can apply the same attitudes and techniques to what has not been accomplished.

5. Look for underlying reasons why you are putting something off. Confront the reason and resolve it so you can move on.
6. Recognize when you need help or support to do something and seek it out without delay.
7. Focus on getting something done, not doing it perfectly. If you get started early, you will have more time to improve it.
8. Don't try to do more than you can physically and mentally handle.
9. Don't commit to goals and plans because of outside pressures; pursue what you want to do, not what you feel you have to do.
10. Don't make time the enemy because you feel you never have enough of it. The more relaxed you are in your attitude toward time, the more you will be able to use it wisely.

Balancing Acts

In a recent article called "Breaking Point," *Newsweek* magazine observed that "Americans move at [an ever] more rapid pace, driven by a staccato sense of time. First, the clock created artificial pressure on our ancestors' inner rhythms. Now we have computer technology based on the nanosecond, an increment of one billionth of a second... Experts say the fatigue of the '90s... the kind that a weekend's rest or reading a trashy book on the beach can't cure—is more widespread." The research behind this article pointed to the fact that far too many Americans are pushing themselves to the breaking point, and that overwork to the point of severe exhaustion is a serious problem in our society. The stresses of family life, work life, financial responsibilities, and the complexities of living in a rapidly changing, technology-driven environment are factors that decrease the very quality of life that people are striving so hard to attain.

What can be done about it? How can you cope with all the things you need to get done without driving yourself to the point of exhaustion? If you have important responsibilities that cannot be set aside while you go to school, your time management plan must take these into consideration.

CHAPTER 2 Taking Control of Your Time   45

Family Responsibilities

If you have family responsibilities, particularly young children, you will need to include them in your time management planning. If they are old enough, explain your decision to attend school and ask for their cooperation. Regardless of your children's ages, it will help if you already have a routine schedule that includes regular meal, bath, and bedtimes. If not, you should consider a family time management system that incorporates more structure into your daily family life. If your child rearing responsibility is shared with a spouse or other adult in the home, a session in which you sit down and discuss any changes that are necessary in division of chores, use of free time, and time spent with the children will get things off on the right foot. It is not wise to assume that your family is going to automatically fall in line and provide the extra help and cooperation you need to complete your education. It is not uncommon for family members to resent the intrusion of study time or changes in your schedule that mean you are absent during hours when they were used to having you at home. Bringing family members into the decisions you make about how many class hours to take, how much time you need to study, and what you expect from them will decrease the level of stress on everyone.

Studies show that women with young children have the most difficult balancing act to achieve when they decide to pursue activities outside of the home. This is because women usually take more responsibility for running the household, even if there is a male counterpart in the family. If you are a woman with family responsibilities, consider whether you need to plan for additional help in order to manage your time effectively. Hiring a babysitter for a couple of extra hours when you have to write a paper or study for an exam may be more productive than trying to work for hours at a time with children under foot.

Plan Stress Reduction

Most people wait until they get stressed out before they do anything about it. Like any other health-related problem, the mind and the body are much better off when stress is prevented. Looking for ways to reduce and avoid stress should be a major part of your plan for managing your time and controlling your life. For instance, no matter what role you play at home as a parent, it is of vital importance that you feel comfortable and secure about your child-care arrangements when you are away from home. Worrying about your children's well being is physically draining, and will interfere with your ability to concentrate. Consider investing in a pager or cell phone so that you know you can always be contacted in case of an emergency.

Another stress reducer to avoid is guilt. Focusing on your long-term goals and what they will mean to you and your family is one way to chase away the temptation to allow family interruptions when you are trying to work at home or to ignore your planned schedule altogether. This may be especially difficult on weekends. This is where your scheduling system can help you. By blocking out your home study hours, you are simultaneously blocking in time that you will be free to spend with your family. Thinking, "I am going to work for two hours on Sunday afternoon and two hours Sunday night" gives you a different mindset than if you approach the weekend thinking, "I have to study—where am I going to find the time?" By blocking out four solid hours with an interval between, you still have plenty of quality time to spend with your family.

Here are some things you can do to reduce stress on a regular basis:

- Get a good night's sleep—whatever number of hours your body normally needs in order for you to feel rested and alert throughout the day. Avoid cutting back on sleep except in an emergency.

> QUOTE
> There can't be a crisis next week. My schedule is already full.
> —Henry Kissinger

- Avoid skipping meals and missing exercising, and don't go on a diet. Well balanced, nutritional meals are energy boosters that help you keep going at a steady level for longer periods of time. Dieting, in the sense of going without food, should be avoided entirely. If you cannot maintain a scheduled program of exercise, do not give up exercising or vigorous physical activity altogether. Physical activity releases tension and keeps you fit for putting in long hours.
- Schedule "down time." This is especially important if you have a tendency to overextend yourself. Plan a long hot bath, buy a new CD and listen to it, or go to see the latest movie. These are all things that can be done in a short period of time and they allow you a period of complete escape from the daily grind.
- Distinguish between necessary haste and "rushing around." The majority of the time an even pace should keep you on your schedule. Feeling rushed or trying to do more than one thing at a time detracts from your ability to concentrate. Often this can result in making mistakes or forgetting something, so that time saved ends up being lost.
- Reduce background noise. Noise contributes to that hectic feeling and also interferes with concentration. If you live with others, you might have to enlist their help in reducing the noise level, not only when you are studying, but also in general.

AVOIDING TIME WASTERS

No matter how good you are at scheduling your time, getting side tracked is easy to do. Be on the alert for these time wasters:

1. The friendly telephone caller: "I just called to talk for a minute."
2. The television set: If you're in charge of the remote control—turn it off. If someone else is in charge, leave the room.
3. The plea for help: "I know you're busy, but I really can't do this without you."
4. Negative thoughts of your inner voice: "I'm tired," "This is too hard," "I was always poor at math," "I can't do this."
5. Positive thoughts of your inner voice: "I wish I was at the beach," "I want something delicious to eat," "I remember all the fun I used to have." Add your own time wasters to this list and make a vow to avoid them.

Time Wasters

Make a list of the things you do or things other people do that cause the biggest waste of time for you. Think of ways to eliminate these time wasters from your life. Make notes on what you are going to do and set a timeframe for your plan to work.

_____
_____
_____
_____
_____
_____
_____
_____

Review and Recall

1. List and explain four techniques for organizing yourself.

   a. _____
   _____

   b. _____
   _____

CHAPTER 2　Taking Control of Your Time

c. _____

   d. _____

2. Explain what it means to prioritize your responsibilities and activities.
   _____
   _____

3. List five important considerations for setting up your class schedule.

   a. _____

   b. _____

   c. _____

   d. _____

   e. _____

4. List five major causes of procrastination.

   a. _____

   b. _____

   c. _____

   d. _____

   e. _____

5. Procrastination is an intentional act. Do you agree or disagree with this statement? Explain your answer.
   _____
   _____

6. Trying to balance too many responsibilities creates stress; it can also be an underlying cause of procrastination. Seeking support and assistance from others is one possible solution. List the resources that are available to you, if you need help in the following areas:

   Course work _____

   Financial _____

   Emotional/mental stress _____

   Child care _____

   Household duties/chores _____

Apply Critical Thinking

A **responsibility** can be moral, legal, or mental. An **obligation** is a course of action that, once chosen, you are morally bound to follow. A **commitment** is an agreement or pledge to do something, usually associated with an emotional attachment. Think of the people with whom you live or who are of great significance in your life. Try to sort out your responsibilities, commitments, and obligations to them. While your responsibilities are unchangeable, consider where you can enlist their help in disengaging you from commitments and obligations that may interfere with your commitment to complete your education. Make a list for each person and decide how you will use it to assist you in achieving your time management goals.

School to Work Applications

SCANS

RESOURCES: *MANAGES TIME*

SYSTEMS: *UNDERSTANDS SYSTEMS; IMPROVES AND DESIGNS SYSTEMS*

1. Review the material that you developed while you were studying this chapter and the suggested tools for developing a time management system. Decide what kind of time management system you want to develop. Go to a stationery, office supply, department store, or computer store and select whatever time management tools you feel you would be comfortable using, or develop your own using the models presented here. Using the materials you have gathered, develop and implement your personally designed time management system. (Keep in mind that it is difficult to determine exactly how well a particular item will suit your needs until after you have used it. You may go through several types before you find the exact tools that are comfortable and easy for you to use.)

2. Time Management System Review: Phase 1
    a. For the next two weeks, in addition to using your time management system, keep a written record of how you actually use your time. During the day and at the end of the evening, record how you spent every hour of the day as closely as you possibly can. This is called keeping a time log. At the end of each week, compare your time log with your schedule and note the areas where they diverge. Circle the things on your time log that are causing delays or postponement of tasks and activities on your daily schedule. Consider how you can cut back or eliminate the things that are disrupting your plans.
    b. How good are you at projecting time needed to complete various tasks and activities? If you find that a lot of your projections have been off the mark, try focusing your efforts to see if you can improve your time-projection skills. During the next week, pick three or four activities related to school, work, or home and estimate how long it will take you to complete them. Compare your estimates with actual performance. How close were you? Did anything unexpected happen to get you off schedule? What did you learn from this time assessment?

3. Time Management System Review: Phase 2

    Place on your calendar an appointment with yourself to review your time management system again two weeks after the completion of Phase 1 above. At this time, answer the following questions about your system:
    a. Have you been able to follow your planned schedule and accomplish the things you need to get done? If not, where does the schedule break down? What kinds of changes do you need to make in order to avoid these problems?
    b. How many of the ideas suggested in this chapter does your time management system incorporate? Are there additional ideas that you could use? What do you need to change about your system to make it work better?
    c. Do you need additional support or resources in order to fully implement your time management system? If so, what are they? How might you go about acquiring these resources?
    d. If you feel it would help, keep a second time log for the next two weeks to help you continue to identify the things that are causing disruption of your scheduled plans. Continue to review your time management system and your activities on an ongoing basis.

SCANS Workplace Application

You are the special assistant to the marketing director of a market research consulting firm. One of the firm's clients has requested a customer survey to find out how its customers feel about the company's products and services. You and your manager have decided that a two-page printed questionnaire should be sent to 300 people to be selected from the client's mailing list. Your firm will handle every aspect of the survey, from acquiring the client's mailing list to preparation and delivery of a complete survey report. Your manager has asked you to make a list of all the tasks necessary to complete this market survey project. She also wants you to make an estimate of the time required to complete each step and give her a target date for the project's completion. Your timeline should allow two to three weeks for return of the questionnaires, before starting to compile and analyze the data. You have adequate people and financial resources available for all tasks. The current date is March 1; the client needs to have the information as soon as possible.

SCANS Personal Progress Application

PERSONAL QUALITIES: DISPLAYS RESPONSIBILITY, SELF-ESTEEM, SOCIABILITY, SELF-MANAGEMENT, AND INTEGRITY AND HONESTY

Self-motivation is a key attribute of a good employee, and every employer wants motivated workers. Beyond that, however, it is always the motivated individual who is best able to ignite the passion that distinguishes an ordinary life from a life of great accomplishment and satisfaction.

A fundamental fact about motivation is that, in most cases, humans do things for one of only two reasons: to move toward pleasure, or to move away from pain. Knowing that can help you identify why you're procrastinating about any activity, and can also help you get the leverage on yourself to overcome your procrastination.

Finding, Understanding, and Using Your Motivation

Identify a task right now about which you're likely to procrastinate (if you can't think of one, use "Doing My Taxes" as a generic procrastination-prone activity). If you procrastinate in doing your selected activity, it is because you believe you will move toward pleasure or away from pain by *not* doing it. For example, if you procrastinate about getting your taxes done, then you either (a) believe it will be a painful process to do them and you want to avoid the pain; or, (b) you believe it will be more pleasurable to do whatever activity you substitute in place of doing your taxes.

No matter whether you believe (a) or (b) or both, the truth is that you can easily convince yourself that doing your taxes (or your selected activity) will avoid pain and give you pleasure. Think about it. What are the reasons that this is true?

Write down these reasons and refer to the list whenever you are tempted to procrastinate completing your activity. A couple of reasons are given in each column below as examples for "Doing My Taxes."

It's only a matter of how much leverage you gain on yourself that determines when you break through your personal procrastination barrier on any given task. A list like the one on the following page can clarify the many reasons accomplishing the task is preferable to putting it off.

REASONS TO GET MY TAXES DONE	
In Order to Avoid Pain	In Order to Get Pleasure
1. Avoid the pain of an all-nighter to finish them.	1. Have the relief of knowing they're done.
2. Avoid the stress of not having enough time to find the receipts I need and thereby losing deductions.	2. Have the pleasure of seeing how big my refund will be this year and taking some time thinking how I'll spend the money.
3.	3.
4.	4.
5.	5.
6.	6.
7.	7.
8.	8.

PART TWO

DEVELOPING YOUR STUDY SKILLS

CHAPTER 3
Applying Study and Research Skills to Mastery

CHAPTER 4
Learning in the Classroom

CHAPTER 5
Learning Through Reading

CHAPTER 6
Writing Your Way to the Top

CHAPTER 7
Preparing for and Taking Tests

THREE

APPLYING STUDY AND RESEARCH SKILLS TO MASTERY

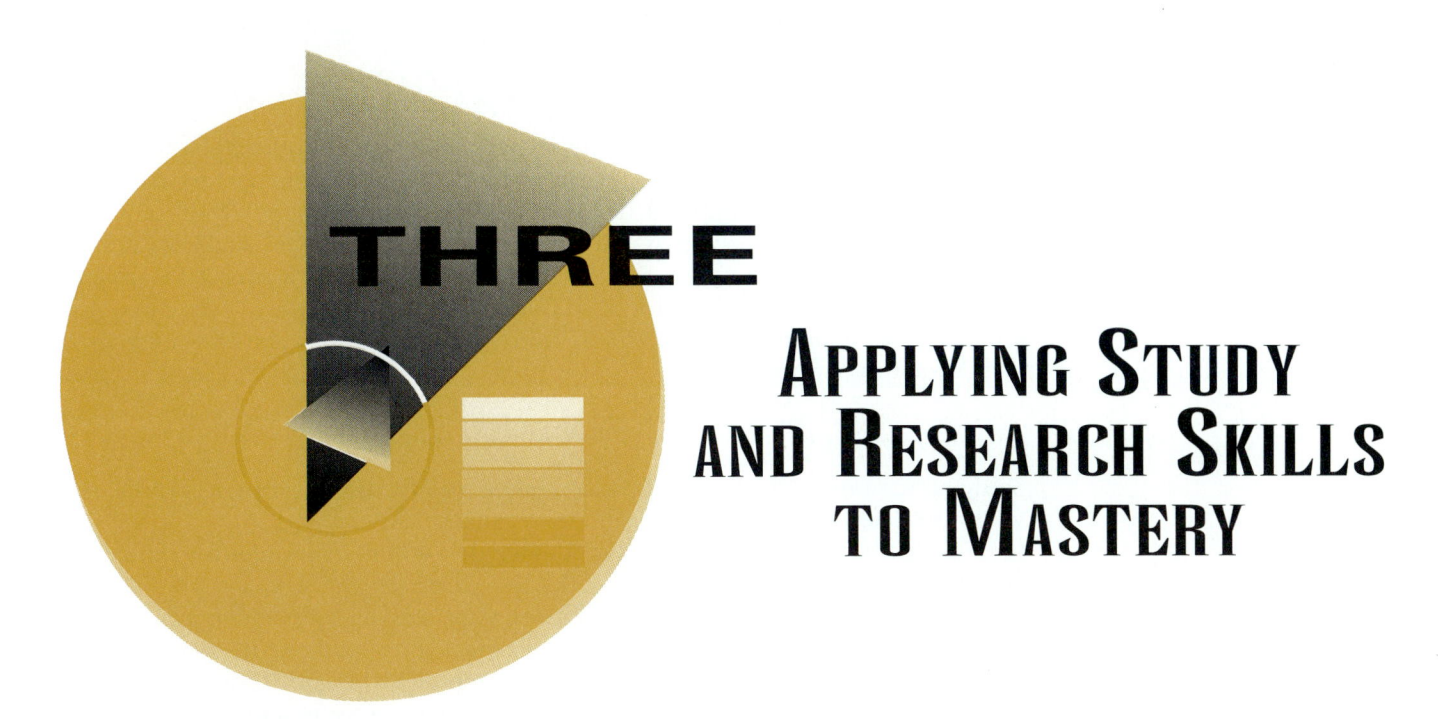

CHAPTER OUTLINE

Preparing for Study Sessions
A Space Where You Can Study
A Space That Works
The Importance of Being Rested
A Clear Head for Productive Studying
Goals for Your Study Session

Study Techniques
Recite
Get a Study Partner
Form a Study Group
Study According to How You Will Be Tested

Developing Your Research Skills
Get to Know the Library
Plan Your Research
Gather the Information

Knowledge will not be acquired without pains and application

—Felton

When we look for an example of mastery in our culture, the athlete naturally comes to mind. Many outstanding athletes start with a special gift, but how do they get to the point of professional excellence? Serious athletes are committed to mastery. They prepare themselves before they apply effort. Then they train long and hard. Just as athletes apply training skills to achieve mastery in a sport, you can prepare yourself and use study and research skills to achieve mastery in a subject area.

Mastery is a "working" knowledge. It means more than the ability to recite key concepts on command. It means understanding how to apply those concepts in valid and useful ways. As a basic foundation for mastery in all of your subjects, you will need to have your research and study skills. While this advice is likely to elicit a groan, consider that a lack of mastery is one of the reasons most people dread these tasks. When and where are they taught? Most of us are left on our own to try to acquire these skills in the early years of our education and most of us are inadequately prepared to handle them at the college level. So, look at this chapter as a way to say good-bye to "hit or miss" strategies of the past and "hello" to a better grade point average.

Preparing for Study Sessions

Consider how athletes prepare before they train. They are not haphazard about where they work out or what they wear. They check their equipment to make sure they have what they need and that everything is in top shape. They free their minds of distractions. They may eat a special diet to fuel their workouts or start with warm-up exercises to get limber. They set goals. To be a successful student, you must approach studying the way athletes approach training. Recognize how environment, equipment, mind, body, and goals, as well as specific "exercises," contribute to your performance.

A Space Where You Can Study

Studying requires a great deal of concentration and focus. Most of you will be able to concentrate best when you are in a quiet place. The fewer distractions, the better. Consider your options and select a space that will help you get the most from your time.

Many of you will do most of your reading and studying in a dorm room or at home if you are a commuting student. In some circumstances, you will be sharing space with other people. Try to find a space that is away from household or dorm activities and allows you to study quietly. If you don't, you will find that interruptions from roommates, family, or friends will distract you and make the job of studying much more difficult.

The library is also a good place for studying. Most libraries have quiet areas set aside, and some may have individual study rooms. Try to go to the same area on each visit. Associating this area with serious studying will help you to concentrate on your work. Studying at the library has several advantages, particularly if you require additional reading materials or need to use a copy machine, do research, or consult with library staff.

> There is no meaning to life except the meaning we give our lives by the unfolding of our powers. To "maximize our potential," we must take advantage of the resources available designed to increase our understanding of ourselves, the people around us, and the life we are now involved in. We become what we indulge ourselves in. The opportunities life offers help us tap our potential and can be explored when we are equipped with the right tools.
>
> —*Erich Fromm, Psychologist*

Study Attitudes

Studying is a very important key to success in college. If you developed good study habits in high school, describe them and tell how you think they will work for you in college and how you might improve them for college level material. If you did little or no studying in high school, record some steps you think might help you get in the habit of studying. Check your suggestions with the suggestions provided in this chapter. If you have ideas that aren't covered in this text, be sure to share them with your class when this topic is discussed.

_____
_____
_____
_____
_____

A Space That Works

Do you usually study while sprawled on the bed with the TV blaring or the stereo blasting? Do you have books, letters, magazines, and other miscellaneous junk cluttering your workspace? Are you munching popcorn and getting up every five minutes for a can of soda or another snack? If any of these habits are typical for you, you could use a little organization and a dose of discipline. Consider the following guidelines to make your study environment a comfortable workplace and one that encourages efficient, productive studying time.

1. Make it a rule to sit in a chair at a desk or table. A straight chair with good back support is best.
2. Check the lighting in your study area. If you don't have a good study lamp, borrow or buy one. Good light will help you avoid eye fatigue.
3. Wear a watch or make sure there's a clock nearby.
4. Clear your desk of any materials that do not relate to your work. Do make room for your reading materials as well as pencils, pens, highlighters, and other supplies.
5. Have everything that relates to the course such as the syllabus, lecture notes, research materials, and a dictionary at your side. If there isn't enough room on your desk, pull up a chair to store all the materials you will be using. Or use a bookcase, small file cabinet, or table for overflow materials. In other words, don't let the Sunday newspaper, laundry basket, or dirty dishes crowd your space.
6. Turn off the TV. The sights and sounds are too much of a distraction. Keep the stereo off, too, unless your style of learning seems to require music in the background.
7. Grab a can of your favorite soda or a bowl of your favorite "comfort food," but hold on before you dig in. No gulps, sweets, or treats until you read ten pages or work through three exercises, or whatever chunk of work you set as a goal to accomplish. This is called the reward system, and it can help you if you apply a little discipline.

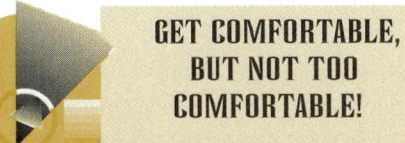

> **GET COMFORTABLE, BUT NOT TOO COMFORTABLE!**
>
> You may question whether studying at a desk in a clutter-free environment is really necessary, especially if your usual pattern is to study on an unmade bed surrounded by your roommate's mess. Well, it is necessary if you believe the research on ergonomics. Basically, ergonomists say that you will be most productive when you are comfortable—to an extent. Sometimes making yourself too comfortable is an invitation to fall asleep. You will be most productive when your back has enough support to prevent a backache, your hands are supported so you don't develop carpal tunnel syndrome (if you're typing or doing some other repetitive motion), and your work is well lighted so that you don't strain your eyes. A clean, organized study area increases your ability to concentrate. A cluttered space is a distraction. So, get comfortable, but do get off your bed and out of that mess!

CHAPTER 3 Applying Study and Research Skills to Mastery

SUPPLIES CHECKLIST

Item	Have	Need
ball point pens	☐	☐
pencils	☐	☐
erasers	☐	☐
marking pens	☐	☐
writing notebooks	☐	☐
glue stick	☐	☐
ruler	☐	☐
stapler	☐	☐
staple remover	☐	☐
paper clips	☐	☐
3 x 5 note cards	☐	☐
Post-it Tape Flags	☐	☐
Post-it Notes	☐	☐
dictionary	☐	☐
thesaurus	☐	☐
bulletin board	☐	☐
calendar	☐	☐
Scotch tape	☐	☐
rubber bands	☐	☐
scissors	☐	☐

FIGURE 3-1 Supplies Checklist

How Do You Study

Take this self-assessment to see if you need to work on your study habits.

Circle One

1. I usually sit on my bed to study.	Yes	No
2. I often fall asleep when I am studying.	Yes	No
3. I like to study with the television or stereo on.	Yes	No
4. I only study before a test.	Yes	No
5. My study area is cluttered and messy.	Yes	No
6. I have a hard time concentrating when I study.	Yes	No
7. I hate to study.	Yes	No
8. I never go to the library to study.	Yes	No
9. I never study.	Yes	No
10. I do not have a special place for studying.	Yes	No

If you answered "Yes" to most of these questions, you need to pay special attention to the study suggestions in this chapter. Look carefully at each item you marked "Yes." Then look through this chapter and highlight the text that discusses that particular study item.

PART TWO   Developing Your Study Skills

The Importance of Being Rested

In order to get the most out of your study time, you need to be well rested. It's true that the amount of sleep needed varies greatly from person to person. However, most adults feel they function best after seven to eight hours of sleep. Yet sometimes the schedule of a college student—filled with classes, errands, meals, socializing, and perhaps a job, children, and other obligations that eat up time—does not permit the desired number of z's. If your schedule leaves you with less sleep than you'd like, you have two options: make room for more sleep or help your body adjust to less sleep.

If you decide you need more sleep, evaluate your daily activities and rank them in order of priority. What can you change to make more time for sleep? You may need to switch some classes around, take fewer classes, work less or at different hours, or attend fewer social events in order to assure a good night's sleep. If you realize there is no way you can spare seven hours of rest, then do your body a favor by maintaining a consistent sleep schedule. Over time, your body will adjust to less sleep each night and you will function just fine.

> **DEVELOP REGULAR SLEEP HABITS**
>
> Irregular sleep is what really causes fatigue. Avoid all-night cram sessions or parties. Your mind and your body will suffer if you make a habit of sleeping two hours one night, ten hours the next, and then five the next night.

Are You Getting Enough Sleep?

Circle One

1. I study in bed. Yes No
2. Reading or studying makes me tired. Yes No
3. I get less than seven hours sleep on school nights. Yes No
4. I fall asleep in class. Yes No
5. I have a hard time staying awake when I study. Yes No

If you answered "Yes" to these questions, you probably are not getting enough sleep. List two or three behaviors you can change to make sure that you get enough rest. (If you do get enough sleep, share your scheduling tips that make this goal possible.)

_____

_____

_____

_____

A Clear Head for Productive Studying

Pick up my paycheck after 2 P.M...get to the bank before 3 P.M...call the dentist to reschedule my appointment...will Randy call about the party on Friday...when is Johnson going to throw that pop quiz at us... Busy students have busy lives, and much of the time you will feel like you have a million thoughts floating in your head. This type of mental mayhem makes it very hard to concentrate and study. To make the most of your study time, take a few minutes to shoo away distracting thoughts. Here are some helpful ways to get focused:

CHAPTER 3 Applying Study and Research Skills to Mastery

- Make a list of pressing concerns so you know that you can "get back to them" when you are done studying. Keep the list nearby to jot down interrupting thoughts.
- Stand and stretch, roll your head and shoulders, shake your body gently to loosen any tension you may be feeling.
- Close your eyes and relax for five minutes. Let the flurry of thoughts die down.
- Open your eyes and look at your particular study assignment. Get a general idea in your mind of the subject matter of this assignment; try to get a "mind set" on the topic.
- Close your eyes and visualize a productive study session. Associate pleasant thoughts with your efforts.
- Open your eyes and get to work.

Goals for Your Study Session

In order to maximize your study time, set goals for each assignment. If you are reading, determine how many pages you will read and set a time limit for that reading session. If you are reviewing materials, list what you must master during the study session. Be as specific as possible, listing the terms you want to memorize or concepts you want to learn and be able to explain.

Start with modest goals at first. You can always increase them. Some students find they need thirty minutes or more to really focus on a subject before taking a break. If you find it difficult to concentrate for long periods of time, try fifteen-minute stretches. Practice setting different time goals for yourself. As you apply study skills and discipline, you will find that your ability to sustain concentration will increase.

Study Techniques

There are a number of techniques that can help you really learn and retain what you study. Some of these techniques can even add an element of fun to your sessions. Take a look at the suggestions listed below. One or more of these techniques may be just right for you.

PART TWO Developing Your Study Skills

Recite

Reciting out loud is a helpful technique when your study task is to reread a passage or review some notes. This technique helps to imprint your memory with details and facts. When you recite, the information traverses several sensory pathways. You not only use your eyes, but also your voice and your ears. Your mind has several opportunities to catch hold of the information. If you are having a hard time staying on task while studying, try reciting. Reciting forces you to pay attention. After all, your mind can't stray easily when you are talking out loud.

To add some spice to this technique, recite while standing in front of a mirror. Pretend you are the teacher and present a lesson on the material you need to learn. Bring a historical figure to life and describe the events you are trying to commit to memory. Use "visual aids" such as maps, diagrams, or tables. As you gaze on your reflection, emphasize certain words and gesture freely. Ham it up! Get inside the material! Be creative and find what works best for you.

Get a Study Partner

Studying with another person helps break the monotony of some study sessions. This technique also provides the advantages of sharing information with one another and quizzing each other on the material. In this case, two heads *are* better than one.

When you look for a study partner, choose someone who really wants to study. To minimize the temptation to socialize, set aside several short break times for that very purpose. When studying with someone else turns into a gab fest, you are better off on your own.

Form a Study Group

Study groups can be fun as well as educational. There are several ways to form a study group. Start by posting a notice on the department bulletin board or passing around a sign-up sheet in class. If that doesn't work, talk to your instructor, who may know other students interested in group learning. Stop recruiting when you have four or five interested students.

A study group serves several purposes: it introduces you to other interested students; it provides an arena for discussion; it exposes you to other perspectives; it can be an excellent way to reinforce the materials you are learning; and it can be fun. If you are involved in forming a study group, you will gain useful leadership experience.

Your study group sessions will be most productive if you plan them well. Some guidelines for organizing and leading a successful study group are:

1. Locate a good meeting place, convenient for all, and with comfortable surroundings.
2. Prepare a schedule of meeting dates and tentative study topics for future meetings. Do this at your first organizational meeting. Encourage group members to offer their suggestions. Be prepared to hold a "brainstorming" session to determine future agenda items.
3. Try to get each member involved in the group process. If your members are serious about learning, they will be willing contributors. If they aren't serious, you need to get students who are. Unless members are willing to work toward the common goal of increased learning, your group won't be successful.
4. Tell people to come prepared. This means each participant should complete relevant assignments and read related chapters before the group meets.

5. Make assignments. If you think additional reference material from the library could help expand your knowledge of a subject, ask for a volunteer. If illustrations or concept maps might clarify your text material, ask someone to make a drawing or map. You might discover an artist in your midst! You can even ask members to take turns bringing a snack or treat.

6. Review your text and class notes together. Compare your notes to see if you share a common understanding of the material with the others. Develop potential test questions and take turns asking and answering questions based on your notes. If you have problems or confusion about the meaning or interpretation of material, pull out the textbook.

7. Assist one another with writing assignments by proofing one another's work. This doesn't mean doing the work for someone else, but everyone could use an extra eye to help catch mistakes. This exercise is a great learning opportunity because it lets you see how others approach an assignment.

> **QUOTE**
> Do not call for black power or green power. Call for brain power.
> —Barbara Jordan

Study According to How You Will Be Tested

At some point in the course of a class, your instructor will ask you to demonstrate what you have learned. When you are asked to discuss the finer points of a subject in an essay test or class discussion, you must remember or recall the information "from scratch." However, if you take a multiple choice or true-false test, you just need to recognize—not retrieve from your memory bank—the correct information. As you probably know from experience, recalling information is harder to do than simply recognizing information. We generally recognize more information than we can recall because we have more to go on. (Plus, multiple choice questions allow for more guess work.)

Most of the time you will not have a choice as to how you are tested on what you have studied. But you do have a choice as to how you prepare. Ask your instructor what form your course evaluations will take, and do so well in advance of examination time. This information will let you know whether to spend your study time practicing the recall or *recognition* of important facts, events, or concepts. In general, it is best to make it your study goal to recall important information. That way, remembering will take place at a deeper level and you will be prepared for any test form.

How Good Is Your Memory?

		Circle One	
1.	I always remember the names of people I meet.	Yes	No
2.	I can remember phone numbers easily.	Yes	No
3.	I can remember the lyrics to many popular songs.	Yes	No
4.	I can remember directions to new locations easily.	Yes	No
5.	I can remember a grocery list of ten or more items.	Yes	No
6.	I can memorize poems and short speeches easily.	Yes	No
7.	I remember the birthdays of important people in my life.	Yes	No
8.	I recall events in the past very clearly.	Yes	No
9.	I think that I have a good memory.	Yes	No
10.	I rarely forget appointments of any kind.	Yes	No

If you can answer "Yes" to at least six of these questions, you have a good memory. For more information and strategies to make your memory even better, refer to the section titled "Improving Your Memory" in Chapter 7.

Developing Your Research Skills

We live in an era that has been dubbed the Information Age. We are constantly bombarded with news, facts, figures, and the latest research findings from around the globe. Computer technology puts information literally at our fingertips *if* we know how to access it. You need up-to-date skills just to get your hands on the information that is important to you. Your research know-how must extend beyond books and periodicals to include new technologies such as CD-ROM and online services.

Get to Know the Library

Although we tend to think of libraries as mainly housing books and magazines, most libraries now carry a variety of other nonprint media sources such as records, compact disks, slide collections, microfiche, and audio and videocassettes.

Check out the library at your school before your first research assignment. Find out what is there and get to know your way around. This will save you time in the long run, especially when you are under a deadline to research a topic. Also check out the county or city library. Some are very well-equipped. If there are other colleges or universities in your area, you may have access to specialized libraries in academic fields such as law, medicine, theology, science, engineering, and music.

Librarian and Staff Assistants. The best thing about libraries is that you can have your own personal guide. Librarians and staff assistants are trained to help visitors find information. These individuals will show you how to locate information on-site and how to access data from other cooperating libraries. They can assist you with the computerized catalogs and other new technologies. Often they will direct you to specific books, articles, and nonprint materials pertaining to your research topic, thus saving you a lot of time.

The Computer Catalog. Most libraries have replaced the old card catalog with a computerized system. The computer catalog is easy to use and allows you to search for materials by author, title, and subject. It also provides helpful information regarding availability. To initiate a search on the computer catalog, use the search feature to type in words relating to your subject. A list of titles will appear on the screen. Information on the screen will tell you if the title is in the library or on loan.

Some systems tell you where a particular book or video is within the system and when it is to be returned. You may also reserve books and other materials through the computer catalog. If you have difficulty finding listings on your topic, ask the library staff to check the *Library of Congress Subject Headings*. This document is an official guide to subject headings and may provide you with other search options.

Books and Periodicals. Your library will contain thousands of books and access to thousands more through library loan programs. It may take a few days or even weeks to get the materials you want and there may be a fee involved. You will also find recent magazines and newspapers on the shelves.

Most libraries carry a variety of popular newsstand magazines as well as professional journals. Many also carry major city newspapers in addition to local papers. Ask library staff to help you find older issues of magazines and newspapers. They often are available upon request from storage or microfiche archives.

HOW DO WE REMEMBER?

Scientists believe a memory is born when nerve cells in the brain change in response to incoming information. According to current theories of memory, the changes take place in either the synapses (where nerve cells meet) or in the chemical makeup of the nerve cells. These changes create what scientists call the memory trace or engram.

Research on memory suggests that the brain can store information on three levels: the **sensory register**, **short-term memory** (STM), and **long-term memory** (LTM). The sensory register is like a brief echo. It provides a perfect image of what you have just seen or heard, but for only about one-quarter of a second. It is the picture you retain in your mind for just an instant after you turn away from your television screen or look up from a book. The next level of memory, STM, is a temporary holding zone for small amounts of information. You've relied on STM to store a phone number you've just looked up or a name you've acquired from a casual introduction. Without rehearsal, information fades from STM after about 30 seconds. LTM is our permanent storehouse of memories. It is created when you attach meaning to something you saw, did, tasted, touched, or heard. In other words, information in LTM is important enough to stay embedded in your mind.

Each level of memory has its usefulness, yet LTM is the storage facility most beneficial to students when they study. Research on LTM suggests that you will get the most from studying when you take the time to really understand critical information—and attach to it personal meaning—before you try to commit it to memory.

Library Literacy

		Circle One	
1.	Have you ever used a computerized catalog system?	Yes	No
2.	Have you used a computerized database at a library for research?	Yes	No
3.	Have you ever enlisted the help of a librarian?	Yes	No
4.	Can you identify three or more types of media available at your library?	Yes	No
5.	Do you know your school library's hours?	Yes	No
6.	Have you ever viewed microfiche?	Yes	No
7.	Do you know what the *Readers Guide to Periodical Literature* is?	Yes	No
8.	Have you ever placed a book on reserve?	Yes	No
9.	Do you know how to locate government documents in the library?	Yes	No
10.	Are you familiar with the library's loan policies on reference materials?	Yes	No

If you answered "Yes" to all the questions above, you are probably quite comfortable using the library and familiar with most of the library's resources. If you had a number of "No" responses, read the following sections carefully and bring your library literacy up to speed.

Print Reference Materials. All libraries contain print reference materials that can assist your search for information. These books often are compilations of facts by topic. In many instances they are not available for checkout; you must request the item at a reference desk. You will be asked to leave identification as collateral and use the material while on the premises.

A general encyclopedia is one such reference. It is a good place to start your research. These comprehensive texts provide articles across a broad range of subject areas. Popular encyclopedias include *Americana, Academic American, Colliers, Comptons, Britannica, New Caxton,* and *World Book.*

Books in Print is a helpful resource which lists most fiction and non-fiction books available in the United States. *The Readers' Guide to Periodical Literature* lists magazine and journal articles alphabetically by topic and author. Listings also are found under headings that indicate the form or media; such as book, compact disk, dance, movie, musical, opera, phonograph records, poems, products, radio programs, short stories, tape recordings, television, theater, videodisk, and videotape.

Other reference sources include:

Special Indexes - titles of articles published in magazines and journals on subjects, such as agriculture, art, biology, book reviews, business, nursing and allied health, computer science, education, demographics, medicine, music, international affairs, conservation, history and current events, humanities, social sciences.

Abstracts - summaries of original academic papers or published articles in a variety of fields, such as psychology, medicine, law, architecture, women's studies, and many others.

PUBLIC LIBRARIES

The first free public libraries in the United States were built by a steel millionaire, Andrew Carnegie. In 1890, he built a library for his steelworkers in Allegheny City, now a part of Pittsburgh, Pennsylvania. Eventually, he built 2,500 library buildings in the United States and Canada. Many of the Carnegie Libraries were built in small, rural towns. You can often recognize these libraries by their classical style and the name *Carnegie* etched on the facade.

Dissertation Abstracts - titles and abstracts of dissertations since 1980.

Directories - names of hundreds of civic, charitable, and professional associations throughout the world.

Specialized Encyclopedias - background information for a detailed technical research assignment. *(Encyclopedia of World Art, Encyclopedia of Chemical Technology, Encyclopedia of American Architecture, Encyclopedia of Authors, Encyclopedia of Geography, Encyclopedia of Sports, Encyclopedia of Banking and Finance, Encyclopedia of Bioethics, Encyclopedia of Associations, Encyclopedia of Education, Encyclopedia of Special Education, Encyclopedia of Educational Research, Religion and Ethics, Encyclopedia of Crime and Justice, Encyclopedia of Physical Science and Technology)*

Unabridged Dictionaries - for more complete definitions and hard to find words. *(Webster's New International Dictionary of the English Language, New Standard Dictionary of the English Language, and Random House Dictionary of the English Language)*

Specialized Dictionaries - another good source of information for a technical or specialized research paper. *(Mathematical Dictionary, Dictionary of Biological Sciences, Dictionary of Quotations, and Dictionary of Biological Sciences)*

Thesaurus - provides synonyms; useful when you find yourself using the same word over and over. *(Roget's Thesaurus, Computer Thesaurus, Music Thesaurus, Medicine Thesaurus)*

Atlases - collections of maps or a book with tables, charts, or plates illustrating a subject. *(United States Atlas, World Atlas, Anatomical Atlas)*

Pamphlets, brochures, maps, clippings - usually located in a large filing cabinet, and contain lots of information that isn't listed in the computer catalog.

Facts on File - summaries of nearly every news story reported in the national press.

Government Documents - thousands of publications on a wide range of subjects printed by the U.S. government which is the largest printing office in the world.

TIP: If the computer catalog lists only one book on your topic, find the book on the shelf and look at its bibliography. You may find other titles that your search did not reveal.

Nonprint Media.
Good research involves using as wide a variety of sources as possible to assure that your information is thorough and accurate. While books and articles are likely to provide much of the information you need for your research paper, nonprint media has a lot to offer. For example, if you are a visual learner, you may get more from a filmstrip about the Vietnam War than from a book on the same topic. You may also find that your topic is covered more fully by nonprint media.

Nonprint Media includes:

- video and audio tapes (talking books)
- films, filmstrips, and slides
- art collections
- record and cassette tapes
- compact disks
- multimedia such as CD-ROMs and laser disks

CD ROMs can contain many media: text, graphics, video, sound, and animation. In addition, they are often programmed so that the user can navigate through the program at will. For example, when you put the *Time Almanac Reference Edition* CD-ROM into your disk player, you can select a decade or look through weekly issues to conduct your search. The almanac contains articles as well as photographs, audiotapes, videotapes, charts, magazine covers, and maps. Imagine how your research on former President Richard Nixon will come to life when you can hear and see him read his resignation speech and locate political commentaries regarding events that led to this action.

Online Information Sources. Online service networks are part of the "Information Superhighway." These networks—essentially a network of computers—join various "servers" to allow you to tap into databases and communicate with other computer users.

Online networks also give you access to the Internet, the world's largest computer network. This world-wide system was started by the Defense Department and was not available to the general public until the early 1980s. The Internet connects users to the most remote parts of the world. It allows the user not only to retrieve information from around the globe, but also to interact via E-mail with people as far away as Japan or Africa.

For example, through an Internet mail connection, you could send a message to a friend or relative in Australia, you could join a discussion group with world-wide participants on topics such as global environmental problems or international study opportunities, or you could request data from the University of Helsinki on the latest cancer therapies.

America Online (AOL), Prodigy, and CompuServe are large online networks that allow users to browse for information on a wide number of topics all over the world. Many colleges and universities are hooked up to an online network and offer free or discounted user privileges to students. Check with your librarian to see what services can be accessed through the library.

MULTIMEDIA MAGIC

You may be asked to prepare a multimedia presentation. Multimedia is just as its name implies—multiple media under one "hat." Right now the most popular multimedia technology is the CD-ROM (Compact Disk Read Only Memory). To view a CD-ROM disk, you need a CD-ROM player attached to a computer with sufficient memory.

An important benefit of CD-ROM technology is its tremendous storage capacity. Because many volumes of text can be stored on one CD-ROM, and because the computer offers search capabilities, the CD-ROM is perfect for exhaustive reference materials. All the major encyclopedias now have CD-ROM versions, and you will also find dictionaries in this medium. Once you learn how to search within these reference tools, you can quickly find a wealth of information—and have fun while you're at it.

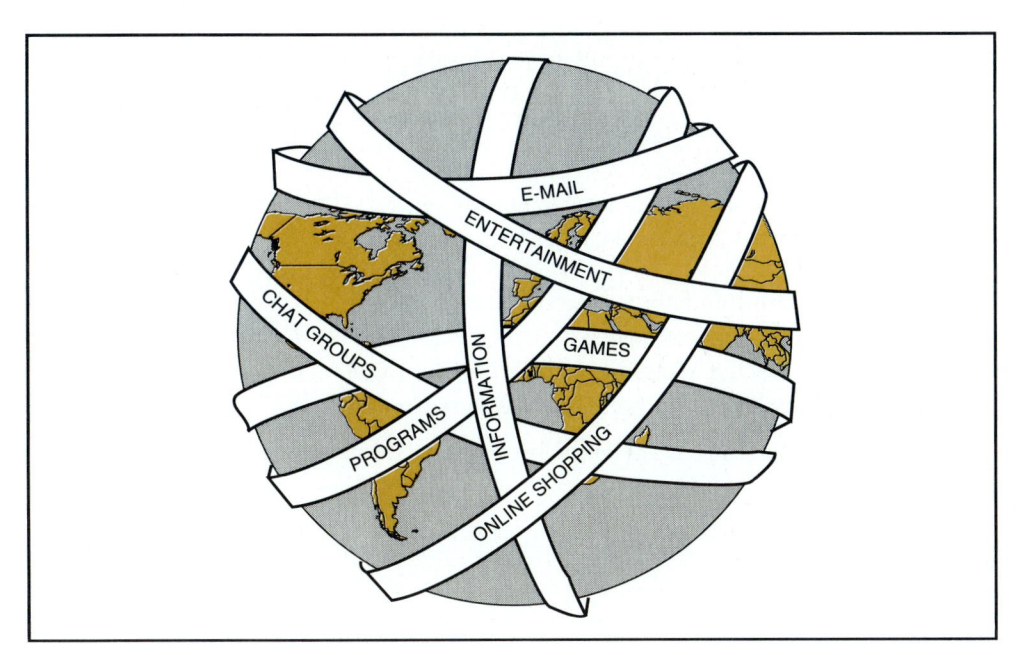

Figure 3-2 Information Superhighway

The menu of the AOL system provides basic services under the following major headings: Today's News, Personal Finance, Clubs and Interests, Computing, Travel, Marketplace, People Connections, Newsstand, Entertainment, Education, Reference Desk, Internet Connections, Sports, and Kids Only. The CompuServe network basic services list looks like this: News, Weather, Sports, Reference and Education, Shopping, Finance, Entertainment, Media, Travel, Home and Leisure, and Computing Support. Other networks have similar categories and new categories and databases are being added daily.

By clicking on to any one of these major groups on a network, you can find information on subjects ranging from pet care to geophysics. You can use a network to connect to reference libraries of science, medicine, law, literature, and many other academic fields. You can access professional journals, consumer magazines, newspapers, specialized newsletters, and published research papers. A database search will allow you to view abstracts of hundreds of articles. The teacher pager feature on AOL lets you post questions to teachers, other students, or other subscribers and receive answers online. The research possibilities are almost endless.

> How ignorant we are! How ignorant everyone is! We can cut across only a small area of the appallingly expanding fields of knowledge. No human being can know more than a tiny fraction of the whole. It must have been satisfactory in ancient times when one's own land seemed to be the universe; when research studies, pamphlets, books did not issue in endless flow; when laboratories and scientists were not so rapidly pushing back frontiers of knowledge that the process of unlearning the old left you gasping for breath.
>
> —Mary Barnett Gilson, Factory Personnel Manager, Economist, Education

Plan Your Research

You will be far more efficient if you approach your research task with a plan that fits your assignment. A specific plan will help you to explore the multitude of resources in the library and locate the information you need to fully develop your topic.

Define the Question. Turn your research topic into a question. This is easy if the instructor has been specific. However, if the instructor has given you a choice or has been vague, it is up to you to focus on a topic. Go to the library and take out two or three books relating to your course subject. Skim through the books until you find an issue or problem that recurs and seems worth pursuing.

> QUOTE
>
> I find that a great part of the information I have was acquired by looking up something and finding something else on the way.
>
> —Franklin P. Adams

Are You Computer Literate?

		Circle One	
1. Do you know how to use a computer?		Yes	No
2. Can you format a document in a word processing program?		Yes	No
3. Do you use a computer to type your school papers?		Yes	No
4. Can you use a spreadsheet?		Yes	No
5. Have you located information stored on a CD-ROM?		Yes	No
6. Have you accessed information through the Internet?		Yes	No

If your answer is "No" to any of these questions, describe what you could do to become more computer literate?

_____

_____

_____

_____

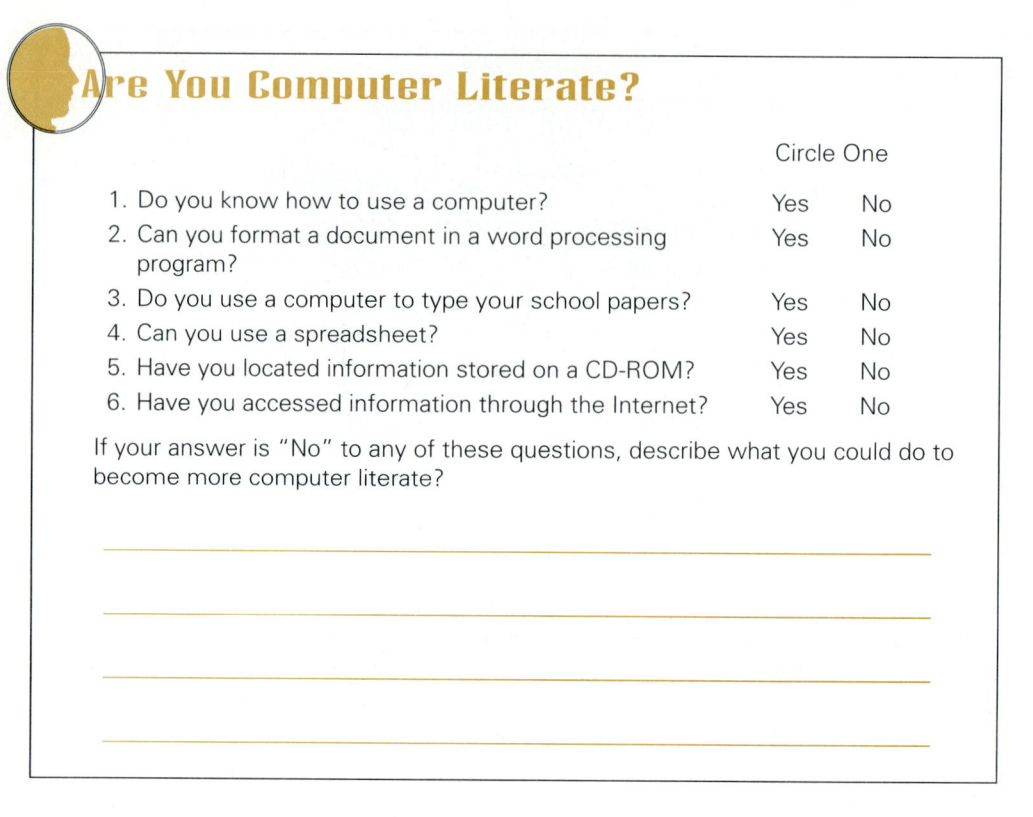

TYPES OF RESEARCH PAPERS

There are several types of research assignments: term paper, essay, report, and data collection. The term paper, sometimes simply called a research paper, is normally quite comprehensive and can be from 20 to 100 pages long. A report is shorter and usually more limited in scope. The term "essay" refers to a short composition asking you to present your own personal views on a literary work. Data collection assignments will vary in both scope and time required. Of course, data collection may be an important part of either a term paper or report.

Each type of assignment requires a different level of research and requires you to plan accordingly. While a term paper will require the most detailed plan, there are general guidelines to follow for any type of research you undertake. Careful planning prior to your library research will increase your efficiency when you actually get the project underway.

For example, books on Vietnam will mention the "domino theory," the My Lai incident, and the Kent State bombings. You would find a great deal of material on any one of these topics, but don't try to cover them all. Narrow the topic to one major issue or event. Then frame a question that you want to answer about the topic. By doing this, you will save enormous time and energy. When you have defined the question, write it on a 3 x 5 card or on your computer. Your research will then be focused on finding answers to the topic question and locating information in support of your answers.

Go Prepared. Being prepared will save you time and irritation. Bring everything that you need to work efficiently such as your course syllabus, your notes on the assignment, relevant notes from lectures or the text, note cards, notebook, pen, pencils, erasers, calculator, and so on. If you want to photocopy a reference book that cannot be checked out, it helps to have change in your pocket. If you plan to spend a lot of time doing research, pack a lunch or snack. Prepare in whatever way that will help you be productive.

Make a List. Jot down where you think you can find information to answer the topic question. Keep in mind that valuable research data can be obtained from nonprint materials as well as books and articles. Head straight to the information desk, if you have any doubt as to where to find material. Library staff can direct you quickly and you'll save time by not having to roam the shelves.

Give Yourself Time. You can't do research in fifteen or thirty minutes. It takes time, so allow a couple of hours or more for your first session. If the assignment is easy and well defined, such as collecting a list of source books for your art project or a list of art galleries in your area, one session may suffice. However, most of your research assign-

PART TWO   Developing Your Study Skills

ments will be more involved. Don't be surprised if your first research session takes longer than you expected. And don't get discouraged. You will become more efficient as you get better acquainted with the various materials in the library.

As you conduct your research, use 3 x 5 cards or your laptop computer to record the title, author, publisher, date, and publishing location. Also note the exact location of each source in the library and the item's call number. Some libraries have collections spread over two or three floors. Pick up a map of the library and use it to find the source locations on your note cards. For books or magazines, note the page numbers where you found the information. Record information that applies to the topic question on these cards. These note cards will provide you with information to build your paper's outline, footnotes, and bibliography. You will also need this information if you want to revisit the text. Steps for writing the research paper are discussed in Chapter 6.

> **USING A LAPTOP COMPUTER**
>
> A laptop computer can be very helpful for conducting research for your writing assignment. If you have a laptop computer, you can use it for taking notes. You can even buy a software program that will arrange your notes to look like 3 x 5 cards. Beware, however, of writing down too much. Key in only the important information and leave lots of white space.

Gather the Information

The nature of your research assignment will suggest certain obvious places to look first for information, but in nearly every case you will start with the computer catalog. Here you will find books and other materials on your topic. However, for most assignments you should look further than the computer catalog. Check the *Readers' Guide to Periodical Literature* or other specific subject area indexes. For example, if your assignment calls for your analysis of the role of international trade associations in North America, look at the *Index on Associations*. If your research paper is an analysis of impressionist art, look at the *Art Index*, in encyclopedias, at slide collections, and art print files. Use our checklist to help make your research session produce results.

Review and Recall

1. Describe how environment affects study habits. _____

2. Four guidelines for organizing a productive study space are:

   a. _____

   b. _____

   c. _____

   d. _____

3. Explain what ergonomists say about productivity and comfort. _____

4. You must always study for at least an hour at a time. True or False? Explain your answer. _____

> **CHECKLIST: SOURCES FOR RESEARCH TOPICS**
>
> - atlases
> - CD-ROMs
> - compact disks
> - dictionaries
> - directories
> - encyclopedias
> - fiction and nonfiction books
> - government documents
> - indexes and abstracts
> - journals
> - magazines
> - newspapers
> - pamphlets
> - records and cassette tapes
> - thesaurus
> - video and audio tapes

CHAPTER 3 Applying Study and Research Skills to Mastery

5. List three techniques that can help you learn and retain what you study.

   a. _____

   b. _____

   c. _____

6. Describe how a study group works and why it is a good study technique.

   _____
   _____
   _____

7. List four places to begin your search for materials on research assignments.

   a. _____

   b. _____

   c. _____

   d. _____

8. Explain the term *multimedia*. _____
   _____
   _____

9. Describe the major advantage of CD-ROM technology. _____
   _____

10. Name three references you could consult for the date of the first landing on the moon.

    a. _____

    b. _____

    c. _____

11. What document would you expect to have a summary of the New York Trade Center bombing? _____

12. List ten subjects that you would find on the AOL or CompuServe networks.

    a. _____   f. _____

    b. _____   g. _____

    c. _____   h. _____

    d. _____   i. _____

    e. _____   j. _____

13. List three planning steps for conducting research for a term paper.

    a. _____

    b. _____

    c. _____

PART TWO   Developing Your Study Skills

14. Most library research can be done in a half hour. True or False? Explain your answer.

    _____
    _____

15. List eight items that you should put on 3 x 5 note cards or in your computer.

    a. _____   e. _____
    b. _____   f. _____
    c. _____   g. _____
    d. _____   h. _____

16. You cannot get into the Internet unless you have your own personal computer. True or False? Explain your answer. _____
    _____

Apply Critical Thinking

Some people feel intimidated or uncomfortable when they enter a library. If having to go to the library makes you think of a million other things you'd rather do, you may need to examine your past library experiences. Analyze your feelings about libraries by answering the following questions in a short essay.

1. What has been your personal experience with libraries?
2. Did you go to the library when you were a child? Describe how you felt about your childhood visits to the library. What made you feel this way?
3. Did you use a library in middle or high school to gather research? If you did, write a paragraph describing one of your research projects.
4. How do you think you can overcome any negative feelings you have about the library and learn to use it as a valuable resource to help you be a successful student?

School to Work Applications

SCANS

RESOURCES: *MATERIAL AND FACILITIES*

1. Evaluate your study space. If you are studying at home, analyze how your study area rates on the following: furniture, lighting, noise levels, convenience, supplies. If your study area leaves something to be desired, make a plan for improving it.
2. What materials do you regularly use to study? Could you benefit from a new set of file folders, assorted colored pens and highlighters, a date book, or a good study lamp? Assess your study "equipment" and visit your college bookstore or an office supply store if your supplies fail to make the grade.
3. Explain why you do or do not use a library.

INTERPERSONAL: *PARTICIPATES AS A MEMBER OF A TEAM*

4. Describe the characteristics of a good "team player." Link these characteristics to the task of studying in a study group. In other words, what qualities can a person bring to a team setting that will contribute to individual and group learning?
5. Form a study group or meet with an existing study group for a class. Analyze the group dynamics and note where the group was effective or ineffective. How did individual personalities influence the group's effectiveness? Suggest ways to strengthen the group's effectiveness.

CHAPTER 3   Applying Study and Research Skills to Mastery

INTERPERSONAL: *TEACHES OTHERS NEW SKILLS*

6. Describe a time when you taught an individual or group a new skill. What was your teaching style? Did you demonstrate or rely only on words? Did you allow for questions? Were you patient with the inexperience of the learner(s)? What did you like or not like about teaching?

7. Offer to tutor another student in a subject you are comfortable with. After a session, describe whether you felt effective or ineffective as a tutor. What challenges did you face? What would you do differently next time, and what might you do the same?

INFORMATION: *ACQUIRES AND EVALUATES INFORMATION*

8. Go to your library and look for information on the following topics: Global warming, Lincoln's assassination, Andy Warhol, and *Citizen Kane*. Locate print and nonprint sources of information on each topic. See if your library offers computer search services. If possible, request a search on one of these topics. Fill out the checklist showing the types of material available for each topic.

	GLOBAL WARMING	LINCOLN	WARHOL	CITIZEN KANE
Abstracts	_____	_____	_____	_____
Audio Cassettes	_____	_____	_____	_____
CD-ROMs	_____	_____	_____	_____
Encyclopedias	_____	_____	_____	_____
Fiction Books	_____	_____	_____	_____
Indexes	_____	_____	_____	_____
Magazines	_____	_____	_____	_____
Newspaper Articles	_____	_____	_____	_____
Nonfiction Works	_____	_____	_____	_____
Print Collections	_____	_____	_____	_____
Slide Collections	_____	_____	_____	_____
Video Cassettes	_____	_____	_____	_____

Use this exercise to get acquainted with your library. Early reconnaissance of the library will make you more efficient when you start your first research project.

9. Pick one of the four topics that you researched and brainstorm ways in which you could put together an interesting multimedia presentation on this topic. Take a 3 x 5 card and write down at least four different media that you could use. Consider how each type of media would enhance your presentation. Be sure to note if these materials can be checked out. For example, would you be able to check out prints or slides of Warhol's paintings; videos on global warming; copies of Lincoln's speeches; a video of *Citizen Kane*?

10. Visualize yourself making a class presentation on the topic you just researched. Make a list of the materials you would use and the steps in your presentation. List equipment needs. For example, if you are going to present slides showing Warhol's paintings, you would need a slide projector; visualize yourself talking about the slides. Consider how you would use the chalkboard or a flip chart to make certain points. Imagine yourself answering questions. If you have a hard time doing this, think of the best instructor you had in high school. Try to recall what this instructor did to make the class interesting. If the instructor used a variety of materials to make the subject more interesting and understandable, how were they presented? Try to find a model in your mind's eye; hang on to this model when you are looking for materials to make your research presentations and reports dynamic and worthy of attention.

11. Look at your course syllabus and choose a topic that relates to one of your courses. If you already know that you will be assigned a research paper in a course, use that topic for this research assignment. If you can't think of a topic, choose from one of the following: Medicare, Mozart, Congressional term limits, or public school desegregation. Check the computer catalog and locate three books on your topic. Fill out the chart below:

    BOOK ONE:
    Title: _____
    Author: (last name, first name, and middle initial) _____
    Year of Publication: _____
    Publisher and Location: _____
    Catalog No.: _____
    Number of Pages: _____
    Location and Call Numbers: _____
    Description of why this book is a good source: _____

    BOOK TWO: _____
    Title: _____
    Author: (last name, first name, and middle initial) _____
    Year of Publication: _____
    Publisher and Location: _____
    Catalog No.: _____
    Number of Pages: _____
    Location and Call Numbers: _____
    Description of why this book is a good source: _____

    BOOK THREE:
    Title: _____
    Author: (last name, first name, and middle initial) _____
    Year of Publication: _____
    Publisher and Location: _____
    Catalog No.: _____
    Number of Pages: _____
    Location and Call Numbers: _____
    Description of why this book is a good source: _____

12. Look for information on your topic in the *Readers' Guide to Periodical Literature*. List the following information derived from one article on your topic:

    Article Title: _____
    Author: _____
    Name and Date of Magazine: _____
    Volume No: _____
    Page Numbers for Article: _____
    Summarize the Article: _____
    Use Checklist to Evaluate the Article. _____

CHAPTER 3 Applying Study and Research Skills to Mastery

13. Check your library's specialized indexes for another source of information on your topic.

    Provide the following information on this source:

    Name of Index: _____

    Year of Publication: _____

    Title of Article: _____

    Author of Article: _____

    Name of Journal and Volume No.: _____

    Page Numbers of Article: _____

    Availability of Article (Is it in the library, on microfiche,
      or must it be ordered?): _____

    Summarize the Article: _____

    _____

    _____

    Use Checklist to Evaluate the Article:

	Excellent	Good	Fair	Poor
Content	☐	☐	☐	☐
Style	☐	☐	☐	☐
Clarity	☐	☐	☐	☐
Detail	☐	☐	☐	☐

SYSTEMS: *UNDERSTANDS SYSTEMS*

14. Ask the library staff to conduct a database search on your topic. Inquire as to how long that might take and if there are costs involved. Ask to see the list of searchable databases. Also ask to see the CD-ROM catalog. Unless you are actually starting your research paper, you will not want to take more of the staff's time, but be sure to note what services are available for future reference. In fact, just browsing the CD-ROM catalog may give you some ideas of what you might like to research.

15. Summarize your research by listing the most important sources of information on your topic. Rank the sources in order of importance and availability. Were there two or three sources that seemed to offer the most promise? Remember, conducting good research means using more than one book or even one medium. In fact, often your professor will be quite specific and require that you provide a varied bibliography.

SCANS Workplace Applications

1. Kyle Finlayson manages a restaurant. The restaurant will be closed for renovation for one week and will reopen with an entirely new menu. Kyle manages a staff of sixteen waiters on two shifts (day and evenings). How can he help his staff learn the new menus? What study skills can he encourage them to try and apply? What activities might be useful to prepare his staff for the "test" of the grand reopening?

2. As assistant to the set designer in a repertory theater, you are asked to provide ideas for sets and costumes for a play that takes place during the Renaissance in Florence, Italy. Sets must be designed to replicate city streets, a castle drawing room, and a peasant's cottage. The costumes must reflect the period dressing for royalty, a court jester, merchants, soldiers, and peasants. List four questions that you could take to the library to help you research ideas for the set and the costumes.

   At the library, locate four sources of information representing at least two media that you and the designer could study to authenticate the architectural style and clothing styles of the Renaissance period in Italy.

   Provide a bibliography of your efforts, your notes, and photocopies of pictures or illustrations you found useful.

PART TWO Developing Your Study Skills

Personal Progress Application

SCANS

THINKING SKILLS: *THINKS CREATIVELY, MAKES DECISIONS, SOLVES PROBLEMS, VISUALIZES, KNOWS HOW TO LEARN, AND REASONS*

Employers want employees who can remember information and put it to use without constant "re-learning" because material presented earlier didn't "stick."

There is a way to guarantee that you'll remember far more of the material presented in your class with far less effort than you've probably been expending. This technique is based on the natural operation of the human brain.[1] The technique is ridiculously easy:

> Be sure to review your notes within 24 hours of the end of class.

Spending as little as five minutes reviewing what was presented, if done within 24 hours after your initial exposure to the material, will add around 30% to your recall. An even better strategy is the 10/48/7 rule: do a review 10 minutes after receiving information, 48 hours later, and once again 7 days later.

Even if all you do is the five-minute review before you go to bed on the day you got the information in class, you will remember much more than if you had not taken this simple step. The far too typical approach taken by most students is to take notes in class and then not look at them again until they start to study for the test. Such a strategy is needlessly stressful. If you let the 24-hour window of opportunity slip by without reviewing the things the instructor talked about in class, when you do get around to studying for the test, you'll have to re-learn the information to a large extent. You will have missed the opportunity for reinforcement provided by a five-minute review session. A graph showing the difference between the two techniques would look like this:

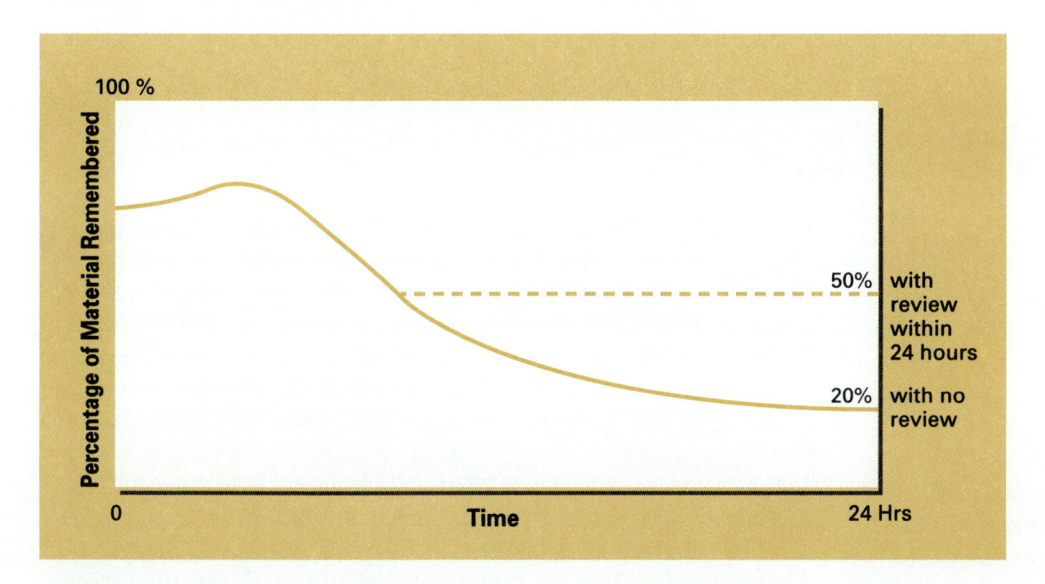

Double Your Recall

Prove this process works by selecting one of your courses as a test case. Within 24 hours after each class, review that class material for at least five minutes. Do this for all the class sessions that will be covered on a particular test. When you study for the test, you'll be amazed at how much easier and faster your studying will go. This is because your brain stores and retrieves information better when reinforcement in the form of review takes place within certain time frames after the material is presented.

After your experiment, congratulate yourself for knowing something about learning that most students don't know, and use this "trick" in all your classes to make better grades on your tests.

[1] A good overview of the concepts behind this exercise can be found in *Use Both Sides of Your Brain* by Tony Buzan, 1989, Penguin Books.

CHAPTER 3 Applying Study and Research Skills to Mastery

FOUR

LEARNING IN THE CLASSROOM

CHAPTER OUTLINE

A Positive Attitude for Learning
　Get Rid of Negative Thoughts
　Connect to Learning
Guidelines for Establishing Good Classroom Habits
　Be Rested
　Get a Good Seat
　Don't Sit with Friends
　Bring Relevant Materials
　Review Notes and Text
　Set Aside Your Assumptions
　Attend Class Regularly
Active Listening Strategies
　Look at the Instructor
　Decide to Pay Attention
　Consider the Instructor's Purpose
　Listen for Key Ideas and Important Phrases
　Pay Attention to Outlines, Formulas, and Data on the Board
Take Notes
　Listen Critically
　Listen to the Very End
Class Participation
　Ask Questions
　Talk to Your Instructor
　Talk to Other Students
After-Class Notes
　Review Your Class Notes
　Summarize
　Coordinate Class Notes with Textbook Notes

If there's been a "surprise" quiz every Friday for the past four weeks, and you spend all of Thursday night studying, this particular Friday the teacher will be absent
　—Tom Royer (Murphy's Law of Learning)

Learning is about gaining knowledge and being changed by that knowledge. It is about actively participating in the educational process, even at seemingly passive times, like when you are sitting in a classroom listening to a lecture. Active listening, taking notes, questioning, making connections to prior learning—these and other classroom learning strategies can make your study time inside and outside the classroom more effective. You will be able to approach your reading, writing, text preparation, and laboratory time with more ease and confidence when your classroom time has been utilized to its maximum benefit.

This chapter gives you a number of ideas you can use to make the most of your time in the classroom. It also encourages you to examine your attitudes toward your role as a learner and the amount of effort you are expecting to exert toward learning. You want to avoid a neutral or negative attitude that can lead you to feeling tortured by the process—as though school is a boot camp where only the strong survive and where the end result of graduation is all that counts. With a positive attitude you can enjoy the learning process for its own sake, and appreciate the knowledge you are gaining, even in courses that may seem irrelevant to your major or to your future goals.

A Positive Attitude for Learning

Your attitude about school will affect how much you learn in the classroom. It can make or break your school experience. When you have a positive attitude, you go to your classes with an open mind and a determination to learn. You realize that to succeed in college you must arrive on time, be prepared, pay attention, participate in discussions when asked, glean important information from lessons, and complete your assignments. Your positive attitude helps you to take responsibility for learning and feel good about the knowledge you are gaining.

How Have You Been Influenced by What You've Learned

Learning is about gaining knowledge and being changed by that knowledge. Describe at least one school learning experience that changed or influenced how you see the world around you.

_____

_____

_____

Get Rid of Negative Thoughts

Let's admit it. There are a lot of things not to like about school. The problem is that most of these are things over which you have little or no control. Even assuming that some college classes bore you, you are the loser if you decide to tune out. You cannot transform a poor lecturer into a brilliant presenter, but you can control how you respond.

Replace the Negative with the Positive. When negative thoughts about school—or other areas of your life, for that matter—pop into your head, make a conscious effort to correct your thinking. If you have a hard time doing this "on the spot," then find the time to sit down with pen and paper and identify typical negative thoughts you may have about school. Then create a positive replacement. If it seems too dishonest to replace, "I hate this class" with a thought such as "I love this class," then create an alternative that has a positive meaning, such as "This class will help me graduate." Remind yourself that the professor has something valuable to offer you, even if that is only a passing grade in a required course.

Act "as if." Psychologists debate the exact relationship between thought and behavior, but most agree that the two influence one another in some way. So it is widely believed that you can influence your thinking by altering your behavior. By adopting the actions of an enthusiastic, motivated student (follow the tips presented later in this chapter if you're not sure what these actions might be), you can encourage and reinforce positive thoughts about school. In addition, positive behaviors set a framework for positive events such as recognition by an instructor and good grades, which in turn can generate positive thoughts and feelings.

Connect to Learning

You can learn more, and with less effort, when you "connect" on a personal level with the material you are trying to learn. For example, if you are taking a composition class to fulfill a degree requirement, you may feel more connected to the course if you focus on the personal benefits of learning to write well. One connec-

> ### Suffering from a High School Hangover?
>
> For each statement, circle NA for "Nearly Always," S for "Sometimes" or R for "Rarely" as it applies to you.
>
> In high school, I…
>
> | | NA | S | R |
> |---|---|---|---|
> | 1. …thought classes were boring | NA | S | R |
> | 2. …skipped | NA | S | R |
> | 3. …daydreamed in class | NA | S | R |
> | 4. …disliked the teachers | NA | S | R |
> | 5. …refused to do homework | NA | S | R |
> | 6. …came late to class | NA | S | R |
> | 7. …doodled | NA | S | R |
> | 8. …considered classes a waste of time | NA | S | R |
> | 9. …was easily distracted | NA | S | R |
>
> A negative attitude carried over from high school will affect your current study habits and in turn, your grades. Are you haunted by old attitudes?

tion you can make is that you will be able to transfer writing skills to the workplace. Another connection is that writing is a great form of self-expression.

Take the time to think about how a course can improve your skills set and your knowledge base. If you're really straining to find a reason or motivation to learn a specific subject but still must complete the course, consider your efforts as practiced discipline. Sometimes in life it is necessary to undergo unpleasant experiences to move forward to a new, more exciting stage of life.

Sometimes just putting forth a little effort—investing energy in a class—can increase your motivation and connection with learning. As mentioned earlier, act as though you care, and eventually you will care. Some ways to show interest in a topic are:

- Ask questions of the instructor.
- Meet the instructor privately to get hooked on the subject.
- Form a study group.
- Hang out with other students who genuinely like the subject matter and are serious students.
- Zero in on any aspect of the subject matter that interests you and research it independently.
- Look for media that deal with the subject in a way that might interest you more.

This last suggestion is a creative way to get a fresh perspective on a topic. It may not work for all of your classes, but think hard and you'll probably find some extension of a subject in popular media. For example, if your history class is covering the U.S. space program and you're having a hard time getting interested, rent *Apollo 13* and experience the adventure of early space exploration.

It may seem like it's the instructor's job to make a dull class a meaningful learning experience, but you really are the key person. It won't always be easy. Sometimes you will have to suffer a windbag instructor with a nasal monotone, but don't let a poor instructor be your excuse for not learning. Choose your classes wisely (remember, you can ask other students and perhaps even the counseling office for recommendations) and then take responsibility for what you get out of them.

Learning Turn-ons

What gets you to turn on and tune in to a class lecture? Describe in a paragraph how the amount of "connectedness" you feel during a class depends on your behavior and how much depends on your instructor's behavior.

_____

_____

_____

Guidelines for Establishing Good Classroom Habits

Just *attending* class does not guarantee that you will absorb and understand what is being presented. You need to prepare your mind and body for classroom learning. While there is no magic formula to make you learn, there are steps you can take that will help you be an efficient student in class—one who listens, takes notes, and absorbs information. Use the following guidelines to improve your classroom habits.

Be Rested

Make every effort to get a good night's sleep while you're in school. If you are sleep deprived, you will have great difficulty being an attentive learner in class. You are the best judge of what constitutes a "good night's sleep." Some people can function well with as little as five or six hours a night. Most people need at least seven or eight hours; some even require ten. If you don't know what your sleep requirements are, keep a log for a month. List the hours you sleep each night and how you feel the next day. Gradually you should be able to determine the best sleep routine for you. Establishing regular sleeping hours will also help you feel more rested. Erratic sleeping patterns over a period of time will lead to fatigue.

Get a Good Seat

This may sound like a pretty simplistic guideline, but it is very important. In order to be attentive in class you must be able to see and hear everything that is going on. Ideally, you should sit up front and in the center. Also, if you are sitting right in front of the instructor, you won't be as tempted to talk to those near you, fidget, or doodle. This is especially a good idea in classes that you expect to dislike or find difficult. Sitting regularly in a seat near the front also helps you to establish a relationship with your instructor. You will become a familiar face, which is a good thing if you're in a large class.

Attentive posture and eye contact, both of which are easier to maintain when you're sitting toward the front of the room, will help you keep focus and impress your instructor as well. It is also easier to participate in discussion if you are sitting toward the front of the room.

> We must continually remind students that expression of different opinions and dissenting ideas affirm the intellectual process. We should forcefully explain that our role is not to teach them to think as we do but rather to teach them, by example, the importance of taking a stance that is rooted in rigorous engagement with the full range of ideas about a topic.
>
> —Bell Hooks, Educator

Don't Sit with Friends

While it seems like a great idea to sit with friends, this can be a big mistake. You are bound to be distracted. The temptation to write notes or make little side comments is very great. In order to be an attentive learner, you need to concentrate and maintain focus. This is a lot easier if you get a good seat and sit by yourself. Of course, as classes progress, you may make friends with people seated around you. Try not to let these new-found relationships become a distraction.

Bring Relevant Materials

Prepare for class the night before by packing a bag with all the materials you may need such as pencils, pens, your text, a notebook, the class syllabus, and a calculator. If you don't come with the right materials you create problems for yourself. For example, if you don't have your notebook, you will have to borrow a loose sheet of paper from a classmate. Taking notes on a borrowed piece of paper is risky—will these notes ever find their way into your notebook and be a part of your studying? If you arrive in math class without your textbook or calculator, you may find that you cannot take part in some of the classroom exercises. You may need your syllabus to note a change in your assignments. Since you don't always know what will take place in class, assume that you need everything.

Review Notes and Text

This is a powerful tool for maximizing your classroom experience. A brief review of your reading assignment and your notes from the last class session will prepare your mind to receive the subject matter. Take time after class to reinforce the new information. Then, try to take a few minutes before class to review the material. This will help you get focused. And by all means, keep up with your assignments. If you don't, you will find that new material presented in the classroom seems a lot more difficult because you are missing the background information.

Set Aside Your Assumptions

All of us approach new experiences with a set of assumptions about people, events, and life in general. Assumptions shape our thinking and actions. Assumptions form the basis for opinions and judgments. Assumptions, however, are not facts. Many of our assumptions are based on casual observations, hearsay, or misinformation.

We don't give up our assumptions when we step on the college campus. The real challenge is to recognize your assumptions and to put them aside, at least temporarily. College students have the unique opportunity to hear other viewpoints and learn about different ideas and cultures. In order for learning to take place, it is important to *open your mind* to the possibilities that all of your assumptions may not be accurate.

If you don't set aside your assumptions, you will block out new information. For example, if you assume that nothing can be done to save the environment, you are likely to tune out any instructor who doesn't share your assumption. You may miss constructive information regarding energy conservation or forest management. You may find yourself using your assumption as an excuse for not listening. If you open your mind, you can always revisit your original assumption after you have listened and evaluated the new information. You may find that your assumption was only partly true or not true at all. Even if you continue to hold the original assumption, it will have been tested against new information. You may come away from the learning experience with even more confidence in your assumption.

Often our learning can be impeded by assumptions about our own abilities. Saying things like "That class is too hard for me" or "I can't read that much material" reflect negative assumptions that you hold about yourself. These thoughts assume that you aren't capable of being a successful student. Such assumptions can be significant barriers to learning.

> **QUOTE**
> We are drowning in information but starved for knowledge.
> —John Naisbitt

Check Your Assumptions

For each statement, circle the response that applies to you.

1.	My teachers don't care whether or not I learn.	Yes	No
2.	Most of the time I know that I won't understand what the teachers are saying.	Yes	No
3.	If I ask a question in class, my classmates will think I am stupid.	Yes	No
4.	If I don't understand what the teacher is saying, there isn't anything I can do about it.	Yes	No
5.	Most people in class are smarter than me.	Yes	No
6.	Nobody wants to be in a study group with me.	Yes	No

If you responded "Yes" to one or more items, you hold assumptions that may make learning more difficult. You can eliminate some of these assumptions by taking an active role in your school experience.

Negative assumptions can become **self-fulfilling prophecies**. This means that you decide not to take a difficult class because you assume that it will be too hard. Or you decide not to talk to your instructor or to join a study group because you assume these individuals are not interested in helping you. Your assumptions cause you to act as if the assumptions are facts. You can short circuit these assumptions in the same way you short circuit any type of negative thinking. Challenge and correct the thoughts behind the assumptions. If necessary, repeat more constructive, reality-based statements over and over in your mind.

Attend Class Regularly

College students are on their own when it comes to attending class. When you're tired or when your schedule is hectic, the temptation to cut can be great. When you are tempted to cut, remember this—succeeding in college without attending class is like trying to row a boat without the oars. It just doesn't work. Much of what you will be tested on will be provided in the classroom. So, resolve to attend *all* classes, lectures, and lab sessions. Let true emergencies or illness be the only reason for missing class. Remember, in order to get the most out of your course work, you need to *be there*.

WHEN YOU DO HAVE TO MISS CLASS

What if an emergency comes up or you become ill? First talk to your instructor. Explain the situation. He/she may be willing to brief you on what has been discussed and what you must do to catch up. Try to borrow lecture notes from a classmate. Remember, this is not the same as going to class. Other student's notes may not be as thorough as yours. Rely on other students' notes only in emergency situations.

Active Listening Strategies

All of us have had the experience of pretending to listen when our minds were miles away. This is not unusual. But if it happens often while you're in class, it can be a problem. Most of the information in your classes will be presented orally. In order to absorb this information, you must **listen actively**. That means you must focus on the speaker or speakers and concentrate on what is being said. To be an **active listener**, you must get involved in the process of listening with your mind. When you listen actively, you process new information, categorize and organize content for retention and recall, and learn more. Perhaps, most importantly, with active listening you reduce significantly the amount of time you will need to study outside of class.

CHAPTER 4 Learning in the Classroom

The first step in the active listening process is to acknowledge that listening is work. Listening is an activity; *it is serious business*. Once you accept this, you are ready to apply the following guidelines to your listening habits in the classroom. You will find that when you make these active listening strategies a part of your classroom behavior, your concentration increases, your homework becomes easier, and your grades improve.

Look at the Instructor

Your attention will stay focused much longer if you look at the person or persons speaking. Concentrate on being attentive and perhaps even respond with appropriate gestures or facial expressions, such as an affirmative nod, a quizzical look, or a surprised expression. Although you may prefer not to look at the instructor for long periods of time, avoid staring at the ceiling, doodling on paper, closing your eyes, or whispering to your seat mate. If you are uncomfortable maintaining continual eye contact in a small classroom, try switching your gaze to a point just beyond the instructor, perhaps looking at the board. Your energy, however, should be directed at concentrating on the person speaking. Looking at the speaker is the best way to achieve this.

Decide to Pay Attention

While looking at the instructor is very important, it does not guarantee that you are hearing and processing what is being said. In fact, you can appear to be listening intently while your mind is planning your vacation, recalling your date last night, or worrying about your car problems. This is where attitude and determination come into play. *You need to decide to listen.* This is an active choice that only you can make. Remember, listening is serious business, so resolve to focus your mind on the speaker.

Making the Grade in Classroom Attention

For each statement, circle the response that applies to you.

1. Do you stay focused in class? Yes No
2. Do you keep your eyes on the instructor? Yes No
3. Do you sit near the front? Yes No
4. Do you take thorough notes? Yes No
5. Do you understand what is presented? Yes No
6. Do you ask questions? Yes No

If you responded "Yes" to most of these questions, you are on the right track. If you responded "No" to several questions, there's room to improve your classroom attentiveness.

There are a number of ways you can improve your attention in class. One way is to put a rubber band on your wrist. Every time your mind wanders, give it a snap. That works for some people. Or make a check mark on your notebook page each time you lose focus. If you have five or more check marks, try taking notes more vigorously. It is hard to lose focus if you are trying to record what is being said.

You will find it easier to pay attention when you are familiar with the subject matter and in tune with the instructor's purpose, which is to explain and expand on the subject matter. In order for you to benefit from a lecture you need to know something about the content that will be covered.

Reviewing past notes and keeping up with reading assignments will give you a focused mindset. You will already have questions in mind and you will be anticipating the purpose of the instructor's lecture.

If you absolutely can't get the assignment read before class, at least take time to scan the chapter so that you are familiar with the major topics. A quick scan of a chapter on private enterprise in a Business Management text might result in questions such as *Just what is private enterprise? Will the instructor explain supply and demand? market competition? bankruptcy? monopolies?* You can generate questions from the topic headings and the sidebars in the text. With these questions in mind, you will arrive in class ready to receive information.

Listen for Key Ideas and Important Phrases

Instructors tend to repeat important information. Be on the alert for repetitions or phrases such as *the importance of, the implications are, in summary, key factors in, for the following reasons, resulted in the following,* and *the definition is.* Another way to tell what the instructor thinks is important is by watching for changes in tone of voice and degree of enthusiasm. If you detect passion or strong emphasis, listen carefully. Your instructor is giving you clues about what he or she believes is important. It is a good possibility that this material will be covered on a quiz or test.

What if you could see your instructor's notes? Would that be helpful? There is a way to find out what's in your instructor's notes—just be sure to write down what is said immediately after you see the instructor glance at them. Often instructors wander off the subject or into related areas that come to mind as they are talking. The reason for looking at their notes is to remember the next *key point* that must be covered. Being alert for these moments is a way to focus your attention and, in a sense, see the instructor's notes. Again, these points are likely to be the ones that will be covered on tests.

Pay Attention to Outlines, Formulas, and Data on the Board

If the instructor has taken time to put information on the board, you can be sure that it is important. Formulas, diagrams, dates, names, places, titles, events, and outlines should be copied into your notebook. Even if the instructor doesn't talk about everything on the board, copy everything anyway. If you are unsure of how the information relates to the course, ask. Most instructors are very up front about what you need to know and why.

Take Notes

It is extremely important to take notes in every class. Taking notes keeps your mind focused on the speaker and helps you to remember the material. Even if you follow and understand your instructor, you will forget nearly all new information very quickly—and by exam time, your recall will be zilch. In fact, studies show that most people forget 80% of what they have heard after two weeks and 95% after four weeks. Taking notes motivates you to listen actively and will help you to prepare for tests.

Taking notes in class differs from taking notes on reading assignments. In class you must listen and concentrate on what is being explained *and* take notes at the same time. It is harder than taking notes on your written assignment because you must keep up with the speaker. Occasionally, you might be able to ask the instructor for clarification or to repeat a statement, but much of the time you simply have to follow the instructor's pace.

Use longhand to take notes. Shorthand or other note taking systems aren't recommended because they have to be transcribed later and you may have trouble deciphering them. Equipment such as a tape recorder or a laptop are not adequate substitutes for good notes. Both of these methods require more time for review than a good set of handwritten notes.

The purpose of note taking is to capture essential points and subpoints in an organized method that provides a tool for recalling the material. The Roman numeral outline system, which works well for text notes, is too difficult to implement when you are taking notes in class. You can have orderly notes by indenting or bulleting subpoints.

Here are guidelines for producing orderly and usable notes.

- Use a separate notebook for each class (put your name and telephone number in each book).
- Write the date and subject before each entry.
- Jot down key concepts, main ideas, major principles.
- Write in phrases by skipping connecting words like *and, but, a, the.*
- Write clearly and neatly.
- Leave white space for adding comments.
- Write more rather than less (you can always eliminate something later).
- Indent when noting supporting data under main ideas or topics.

A well known system of note taking is the Cornell Note-Taking System developed by Walter Pauk at Cornell University. This system requires that you divide your notebook page into two columns. The right side column is wider than the left to allow space for recording phrases that describe major points, concepts, and examples. The left column is used to reduce the phrases to "cue" words that will help you remember the major point. For example, opposite the cue word "Watergate" the right column might contain the following phrases: "break-in at National Democratic Headquarters," "orchestrated by Republican party," "political scandal," "led to Nixon resignation." Subordinate information might include the dates of the break-in and the associated senate hearings. Cue words also can be turned into questions that relate to the information in the right column: "What was the significance of Watergate?" or "How did Watergate affect American politics?"

Listen Critically

This may be the most difficult technique to put into practice. You may feel unable to apply thinking skills during class lectures because you are busy keeping up with the flow of speech. In time and with some effort, you can evaluate and process what you hear *as* you hear it. As you become a more experienced listener, you can jot down questions that arise during the lecture. When you review your class notes, think about your questions. If these questions lead you to disagreement with your instructor's explanation or analysis of a topic, discuss your questions with someone else in the class or meet with the instructor. Often, simply discussing an issue can help clarify murky points. Remember, too, that you do not have to agree with everything that is presented to you. However, you need to listen and understand an issue before you can engage in a debate.

Listen to the Very End

Most people get restless toward the end of class. This is when they begin to put away their materials and think about what they plan to do next. Unfortunately, the last few minutes may be the most important part of the class. This is often when the instructor summarizes what has been presented in class. So stay tuned during the last five minutes of class. Resist the temptation to mentally check out. Focus on the instructor's parting words and listen for summary statements, information about the next class session, new assignments, or changes in due dates. Make sure you write down this information, even when you think it is something you are unlikely to forget.

Class Participation

Your opportunities to participate in class depend on several factors: the number of students in the class, the setting (small classroom vs. lecture hall), and the instructor's teaching style. Your level of participation will vary according to these factors. In some classes you will be encouraged to ask questions and join discussion groups. Be prepared to be an *active* participant in those classes where it is encouraged. Asking questions and taking part in discussion is an excellent way to get involved with the subject. It also gives you the chance to improve your ability to speak with and in front of other people.

Ask Questions

Do not be afraid to raise your hand in class. Most instructors welcome questions from students. As long as you ask a serious question, you will get a serious answer. Questions should relate to what the instructor is speaking on at the time; if you have other unrelated questions, it is best to wait until after class or meet with the instructor during office hours.

Questions that you and other students ask can help to get the instructor to expand on a difficult concept, issue, or formula. However, don't ask questions that might antagonize the instructor. You are entitled to voice your opinions in class, but there is nothing to be gained by attacking your instructor publicly. If you strongly disagree with an instructor's point of view or the style of presentation, your best strategy is to talk with the instructor privately.

Listen to questions posed by other students. Student questions may cause the instructor to expand and clarify difficult concepts; sometimes a second or third explanation is what you need to really understand. By focusing on the student asking the question, you are keeping your attention on the subject matter. Even if you think you know the answer to the question, listening will help reinforce your learning.

Talk to Your Instructor

Sometimes you can talk to your instructor before or after class. However, if you expect to have a serious discussion or if you have a lot of questions, it is best to arrange a visit with the instructor during posted office hours. Sometimes you can schedule an appointment with the department secretary to avoid a long wait. Prepare for your visit by bringing a list of questions or notes on what you want to discuss. Your time and the instructor's time is valuable; use the time productively.

Talk to Other Students

Try to get to know some of the students in each of your classes. Exchange names and phone numbers with students who appear to be serious and on whom you could rely for accurate information when you need assistance. When you want to clarify something heard in class or if you have to miss a class, call one of these classmates. Discussing your class material with others is an excellent way to reinforce learning. Your arrangement with other college students could turn into an ongoing "study pal" relationship or it could lead to forming a study group as suggested in Chapter 3.

After-Class Review

It is hard to remember all that you hear in class. Most of the time the lecture is your first exposure to the material. Simply attending class and taking notes will not put the information into your long-term memory. In order to process the information you heard and noted in your brain, you must review it daily. It is best to review within 24 hours after each class if your schedule permits it. If not, schedule review time later in the day or evening. Many of the study techniques presented in Chapter 3 can be used for your review sessions.

Review Your Class Notes

Your notes provide a route back to the important concepts and main facts introduced in the lecture. Review them to give them a permanent spot in your memory banks. As you go through your notes, mark any areas that are still unclear. Highlight key words. Fill in gaps or missing data. If you used the "cue" notetaking system, turn the cues into questions. Pretend you are the instructor making up test questions. Be sure you can answer the questions!

If you are having difficulty understanding the lecture material, find a way to increase your knowledge. You may decide that you need to go back to the textbook or go to the library and get other books on the subject. You may decide to make a list of questions to ask your instructor or your study group. Use your notes to determine what you understand and what you may need to learn more about.

Once you understand the content of your notes, imprint key words and ideas in your memory so that you can recall them. Read your notes out loud. Then cover a page of your notes and talk out loud about the major idea. Use your own ideas. Hold a discussion with yourself. Ask questions and talk to yourself about the information until you have looked at it from a number of angles. If you have not been in the habit of reading out loud, you may find it awkward at first, but this is a very effective technique for remembering information.

Summarize

After you have reviewed your notes and discussed them out loud, you are ready to write a summary. This is where you try to organize the lecture information into a concise paragraph. Cover the key idea or ideas in three to six sentences. Your summary should cover global (big picture) concepts, not the details. A good summary will trigger recall of the more specific details that you have recorded in your notes.

Summarizing your notes has a big payoff. When you are able to write a clear summary of the day's lecture, you are demonstrating that you understand the material. You are reinforcing learning by condensing the material into a handful of key thoughts. Make a habit of writing a summary at the end of your notes following every lecture you attend. A sample summary is shown below.

SUMMARY PARAGRAPH OF DAY'S LECTURE NOTES

The Civil War was triggered by the secession of the Southern slave states from the Union. Economics, states' rights, and slavery were contributing issues. The interests of Northern capitalists, laborers, and farmers were fundamentally different from those of the Southern plantation owners.

Coordinate Class Notes with Textbook Notes

If your instructor is very well organized and sticks closely to the text, you can combine your notes from both sources on one page. Do this by drawing three lines down your paper with "cues" or "questions" in the left column, text notes in the middle column, and lecture notes in the right column. When the text and lecture materials are not coordinated, keep separate notes until they begin to line up. Review your class and lecture notes by topics and blend them into a new set of notes. It will take more work to combine materials when they are not parallel, but it is a good learning exercise.

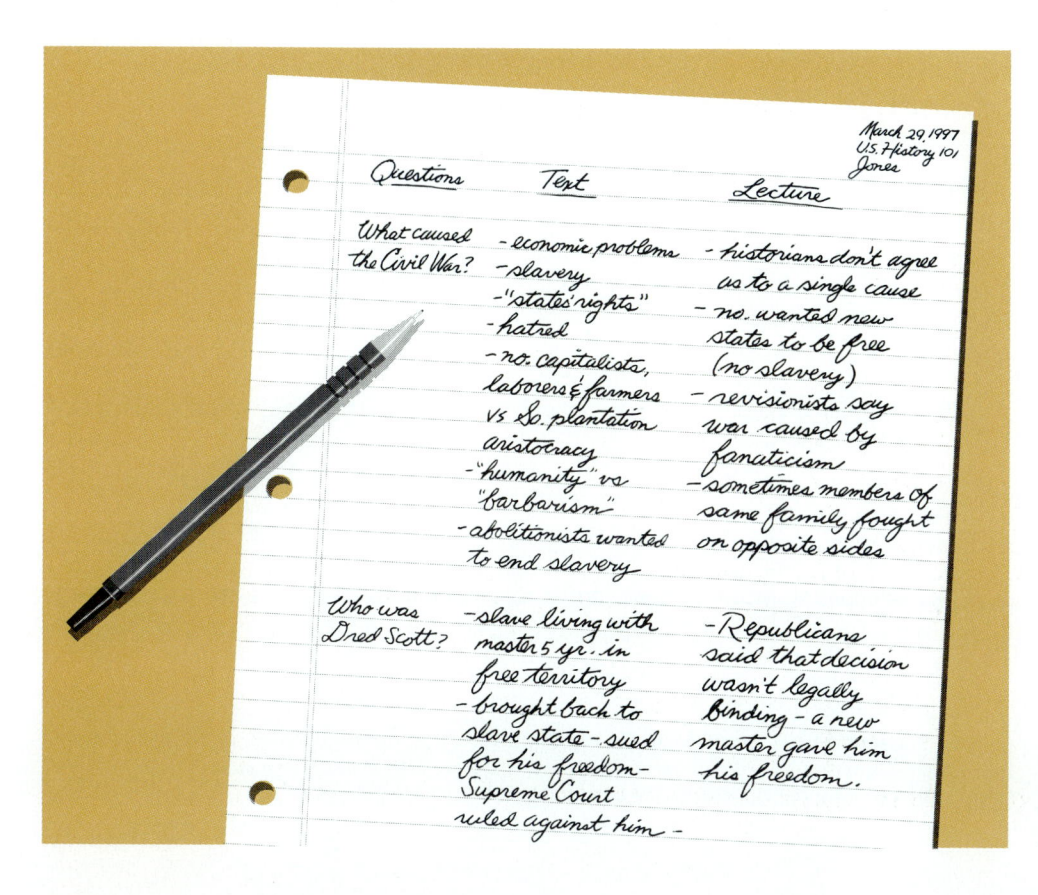

FIGURE 4-1 Text and Lecture Notes Side by Side

Review and Recall

1. Describe why, in the classroom, it is best to sit up front and in the center.

   _____

   _____

   _____

2. List four things you can do to get more out of your classroom experience.

   a. _____

   b. _____

   c. _____

   d. _____

3. Explain what you can do before class to help you understand the purpose of a lecture.

   _____

   _____

   _____

CHAPTER 4   Learning in the Classroom

4. It is not important to copy data and formulas from the board. True or False? Explain your answer.
   _____
   _____

5. List six principles for good notetaking in class.

   a. _____

   b. _____

   c. _____

   d. _____

   e. _____

   f. _____

6. Describe two techniques you can use when you start to lose concentration in class.

   a. _____

   b. _____

7. Describe the recommended format for lecture notes.
   _____
   _____

8. Describe the Cornell Note-Taking System.
   _____
   _____
   _____

9. Explain what it means to listen critically. How should you apply this in class?
   _____
   _____
   _____

10. What three techniques can you use to place information in long-term memory after class?

    a. _____

    b. _____

    c. _____

Apply Critical Thinking

Get together with a classmate after a lecture and compare notes. Did you both record the same information? Who provided more detail? Was the detail necessary? Did your classmate's notes call to attention anything you may have missed or misunderstood? Make notes on what you learned from this exercise and how you will apply it to your note taking from now on. Be sure to include any insights you get about your classroom habits.

School to Work Applications

INFORMATION: ORGANIZES AND MAINTAINS INFORMATION

1. Go to class prepared to ask two or three questions about your reading assignment or the topic of the day's lecture. Listen and take notes with these questions in mind. If your questions are not answered, ask them during the lecture or at the end of the period. Did your questions help you to focus in class? Did you recognize the answers when they were discussed or did you have to ask the questions to get the answers? Will you apply this technique again?

2. Use the Cornell Note-taking System to take notes in a class, then answer the following questions. Was it easy or hard to use the system? How do these notes compare to notes you have taken on other occasions in terms of readability and content? Does the Cornell system work for you?

3. Pick a class in which the instructor welcomes student input. Go to the class and make observations based on the following questions. Does everyone participate or do only a few speak out? What types of questions or comments do you find most helpful? Were any questions unhelpful or distracting? Does your instructor make sure that all questions are answered before proceeding?

INFORMATION: INTERPRETS AND COMMUNICATES INFORMATION

4. Identify some of your assumptions related to any of your current classes. How might these assumptions affect what you learn? What are the bases for your assumptions? Are you willing to open your mind to conflicting ideas? What can you do with assumptions that interfere with learning?

5. Practice summarizing your notes by assuming you must communicate the most important messages from a lecture in five key phrases. Use these key phrases to then restate out loud the essential elements of the lecture.

6. Use your notes from a class to practice the techniques of after-class reviewing. Review your notes, write a summary statement, and coordinate class notes with notes from your textbook. How well do you know the material after this exercise?

Workplace Application

You work for a property management firm and need a real-estate license to qualify for promotion. You are enrolled in a course to help you prepare for the licensing test. The class doesn't start for a week but you already have the class syllabus, a textbook, and a copy of a real-estate license exam. What can you do to prepare to get the most from your classes? What will you do between classes to reinforce what you need to learn? Be as specific as possible.

CHAPTER 4   Learning in the Classroom

SCANS Personal Progress Application

THINKING SKILLS: *THINKS CREATIVELY, MAKES DECISIONS, SOLVES PROBLEMS, VISUALIZES, KNOWS HOW TO LEARN,* AND *REASONS*

As a student, one of your opportunities is to interpret the information you get in your courses and communicate that information to yourself so that you learn it well and remember it for future use. A powerful technique for doing this is the graphics organizer. One kind of graphic organizer is the concept map.

When you review the material in your class, sketch a quick map of the information that shows relationships among the concepts presented. Near the top of the page are the big, overall concepts, and they're linked to sub-concepts farther down the page. The connecting lines between the concepts make a statement about the connection. For instance, here's a concept map about the classroom habits section of this chapter:

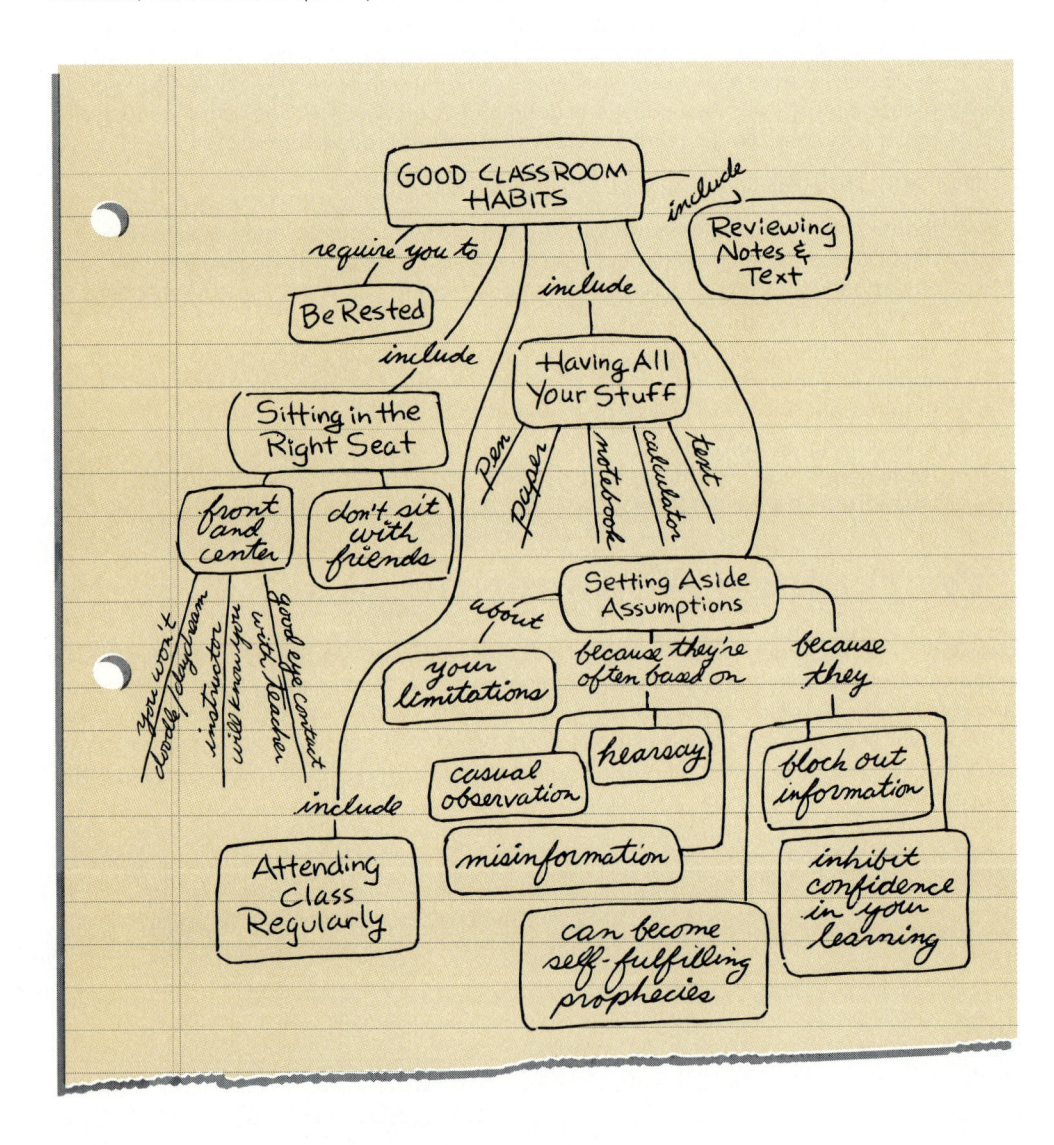

Your concept map doesn't have to be pretty, and you don't have to spend a lot of time drawing it. If you ever find yourself stumped, however, about how concepts and sub-concepts relate to each other, that may be a sign you're not quite clear on some of the information. That's good to know at the time you do the map because you've got the opportunity then to clear up your confusion by checking the text, your notes, or talking with your teacher. Finding this confusion exists when you get a test back with your incorrect answers because of your confusion is *not* such a good time to realize you didn't clearly understand the material.

Many texts have listings of key words or concepts at the end of each chapter. Put those terms on your maps. If your text doesn't have such listings, pull key words from chapter headings, sub-headings, and topic sentences of paragraphs.

Summarizing Concepts Presented in Class

Create a concept map right now of the "Active Listening Strategies" section of this chapter.

FIVE

LEARNING THROUGH READING

CHAPTER OUTLINE

The Case for Active Reading
Active Reading Improves Performance
The Payoff from Active Reading

Active Reading Techniques
Know Your Purpose
Preview the Material
Connect New Material to Your
  Prior Knowledge
Pose Questions and Then
  Read to Find Answers
Visualize
Use Graphics to Aid Understanding
Reread
Talk It Out
Underline and Highlight
Take Notes
Read Beyond Your Textbook
Pay Attention to Word Hurdles
Chase Away Mental Blocks
Additional Techniques for Specific Subject
  Matter

I hated every minute of the training, but I said, "Don't quit. Suffer now and live the rest of your life as a champion."

—Muhammed Ali

Most of us take reading for granted. People with serious reading difficulties or those who have English as a second language get help with their reading. The rest of us go on with whatever level of skill we attained early in our educational lives. Yet reading to decipher, comprehend, and retain information is a very complex skill which becomes even more challenging when the reading material is textbooks, professional articles, and other kinds of technical material.

Just as the runner trains to become a better runner, you can train to become a better reader. Training is practice of an activity combined with a methodology for excelling. One methodology to improve learning through reading is called active reading. With active reading you can increase your reading comprehension and retention. You can learn to stay focused and accomplish more in less time. By using active reading strategies, you can become a more effective, more efficient reader and strengthen your overall performance as a student.

The Case for Active Reading

When you read the newspaper or a magazine article you are engaged in **passive reading.** Passive reading is fine when you are reading for pleasure. It is perfectly appropriate if you know you won't be tested on information and have no pressing need to retain what you read. But if you want to understand and retain information, you need to read actively.

When you read actively you do things that will help you retain information. **Active reading** is like studying, but it is much more. When you study, you review material you have already read or heard to reinforce it and improve your retention. Active reading means you do most of your learning the first time around. Your reading is a much more dedicated, intensified workout. Active reading means you, the reader, engage all your senses in your task much as the runner does when running.

FIGURE 5-1

Training in active reading techniques teaches you to do the following:

- Have a purpose for reading.
- Preview the content to help you anticipate and channel what you read.
- Look for ways to apply what you read to what you already know.
- Think as you go and try to answer your own questions.
- Create mental pictures to help you retain important concepts.
- Pay attention to graphics and grasp their content.
- Reread sections that are particularly difficult to improve comprehension.
- Talk out loud to explore what you think the author is saying.
- Underline, highlight, and take notes to reinforce the content on several sensory levels.
- Look to other sources to reinforce the material.

Active Reading Improves Performance

Research shows that active readers become good students in whatever area they study. The reason is that the techniques help students understand what they read and retain important information. So you can apply active reading to more than just your literature, humanities, and history courses. Active reading can make you a more successful student of math, science, business, and technology as well.

Check Your Reading Habits

Answer the following questions that describe your reading habits as they relate to school assignments and reading for pleasure.

		Circle One		
1.	I read for pleasure.	Often	Sometimes	Never
2.	I read a daily newspaper.	Often	Sometimes	Never
3.	I read popular or hobby magazines.	Often	Sometimes	Never
4.	I read fiction stories and books.	Often	Sometimes	Never
5.	I complete my reading assignments.	Often	Sometimes	Never
6.	I take notes on my reading assignments.	Often	Sometimes	Never
7.	I read difficult assignments more than once.	Often	Sometimes	Never
8.	I summarize my reading assignments.	Often	Sometimes	Never
9.	I use a highlighter or underline text material.	Often	Sometimes	Never
10.	I examine pictures and graphs in the text.	Often	Sometimes	Never

Take a highlighter and mark the "Never" responses. For each highlighted response, describe how that habit could be interfering with your success in mastering college-level reading material.

The Payoff from Active Reading

Because you must adopt new behaviors to become an active reader, you may not be excited by the idea. Your mind may be arguing that active reading takes too much effort or too much time. And realistically, it's hard to change just about anything in our lives. But consider your alternative. You can muddle along in your course work, reading your textbook assignments without any particular purpose or strategy. By test time you will have spent as much or more energy as you would with active reading techniques because you probably had to reread and "cram" to attain a sufficient level of learning.

If you want to become a more efficient, effective reader, and if you'd like a little less stress in your life as a student, consider what active reading can do for you. Focus on the payoff from active reading to motivate yourself to enter a new relationship with your textbook.

The "effort" of active reading will keep you on task, and staying on task will get you results. Your mind is less likely to wander when you have something to do as you read. You have purpose and your purpose will keep you focused. When you stay focused, you learn.

The time you spend in active reading is productive time. Learning takes place when you apply active reading techniques. Ask yourself this: Do you want to spend time rereading material? Or, would you rather log a little extra time up front to really get inside the material and get the material inside of you?

> QUOTE
> To read without reflecting is like eating without digesting.
> —Edmund Burke

If after you've read this chapter, you're still not convinced that active reading will improve your ability to learn from your text, put active reading to the test. Select two different reading passages and read one "passively" and the other "actively." Would you be able to explain the contents of both passages equally well in an essay? Active reading pays off when it comes time to apply the information you've read.

How Well Do You Retain Information?

When you read and find that you have not fully understood or retained important information, what do you do to improve your reading effectiveness? Do you stop to assess retention of the materials as you go or do you wait until you have finished an entire chapter? What would you like to do differently? Answer these questions in a paragraph.

_____

_____

_____

_____

Active Reading Techniques

Active reading is really a philosophical approach. It suggests that you must interact with material in order to internalize its content. So active reading is not so much a formula for success as it is an approach that is applied through a variety of techniques. Some are entirely necessary, others are not essential but can be used to good effect in certain situations. The more you take active reading to heart, the more techniques you will likely apply. Here are the techniques that will make you an active reader.

Know Your Purpose

Consider why most people finish a good book. They want to know what happens. That purpose motivates them to read on. You too need motivation to get through your reading assignment, but it needs to be more than just to make it through 30 pages before your favorite TV show comes on. If you are motivated to find out about X or to define Y, you have a reason to turn the page; to keep moving. Use your purpose as a way to get and stay involved with what you are reading.

Identify why you are reading before you dig in. Are you trying to understand a waste management philosophy? Or, are you reading to find out how worldwide pollution has become a serious problem in the twentieth century? In the first instance you read to discover the key points of the philosophy and perhaps determine how it differs from other approaches to waste management. In the second instance you are on guard for facts that point to a global crisis. In both cases you hope to extract a concrete illustration, for example, the philosophy applied to a real waste management task, or a specific incident of global pollution. When you know your purpose, you know what you are looking for and what you need to get from the material.

Each time you plan a study session that includes reading, write down the purpose of the reading assignment alongside the name of the material. The purpose statement should be what you need to learn from the material, not what you are intending to do. "To prepare for tomorrow's class" is not the purpose of reading a chapter in your General Business text. "To understand the three main types of business entities and how they are organized" is the real purpose for doing the reading. Most texts have learning objectives listed at the beginning of each chapter or an introductory section that explains the purpose of the material (as is done in this text). Use this to guide you, but it helps to rewrite the information in your own words and to try to personalize it where possible. For example, a purpose for reading this chapter is to "improve my ability to understand and retain the information in textbooks."

Preview the Material

A movie preview lets you know what a movie is about before you see it in its entirety. Similarly, your reading preview will give you a feel for what the material is about before you read it carefully. Previewing provides a mental map that helps you see where the author is going with the content. You get a feel for how the material is arranged, connected, and organized. Then when you do read more thoroughly, you have an idea where you're headed—from major point A to major point B to major point C. With this map as your guide, you can stay on track.

Your Textbook Preview.
Even *before* you get your first reading assignment, you can preview your textbook. The following activities will acquaint you with your textbook so that when it comes time for intensive reading you can get right to work.

> **YOUR TEXTBOOK IS ON YOUR SIDE**
>
> Your textbook is fundamental to success in your course work. View it as your ally, and you may be more inclined to spend time with it. Remember that its purpose is not to entertain you but rather to convey information that the author (and your instructor) believes is necessary to gain mastery of a subject.

- Review the table of contents to learn how the material is organized at the unit and chapter level.
- Consider the overall length of the book and the average length of each chapter or main section.
- Look for information about the author(s) that might give insight into the text's point of view.
- Look for objectives or introductory statements at the front of each chapter and read one or two to get a feel for the content at the chapter level.
- Look for concluding paragraphs or summaries at the end of each chapter and unit.
- Note the use of illustrations such as pictures, tables, and graphs.
- Check the back of the book for appendices, a glossary, and a detailed index.
- Note how the publisher uses different type styles, type sizes, and colors to emphasize important information.
- Look to see what kind of review questions and suggested activities are included at the chapter and unit level.

Whether your textbook is colorful, nicely formatted, and written in an easy, conversational style or is in black and white, wordy, and just plain dry, remember this: it contains information that you need to become a successful student!

Your Reading Assignment Preview.
The best way to preview a reading assignment is to scan through it. **Scanning** is rapid, selective reading. You scan by looking at topic headings, text in different formats (boldfaced or bulleted lists, for example), charts, drawings, diagrams, and pictures. Read introductory and summary statements. These will clue you in to important concepts as well as the logic behind the organization of the material. If you spend some time looking ahead, you won't get lost once you've started reading.

Let's apply previewing to an imaginary reading assignment on creative writing. You are to read a 20-page essay titled *Discipline and the Creative Form*. The essay appears in a textbook and is followed by several discussion questions and a vocabulary list. It is formatted with headings and some italicized text. By "previewing" the questions, vocabulary, headings, and italicized passages you learn that the essay explains how creativity is hampered by lack of discipline, how a writing regimen can actually promote creativity, and how several authors have imposed self-discipline for positive results. You don't have the specifics yet, but your preview tells you just enough so that you can anticipate and intelligently digest what a close reading will fully develop.

Connect New Material to Your Prior Knowledge

Any connections you can make between new information and your **prior knowledge** (what you already know) can help you to retain material. These connections act like a glue to hold the new information in a place where you can retrieve it. It lends credibility to the new information.

To apply this technique, be on the lookout for how the new information you read relates to what you already know about this subject. Take the topic "causes of water pollution." You may not have a clue to the causes, but you probably have seen the effects. How about that vacation lake that was so clear and pristine when you were a youngster? What does it look like today? Are you concerned about the drinking water in your community? There is likely to be something in your experience that will help you to integrate the new information with your existing knowledge. This will increase your motivation to learn more and heighten your level of interest in what you are reading.

Pose Questions and Then Read to Find Answers

When you have questions, your natural tendency is to look for answers. In this way, knowing the questions that your reading material will answer will motivate you to uncover the answers. They will strengthen your sense of purpose. But posing questions does even more by putting your mind on alert to key information. You will be more prepared to recognize the answers when they're presented.

> **BREAK IN THAT NEW BOOK**
>
> In order to make a new book easier to physically handle and read, break it in. Place it on a flat surface and open the front and back covers slowly. Then take a few pages near each cover and flatten them down. Work your way into the middle until the whole book has been flattened. This may sound like a silly thing to do, but it serves two purposes. First, it is good for the book; second, it makes it a lot easier to turn the pages. And you'll never again find yourself wrestling with a book that doesn't want to stay open.

CHAPTER 5   Learning Through Reading

> Not all learning comes from books. You have to live a lot.
> —Loretta Lynn

Before you start reading, ask yourself why the material was assigned. Do you know how it relates to the course goals? Look at the course syllabus and any other introductory materials that were given to you. Did your instructor already identify key questions? Does your textbook contain end-of-chapter questions? Go ahead and use them, and save yourself some time. If you do need to create your own questions, phrase them in terms of what you want to learn. Use the information you gleaned from your preview of the material to be as specific as you can.

You may want to write your questions in the margin of your text. You can rewrite headings and subheadings as inquiries and then seek the answers as you read. Later you can test your recall by covering the text and reading your questions in the margin. Do you know the answers? If not, then reread until you have a good grasp of the material.

You can create questions to guide you through literature as well as standard textbooks. Ask yourself what the author's purpose is, who the characters are, and how the characters are developed. These questions will help you tune in to the material and zoom in on the answers.

Visualize

Dreams prove that people have the ability to create vivid mental pictures. So, if you dream, you can visualize. Visualizing provides a way to interpret, connect, and store information. It helps you to "see" in the mind's eye what you are reading about. When it comes to retrieving that information, particularly complex ideas, mental pictures provide quick access to your brain's filing system.

As you read, try to get a visual image from the words on the page. Illustrations or diagrams in your text can give you a head start. Whether your mental picture includes people, landscapes, equipment, or events, try to keep it simple. Think of visualizing as making a silent movie of the text material. Using pictures will help you retain the information and recall it more easily when you need it later.

Use Graphics to Aid Understanding

The term "graphic" means anything in a visual form. Textbooks, newspapers, and magazines are loaded with graphics that contain important information. Many texts label their graphics as figures or tables. Figures may contain bar graphs, line graphs, pie charts, diagrams, drawings, photographs, or maps, while tables contain data (text, symbols, or numbers) arranged in columns and rows.

Sometimes students think that they can just gloss over the graphics in a textbook, but they are making a big mistake. As you read, it is extremely important to pause and examine each and every figure and table carefully. Figures and tables are a convenient way of summarizing data that the author considers important. They are designed to present large chunks of information in an easily understood format. A thorough understanding of the graphics in your reading material will help your retention and recall of important subject matter. If your preferred learning style is visual, you may need to rely heavily on the graphics in your texts.

Bar and Line Graphs. Bar and line graphs are frequently used to show how values change over time or categories. Values appear on a vertical axis with designated timeframes or categories along a horizontal axis. Values for a bar graph are plotted with bars; for a line graph they are plotted with different colored lines. These types of graphs convey a great deal of information quickly and easily. Line graphs reveal patterns or trends (noted by a line that consistently rises or falls). For example, you can look at a line graph that shows sales for several products

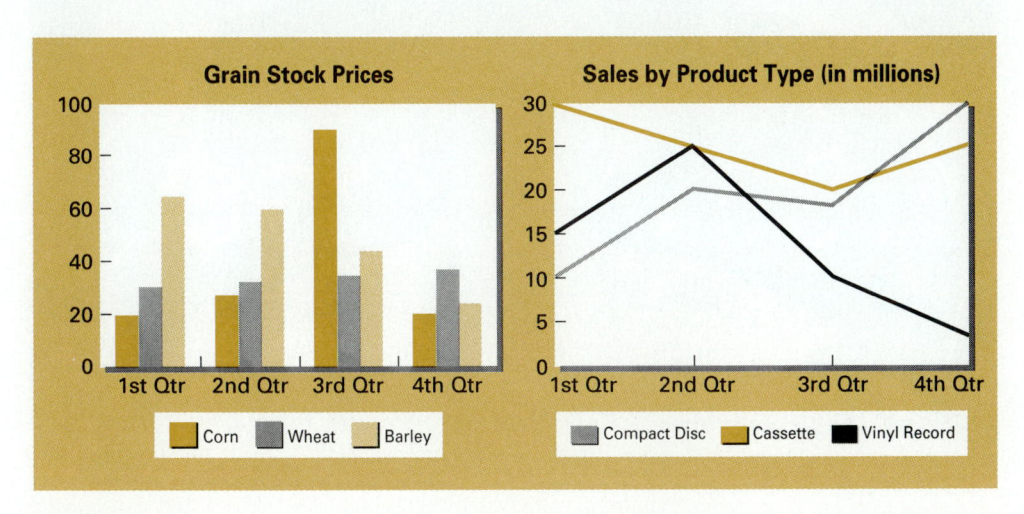

FIGURE 5-2 Bar and Line Graph

CHAPTER 5 Learning Through Reading 99

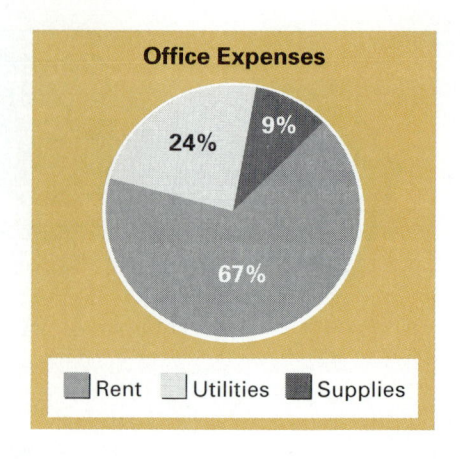

FIGURE 5-3 Pie Chart

over a year's time and see at a glance whether sales are increasing or decreasing for a particular product. You can also observe how the sales compare. A bar graph allows for very clear comparison of values.

Pie Chart. A pie chart is useful for showing the relationship of parts to a whole. The pie is the whole, or 100 percent. Each value is translated to a piece of the pie as a percent of the whole. For example, a pie chart can show how the cost of office supplies contributes to the total expenditures for office expenses, or how our nation is divided by age groups.

Diagram. A diagram is used to clarify and explain a process, an event, or relationships. For example, a geography text may use a diagram to show the relationship of the Earth's interconnected spheres, which play important roles in the mobilization, transport, and deposition of chemical elements.

Drawings. Sometimes a drawing or sketch is used to illustrate a concept, an event, or an object. With the price of paper these days, they are not included just because they're attractive! Study each drawing or sketch and make sure you understand how it connects to and expands upon the written material.

FIGURE 5-4 Diagram

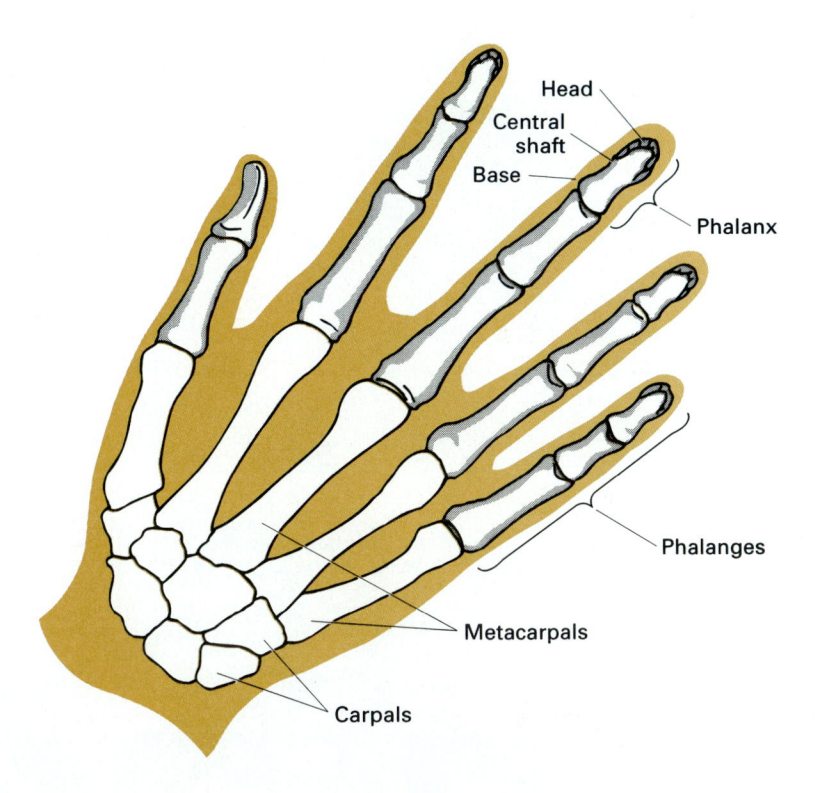

FIGURE 5-5 Anatomical Drawing of a Hand

The function of drawings or sketches in most of your reading assignments will be obvious. Anatomy texts present detailed drawings to show the muscle and bone structure of humans and other vertebrates. Architectural texts use drawings to illustrate different home or building styles.

Photographs. Photographs can show people, places, and things as they were or as they are. They often are used in connection with historical and current events. Sometimes a picture becomes the symbol of an event. For example, the Raising of the Flag on Iwo Jima has come to symbolize the victory of the U.S. troops in the South Pacific during World War II. If you spend time looking at a picture of an important event, you can use the visual memory to attach all kinds of facts for easy retrieval.

Maps. Maps depict the location or terrain of significant areas. A history text will include maps of explorer's routes or battle sites. A geography text will include maps of various landscapes. An astronomy text will include maps of the constellations and the Solar System.

Tables. Tables present numerical and other data in columns and rows. Vast amounts of information can be displayed in a table, for example, data on population, school enrollment, mileage, car production, restaurant sales, movie attendance, housing, investments, industrial production, goods and services, and career opportunities. Most tables in a textbook are constructed to provide summary information for the reader.

A PICTURE IS WORTH A THOUSAND WORDS

How long does it take you to read a thousand words? Fifteen minutes or more? Then don't shortchange yourself by glossing over the graphics in your textbook. Take a few minutes to study each graphic as you come across it in a reading assignment. Linger a bit longer if the graphic is detailed or complex. If a picture is indeed worth a thousand words, your time will be well spent.

Reread

The goal of active reading is comprehension. That is why active readers reread when necessary. You may be reading material on a topic you know very little about. It isn't a sure thing you will get the message on the first go-round. Don't hesitate to revisit a paragraph or entire chapter if you are foggy about the content.

CHAPTER 5 Learning Through Reading

FIGURE 5-6 Flag Raising at Iwo Jima. (Photographer: Rosenthal; AP/Wide World Photos)

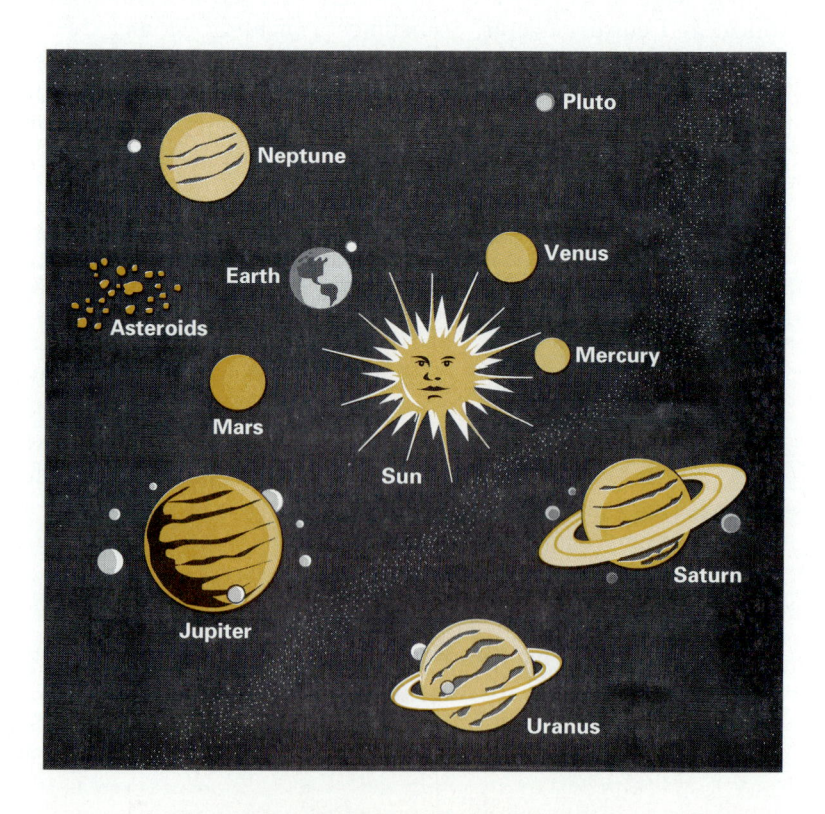

FIGURE 5-7 Map of the Solar System

102   PART TWO   Developing Your Study Skills

ENROLLMENTS BY AGE, UNIVERSITY POST-SECONDARY SYSTEMS, FALL 1986 AND FALL 1996						
	19 OR YOUNGER	20-24	25-34	35 OR OLDER	AGE UNKNOWN	TOTAL
Community Colleges						
1986	9,054	11,217	8,407	5,223	3,187	37,088
1996	14,216	16,933	13,549	11,332	555	56,585
State Universities						
1986	10,809	21,246	7,749	4,853	2,181	46,838
1996	10,690	27,023	9,852	8,034	844	56,443
Technical Colleges						
1986	12,493	12,636	8,945	3,666	1,670	39,410
1996	7,679	12,432	11,553	13,141	6,166	50,971
University of Minnesota						
1986	11,197	25,686	13,334	3,707	2,119	56,043
1996	9,070	22,098	12,472	4,537	347	48,524
Private Colleges and Universities						
1986	13,423	18,699	5,546	2,830	259	40,757
1996	12,930	20,093	10,805	11,438	245	55,511
Private Professional Schools						
1986	0	727	1,944	622	21	3,314
1996	0	759	1,452	1,171	42	3,424
Private Career Schools						
1986	2,471	3,853	2,199	484	717	9,724
1996	1,350	3,191	2,220	969	237	7,967
All Systems						
1986	59,447	94,064	48,124	21,385	10,154	233,174
1996	55,935	102,529	61,903	50,622	8,436	279,425

FIGURE 5-8 Example of a Table

As you read, check to make sure you understand the material. Is your purpose for reading still clear? Are you finding answers to your questions? If not, backtrack to more familiar territory. Expect to reread passages that explain complex ideas, historical events, or formulas. A second and third time through a section or chapter may set off the light bulb *and* help to lay down a well-worn path to your memory banks.

Talk It Out

Sometimes talking out loud about what you are reading facilitates understanding and helps to imprint details and facts in your mind. It helps you to see if you really have absorbed what you have just read.

Check your comprehension by talking it out at different intervals during your reading. When and where you stop to do so will depend upon how your reading material is structured. For example, after a new idea is introduced, stop and explain out loud in your own words what you have just read. If you are reading about global warming you might start with something like this: "The author says that some scientists believe increases in carbon dioxide cause global warming and the accompanying rise in sea levels. More data are needed to determine if this is a long-term trend, and improved climate models will predict changes in the rate of global warming." For variety, you could try talking it out as though you are explaining the material to someone else. This applies well when the material is about a process or event.

Underline and Highlight

We said that active readers use more than their eyes to read. They get involved with their reading material. One way to get involved with your material is to mark it. The physical act of underlining or highlighting actually helps your mind stay on task, assimilate new information, and retain that information. Experiment with different color highlighters. Many students find that the color called *hot pink* is the most effective.

If you own your textbook, don't be afraid to mark it. Textbooks are learning devices and marking them will help you learn. As you read, underline key phrases with a pen or highlighter to make your second reading or review much easier. You will be able to locate important points quickly and easily. Too, you can use underlined text as the basis for your notes.

Don't be in too big a hurry to start underlining. Read the entire paragraph first. Then ask yourself, What is the most important idea in this paragraph? Don't start underlining until you have answered that question. Underlining is only effective if it is used carefully and sparingly. Take a look at the examples below.

EXAMPLE A: NOLAN'S UNDERLINING

A local area network (LAN) links computers. <u>Many businesses use LANs to increase worker productivity and to save on equipment costs. LANs let users share files, software applications, and hardware, such as printers.</u> There is a limitation with LANs, however. <u>They are confined to a relatively small geographical area.</u> The computers can be located in several buildings but must be housed within the designated area.

EXAMPLE B: MARISSA'S UNDERLINING OF THE SAME PASSAGE

<u>A local area network (LAN) links computers.</u> Many businesses use LANs to increase worker productivity and to save on equipment costs. LANs let <u>users share files, software applications, and hardware,</u> such as printers. There is a limitation with LANs, however. They are confined to a relatively <u>small geographical area.</u> The computers can be located in several buildings but must be housed within the designated area.

In Example A, Nolan underlined almost everything, which will provide no help when he tries to take notes. In Example B, Marissa found the main idea and three key phrases. She reduced 65 words to 17 words. Because she has been selective, Marissa will be more likely to remember these key words. She can also transfer them to her notes for later review.

We have stated that you can choose to underline or highlight as you read. But actually the two methods are not equally effective. Studies have shown that highlighting is not as useful a technique as underlining. The pastel colors of the highlighter draw your attention to the location of certain words on the page but do not help you to remember these words. According to the Von Restorff phenomenon,* words that are highlighted have less meaning for the reader and are actually more difficult for the reader to visualize.

Take Notes

You may wonder why you have to take notes if you have already read and underlined a passage. That's a fair question. For most of us, one read-through

---

> **NOT EVERYTHING IS IMPORTANT!**
>
> We often think everything is important. However, most of us can't remember everything. We have to distinguish between what is "nice" to know and what we "need" to know. Unless you have a photographic memory, reduce your reading material to key facts and concepts that you can understand and recall. Two active reading techniques—underlining important information and taking notes—will help you to do this quickly and efficiently.

---

*Monte, Christopher F.; *Merlin: The Sorcerer's Guide to Success in College.* Belmont, CA: Wadsworth 1994.

of difficult material will not make a sufficient imprint on our brain for even short-term recall. Copying or paraphrasing underlined points in your own handwriting deepens the impression on your brain. The active note-taking process also helps you to look at the material again and test your understanding of it.

It is important to read and comprehend at least a paragraph before you attempt to transfer information to notes. Read until you grasp an important idea or fact. Reread if the meaning is unclear. Then stop to jot notes in the text itself or in your notebook. Your notes should emphasize, clarify, and reiterate the substance of the material you have just read. Good notes capture mountains of information in chunks that you can remember.

Some of you will find it too disruptive to underline *and* take notes while reading. An alternate method is to underline on the first read-through, then reread and take notes based on the underlined material. Experiment to see which sequence works best for you.

Margin Notes in the Text. If you own your textbook, go ahead and write notes in it as you read. List or summarize major points in the margins. Use arrows to clarify relationships and enumeration to establish a sequence or series. Draw pictures to illustrate a relationship or concept. Use notes that further your comprehension and that will help you when you revisit the text at another sitting.

Notes in a Notebook. You can also use the more traditional method of writing notes in a spiral or three-ring notebook. The three-ring notebook allows you to insert or remove pages easily. Open your notebook and keep a pen in your hand as you read. Identify your reading assignment and the date at the top of the page. Then proceed to take notes in whatever fashion works for you. You can apply the same note-taking system that you use in the classroom. Reread Chapter 4 if you need a refresher on how to take good notes.

Notes on Your Computer. The computer is an effective tool for storing information, yet so is a spiral notebook. One important distinction is that with the computer, you can manipulate information as you see fit once it is stored in a file. For example, you can code key words in boldface or make bulleted lists of examples supporting key ideas. You can print a hard copy and make changes at a later date.

If you have access to one, try reading next to a computer and keying your notes. Whether you begin your note taking at the computer or simply transfer your written notes to an electronic file, you are doing yourself a favor. Your mind gets to process the information one more time, and that improves recall.

Read Beyond Your Textbook

The textbook is often the primary vehicle for instruction in a course. But not all textbooks are created equal. If you find that a textbook is very confusing, too difficult to read, or just plain irritating, then look for other sources of information on the subject.

You might be able to find another textbook on the same subject that is more user friendly. Or you may want to seek out a different medium. Go to the library and look for books, videos, journals, and magazine articles on the subject. An encyclopedia may be a useful resource. Ask the librarian for help. In other words, do your own research on the subject if you simply cannot manage the text. In fact, even if the text isn't giving you difficulty, going to other sources to enrich your understanding of the subject matter will pay dividends at test time.

DON'T GIVE UP ON YOUR TEXT TOO SOON

Give yourself time to warm up to your textbook. Remember, you don't have to read it in a day or a week. Instructors tend to assign reading material according to chapters, which can vary in length, with the average chapter running about 30 pages. Also, class lectures often will shed light on chapter content. A textbook may be overwhelming at first, but if you read it chapter by chapter you can handle it.

READ MORE, READ BETTER

The more you read, the better you will become at reading. This is true whether you spend your time buried in a fashion magazine or a murder mystery, *The New York Times* or the *Encyclopedia Britannica*. Any reading is practice that will improve your textbook reading ability. Your vocabulary will grow. Your prior knowledge will expand. Your reading speed will pick up. So try to read more in your spare time. And enjoy it!

List three subjects you enjoy reading about (for example, cooking, hobbies, famous people, mysteries, romance, science fiction, or general fiction.) What format do you usually choose (book, newspaper, magazine, or other)?

_____

_____

_____

Pay Attention to Word Hurdles

Words that you do not know or that convey complex ideas can be hurdles to understanding. Keep a dictionary handy when you read so that you can quickly look up words that are stumbling blocks. If you are taking notes on your computer, use your on-line dictionary.

If you find it too disruptive to look up words while reading, make a list and then define the words at some later point. Note on what page a word appears so you can revisit its context. Definitions need context to really make sense.

Words pack a lot of meaning. Thus one or two skipped or misunderstood words can really hinder your comprehension. So get to know all of the words that block understanding. You'll be better able to grasp the author's message.

Chase Away Mental Blocks

Nearly everyone experiences mental blocks from time to time. **Mental blocks** occur when, no matter what you do, you just can't concentrate. Mental blocks when you are reading, may be caused by text that is too difficult, confusing, or boring—or because you dislike the subject. Whatever the cause, you can overcome these blocks.

If you think it is the text's difficulty that is causing a block, go to the library or bookstore and look for material on the subject written in an easier, more comfortable style for you. A different author's presentation may help clarify material in your assigned text. Another excellent way to chase away a mental block is by viewing multimedia presentations of the subject matter. Seeing or hearing information on a CD ROM or tape brings material to life in a way that texts don't. When your mental block is caused by your attitude about a subject, engage in some "self talk." Try to recall why you dislike the subject. What past experiences shaped your attitude? Did you get a poor grade in high school? Was the instructor poor or boring? Was the class disruptive? Work your way through the reasons that you feel the way you do about this subject. Resolve to change your attitude. After all, this is a different time in your life, and you have a different instructor, class, and textbook.

If you can't change your attitude about the *subject*, focus on *why* you need to learn the material. Maybe it is simply a required course and you have to get a passing grade in it. Maybe it is a prerequisite for a course you really want to take. Concentrate on how success in this course relates to your future work in school. A positive attitude and determination to succeed will help you get through courses that you may not like but that you *need*. If these steps don't help, talk to your instructor, who may be able to provide you with supplementary materials.

Additional Techniques for Specific Subject Matter

Using active reading techniques will improve your reading and comprehension in every area of study. In addition, you can improve your reading skills even more by understanding the differences in how subjects are presented. Recognizing the characteristics that govern the presentation of various subjects allows you to tailor your reading activities to the subject matter structure. Use the following tips for approaching reading assignments in the following areas.

Science. Science deals with understanding the order of the universe through observation, identification, description, and experimental investigation. The results of scientific inquiry are methodically recorded by categories, classifications, systems, or analyses of cause and effect. While sciences may seem difficult, with a little extra effort, you can master these subjects.

The key to mastering science material, is to apply a *scientific* method to reading your assignments. This means being disciplined, methodical, and orderly. Put yourself in the role of a scientist and look for categories, processes, causes and effects, and relationships. Take careful notes. Make lists including major points, draw diagrams to show relationships, and form questions on topics that need more study or research. For example, after reading about the solar system, list the nine major planets in your notebook.

You need to sharpen your memory skills for science courses. For example, in biology you may be expected to memorize the classes of vertebrates and invertebrates. Or in chemistry, the instructor may insist that you memorize the elements on the *Periodic Table*. Memorization techniques are covered in detail in Chapter 7.

Literature. You will be required to read essays, poetry, short stories, plays, and novels for literature courses. There are certain general principles that help your reading in any of these categories. Before you start your reading assignment, put the following headings on a page in your notebook: Setting, Characters, Point of View, Plot or Theme, Issues, and Outcome. As you start reading, write down where the action takes place. For example, if you are reading the novel *Ethan Frome* by Edith Wharton, note that the story takes place in New England. As you read, ask yourself how the setting affects the action. List the main characters. As the plot evolves, summarize the actions. Describe the issues that this story raises and the outcome. Since a major point of this story is *irony*, be prepared to discuss the meaning of irony and how the concept is illustrated by events in the novel.

> ...often in the heat of noonday, leaning on a hoe, looking across valleys at the mountains, so blue, so close, my only conscious thought was, "*How* can I ever get away from here? How can I get to where they have books, where I can be educated?" I worked hard, always waiting for something to happen to change things. There came a time when I knew I must make them happen; that no one could do anything about it for me. And I did.
> —Belinda Jelliffe, Nurse

Mathematics. Just the thought of Trigonometry or Calculus triggers fear in some students. Immediately, thoughts of impossible formulas and equations come to mind. Fear of math, sometimes even simple math, is very common. For most people, this fear is rooted in the belief that math is just too hard. This fear is often called **math anxiety**.

You can overcome math anxiety by changing your attitude toward math and by applying extra effort. Even if you don't have some math anxiety, expect to devote a lot of study time to your math course. Allow time to read, do problems, and reflect. Be prepared to read difficult formulas and explanations several times! Math courses rely heavily on the textbook. Don't skip anything. Do *all* the problems and answer *all* the questions. Plan to spend time on memorization of certain equations and formulas.

Your study of math can't be hurried. Read until you understand the material. Much of math is cumulative; that is, one principle builds the foundation for the next. If you skip the foundation work, you will soon be lost. If you can't clear up questions by rereading, write down your questions and find time to meet with your instructor. You also may be able to find a student tutor. Another excellent way to improve your math ability is to join a study group.

History. History courses focus on events, trends, theories, and causes. You will be provided with enormous detail to support the author's descriptions. Don't let yourself get bogged down in the details. Previewing is especially important. Look for the big picture and then fill in only the most important supporting arguments or details. For example, if the topic is the Viet Nam war, you will not be expected to recall every single battle. But you will be expected to know the reasons the United States government gave for entering the war *and* the reasons put forth by war protesters. You will be expected to understand such things as: 1) what is meant by the *domino theory*, 2) what happened at My Lai, 3) what happened at Kent State University, and 4) how the experience of Viet Nam affects the United States' current policies on war.

You may be required to read more than just your textbook for history courses. Text and outside reading assignments may be extensive, so plan for long blocks of reading time. Keep up with the assignments. Resolve to read the assignment before going to class. After class, read your lecture notes. Locate the outside reading assignments early on (they will probably be listed on the syllabus). Don't wait until the end of the quarter or semester to do the outside reading. If you do, you may find that the books aren't available and that you don't have time to complete the readings.

Review and Recall

1. List two ways that active reading can make you a more efficient reader.

   a. _____

   b. _____

2. What is the purpose of posing questions as you read?

   _____

3. Explain how *previewing* a reading assignment can make your reading assignment easier.

   _____

   _____

4. Most people are unable to use visualization techniques. True or False? Explain your answer.

   _____

   _____

5. Name and explain four types of graphics.

   a. _____

   b. _____

   c. _____

   d. _____

6. Give three reasons why you might have to *reread* an assignment.

   a. _____

   b. _____

   c. _____

7. The more you underline, the better you will understand the material. True or False?
   Explain your answer. _____

8. Why is highlighting considered less effective than underlining? _____
   _____

9. The only way to take notes on reading is with 3 x 5 note cards. True or False?
   Explain your answer. _____
   _____
   _____

10. List two ways to cope with mental blocks.
    a. _____
    b. _____

Apply Critical Thinking

Review the Table of Contents at the front of this text. In your notebook write down each of the chapter titles and, below each one make a list of questions that you would like to have answered on the subject matter. Review this list as you complete each chapter (think back through the chapters you already read). Keep a list of those questions that have not been answered or where you want to acquire more information and explore finding the answers on your own, using additional reading materials such as magazine or journal articles and self-improvement books and tapes.

School to Work Applications

SCANS

INFORMATION: *ACQUIRES AND EVALUATES INFORMATION*

1. Select a magazine or newspaper article and apply at least two active reading techniques to improve your comprehension. Record the techniques you used and write a short summary of the article. Then evaluate how well the reading techniques helped you to understand and recall the article's content.

2. Find a textbook with graphics. Flip through several chapters and note the type of graphics it contains. Find three examples (bar graph, line graph, pie chart, diagram, drawing, map, photograph, or table) and summarize the information provided by each. Evaluate whether the form the information takes enhances communication. Could the information be communicated more effectively in another manner?

3. Select a newspaper article. On the basis of the title, jot down any prior knowledge you have of the subject. Then read the article from beginning to end. As you read, think about how the new information relates to what you already know or have experienced. Now create three questions that ask for specific information about the article's content. Test your recall of the new information by answering the questions after 24 hours. How did you do? *Note: Don't cheat by rereading the article before answering the questions!*

4. Select a 50+ word advertisement. Read the ad, then reread and underline no more than 10 key words or phrases. Are you able to recall the main points of the ad (likely the "selling features") by glancing at the key words?

5. After reading several paragraphs in a textbook, corner a friend or sit in front of the mirror and "talk it out." Are you able to communicate the information you read by paraphrasing? Do you need to refer to the text or are you able to talk from memory? How does this technique work for you?

CHAPTER 5   Learning Through Reading

6. Read a newspaper or magazine article on a topic that interests you—it can even be a "Dear Abby" column. Then find a friend or fellow student and summarize what you read. How well are you able to convey the main ideas of what you read? What are your stumbling blocks, if any? Notice how your retention increases with your level of interest.
7. Read a short story, novel, or magazine article (25 pages or more). Just do it to give you more reading practice and to help you make reading part of your lifestyle (if it isn't already).

SCANS Workplace Application

You work in the human resources department of a manufacturing company. Recently the company added a dental plan to their employee benefits package. You need to read the document describing the new plan so you will be prepared to answer questions from employees. Apply active reading techniques as you read the dental plan. Then answer the questions that follow the passage without referring back to the dental plan. How did you do?

DYNAMICS DENTAL PLAN

Helping you to maintain your dental health!

DYNAMICS DENTAL PLAN Eligibility

All full-time employees currently enrolled in the DYNAMICS HEALTH CARE PLAN are now eligible for the DYNAMICS DENTAL PLAN described here. New hires are eligible for the DYNAMICS DENTAL PLAN three months after hiring date. Coverage also applies to employee dependents (spouse and children under age 21 or over 21 and enrolled in school).

DYNAMICS DENTAL PLAN Benefits

The DYNAMICS DENTAL PLAN umbrella of care covers 100% for preventive dental services (up to two checkups and cleanings per year per enrollee), 75% for invasive services (fillings, simple extractions, root canals), and 30% for reconstructive procedures (crowns, dentures). In addition, the DYNAMICS DENTAL PLAN offers $1,500 per lifetime coverage for orthodontic services.

Questions for Dynamics Dental Plan Reading Passage

1. How long must an employee wait before becoming eligible for the plan?
2. Name the dependents eligible for the plan.
3. What percent of a root canal does the plan cover?
4. Does the plan cover any services provided by an orthodontist?

SCANS Personal Progress Application

BASIC SKILLS: *READS, WRITES, PERFORMS ARITHMETIC AND MATHEMATICAL OPERATIONS, LISTENS, AND SPEAKS*

THINKING SKILLS: *THINKS CREATIVELY, MAKES DECISIONS, SOLVES PROBLEMS, VISUALIZES, KNOWS HOW TO LEARN, AND REASONS*

Extracting information is vital for employees today because the information often comes buried within a great deal of material.

There's an enjoyable way to develop the ability to extract critical information from all your classes. As a bonus, this techniques will make your classes more interesting and will develop your self-confidence as a learner.

The process is simple: (a) read the assignment before class; (b) outline or make a concept map of the material; (c) take notes in class; (d) after class, compare your outline or concept map to what was covered in class. You'll quickly find that this process tunes you in to the way your instructor thinks about the material. When that happens, you'll start reading your textbook "through your instructor's eyes." Doing so will help you anticipate the flow of the class and will give you a much better understanding of what it is your teacher wants you to learn.

You've summarized the information in your textbook and the class when you've boiled it down to the key points you know the instructor wants you to learn. The above process will help you do that. This technique will also develop one of the important skills employers want you to have.

Train to be a Better Reader

Right now, do steps (a) and (b) of the process described above for the next assigned chapter or section in one of your courses. Then take notes in your upcoming class and compare what you produced in (a) and (b) with what your instructor actually covered. Make adjustments to your "pre-notes" based on the notes you took in class, then save the adjusted "pre-notes" as study guides for the test on that material.

SIX

WRITING YOUR WAY TO THE TOP

CHAPTER OUTLINE

Messages that Make Their Point
 A Clear Message
 A Concise Message
 A Considerate Message
A Method for Good Writing
 Plan Your Attack
 Take a Stab at It (First Draft)
 Make It Better (Second Draft…)
 Make It Perfect (Final Draft)
Specific Writing Assignments
 The Journal Entry
 The Essay
 The Report
 The Research Paper
Electronic Help for Writers
 Word Processing and Desktop
  Publishing Programs
 Electronic Storage
 Formatting Capabilities

*Of all those arts in which the wise excel
Nature's chief masterpiece is writing well.*
—Buckingham

Words have amazing power. In the context of good writing, words deliver important information and ideas. They can influence readers to feel, think, and act in a desired manner. Similarly, words can misinform, offend, and literally "turn off" readers. You have the power of words at your fingertips. Are you able to write to get the results you want?

Like other skills, writing skill does not come naturally. Good writers are made, not born. Whether they are writing the great American novel or a research paper, good writers follow a method or process when they write. They adhere to certain rules of grammar and composition, and they revise their work until they are satisfied with it. Behind every good writer is a wasteland of poorly written sentences. That's because good writing takes practice, and practice means trial and error. If you recognize that writing is a desirable skill, you will take the time to make mistakes, try again, and get better.

Writing is a necessary skill in our culture. After all, to complete college-level courses, you must be able to communicate what you have learned in writing. If you can learn to write well in school, you will be able to apply your writing skill to work situations as well. Just to fill out a job application, you need a good command of written English. In addition, most entry-level positions, and certainly all professional and management positions, require some writing skills.

Messages that Make Their Point

Unless you are a budding novelist or playwright, or an avid letter or journal writer, most of the writing you will do in your lifetime will take place in the classroom or the workplace. Writing "assignments" in both settings is **goal oriented**, that is, the writing has a specific purpose, and generally that purpose is to convey information. The writer's challenge is to write so readers understand the message.

How can you write a term paper or essay that is easy to understand? Get to the point and stay there. This advice sounds very simple, yet there are many, many ways to express a thought. The English language is filled with thousands of words that can be combined in millions of ways. Fortunately, there are rules and guidelines on how to form phrases, sentences, and paragraphs. The rules make up what we call "grammar" and the guidelines dictate usage. Grammar rules and usage guidelines will help you to control your message. After all, if you don't take control of your written product, no one will!

There are several elements of your writing that you can control that will affect whether your reader(s) "get" your message. Is your message clear? Is it concise? Is it considerate of your readers (in other words, not offensive to anyone in any way)?

Writing is a great way to connect with other people to convey thoughts, feelings, ideas, and other information. Describe in several sentences a specific example of how you have used your writing skills to communicate with others.

_____

_____

_____

_____

Check Your Writing Skills

For each statement, circle "Yes" or "No" as it applies to you.

1. Do you like to write?		Yes	No
2. Are you confident about your writing ability?		Yes	No
3. Do you enjoy having others read what you've written?		Yes	No
4. Do you welcome writing assignments?		Yes	No
5. Can you easily overcome writer's block?		Yes	No
6. Do you regularly revise what you've written to make it better?		Yes	No

If you responded "Yes" to most of these items, you are ready to improve the writing skills you already have. If you responded "No" to several of these items, you may have to expend extra effort to improve your writing comfort and ability.

A Clear Message

If you don't write clearly, you can lose your readers at several levels when you write. You can lose them at the *organizational level* if your information flows illogically. You can lose them at the *paragraph level* if your sentences do not build upon or relate to one another. You can lose them at the *sentence level* if your sentences are poorly constructed. Lastly, you can lose your readers at the *word level* if the words you use are inaccurate, too broad, too difficult, or too abstract. Check your writing at all of these levels to make sure your meaning is intact.

Clarity at the Organizational Level.
You can craft a clear message at the organizational level by immediately and directly stating your main idea and then telling your reader when you are introducing and developing supporting ideas. Start by telling your reader what you plan to do. It may seem simplistic, but many good papers start with a variation of "This paper discusses…" or "In this report, I will examine…." Such straightforward openings are helpful. For one thing, if readers get lost, they can go back to the opening and find direction, that is, by realizing "Aha, she's examining the relationship between Galileo and the Catholic church. That's why she's describing the Catholic church during the seventeenth century."

Transitional words, phrases, and sentences serve as organizational "glue" to hold your message together and lead your readers from point A to point B. Go ahead and say, "There are two reasons why Galileo was in conflict with the Catholic church. The first reason is…The second reason is…" Then develop each reason. When giving an example, say so by leading in with "for example," "for instance," "in particular," "namely," or something similar. When you want to contrast two ideas, use "yet," "on the other hand," "in contrast," or "however." If you want your readers to follow a sequence of activities over time, use words like "initially," "first," "next," "eventually," and "finally."

Clarity at the Paragraph Level.
A good paragraph presents an idea and then develops that idea in a logical manner. This simple, **deductive paragraph construction** is very effective. If you want to take a slightly different approach, you can begin with supporting information and build to your main idea. This is called **inductive paragraph construction**. In any event, make sure that your paragraphs do not derail your readers. Develop one train of thought per paragraph!

> SAMPLE DEDUCTIVE PARAGRAPH:
> My function on the sales floor was to be a "floater." Generally, I provided assistance where I was needed. I worked in a variety of departments rather than in one department in particular. When a sales assistant was sick or a department was short-handed, I filled in by handling sales and assisting customers. I also participated in weekly sales meetings.

> SAMPLE INDUCTIVE PARAGRAPH:
> When a sales assistant was sick or a department was short-handed, I filled in by handling sales and assisting customers. I also participated in weekly sales meetings. I worked in a variety of departments rather than one department in particular. In this way my function within the department store was to act as a "floater," meaning that I helped out where I was needed.

Clarity at the Sentence Level.
Sentence meaning will be fuzzy to your readers if you tend to write run-ons, dangle your modifiers, or use a lot of complex constructions. When you are aware of these pitfalls in your writing, you will be better able to correct them or avoid them altogether.

Run-ons are really two or more thoughts presented as one thought. They usually can be fixed by breaking the run-on sentence into two or more sentences or adding a conjunction and the appropriate punctuation (comma or semicolon).

> RUN-ON:
> My favorite restaurant is closed on Tuesdays we can't eat there tonight.

Rewrites:
My favorite restaurant is closed on Tuesdays. We can't eat there tonight.
My favorite restaurant is closed on Tuesdays, so we can't eat there tonight.
My favorite restaurant is closed on Tuesdays; we can't eat there tonight.

Dangling modifiers are clauses or phrases that, because of their position within a sentence, convey incorrect meaning. Be careful to place clauses and phrases in a logical sequence.

Dangling Constructions:
Having won an Oscar, the director was pleased to have the actor commit to the film.
When she was twelve, Sarah's older sister graduated from medical school.

Rewrites:
The director was pleased to have the Oscar-winning actor commit to the film.
Her older sister graduated from medical school when Sarah was twelve.

Complex constructions are not bad in and of themselves. There will be times when it is entirely appropriate to state a complex idea in one sentence with several clarifying clauses. However, keep in mind that overly complex writing is hard to read. Always look for ways to simplify your message. Eliminate or rewrite complex constructions to increase the clarity of your message.

Complex Construction:
Overall recall for the two groups should be equal, since this study proposes that not only are feeling words better retained over neutral words, but they are better learned because we process words with emotional meaning more deeply than we do words that have no emotional trigger.

Rewrite:
[Note that this rewrite breaks the complex construction into two sentences and eliminates the "not only…but also" construction, which is difficult for readers to follow.]
Overall recall for the two groups should be equal. This assertion is based on the reasoning that feeling words are better retained and learned than neutral words because we process words with emotional meaning more deeply than we do words that have no emotional trigger.

Clarity at the Word Level. Words differ greatly in terms of how much meaning they carry. Some words are very broad (for example, animal), others are exceedingly specific (such as English cocker spaniel). Some words are abstract (pleasure), others are concrete (laughter). It is always helpful to your readers to be as specific as possible. That is, unless you intend your meaning to be quite broad. Clarity at the word level helps your readers understand your exact meaning. It also adds interest and depth to your message.

Poor Word Clarity:
The trees on the stage set were made of a hard material and were covered with greenery.
The dismal news sunk in quickly.

Rewrites:
The trees on the stage set were constructed of wood and were roughly textured with what looked like lichens and moss.
He was deeply saddened when he heard of his father's death.

A Concise Message

Good writing is tight. It uses an economy of words to express information. Streamline your message by carefully choosing your words and sticking with your point. By doing so you avoid wasting your own and your readers' time. Certainly, your instructors will agree with this "less is more" philosophy. In most cases, they have many papers to read; concise writing is appreciated.

You can easily eliminate redundancy in your writing by paying close attention to your use of adjectives and adverbs. Are you using two or three when one will do? Also consider how you write transitions. Do you rely on phrases when one word will convey the same meaning? Here are some common phrases that contain more words than necessary and their more concise counterparts:

> **QUOTE**
> The most valuable of all talents is that of never using two words when one will do.
> —Thomas Jefferson

WORDY	CONCISE
at the present time	now
change over	change
discuss about	discuss
discuss further	discuss
exactly alike	alike OR identical
for the purpose of	for
in between	between
in order to	to
so that	so
in the event that	if
move on	move
repeat again	repeat
very obvious	obvious
very unique	unique

A Considerate Message

If you want to write so others receive your message, treat your audience as you would like to be treated. Show respect. Be aware of how your words will be perceived by others. One way to show respect is to be aware of evolving language. Another way to show respect is to talk *to*, rather than *at*, your reader.

Evolving Language. Language changes in response to new ideas and trends. Usage that was acceptable ten years ago may no longer be "okay." One important example is gender-based references. In the past, the masculine gender—words like "mankind and chairman"— was used to refer to men and women in general. This usage is considered offensive today.

Inclusive language that does not assume gender should be used. Often you can avoid a gender reference by using the plural form. Instead of "If a *student* works over summer break, *he* may find it difficult to attend summer session" you can write "If *students* work over summer break, *they* may find it difficult to attend summer session." If it is impossible to avoid referring to gender, see if "he or she" or "him or her" works in place of one pronoun. Of course, it is always appropriate to use gender if you are certain of the sex of the individual(s) to whom you are referring.

> Luck is a matter of preparation meeting opportunity.
> —Oprah Winfrey

Be aware of how job titles have changed in the past decade to reflect the blurring of gender lines in the workplace. Because jobs are no longer off limits to one or the other sex, job titles have been changed to gender-neutral equivalents. For example, not everyone on the police force is a "man," therefore it is more appropriate to use "police officer" rather than "policeman." Similarly, there's no excuse for using "Dear Sir" or "Gentlemen" when writing to a business or agency. Good letter writers do their homework and get the name and title of their intended reader (or at a minimum, address the letter to a specific department) before sending correspondence.

Here are some titles that are gender-biased and their more acceptable alternatives:

Gender-Biased Titles	Gender-Neutral Titles
Chairman	Chair or Chairperson
Councilman	Council Member
Fireman	Firefighter
Steward/Stewardess	Flight Attendant
Waiter/Waitress	Food Server

Words that Respect Your Readers. Consider the reading ability and background of your audience before you write. If you are writing for a class taught by a college professor, you can write at a higher level than if your message will be read by adults for whom English is a second language. Similarly, you can use **jargon** (words that describe activities and objects specific to a line of work or expertise) when you know the jargon will be understood and perhaps will be expected by your readers. Don't use it to try to impress people with your knowledge. Avoid jargon unless you are certain your readers will know what you are talking about. At a minimum, always define your terms.

Use three- and four-syllable words sparingly when you write. Why say "utilize" or "incorporate" when "use" will do? Long and unfamiliar words are hurdles that your readers must leap over to get to your meaning. Remember the purpose you want to serve and "keep it simple."

Certain words and phrases can convey a smug attitude. "Obviously," "as anyone can see," and "in my estimation" are examples of words that will turn off your readers, especially if your point is not as clear as you believe it to be. College instructors will quickly detect a superior attitude if it appears in your writing, so do away with such posturing immediately. After all, your instructors are looking to see if you can provide a straightforward, intelligent discussion of ideas in your writing assignments, not a show of your mental superiority.

Grammar Review

The English language has many rules of grammar. If you ignore them, intentionally or unintentionally, you send a message to your readers that you either do not care or that you are uninformed. What follows is a quick review of grammatical rules many writers overlook. If you find that your grammar is quite rusty, consult a grammar or style book for a more comprehensive review. In fact, it's a good idea to invest in a grammar reference book. Even experienced writers rely on reference books from time to time to produce writing that is free of grammatical errors.

Make your subjects and verbs agree
Use single verbs with single subjects and plural verbs with plural subjects.

EXAMPLES:
The person who signs the checks is also a notary public. (NOT *The person who signs the checks are also a notary public.*)
The instructors are a diverse group. (NOT *The instructors is a diverse group.*)

In most cases, compound subjects are plural. However, when "each" and "every" appear before a compound subject, the subject is singular. Similarly, it is incorrect to use "each" *after* a compound subject.

EXAMPLES:
Every employee and customer is entitled to the sale price. (NOT *Every employee and customer are entitled to the sale price.*)
The managers and the staff have separate lounges. (NOT *The managers and the staff each have separate lounges.*)

Use consistent verb forms
Maintain the same verb tense when using compound verb phrases.

EXAMPLES:
The clinician took the samples and examined them thoroughly. (NOT *The clinician took the samples and examines them thoroughly.*)
The officials realize the mistake and want to correct it. (NOT *The officials realize the mistake and wanted to correct it.*)

Use the right pronoun:
When the pronoun is the subject, use the subjective case (I, we, he, she, they, who, it, you).

EXAMPLES:
Nan and I are ready to go. (NOT *Me and Nan are ready to go.*)
Who has the book? (NOT *Whom has the book?*)

When the pronoun is the object of a verb or a preposition, use the objective case (me, us, him, her, it, them, whom, it, you). Note: You can check if the pronoun is an object by asking "who" or "what." If the pronoun does not answer either question, it does not take the objective case.

EXAMPLES:
The concept was developed by him and me. (NOT *The concept was developed by he and I.*)
These are the people for whom I work. (NOT *These are the people for who I work.*)

Be consistent with pronoun usage within your writing.

EXAMPLES:
When a student attends the seminar, he or she receives a free pocket calculator. OR Students who attend the seminar receive a free pocket calculator. (NOT *When a student attends the seminar, they receive a free pocket calculator. OR Students who attend the seminar receives a free pocket calculator.*)
If anyone is worried about the program, he or she can speak to the director. (NOT *If anyone is worried about the program, they can speak to the director.*)

Use adverbs and adjectives appropriately
Remember that adverbs modify verbs, adjectives, and other adverbs, while adjectives modify nouns and pronouns.

EXAMPLES:
The machine works excellently. (NOT *The machine works excellent.*)
The driver felt bad about the accident. (NOT *The driver felt badly about the accident.*)
The musician plays really well. (NOT *The musician plays real well OR really good.*)

Use the comparative form when using adverbs or adjectives to compare two things. Use the superlative form if you are comparing more than two things.

Examples:
Of his two movies, we liked the director's first effort more. (NOT *Of his two movies, we liked the director's first effort the most.*)
The previews were more entertaining than the movie. (NOT *The previews were the most entertaining compared to the movie.*)

A Method for Good Writing

When it's time to complete a writing assignment, many students just sit down and expect to get it done in one sitting. An hour later they find themselves still staring at a blank page—or at a blinking cursor on a blank computer screen. The problem is, they don't know quite how to get started. They have not prepared for the assignment, and the deadline panic has set in to short circuit their half-hearted attempts at a serious composition. What's wrong with this picture?

What's wrong is that these students have no "method" to their "madness." They have not thought through their assignment or planned their attack. Without a plan, they're winging it, and you know from experience what happens when you wing it. Sometimes you win, sometimes you lose. But with a step-wise, methodical approach, you can tackle a writing assignment and produce a respectable, winning piece of writing every time.

The method that is used by many (but not all) successful writers involves some variation of the following four steps: 1) plan your attack, 2) take a stab at it, 3) make it better, and 4) make it perfect.

Plan Your Attack

The first step to any writing assignment is to think about your purpose for writing and decide what you must do to achieve that purpose. For example, your purpose

> ### Check Your Approach to Writing
>
> For each statement, circle "Yes" or "No" as it applies to you.
>
> | | | |
> |---|---|---|
> | 1. I take time to formulate my approach before writing a paper. | Yes | No |
> | 2. I create an outline. | Yes | No |
> | 3. I refer to my outline as I write. | Yes | No |
> | 4. I consult a dictionary, thesaurus, and/or grammar book as needed. | Yes | No |
> | 5. I write several drafts before my final paper. | Yes | No |
> | 6. I proofread for spelling and grammatical mistakes. | Yes | No |
>
> If you responded "Yes" to most of these items, you are already following a process as you write. If you responded "No," consider how you can adopt a process to help you tackle your writing assignments.

may be to compare and contrast two nineteenth-century writers for a humanities paper. To achieve that purpose, you must identify two authors and isolate characteristics of their writing to support comparison and contrast.

As you narrow your topic, consider your target audience and the best way to convey your message to the intended reader. Your instructors will appreciate a fresh perspective and may assign a poor grade to a well-written paper that merely rehashes common knowledge. Remember that the papers you write for college are assigned so that your instructors can evaluate your verbal and reasoning skills, your ability to generate new ideas, and your understanding of the subject area. Choose a topic that helps you do all these things.

Unless your topic is clearly defined, you will need to spend time identifying the subject area and the specific aspects of that subject area. Once you have narrowed your topic, you can use it to generate questions that you will answer within your writing. These questions can help you determine the research you need to conduct. They also can be used as an outline.

An outline provides a framework for the piece you plan to write. It lists your major topics and subtopics and serves to tell you the order in which to develop key points. Most outlines are written using a combination of arabic or roman numerals and uppercase or lowercase letters (see Figure 6-1).

Another way to plan your writing is to formulate questions. Imagine you have been assigned a four-page essay in your classic literature class. Your instructor says you may choose any topic relating to the writing style of the five Greek authors on your reading list. The five authors are Homer, Euripides, Sophocles, Aristophanes, and Aeschylus. You choose Aeschylus because you read his work most recently. Next you flip through your reading assignments by and about this author to narrow your topic. Finally you settle on this aspect of Aeschylus' writing style: his use of animal imagery in his trilogy of plays *The Oresteia*. Next, you formulate questions to guide your research and the actual writing of your essay. Your questions may look something like this:

- How does the imagery support the themes in Aeschylus' writing?
- How does the imagery support character development?
- Is the imagery consistent across the plays? Does it change?
- How does the imagery reflect the characteristics of Greek culture at the time?

> **SAMPLE OUTLINE**
>
> Subject: Life and Career of C. Everett Koop, M.D.
>
> **I.** Early Days
>   A. Childhood in the Bronx
>   B. Early desires to be a physician
>   1. Practiced surgery techniques
>   2. Observed surgeries
>   3. Volunteered at hospitals
>
> **II.** College at Dartmouth
>   A. Met future wife
>   B. Studied zoology
>
> **III.** Medical School at Cornell
>
> **IV.** Residency at University of Philadelphia
>
> **V.** Career
>   A. Surgeon-in-chief at Children's Hospital of Philadelphia
>   1. Helped establish pediatric surgery as medical specialty
>   2. Educated public/medical community on abortion/infanticide issues
>   B. Surgeon General
>   1. Worked above politics for sake of nation's health
>   2. Addressed controversial subjects
>   a. Smoking
>   b. AIDS
>   c. Abortions/infanticide
>   C. Current activities
>   1. Founded the Koop Institute at Dartmouth
>   2. Founded the C. Everett Koop Foundation

FIGURE 6-1 Sample Outline

- What other purpose(s) does the imagery serve (for example, is it a vehicle for irony or foreshadowing)?

If indeed Aeschylus used animal imagery throughout his trilogy of plays, your work is clearly cut out for you. You can start answering the questions you have posed by scanning through each play to find examples of the imagery and studying those passages to see how Aeschylus used these images. You can also add to your research by reading what critics have written about the imagery in Aeschylus' work. Pretty soon you'll have enough information to attempt a first draft.

Take a Stab at It (First Draft)

When you write, keep a dictionary, thesaurus, and grammar book at your side. That way, if you stumble looking for the right word or proper construction, you will have the resources you need at your side. If you are working on a computer, you probably have these tools at your fingertips within your word processing program.

When you feel you know what you want to say, go ahead and start writing. You do not need to be concerned about grammar or style at this point. Your main objective is to get your ideas on paper in a logical sequence. If you find that you are really struggling to get words on the page, then go back to your plan. You may need more information, more factual evidence, or a clearer vision of your main thesis. Another thing you can do to get yourself going is to talk to a friend or classmate about what you plan to write. Sometimes explaining something out loud helps you transition to saying something in writing.

It is easy to get hung up on the introductory paragraph. After all, it is the first impression of your paper and it is very important. However, if you are so hung up that you begin to lose valuable time, move on. Start developing your first main point and keep going. Sometimes it is easier to write an introduction to a paper that is finished. You know what you covered and therefore, you are better able to write the all-important gateway paragraph.

End your composition with a well-crafted summation. It may take several paragraphs to summarize your main points, or you may be able to tie things up in a three-sentence paragraph. In any event, make sure that your final words capsulize your main points. Your instructor probably will stop reading your paper here, so make a good impression. The grade comes next!

> **QUOTE**
> Nothing you write, if you hope to be good, will ever come out as you first hoped.
> —Lillian Hellman

Make It Better (Second Draft...)

Once you have your first draft, revise, revise, revise. Move a sentence from here to there or reverse the order of several paragraphs if it improves clarity. Keep your eye out for places where you may have repeated yourself or gotten off track. Cut the fat. You've probably said what you need to say in your first draft, but chances are you need to tighten or rework what you've written.

Remember that all you have written should relate to your topic. Your readers should not have to struggle to figure out why you mention fact A or quote passage B. If you stray from your topic, something is wrong. As you revise, check that you are staying in line with your purpose and your outline.

Most writers generate at least two drafts of a document before they move to the proofreading stage. However, there is no formula for a perfect paper. Keep writing until you get it right. If you are an inexperienced writer, don't be surprised if you are not happy until your fifth draft. It takes time and practice to become skilled at writing. Your writing speed and ability will quickly improve as you tackle more and more writing assignments.

Make It Perfect (Final Draft)

Now is the time to weed out the extra comma, the transposed letters, the misspelled words, and the misplaced quotation marks. Read slowly and carefully, using a red pen to mark needed corrections. At this stage you are doing a cleanup job—the construction stage is over. If you are tempted to rewrite more than a transition or two, move back to the revision stage and stop worrying about stray commas.

Use the following checklist to guide your proofreading:

- Are all words correctly spelled?
- Are commas, colons, semicolons, parentheses, apostrophes, and end-of-sentence punctuation used correctly?
- Are words hyphenated correctly?
- Are upper-case and lower-case letters used appropriately?
- Are all quotations presented and punctuated correctly?
- Are headings and subheadings consistent in form and presentation?

PROOFREADER'S MARKS

When it is time to edit your own work, either at the revision or the proofreading stage, it is useful to use proofreader's marks. These standard marks let you quickly indicate changes to your writing. They also make it easy to interpret what you must do when you go to make the changes.

It is common to get a "lazy eye" when proofreading your own work. Because you are familiar with your own writing—too familiar than you care to be by your third or fourth draft—your brain unconsciously corrects your errors while leaving them on the page. For this reason, you may want to enlist a classmate to proofread your work. This can be mutually beneficial. Swap papers with one another, and you can each proofread for errors the other may have overlooked.

PART TWO   Developing Your Study Skills

style of type

wf	Wrong font (size or style of type)
lc	lower case letter
lc	Set in LOWER CASE
C	capital letter
Caps	SET IN capitals
c+lc	Set in lower case with INITIAL CAPITALS
sc	SET IN SMALL CAPITALS
c+sc	SET IN SMALL CAPITALS with initial capitals
rom.	Set in roman type
ital.	Set in italic type
ital. caps	SET IN ITALIC capitals
lf	Set in lightface type
bf	**Set in boldface type**
bf ital	***Set in boldface italic***
bf caps	**Set in boldface CAPITALS**
	Superior letter b
	Inferior figure 2

position

]	Move to right
[	Move to left
ctr	Center
⊔	Lower (letters or words)
⊓	Raise (letters or words)
=	Straighten type (horizontally)
‖	Align type (vertically)
tr	Transpose
tr	Transpose (order letters of or words)

spacing

ld in	Insert lead (space) between lines
ld	Take out lead
⌢	Close up; take out space
#	Close up partly; leave some space
Eq #	Equalize space between words
#	Insert space (or more space)
space out	More space between words

insertion and deletion

the/	Caret (insert marginal addition)
𝒹	Delete (take it out)
𝒹	Delete and close up
e	Correct letter or word marked
stet	Let it stand (all matter above dots)

paragraphing

¶	Begin a paragraph
No ¶	No paragraph
Run in	Run in or run on
flush	No indention

punctuation

(Use caret in text to show point of insertion)

⊙	Insert period
↗	Insert comma
:/	Insert colon
;/	Insert semicolon
ʺ/ʺ	Insert quotation marks
ʼ/ʼ	Insert single quotes
ʼ	Insert apostrophe
set ?	Insert question mark
!	Insert exclamation point
=/	Insert hyphen
1/M	Insert one-em dash
(/)	Insert parentheses
[/]	Insert brackets

miscellaneous

×	Replace broken or imperfect type
○	Reverse (upside down type)
sp	Spell out (twenty gr)
Au/?	Query to author
Ed/?	Query to editor
∫	Mark off or break; start new line

FIGURE 6-2 Proofreader's Marks

If you are typing your paper, always proofread the printout instead of proofing the document on the computer screen. You will avoid eye strain and be more likely to catch all of your errors. Once you have marked any errors, you can make corrections, and save and print the new copy. Then compare this new copy one last time to your marked copy to ensure that you've made all the corrections.

Specific Writing Assignments

As you go through school, you will probably encounter four types of writing assignments: the journal entry, the essay, the report, and the research paper. The specific form you must follow for each will vary according to your instructor's preferences and the area of study. What follows are general guidelines to familiarize you with each type of writing assignment.

The Journal Entry

A journal is like a diary. In the journal entry, you are required to describe, on a personal level, something you have experienced or learned. The emphasis is on the subjective; your instructor wants to know your thoughts and feelings rather than facts and figures.

Instructors frequently use the journal entry assignment to encourage students to improve their writing skills and to explore how a subject area has personal significance. Some individuals thrive on this type of writing, while others find it very difficult to share personal thoughts for the world to see.

To write a good journal entry, use descriptive language and provide as much detail as possible. Fill your writing with adjectives and adverbs to paint a picture for your readers. For example, if you are writing about how gloomy weather influences your mood, describe the weather and how it affects you. Rather than writing "Rain makes me feel sad," you might write, "Whenever rain falls in gray sheets against the window, I feel my chest tighten and my eyes sting with tears." Actually, you would probably write that passage in a different, totally unique way, and that is what it's all about. It is the intensely personal and creative nature of the journal entry that makes it a challenging and exciting form of writing.

> I can shake off everything if I write; my sorrows disappear, my courage is reborn. But, and that is the great question, will I ever be able to write anything great, will I ever become a journalist or a writer? I hope so, oh, I hope so very much, for I can recapture everything when I write, my thoughts, my ideals, my fantasies.
> —Anne Frank, Dutch Jewish Diarist

Here's another way to think of detail in your journal entries. Consider, for example, that you are writing about taking the city bus. You might begin, "Every day I take the bus. I always sit in the same seat. I avoid eye contact and read the newspaper." So far you have provided some details, but without much elaboration. Why do you take the bus? Where are you going? Why do you sit in the same seat? Do you have an emotional attachment to that seat? How would you feel if one day you got on the bus and someone else was sitting there? You can add meat to your entry by writing about how you perceive the sights, sounds, and smells of the bus environment. Your entry will be much more fascinating if you recreate your experience so readers can really understand what you are saying. It may turn into something like this:

> *At 8 a.m., every day, Monday through Friday, I take a fifteen-minute bus ride aboard the 21A to get to my job at the Burger Palace. I always sit in the same seat, second from the back on my right as I enter. By now I know by heart all its cracks and stains, though sometimes I'm surprised by new graffiti or a boldly placed wad of gum. The familiar ritual, making my way down the pleated rubber path to secure my seat, gives me a feeling of ownership as I ride the city line. I'm not sure what I would do if someone were to be sitting there before I could stake my claim—it's never happened in the two years I've been riding.*

The Essay

Essays are discussion papers that present an opinion and support for that opinion. Most essays are rather brief, running about three to five pages in length. As with all papers, it is important to narrow your topic and think carefully about how you plan to develop it. For your essay, ask yourself if the opinion you plan to state is valid. That is, can you muster enough support for it? You need to go on more than just a hunch or a feeling. You need the kind of support provided by quotes or observations from reading materials, lectures, interviews, or films. For each point you want to make, try to find three or four supporting details.

The first paragraph of your essay is very important. In it you must state your opinion and let your readers know where you plan to take them. Here is a sample introductory paragraph from an essay written for a class in English literature:

In William Shakespeare's historical play Richard II, *Richard and the usurper of his throne, Henry Bolingbroke, are men of different breeds. As men of ambition they both share certain qualities, but for the most part they differ in their psychological makeup. As the play proceeds the contrasts in their personalities are developed, and it is the overwhelming intensity and flamboyance of Richard's character that make his appeal greater than that of Bolingbroke's. Taking account of both their weaknesses and their strengths, Richard comes across as a more accessible individual than the cold and calculating Bolingbroke. Though Richard is not the realist that Bolingbroke is, he is ultimately more real to the reader because he allows his weaknesses to show.*

Later in the essay the writer develops the theme of the contrasting natures of Richard and Bolingbroke by citing Richard's actions and directly quoting him. In this way readers begin to get a picture of how the two men differ.

The differences in personality between Richard and Bolingbroke are what make the former a likeable figure and the latter merely another greedy political hound. Richard may be a poor politician, as shown in his financial bungling and his failure to follow the Duke of York's wise advice against seizing Bolingbroke's lands. Yet, he is much more grand than his dull challenger. He speaks in eloquent and adorned speech and he cannot keep his thoughts to himself. He even corrects himself aloud and, after much equivocating, chastises himself by saying, "I had forgot myself: am I not King?" (III.ii.83).

The Report

A report is a factual presentation. The types of topics handled within reports are quite broad. You may be required to write a report to discuss a historical event, a research project, to summarize a reading, or to "review" an article or book. In your own words and with detailed support (quotes or factual evidence), you must describe the topic. When reporting facts, you should avoid adding your opinion to the equation. However, many reports do require you to offer your conclusions, recommendations, or both.

Here is an example of the introductory paragraph from a report on an article. Notice how the writer uses words such as "contends," "believes," and "argues" to let readers know that the author of the article is presenting his opinion, and the writer is merely reporting on that opinion piece.

*In Leon Hollerman's article "International Economic Controls in Occupied Japan" (*Journal of Asian Studies, *vol. XXXVIII, No. 4; August 1979, pgs. 707-719), the author contends that the Supreme Commander for the Allied Powers for the Occupation and control of Japan (SCAP) failed in its supervision of Japanese economic policies in two ways: 1) by increasing restrictive controls and 2) by promoting a government bureaucracy. SCAP, Hollerman believes, is responsible in large part for the protectionist foreign trade and foreign exchange policies operating in Japan today. To support his belief, Hollerman points out the inadequacies in SCAP management of economic affairs conducted through the existing Japanese government bureaucracy and the lack of foresight in SCAP decision-making. These weaknesses, he argues, directly resulted in an increase in bureaucratic red tape for the business community and an escalation in black market activities.*

Depending on the length and depth of your paper, you may want to begin with an introduction and then divide your report into several sections. As necessary, use headings and subheadings to guide your readers. Always present headings and subheadings in a consistent format such as all nouns or verb phrases. In addition, be careful to present headings so readers can follow the organization of the report. For example, present main headings flush left and in all-capital letters;

first level subheadings flush left with upper- and lower-case letters; and second level subheadings flush left with upper- and lower-case letters, underlined, and punctuated.

The Life of Abraham Lincoln	[Title]
HUMBLE BEGINNINGS	[Main Heading]
Life in a Log Cabin	[First Level Subheading]
Nolin Creek, Kentucky.	[Second Level Subheading]
Gentryville, Indiana.	[Second Level Subheading]
Career Trials and Errors	[First Level Subheading]

The Research Paper

Research papers can vary in length and depth, but they all involve a significant amount of background work to gather detailed information on your topic. The topic of your paper can be broad or narrow; your instructor's wishes will guide your decision-making here. Research papers can run from about 5 to 50 pages in length, depending on the depth to which your instructor wants you to research your topic.

Some instructors will want your paper to follow a specific format. For example, most psychology professors expect their students to write reports like those that appear in psychology journals. These reports contain five sections: abstract, method, results, discussion, and a list of references. Check with your instructor early in the course if you are unsure of what format you are required to follow.

Plan to spend a lot of time in the library before you write your research paper. Most instructors assign research papers at the beginning of a course, so generally there is no excuse for putting it off until the last minute. Remember that when you go to the library, there will be times when the materials you want are not available for check out. Don't let other students get a jump on you. When you know what your topic will be (or to help you narrow your topic), check out the books you need well in advance of your paper's due date. Refer to the chapter on library research in this book for guidance in getting the most out of this valuable resource. Use your time management system to plan the stages of developing your report.

Use notecards or some type of note-taking system as you research your topic. When you are drawing from several sources, it is nearly impossible to keep track of where you found information without notes of some sort. It helps to have organized notes when it comes time to write and when you must cite your sources (including page numbers) in a bibliography.

Electronic Help for Writers

From a mechanical standpoint, the writer's job is much easier than it was just thirty years ago. With computers and word processors, students are spared the painstaking process of writing and rewriting assignments in longhand. Some people still prefer to draft with pen-on-paper, but generally, when you are freed from the physical work of writing, you can put more energy into the creative process and spend more time polishing your message. In short, with the aid of technology, writers have more time to write.

You may already know how to use a computer. If so, consider this section a review and see if you can learn something new to apply. If you are one of those unlucky individuals whose high school's budget did not

---

FOOTNOTES AND BIBLIOGRAPHIES

Always cite your sources when you quote or **paraphrase** (restate a passage using your own words) material. Several formats are acceptable, although your instructor may dictate the format you use. You may cite the source immediately following the quote by placing the author's name, the year of the publication, and the page from which you obtained the material in parentheses. The complete source must then be listed in a bibliography or list of references at the end of your paper. Another format for crediting your references is the footnote. When you use a footnote, you place a number at the end of the quoted material and then cite the corresponding number and complete reference at the bottom of the page (or at the end of the paper).

Footnote entry citing a book:

1. Wing, Lorna, *Early Childhood Autism*, Permagon Press, Great Britain, 1976: 32-45.

Footnote entry citing a journal article and with multiple authors:

2. Bower, Gordon H., Gilligan, Stephan G. & Monteiro, Kenneth P. "Selectivity of Learning Caused by Affective States," *Journal of Experimental Psychology: General*, 1981, Volume 110: 451-471.

Bibliography format:

Bruch, H. *Eating Disorders: Obesity, Anorexia and the Person Within.* New York: Basic Books, 1973.

include cutting-edge technology, get excited, because you are about to discover a wonderful, time saving device. One last note for those of you who are new to computers: Don't despair if you do not have keyboarding (typing) skills. Find a keyboarding textbook and teach yourself how to type. It's similar to learning how to ride a bike. Just learn how to position yourself (your fingers) and then go for it. Once you learn, you'll never forget, and you'll become faster with practice.

Word Processing and Desktop Publishing Programs

> QUOTE
> I write to keep in contact with our ancestors and to spread truth to people.
> —Sonia Sanchez

Computers, monitors, keyboards, modems, and printers are called hardware and are your "equipment." The stuff that makes the computer do what you want it to do is called software. You will need to know how to use a word processing or desktop publishing software application to produce your writing assignments. Word processing software allows you to create a variety of documents with standard formatting. Desktop publishing software gives you many formatting possibilities.

Most word processing applications let you edit your document as you create it. With *insert* and *delete* keys and *cut and paste* functions, you can move, replace, and copy chunks of text with a keystroke. In addition, most programs contain a dictionary, thesaurus, spell-checker, and grammar-checker to help you produce an error-free draft. (Note: Always proofread your paper even when you use a spell-checker. You can't rely on the computer to catch errors that are determined by context, such as when "their" should be "there.") You can print as many copies as you like, edit the printed draft, and then enter your changes. You can keep as many versions as you like and make changes until you get it right. Computers are the best shortcut a writer can take when creating a grade A paper.

There are many software application programs on the market. Learn the program you have access to if you do not own your own system. Take a course or sit down at the computer and teach yourself. Most programs contain tutorials that introduce you to the application features and "help" facilities that provide immediate assistance while you are in the application. You may want to get a book from the library or bookstore that shows step-by-step instructions for learning to use your specific program.

Electronic Storage

Computers have an edge over the standard typewriter in part because they allow you to store your work. Electronic files can be saved internally, that is, on the computer's hard drive, or externally, on floppy diskettes. These files can be retrieved at a later date and can be changed, copied, and resaved as necessary. To avoid losing your work, it's a good idea to make a habit of saving files in both places. That way, if your hard drive malfunctions or you lose the disk, you have a backup file.

Formatting Capabilities

You can dress up your document when you know the formatting capabilities of your software application. When used sparingly, **boldface** and *italic* text effectively direct readers to important information. You can also vary fonts and font sizes for headings, tables, or inserts.

All applications allow you to customize the spacing and margins of your document. In addition, you can make the text appear flush left with a jagged edge, centered, flush right, or flush left with a justified edge. Most programs let you format text in columns or tables. You may also be able to create simple bar, line, or pie charts. These elements serve to add important information and give your document a professional appearance.

Flush left with jagged edge	In addition to the designated holidays, there are three personal days which may be used for religious holidays or personal business. Personal days should be scheduled and approved in advance.
Centered	In addition to the designated holidays, there are three personal days which may be used for religious holidays or personal business. Personal days should be scheduled and approved in advance.
Flush right	In addition to the ten designated holidays, there are three personal days which may be used for religious holidays or personal business. Personal days should be scheduled and approved in advance.
Flush left with justified edge	In addition to the ten designated holidays, there are three personal days which may be used for religious holidays or personal business. Personal days should be scheduled and approved in advance.

FIGURE 6-3 Sample Paragraph

Use formatting to create a paper that is easy and interesting to read. Sometimes that means using many of the formatting features available, but often it means using only one or two capabilities. Experiment with the features on the software application you are using so that when it is time to write a paper, you know what is available and how to use it.

Review and Recall

1. Why is writing a necessary skill in our culture?

2. Discuss ways in which you can make your message clear to your readers.

3. Explain how you can write concisely and why it is important to do so.

4. Discuss how you can avoid gender-biased language.

5. Pick two grammar pointers from the Grammar Review section and create two examples illustrating the correct and incorrect use of each rule. Note: Pick two pointers that challenge you.

   a.

b._____

_____

6. What are the four steps of the writing process?

a._____   c._____

b._____   d._____

7. Why is the planning process important?

_____

_____

_____

8. Identify three tips for proofreading.

a._____

b._____

c._____

9. Compare and contrast two of the following types of writing assignment: the journal entry, the essay, the report, and the research paper.

_____

_____

_____

_____

10. List four advantages of using a computer as a writing tool?

a._____

b._____

c._____

d._____

Apply Critical Thinking

Write a paragraph describing the type of writing you like or would like to produce. Consider all types of writing, from creative (advertising copy, poetry, short stories, plays, novels) to critical (opinion pieces, letters to the editor) to business (reports, research documents, technical writing). Explain why you enjoy this type of writing.

School to Work Applications

SCANS

INFORMATION: *INTERPRETS AND COMMUNICATES INFORMATION*

1. Read a letter in an advice column without looking at the response by the columnist. Next, write your reply to the letter, showing your understanding of the problem and communicating your solution. Compare your reply to the columnist's reply. Briefly describe how your responses are alike or different.

CHAPTER 6 Writing Your Way to the Top

2. Rewrite the following paragraph to correct grammar and spelling and improve clarity.

   Both Truman and Eisenhower, each in there quest for containment of Soviet aggression, both ended up supporting right-wing governments around the world becuase they were 'pro-western.' Eisenhower himself come up with a doctrine of his own which called for U.S. intervention for containing communist aggression in the Middle East. Truman, sought strength through nuclear armaments, and went as far as to use the atom bomb in Hiroshima and Nagasaki to end the war and also to flex America's military muscle in hopes of frightening Russia. Eisenhower picked up on this trend with the 'new look' in military spending which involved a cut in traditional ground troops and artillery and an incrase in nuclear arms, which led to the foreign policy of massive retaliation and Brinkmanship.

3. List at least two synonyms for the following words. Use a thesaurus if you need help.

idea	like
important	many
agree	uncertain
make	delay
deny	explain

4. Rewrite these sentences to simplify the message. Use a dictionary if you are unsure of a word's meaning.
   a. The swindler was subject to swift retribution.
   b. Jim was mortified by the defamatory communique.
   c. The depravity of the interloper was legendary.
   d. The criminal's defense was inconceivable.
   e. The clerk was genial to the petulant customer.

5. Write a two-page essay on a topic of your choosing. Cite your sources.

INFORMATION: *Uses Computers to Process Information*

6. If you have access to a computer and a word processing application, identify the application and explain how to perform the following functions:
   a. center a title
   b. indent a paragraph
   c. change a selected passage to boldface
   d. move a paragraph
   e. double space a document
   f. save a file
   g. change a font
   h. obtain Help

7. Use a computer to retype a newspaper article (at least four paragraphs in length). Use the following features to "dress up" the article: boldface, large fonts, indents, italics, centered text, right-justified text.

8. Use the dictionary and thesaurus available with your word processing application to look up the words below. Record the information you find.
   a. category
   b. schedule
   c. recognize
   d. proceed
   e. separate

SCANS Workplace Application

You work for a community newspaper, *The Northern Sun*. This week you have been asked to write an editorial, about five paragraphs in length, describing how you feel about the current level of violence in movies. In the editorial, state whether you believe violence is a problem and support your position with examples or facts. Describe the appropriate roles of movie makers, the government, and viewing audiences in finding solutions to the problem or accepting the status quo.

Now imagine that you are a reader who disagrees with your editorial piece. Write a letter to the editor contradicting the position you argued in the editorial.

Personal Progress Application

SCANS

BASIC SKILLS: *READS, WRITES, PERFORMS ARITHMETIC AND MATHEMATICAL OPERATIONS, LISTENS, AND SPEAKS*

THINKING SKILLS: *THINKS CREATIVELY, MAKES DECISIONS, SOLVES PROBLEMS, VISUALIZES, KNOWS HOW TO LEARN, AND REASONS*

Did you notice that reading and writing are among the basic skills employers want? Poor writing skills will limit your advancement in your career. The good news is that there is a method to make your reports "write themselves." It consists of the following steps:

1. Find out what you're supposed to write about. Ask questions to clarify exactly what the reader (meaning, in the case of class assignments, the teacher) wants to see in your report. One question to ask your reader might be, "What are the things you hope to know *after* reading my report that you might not have known *before* you read my report? Write down the answers you get as a result of clarifying the purpose, subject, and expected outcomes of your report.
2. Take those answers to the library. Find a librarian. Show him or her the topic of your report and what you're supposed to find out. Ask the librarian how to find the references that will provide the information you'll need to produce your report.
3. Do what the librarian says to find the books, on-line resources, magazines, journals, or other sources that contain the information you need for your report.
4. In each source, examine the table of contents, the index, the chapter or topic headings, the charts and illustrations, and use any other skimming techniques the librarian might suggest to zoom in on parts of the material that will be helpful in addressing the questions you're trying to answer in your report.
5. For each section in a source that addresses one of the topics you're supposed to cover, write a summary of what that section says on a separate 3x5 card. On the same card, write any quote you think might be particularly effective in helping your paper answer the questions it's meant to address. Finally, on the same 3 x 5 card, make some kind of notation about the source from which you took the quote and/or your summary. (Many people keep a separate sheet of paper on which they number the sources as they go through them. They write down the bibliographic information about the source, and then put that number plus the page number of the summary and/or quote on the 3 x 5 card. You can easily transfer this information to a database using your computer.) With the bibliographic information about the source recorded, you will be able to include it in your report without having to go back to the library to find it again.
6. After making sure you've found answers to all the questions your report is supposed to cover, gather your 3 x 5 cards. Sort the cards into stacks grouped by topic, then arrange the cards in each stack into a logical order based on the easiest way to understand the information. Finally, arrange the stacks in logical order using the same process, or key the information into your computer.
7. The "big picture" of your paper is now complete. Each stack of cards (or segment of computerized notes) is a topic in the paper, and the order of the information is the order in which you'll present the topics.
8. Refer to the sections in this chapter on report and research paper writing, and to the section in Chapter 3 on library research, to actually write your report. If you're not an accomplished report writer, don't be intimidated—steps 1-7 above have guaranteed you won't stray from your topic. At this point, even if all you can manage is to put what's on your cards into sensible paragraphs with decent

topic sentences, you'll be able to create an acceptable report. The final step will be to add an introduction and a conclusion.

After using this process a few times, you'll get to know how to do research well enough to at least start the process without having to stop at the reference desk of the library as your first step. However, even after you become more experienced with research, always check with the librarian. Today's information explosion means new resources are becoming available rapidly, and you don't want to miss out on an important source just because you didn't know it existed. Your librarian's job is to know about those sources, so use that expertise.

Research and Write a Paper

Use the above steps to write your next report. If you're a kinesthetic learner, you'll find working with the 3 x 5 cards to be helpful as a hands-on experience. If you're an auditory learner, read your report into a tape recorder and then play it back before turning the report in—this will be a good way for you to catch any illogical statements or holes in your report. If you're a visual learner, seeing the stacks of cards in order and the individual cards ordered within each stack on the table will be very helpful for fine-tuning the layout of the report.

SEVEN

PREPARING FOR AND TAKING TESTS

CHAPTER OUTLINE

Preparing for Tests
Strategies to Help You Win
 Schedule Study Time
 Develop a Study Plan
 Apply Sound Study Techniques
Improving Your Memory
 Examine Your Attitudes
 How Memory Works
 Memorization Techniques
Test-Taking Strategies
 The Day of the Test
 Answering Objective Test Questions
 Answering Subjective Test Questions
 Handling Test Anxiety
 Appraising Your Performance

Even if you're on the right track, you'll get run over if you just stand there.
—Will Rogers

Question: Fifty percent of adults in the United States say they would rather have their teeth drilled at the dentist than take any kind of a test. True or False? *Question:* When told that the test will help determine a school grade or consideration for a job, the number increases to: (a) 75% (b) 85% (c) 95% (d) None of the above.

If you took a guess and answered these questions, your answers may be an indicator of how you feel about taking tests. If you answered "True" to the first question (and maybe even wondered why the percentage was so low) and "a," "b," or "c" to the second question, you probably have some negative feelings about tests. You may feel that you don't generally do well on tests and that you don't have a solution to this problem. If you answered "False" and "d," there is a good chance that you feel comfortable taking tests and tend to feel that whether or not you do well on tests is something that you can control.

This chapter will help you come to terms with your personal attitudes about tests and improve your skills at preparing for and taking tests. The goal is to help you improve your performance and feel more comfortable with the process. Whether you just need to hone your skills or you need to develop a whole new approach, you will find some useful information here.

Preparing for Tests

Studying for a test is a specific task that takes place in one, two, or several sessions just prior to taking a test. *Preparing* for a test, however, is a process. How well prepared you are for a test is directly related to the time and effort you have put into the work for a course prior to test time. This includes:

- attending classes regularly
- reviewing lecture and class discussion notes regularly
- reading all assigned material
- completing laboratory and homework assignments

These activities form the basis of the learning process. Even though you may feel that you forget much of what you learn in advance of tests, the information does not totally escape your mind. At test time, further review and study will revive your memory and reinforce what you already know—even if you didn't know you knew it. On the other hand, facing new material when it is time to study for a test places an extra burden on your mind. You will not be able to absorb everything in time to master it. In addition to not being well prepared in this situation, you are more likely to suffer the nervousness and anxiety that contribute to poor test performance.

Being prepared for a test begins with the development of good study habits and continues with the key skills that have been discussed in preceding chapters of this text. These include:

> There is no meaning to life except the meaning [we]... give [our lives]... by the unfolding of [our}... powers. To "maximize our potential," we must take advantage of the resources available designed to increase our understanding of ourselves, the people around us, and the life we are now involved in. We become what we indulge ourselves in. The opportunities life offers help us tap our potential and can be explored when we are equipped with the right tools.
> —Eric Fromm, Psychologist

- Developing a time management strategy that includes two hours of study time for every hour of course time per week.
- Taking stock of your preferred learning style and discovering ways to supplement your learning in courses that do not favor it.
- Using critical thinking skills to help you retain knowledge and adapt your learning to situational needs (see Chapter 8).
- Practicing active listening, notetaking, and participation in class.
- Practicing active reading through techniques such as taking notes, reciting, and rereading.
- Utilizing all of the features of your textbooks and learning materials to aid in your understanding and retention.

If, at any time, you find yourself feeling unprepared at test time, you need to review these chapters and put the ideas into practice.

Strategies to Help You Win

In many ways tests are like a game between you and the instructor. The instructor devises an instrument to challenge you to prove that you have mastered the course material. How well you rise to the challenge determines your score, or grade. To win at test taking, you need solid preparation and testtaking skills. Like winning a game, you also need the will to do your best and the confidence that you can pull it off. Positive strategies that work for you will improve your chances of excelling in the game of test taking. Now is a good time to analyze your past habits and devise some fresh, workable approaches that will put you ahead in the game.

Your Test Study Habits

By now you have experienced (or suffered through) years of studying for tests. Have you ever analyzed your preparation and study methods? Do you usually feel relaxed and prepared or anxious and unprepared? List all of the things that you normally do to prepare and study for tests. Which of your habits are positive ones? Which are negative ones? Keep this list available as you study the rest of this chapter and make notes on it as you go along.

_____
_____
_____
_____
_____
_____
_____
_____

The following section discusses some suggested strategies for test preparation and study. How many of them are you already utilizing?

Schedule Study Time

In the days before a test or an important exam, make sure you schedule the amount of study time you feel you need for each course. This may be a time when you will have to put other activities aside, postpone social activities, or get some help with home responsibilities. Whatever you do, don't put off your study time. If you are having trouble with a course—maybe you didn't do well on the last test—don't let the problem turn into anxiety or fear. Remember, you are more likely to procrastinate—put off "facing it"—when you feel anxious about something. Instead, take control. Get out your calendar and plan how much additional time you can spend on studying for a test. Then, refuse to allow other forces—external or internal—to keep you from your appointed study time.

Develop a Study Plan

You have a number of tools at your disposal when you need to study for a test. Rather than just diving in, decide how you can best use each tool to accomplish your goal, which is to feel confident and do well on the test. Following is a five-step plan that you can adapt to include other methods that already work for you:

1. Assemble the tools available: reading and lecture notes, texts, homework, lab work papers, previous tests, course handouts, and any other course-related materials.

2. Review homework assignments, tests, and previous papers to assess your past performance. These items will help you identify areas in which you are already strong and areas in which you need to concentrate your study.

3. Based on everything you have before you, try to predict the areas that are likely to be the focus on the test. For instance, handouts on particular topics

CHAPTER 7   Preparing For and Taking Tests   **135**

indicate things the instructor feels are important. Likewise, details from your notes, such as charts, formulas, and lists that supplement the text material probably contain key information.

4. If you don't know, try to predict the type of test you are studying for. Tests usually fall into one of three categories or a combination of these categories:
   - Subjective tests, which require you to write short or long essay answers.
   - Objective tests: fill-in, multiple choice, true/false, short answer.
   - Practicum or skill tests, where you actually demonstrate the performance of a skill. Tests for courses such as keyboarding, electronics, and computer applications often fall into this category.

5. Organize the materials according to the areas you have identified in step 3 and the methods you think will be used according to step 4. Then, write down the key areas in which you plan to concentrate your studies and assign a timeframe to each one of them. You may wish to design this as a checklist (see Figure 7-1).

STUDY CHECKLIST

COURSE _____

TEST DATE _____

TOPICS TO STUDY	DONE/DATE	TO DO/DATE	NOTES

FIGURE 7-1 Study Checklist

Apply Sound Study Techniques

Following are some tips on how to use the study tools and materials you have available.

- *Organize notes.* Read your notes from class lectures, readings, lab work, and so on. On a separate sheet of paper, list the key topics that will be covered on the test along with study notes that summarize or list key information. (You may wish to put each topic on a separate sheet so you can prioritize them.) Then, with the notes covered, go over each topic and recite out loud or summarize the ideas, themes, concepts, or facts to be memorized. Check your answers against your notes to identify areas that need more study.
- *Text materials.* If your instructor has relied heavily on a core text or other printed supplements to teach the course, use these materials to test yourself while studying. Most texts use key elements for presenting material. These include lists of learning objectives, lists of facts or key principles, skills checklists, charts, graphs, tables, chapter summaries, lists of key terms, review questions, and exercises. Use these elements to determine where you need to concentrate your efforts. For instance, check off the key terms you know, and circle those you need to go back into the chapter and review. Read the review questions and check off the ones you have trouble answering. Using the text elements in this way will help you identify the areas in which you need to spend the most time.
- *Create learning aids.* Use your creativity to develop your own learning aids. This method is particularly useful in transferring information from one medium to another to accommodate your preferred learning styles. Key terms may be placed on flash cards with definitions on the back. If you are an aural learner, make a tape that you can listen to while exercising.

You can also create diagrams, information charts, concept maps, and sketches as aids to trigger the recall of information. These visual pictures will become imprinted in your mind, and they are reinforced by the writing activity that accompanies them.

TURN ON THE LIGHT

Don't study "in the dark" unless you have absolutely no alternative. Before you begin intensive study for a test, get as much information as you can about what the test will cover and what kinds of questions to expect. The primary source for this is, of course, the instructor. Whatever you do, don't miss the class preceding an important exam. Some instructors tell students exactly what to expect, others wait to be asked, and others will not tell. Don't be reluctant to ask, and try to elicit as much information as possible. Sometimes, even if an instructor doesn't want to answer a specific question (such as "Are all of these technical terms going to be on the test?"), you may get a clue from the body language. Other sources of advance information include:

- students who have previously taken the course
- previous tests (check with the department that oversees the course)
- homework assignments, which give clues to things the instructor considers to be important

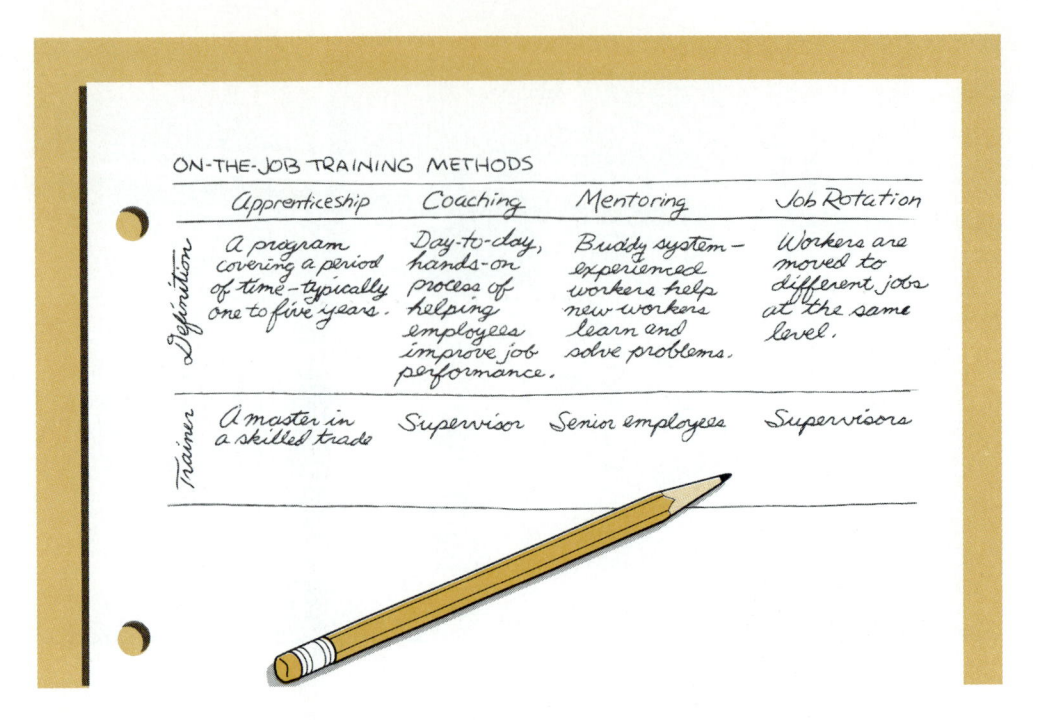

FIGURE 7-2 Information Chart

Improving Your Memory

Much of the fear suffered by people who become anxious over tests has to do with worrying that they will forget what they know. When you know you aren't well prepared you may adopt a fatalistic "let the chips fall where they may" attitude, which will tend to make you less nervous. After all, you have chosen to approach the test in this manner and you accept that you will have to suffer the consequences. But when you have studied hard—possibly even crammed—it is extremely frustrating to forget information that you're sure you were in command of the night before. How

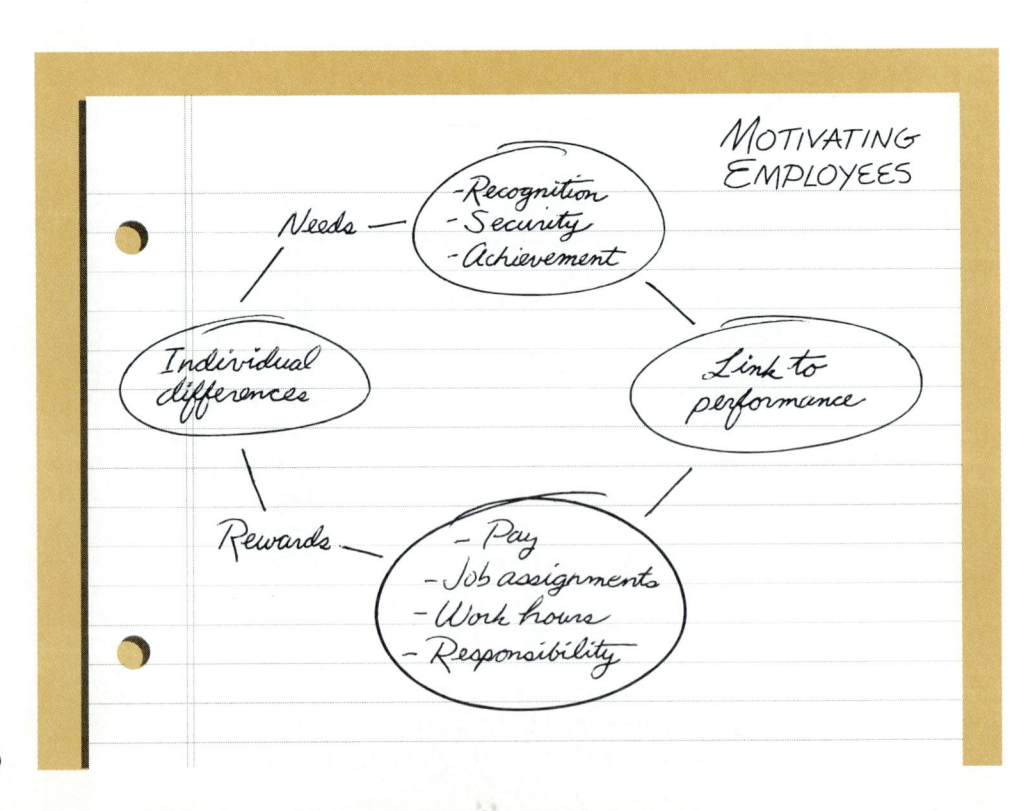

FIGURE 7-3 Concept Map

PART TWO Developing Your Study Skills

can you improve your ability to remember? Experts offer all sorts of neat tricks and advice, but before we get to those, let's look at the groundwork that must be laid.

Examine Your Attitudes

Do you have a "good memory" or a "bad memory"? Your answer to this question may be related to some of the issues discussed earlier in this text—self-image, self-esteem, and preferred learning styles. If you have not done well on "recall" types of tests in the past, examine the possible reasons.

- If past experience has caused you to think you have a bad memory, have you stopped trying, thereby making the conclusion a self-fulfilling prophecy?
- Do you have a "bad memory" about everything? Most healthy people do not, in which case your memory problem with educational situations, such as tests, probably stems from other factors.
- Do you remember things that interest you and forget things that don't? If so, this is a habit you can change by focusing on how interested you are in the future benefits of mastering the knowledge and getting a good grade in every course you take.
- Do you find it easy to memorize information in some types of courses and very difficult in others? This problem may be related to your preferred learning style. If you are a visual person you may find it easier to memorize information in science and math courses, which use a lot of charts, diagrams, and illustrations to impart information. Courses such as social science and English, which require reading text, may be more difficult for you. Remember, being aware of your preferred learning styles opens up an opportunity to strengthen your performance in areas in which you may have been weak in the past by finding alternative ways to learn in courses that do not suit your preferred style.

> **STUDY GROUPS**
>
> If you learn better when working with others, find someone to study with you or join a study group. Within the group you can brainstorm possible test questions, take turns quizzing each other, share notes, help others where you are strong, and get help where you are weak. However, be sure that you don't let the group become a distraction. Consider time needed to travel back and forth to wherever a group may need to meet, plus social time that will surely be included. Add on time devoted to helping others with things you may not need to concentrate on, and then conclude whether the balance is in favor of working or not working in a group.

How Memory Works

Why do we remember some things and forget others? Because in order for information to stay in your mind, it must pass through three stages as follows:

Stage 1: **Sensory memory:** The very brief recognition by the mind of what the senses take in through vision, hearing, touch, smell, and taste. Most sensory impressions are discarded almost immediately because the mind has no need to record them. When the mind does pay attention to a sensory impression, it enters the second stage of memory.

Stage 2: **Short-term memory:** The small amount of material that you can consciously think about at any one moment. Most experts believe that short-term memory can hold no more than six or seven items. This material will be forgotten in five to ten seconds, unless it is continually repeated or transferred to long-term memory.

Stage 3: **Long-term memory:** The limitless information that can be held in your mind indefinitely. While this information is no longer in conscious thought, it is stored for potential recollection.

Remembering can be defined as learning and storing information so that it can be retrieved at some future time. Thus, successful remembering consists of **encoding**—getting information solidly into long-term memory and **retrieval**—recalling information when it is needed.

Encoding. Researchers use the term *encoding* to describe the process of getting information into long-term memory. Encoding may consist of a number of mental tasks, such as paying attention to something, reasoning it through, associating it with something already known, analyzing it, and elaborating on the details. Often these tasks are performed automatically without any conscious effort on your part. These tasks give deeper meaning to the information and strengthen your chances of remembering it.

Retrieval. Retrieval is the process of getting information from long-term memory into the conscious state of short-term memory. Most memory complaints center on the inability to bring to mind information on demand. In actuality, however, your ability to find a piece of information in your vast storehouse of memories and bring it to awareness is truly amazing and happens easily most of the time.

There are two ways in which information you have processed and stored in long-term memory is retrieved: **Recall**—a self initiated search of long-term memory for information and **recognition**—receiving information that is presented to you as something you already know.

In most cases recognition is easier than recall. When you say "I can't remember," you usually mean "I can't recall." Even though you cannot recall the name of your representative in Congress, you may easily recognize the person when you see him or her. It may be hard to recall the name of a particular TV show, but you recognize it easily when you see it in the *TV Guide*.

Recall of information is often triggered by a cue. A **cue** is an event, thought, picture, word, sound, or so forth that triggers the retrieval of information from long-term memory. For example, you may be able to recall the last name of your Congressional representative when prompted with the first name. This triggering information, the first name, is a cue.

People often say, "I can't remember names, but I never forget a face." The reason we remember faces easily is that they present themselves for *recognition*.

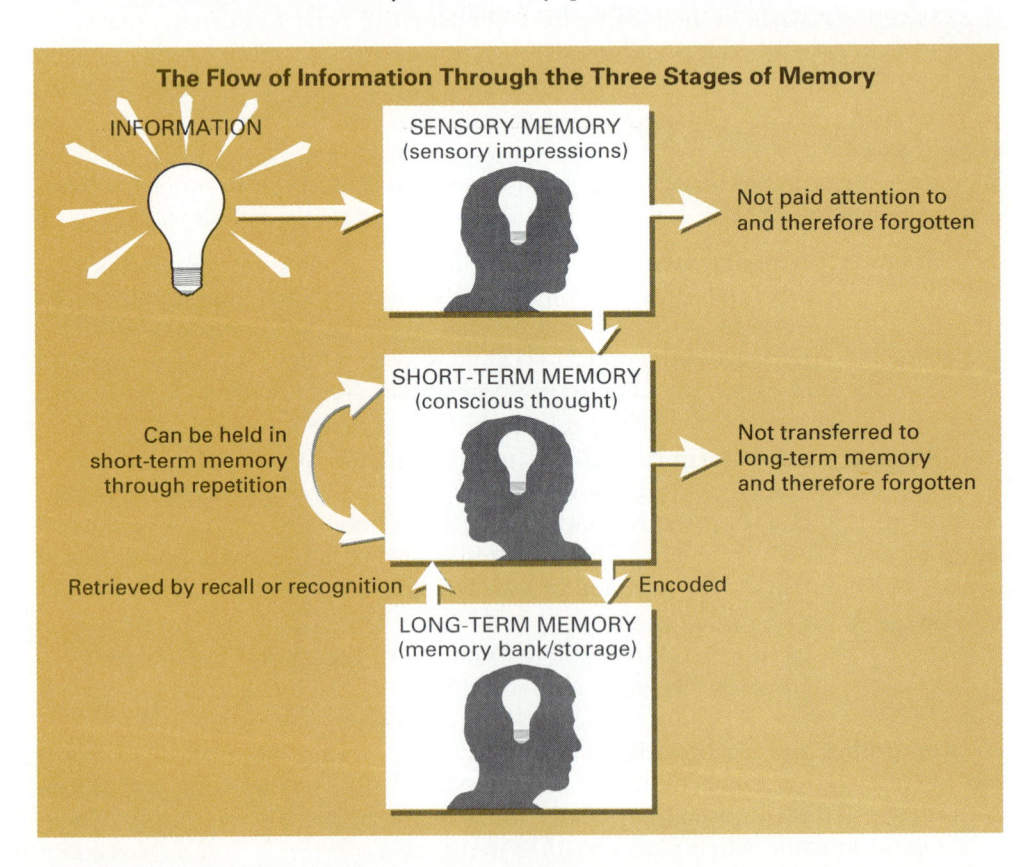

FIGURE 7-4 A Model For How Memory Works

The Flow of Information Through the Three Stages of Memory

INFORMATION → SENSORY MEMORY (sensory impressions) → Not paid attention to and therefore forgotten

↓

SHORT-TERM MEMORY (conscious thought)

Can be held in short-term memory through repetition

Not transferred to long-term memory and therefore forgotten

Retrieved by recall or recognition ← | → Encoded

LONG-TERM MEMORY (memory bank/storage)

140 PART TWO Developing Your Study Skills

Remembering names, on the other hand, involves *recall* of information from long-term memory, for which the face is only a cue. When we are searching for a name or other piece of information, we can think of related facts, which may serve as cues, and will often trigger the desired piece of information. For example, if you are having trouble recalling what course you took in summer school, you might think about where it was held, who was in the class with you, and the subjects you have taken in the past.[1]

Memorization Techniques

You should practice memorization techniques during every study session, not just when you are studying for a test. This will help you store more information in long-term memory, making it easier to recall and recognize at test time. Following are some helpful memorization techniques. Select them according to your learning style, the time you have to spend, and the subject matter that you are studying.

Association. There is so much information to remember when studying and so much of it does not relate to anything that is familiar to you. This is what makes it easy to forget. Memory is enhanced when you are able to associate something you want to remember with something you already know. The thing you know may be related to the topic, it may be a personal association, or whatever works for you. For instance, suppose you need to remember the X and Y theories of management. The Y theory has a positive view of people. It says that employees are self-motivated and can be trusted. The X theory takes a negative view. It says that employees will only do what is required of them and need constant supervision. You can use association to remember which is X and which is Y. For example, you can associate the X theory with the act of crossing something out. You cross out something you want to get rid of it. As an employee you want to cross out, or "X" out, the X theory of management because it views you in a negative light. Now you can remember which theory is the positive one and which is the negative one.

Visualization. Create a picture in your mind that contains the information you are trying to remember. This method works especially well with information that has already been presented to you in visual form, such as a textbook line drawing with labels giving the bone structure of the human body. When you study, stare at the picture and memorize the position and name of each label on it. Then, close your eyes and place each label on the visual picture in your mind. Also, memorize the number of labels to make sure you have named every part. You can create a similar picture in your mind by visualizing a map for a geography exam, a formula for a math test, or a scene in a play you read for a literature course.

Rote Memorization. The idea of rote memorization has lost favor in the field of education over the years. Today, educators and students alike prefer to think that learning is not about just memorization. However, this technique aids learning and retention, as anyone who still remembers their multiplication tables will attest. Rote memory is the opposite of association. It does not take into account a relationship or a context. It is simply a matter of closing your eyes and repeating or having someone test you until you can repeat facts "by rote." You can make use of this technique, for example, when you need to memorize definitions of key terms, the meanings of acronyms, the characters in a play or novel, the functions of your word processing software, or any information that is simply easier to learn and remember with this method.

[1] Pages 139-140 are adapted with permission from Fogler, Janet and Lynn Stern, *Improving Your Memory*, Baltimore: The Johns Hopkins University Press, 1994.

Making flashcards is useful when you want to achieve straight memorization. Again, using the example of key terms, you can write the word on one side and the definition on the other. After going through the cards a couple of times, place the ones you don't get stuck on in a separate pile. Watching that pile grow will help you feel a sense of accomplishment as you progress through your study period.

Mnemonics. Mnemonics is a system that uses the creation of new words, phrases, sentences, or rhythms that are easy to remember and that will trigger recall of more complex information. They are particularly useful for memorizing formulas; unrelated ideas; and important terms, names, places, or events. A fairly common mnemonic device involves making a sentence out of the first letters of words. For example, you can apply this device to the task of memorizing the main layers of the earth's atmosphere (*ionosphere, mesosphere, ozone layer, stratosphere,* and *troposphere*). Your letters are i, m, o, s, and t. The sentence "I must observe such things" uses these letters, is easy to recall, and will lead you along the mental path where the key words are stored.

Another mnemonic device that works is rhyming. Rhymes give your brain cues that shortcut the retrieval effort. If you can create a ditty that combines meaning and rhyme, you will have a helpful memory aid. For example, to remember an important rule in spelling, you may have been taught this rhyme in school: "I before e, except after c."

Physical Activity. Using physical activity in combination with your mind work can help your retention and recall. Stand up and talk out loud to yourself or look in the mirror and pretend you are giving a lecture. Change your setting while focusing your mind on one particular area. For instance, go for a walk or a bicycle ride or get on your treadmill for a while. Later, the picture of yourself doing this activity will trigger the memories associated with what you were studying at the time.

Test-Taking Strategies

On the day of the test you need to feel mentally and physically prepared. If you planned your test preparation time carefully and used it wisely, you should be able to get a full night's sleep the night before an important test. During mid-terms and finals, when you are taking several tests in one day, this is absolutely crucial if you want to avoid "hitting the wall" at some point during the day. Whatever you do, don't stay up late drinking coffee (avoid a lot of coffee, even if you go to bed early—it's likely to keep you awake). An overdose of caffeine may make you feel debilitated and slightly "shaky" the next morning, just when you need to be at your strongest and most alert.

The night before the test assemble all the supplies you will need: paper, pens, pencils, notebooks, calculator, text (if open book). This will save you time and stress in the morning.

The Day of the Test

Try to avoid stress at home on the day of the test. Setting your alarm a little earlier, and getting organized the night before for whatever tasks you have to do in the morning, will ensure that you leave the house in a calm frame of mind. If you drive, make sure you have plenty of gas. If you use public transportation, try to get an earlier start than usual. The last thing you need is to be stressed out over possibly being late or missing the test. Whatever your usual morning routine, think it through and plan ahead to do whatever you can to make it run smoothly and to have time to spare.

Following are some additional ideas that may help you improve your performance:

- If exercising is a part of your routine, the stimulus of a workout—even a short one—would be a good way to get yourself physically relaxed and mentally alert.
- Eat a light breakfast.
- Wear comfortable clothing.
- Make sure you have the supplies you need. Take a good pen that doesn't run and a pencil in case you want to write notes or make checkmarks on the test paper to erase before turning in the test.
- When you get to class, sit and relax for a moment. Do some deep breathing exercises if you feel anxious.
- Avoid conversing with classmates about the test or listening to conversations about the test. Anything others may say about the test that is in sharp contrast to what you are thinking could make you feel anxious.
- Remember to wear a watch, so that you can easily keep track of the time during the test. Looking up at a clock in a room may cause you to glance around, which can break your concentration. Noticing what other students are doing, or that someone else is already finished, may cause you to feel anxious.

Answering Objective Test Questions

Often instructors include several different types of questions on one test. **Objective tests** consist of questions that have only one correct answer. These include multiple-choice, true/false, fill-in or short answer, and matching. Experts recommend a number of different strategies that can improve your performance on different types of test questions. As you read the following section that describes some of these strategies, you will probably find that you are already using many of them. Some you may be applying consciously, and others may have become automatic over your years of taking tests. Whatever the case, this is an opportunity to refine the strategies that have worked for you in the past and possibly pick up some new ones to try.

Multiple-Choice. Most multiple-choice tests offer four or five possible answers. Often the last answer is "None of the above" or "All of the above." Make sure you read the directions carefully to see whether there is only one possible correct answer. This is usually the case, but not always. First, read the question carefully with the answers covered, and try to come up with the answer on your own. Sometimes reading the answers before thinking on your own can cause you to become sidetracked or confused by the choices before you. If you have second thoughts about your own answer after reading the others, trust yourself, unless you are absolutely sure you were wrong. Usually, the first answer you think of is the correct answer.

Answer all the questions you know first, and then go back to the ones you are unsure of. It's possible that clues to these answers are contained in the other questions or that your memory will have been jogged as you went along. Don't leave any questions unanswered. Guessing gives you a one in four or five chance of getting the question right. To guess, narrow down your choices. Eliminate any that you know to be wrong. Words that *seem* out of place or totally unfamiliar to the context probably are. If there are two choices that are very similar, chances are high that one of them is the correct answer.

True/False. The main thing to remember about these kinds of questions is that there usually are one or two key words that make the statement true or false. A word that describes an absolute, such as *never* or *always* usually indicates a false statement, because there are exceptions to almost everything. Words such as *do not, may not, can, all, rarely,* and *sometimes* are other key words that can change the meaning of a statement.

TEST ETHICS

Cheating is not an option. Most people do not cheat simply to take the easy way out. Instead, they rationalize it in their minds to try to make it right. They justify spending enough time studying; blame the instructor because the material is too hard or there was too much to cover; tell themselves that the risk of a bad grade is too high, and promise themselves they won't do it again; and convince themselves that it's a common practice used by students who know how to "work the system." Don't fall into this trap when panic takes over. It will never be worth the risk and what you stand to lose as a consequence. Cheating is taken as a serious offense at the college level and most colleges will suspend students caught cheating. At the very least, you will have to appear before a disciplinary board of your peers and/or instructors.

Short Answer/Fill-In. When answering these questions, you are more dependent on your recall ability. Otherwise, the same techniques apply: Quickly go through and answer the questions you know immediately; look for clues and memory associations within the questions; trust your first idea; guess as a last resort.

In fill-in questions, the number of blank lines provide a clue to the answer. At least you can eliminate answers that don't fit. Be careful with fill-in questions that can have a variety of answers. Keep in mind that the instructor is looking for a specific response that comes from your course material. For example, the question, "Communication problems can be directly attributed to _____ and _____" could have many answers. However, there are two specific words that the instructor is looking for (*misunderstandings* and *inaccuracies*), based on the reading of the course textbook.

Matching. Most students like these kinds of test items because they are among the easiest. Answers are provided and choices are narrowed once you go through and answer the items you are sure of. Usually, the process of elimination allows you to answer the rest. Some instructors increase the difficulty of matching tests by having an uneven number of items to be matched. With terminology, for example, you might have more definitions than terms to be defined. Nevertheless, all the information is placed before you, and if you are prepared, you should be able to get a high percentage of correct answers.

Answering Subjective Test Questions

Subjective or **essay tests** are broader in nature, requiring the discussion of more than one concept or idea. Usually there is a wider range of acceptable answers. Essay questions may require short or long responses. Students have widely varying feelings about essay tests. Generally these feelings are related to how you feel about your critical thinking and writing abilities. If you feel uncomfortable as a writer, essay exams will be harder for you. There is no easy solution to this, short of working hard to improve your ability to write clear sentences and concise paragraphs. Before you can do this, however, you must understand what it is you want to say.

Preparing thoroughly and writing down answers while you are studying is the best way to boost your writing confidence. Students who feel comfortable writing tend to prefer essay exams because the questions provide more leeway, and points can be earned even if the answers are not all that the instructor was looking for. Good students tend to appreciate the opportunity to "fudge" if necessary on essay exams, or to earn extra points by going beyond the questions, whereas objective questions do not offer this possibility. Consider this question: "Explain how computer technology has improved business communication in the modern office and name three trends that are predicted for the future." Your answer may earn you extra points if you were to add some information about the coming trends in addition to just naming them.

When answering essay test questions, here are some strategies that will be helpful:

Look for Key Instruction Words. Read the questions carefully to determine what type of answer is needed. Since most essay questions are designed to test understanding, you need to look for key words that request a specific "take" on the answer. These words include *analysis* or *analyze, describe, list, explain,* or *list* and *explain, compare* and *contrast*, and others. For example, an essay question on a literature exam may quote two passages on the same topic and ask you to compare and/or contrast the two authors' points of view. See Key Words in Essay Test Questions for a list of key essay question words and their definitions.

Plan Your Time. For long-answer essay questions, check your time and determine how much time you can spend on each question. Make sure you don't go over and have to skimp on the last question.

Outline Your Ideas. Think through your answer and formulate key points in your mind before you begin to write. After you have arrived at the general direction you plan to take in your answer, double check the question to make sure your intended response is on target. Then, jot down key words in a short "outline" to guide you in your writing. (You can write this on a separate sheet of paper if you are allowed to have it, otherwise, use the margin of the test paper.)

Use Good Writing Form. Remember to begin your paragraphs with topic sentences. These sentences will contain your key ideas or point of view. Each paragraph should have several supporting sentences and as much detail as necessary. Make sure your answer has a clear beginning, middle, and end. Your concluding sentence should relate to your opening topic sentence. Keep you writing clear and concise. Instructors can spot "hot air" a mile away. It is a good idea to leave space between paragraphs, in case a new thought comes to you when you reread your answer.

Reread and Proofread. Reread the question before you reread your answer. Make sure that your answer covers each key element in the question. (You may want to underline the key element words before you begin writing.) Students have been known to get carried away with the first element and forget about subsequent ones. Your "mini-outline" should also help you in this regard. When you reread, look for grammar and spelling errors. Cross out errors neatly with one line and write the correction above it. Remember, in the eyes of most people, neatness counts! This means legible handwriting, straight lines, and as few cross-outs as possible. While most instructors have trained themselves to overlook form for content, it is logical to assume that when your answer is not all the instructor would hope for, a messy paper or one with too many errors will probably not invite second thoughts about a negative evaluation.

Other Kinds of Tests

While the types of tests you have just been reading about are the most commonly used, they are not necessarily the only kinds of tests you will encounter. Teachers are creative and are continually thinking of new ways to improve their ability to evaluate students' performance. Some additional kinds of tests you will likely encounter include computerized tests, performance-based tests, and open-book tests.

Computerized Tests. As technology advances, the computer will play an ever larger role in the testing process. One of the most common uses of computers in testing takes place behind the scenes. Instructors can create or purchase **computerized test banks**, which allow them to generate tests that are tailored to the needs of each of their classes. These tests save instructors valuable time and make it easy for them to create new tests each semester, or to even generate different versions of the same test for one class (to discourage unethical practices by students).

KEY WORDS IN ESSAY TEST QUESTIONS

Discuss: This is probably the most open-ended type of essay question. Normally a particular aspect of a topic will be requested as the focus of the discussion. Here, it is important to think back to lectures on the topic. Your instructor is probably looking for key points that were emphasized when this topic was discussed in class. When answering this type of question, it is important to focus on major points and not get caught up in side issues or details that may also have been covered concerning the topic.

Trace: This word indicates that you should discuss the stages or phases of something, such as a political movement or change in scientific thought over a specified period of time.

Explain: This word indicates a specific question that relies on reasoning. You will often be asked to explain "why" or "how." Logic is important in a question that calls for explanation. Remember not to confuse reasons with facts. This is sometimes easy to do when you have been studying facts. Consider the question, "Explain how the threat of nuclear war changed the balance of power among the Western allies after World War II." An answer that gives facts about how nuclear weapons were first introduced and used does not answer this question. The word **state** is sometimes used to request a very precise explanation, or piece of information. For example, "Explain how the Electoral College determines the outcome of Presidential elections and *state* the Presidential election in which it was first enacted."

Define: This is a form of explanation, but one that is confined to the meaning of something. For example, "Define the purpose of the North American Treaty Organization (NATO) as set forth in its charter."

Compare and contrast: *Compare* means to show similarities, and *contrast* means to show differences. However, sometimes the word *compare* is used to mean similarities *and* differences. Use your judgment, depending on the subject matter, when you see the word

continued on page 146

CHAPTER 7   Preparing For and Taking Tests

KEY WORDS IN ESSAY TEST QUESTIONS

continued from page 145

compare used alone. You may be asked to compare/contrast properties or characteristics, points of view, strategies, or other elements—usually of no more than two things. The best approach for most topics is to compare/contrast on a point-by-point basis, rather than discussing all the points for one and then all of the points for the other.

Analyze: To analyze something means to identify its components and explain something about them. What you need to explain should be clearly stated in the question. In fact, an analysis is really a sophisticated form of explanation. It implies that, having studied the topic, you would have greater insight than someone who has not. For that point in time you become an "expert" on the topic, giving your insights—much as a political analyst tells us what the President "said" right after we have listened to a nationally televised speech. The word *interpret* is used in a similar fashion, but an interpretation is more likely to be based on your personal opinions and ideas, whereas an analysis is more frequently based on facts.

Summarize: A summary is a brief overview, covering important points without going into great detail about them. In a summary, you will often draw a conclusion about the subject based on the points summarized.

Describe: This term calls for details of, for example, a physical object, a process, or a concept. It might call for a description of features, ideas, characteristics, or other elements.

Other key terms:

Criticize	Identify
Relate	Illustrate
Outline	Support
Prove or Demonstrate	
List or Enumerate	

Instructors with computerized classrooms or laboratories have the advantage of being able to use tests that students take on the computer. Some of these tests are **interactive**, that is, they give instantaneous feedback on answers. Others score the tests and give the teacher a printout to use for grading. Testing in this format may take some getting used to at first, but most students find it interesting and challenging. The ability to integrate graphics and other features, including CD-ROM technology, which can bring in audio as well as video, opens up a whole new world of testing that is more creative and possibly more on target to test skills and abilities in a way that cannot be done with paper and pencil testing. Your comfort level with computers will affect how well you do on computerized tests in the beginning, but you can rest assured that your performance will improve with experience.

Performance and Laboratory Tests.

There are some courses that are essentially **performance-based**, which means that performance of a specific set of skills is of equal importance to the knowledge base. Examples are courses in the health and science fields, computer skills, automotive mechanics, and others where overall competence encompasses the ability to perform hands-on tasks, such as drawing blood, repairing an engine, or writing a computer program that works. Academic courses such as biology and chemistry also have hands-on components that are usually conducted and evaluated in a laboratory setting. Many students actually enjoy these kinds of tests or at least prefer them to the standard way of testing. For kinesthetic learners they are definitely preferable. You may find such tests set up as a series of workstations, where students rotate after spending a set amount of time on each problem or task. You may have to make an observation and note your findings, perform a task and have it evaluated by an observer, or demonstrate a skill in some other specified manner. As with other kinds of tests, timing is a key factor because of the need to evaluate all students, even in situations where you may be performing a task that would not be timed in real life. If you know what you are going to be tested on in advance, practice the activity using a timer to find out the average amount of time you need and then consider where you can cut back if necessary. Concentration is also important because it is easy to get distracted by other students or by the person who is evaluating you. Generally in such testing situations, nerves calm down after the first couple of tasks have been completed.

Open-Book Tests.

There is a tendency to shout "hooray" at the announcement of an open-book test, but this is not always the relief it appears to be on the surface. Most instructors do not give open-book tests that simply require you to go into the text and find the answers to straight-forward questions. In fact, open-book tests can sometimes be much harder than closed-book tests. While you are allowed to rely on the text, often the purpose of an open-book test is to force you to think beyond the information it contains. The questions may be conceptual and multi-layered, requiring you to synthesize information and solve problems that go beyond the factual information and examples presented in the text. To prepare for an open-book test, the first thing you need to do is know how to find the information. You should be completely familiar with the index, the table of contents, and other features such as appendixes, tables, formulas, and graphics that will help you locate information quickly. Review chapter objectives and summaries to remind you of the major concepts you need to understand. Also review any problem-solving activities that appear in the text, study guide, or lab manual, and review homework assignments that required you to apply problem-solving and critical-thinking techniques.

Handling Test Anxiety

Being prepared is the best way to avoid having test anxiety. A minor case of nerves—some butterflies in the stomach, a dry mouth—are normal. A rush of adrenaline just before the test will boost your energy and improve your concentration level. Some factors that commonly heighten test anxiety include:

- lack of preparation
- inadequate rest
- dwelling on poor performance in the past
- low energy level due to lack of proper nutrition
- listening to others' ideas about the test
- being a "worrier"

Most of these problems can be eliminated by following the preparation strategies discussed in this chapter. For those who do experience nervousness, some techniques that may help include:

- Talk positively to yourself. Tell yourself you're going to do well, reassure yourself that you are prepared, and believe that your memory will be sharp and accurate.
- Arrive early so you have time to look over notes at the last minute instead of frantically reviewing them in your head.
- Avoid distracting conversation with friends and classmates.
- Schedule time to exercise just before the test.
- If you're allowed to eat, bring along one of your favorite snacks.
- Do deep breathing, meditation or other relaxation techniques to get yourself mentally focused.
- Don't get hung up when you don't know an answer. Losing time by dwelling on a hard question will increase your anxiety because you will have to rush to complete the test.

If you suffer from persistent anxiety that is severe enough to lessen your performance, it would be wise to see a counselor or health professional for help in dealing with the problem.

Appraising Your Performance

Students who do poorly on a test rarely want to look at it again. The worse the grade, the more you want to toss it in the nearest wastebasket. But wait! This is a defeatist attitude. If you intend to do better next time, a careful review of your test will be a tremendous aid. Looking at it closely will help you focus on where you need to improve. Were there certain types of questions that you missed? Was your timing off? Were your essay answers weak or your multiple-choice answers mostly guesses? Take notes and incorporate them into your study preparation and test-taking strategies for next time.

> **QUOTE**
> Successful people succeed because they learn from their failures.
> —Bettina Flores

Over a period of time collect a number of tests and look for patterns in your mistakes. For instance, do you tend to misread directions, have calculation errors on your math tests, skip problems and forget to go back, have questions at the end that you didn't have time to complete? Analyzing

FINDING A TUTOR

There are many sources for finding help when you need a tutor. Most colleges have some kind of free tutoring system or open lab where you can seek help. Contact the counseling office or the department office of the subject area in which you need help. Some colleges have on-line tutoring systems where students from the honor society answer questions from other students in all subject areas. The Internet also has tutoring groups in all subjects. America Online has an excellent education section where you can ask any question about any school subject.

your previous tests can help you identify problems that may be easy to correct once you are aware of them.

If, after reviewing your test, you really feel that you have a problem with your ability to master the material, talk with your instructor about your performance. Seek help from him or her or try to find some other source for help. Do you need a tutor? Would it help to join a study group? Do you need a different mode of learning to supplement the mode used by your instructor? Whatever the problem, be persistent in looking for a solution. Facing your poor performance, taking responsibility for it, and analyzing it will release the tension and frustration that you feel about doing poorly. It will allow you to rebuild your feeling that you are in control, which is essential to keep you from going into a downward spiral. Developing this process of dealing with a failure or a disappointing performance will transfer into how you deal with similar situations in other areas of your life.

When your performance is good, reward yourself. This will reinforce the positive feelings you have about the effort you put into studying. In fact, planning how you will reward yourself in advance can motivate you to study beforehand. So, think of something that will really make you happy and go for it—you deserve it!

Test-Taking Plan

Go back to your initial entry and review what you wrote in the context of what you just read. Now, create a personalized plan for improving your test preparation and test-taking strategies and skills. With which types of test questions are you most and least comfortable? How do you feel about your writing skills on essay tests? What are three things you can do to improve your test preparation? What are three things you can do to improve your test performance?

_____
_____
_____
_____
_____
_____
_____

Review and Recall

1. List five study habits that can help you be better prepared for tests.

   a. _____

   b. _____

   c. _____

   d. _____

   e. _____

2. Describe five steps in developing a sound plan for studying for a test.

   a. _____

   b. _____

   c. _____

   d. _____

   e. _____

3. What are the three stages of memory?

   a. _____

   b. _____

   c. _____

4. Define the following terms related to the process of remembering:

   a. encoding: _____

   b. retrieval: _____

   c. recall: _____

   d. recognition: _____

5. List and describe five memorization techniques. Give an example (different from those in the chapter) of each technique.

   a. _____
   _____

   b. _____
   _____

   c. _____
   _____

   d. _____
   _____

   e. _____
   _____

6. Name three things you can do on the day of a test to reduce anxiety.

   a. _____

   b. _____

   c. _____

7. What is the difference between an objective test and a subjective test?

   _____
   _____

8. List five techniques for answering objective test questions: multiple-choice, true/false, short answer/fill-in, and matching.

   a. _____

   b. _____

   c. _____

   d. _____

   e. _____

9. List five techniques for answering essay questions.

   a. _____

   b. _____

   c. _____

   d. _____

   e. _____

10. Explain the meaning of the following key words when they appear in directions to essay questions.

    a. analyze: _____

    b. describe: _____

    c. summarize: _____

    d. compare/contrast: _____

    e. discuss: _____

Apply Critical Thinking

Get some file folders and make files to collect copies of the different kinds of tests you take over the course of this semester—essay, short answer, and so on. At the end of the semester, do an in-depth analysis to identify error patterns in your test taking. Make a list of the kinds of errors you consistently make and examine this list in conjunction with your test study plans. Develop a new study plan that focuses on correcting the areas in which your performance is weak.

150 PART TWO Developing Your Study Skills

School to Work Application

SCANS

INFORMATION: *INTERPRETS AND COMMUNICATES INFORMATION*

1. Using the information in this chapter on answering objective and subjective test questions, create an information chart or some other visual diagram to use as a study tool for remembering the techniques suggested for each question type. Use the format shown in Figure 7-2 or any other format that is comfortable for you.

INTERPERSONAL: *PARTICIPATES AS A MEMBER OF A TEAM; TEACHES OTHERS*

2. Get together with a group of three or four students in your class and compare your visual learning tools. Discuss the pros and cons of different formats used. Review the test-taking suggestions and discuss additional ideas of members of the group. Add the ideas that you want to use to your study plan.

3. Do some research on relaxation techniques if you are not familiar with them, or select a technique that you already use. Prepare a short oral presentation with an accompanying illustration such as a concept map, diagram, or other visual to explain a technique that works for you. Explain how to do it, what it is designed to accomplish, and in what situation it is most likely to be effective. Include any other information that you feel would be useful to others.

TECHNOLOGY: *SELECTS TECHNOLOGY*

4. Find out if any of your instructors plan to use computerized tests. This may include computer-generated tests, which the instructor then prints out, or interactive tests where students actually do the test on the computer. If you have an instructor who is using such material, ask him or her to demonstrate it to you. Take notes on how the computerized program works. Find out if there are any skills required of students that would not be required on a traditional test. Report your findings to the class.

Workplace Application

SCANS

The kind of pressure you feel to do well on a test creates some of the same kind of performance anxiety that employees feel on the job when faced with an important task or project. Some of the same factors apply:

- Making a personal investment of time and effort
- Revealing what you know and don't know to someone who is going to judge you
- Having your performance compared to others
- Accepting someone's evaluation of you and dealing with your feelings about it

Working with a partner in your class, place yourself in the role of the supervisor who must appraise the performance of a subordinate. You are to assess each other's performance on their job as a student, specifically as it relates to the performance of study skills. Conduct the performance appraisal in the following manner:

1. Using the information you have learned in this course, work with your partner to develop a list of study skills competencies.
2. Develop a system for rating the level of the performance of each competency.
3. Design an evaluation form.
4. Each partner should fill in two copies of the form. One is a self-evaluation and the other is an evaluation of your partner based on your observations of them in class and anything you may have learned about them outside of class.
5. Agree on a time to meet with your partner and exchange forms. Allow about a half hour for a discussion of each partner's performance, and another fifteen minutes to develop a plan of action for improved performance.

SCANS Personal Progress Application

PERSONAL QUALITIES: *DISPLAYS RESPONSIBILITY, SELF-ESTEEM, SOCIABILITY, SELF-MANAGEMENT, AND INTEGRITY AND HONESTY.*

You can use the natural way your brain functions to make studying for tests easy. The process involves reviewing information in a cumulative fashion throughout the duration of the class.

Researchers have verified the powerful effect review has upon memory. The most surprising part of their findings may be that the amount of review needed is really very little in order to bring about very big jumps in memory retention.

The way you can take advantage of this aspect of brain function is to use the flash card technique.

Never Cram Again!

Use 3 x 5 cards to make flash cards of the information in your reading assignments. When you highlight a section of your textbook, figure a way to make a question out of that highlighted section, then write the question on one side of the card and the answer on the other. Also mark on the card the page number in the text from which the question came in case you want to go directly to that part of the text in any future study session for more detailed information.

After the class in which the instructor covers the information, create any additional cards from your notes that may be necessary.

Accumulate these cards throughout the course. Carry them with you from time to time and pull them out at odd moments (waiting at traffic lights, in line at the bank, in line at the post office, when you're at the laundromat, and so on) to test yourself with them. Sometimes look at the question and try to come up with the answer. At other times, look at the side of the card with the answer, and try to create the question, and maybe even other questions that could have the same answer.

This constant reinforcement of the material in the class will fix the information in your memory very quickly. Studying for tests then becomes a simple matter because you've kept up with the material and have constantly reviewed it.

The beauty of this process is that it is accomplished at odd, otherwise unproductive, moments, and you don't have to set aside special study hours.

PART THREE

DEVELOPING YOUR PERSONAL SKILLS

CHAPTER 8
Using Critical Thinking Skills

CHAPTER 9
Relationships

CHAPTER 10
Taking Care of Yourself

CHAPTER 11
Managing Your Financial Resources

EIGHT

USING CRITICAL THINKING SKILLS

CHAPTER OUTLINE

Critical Thinking Skills Are Important
What Is Critical Thinking?
  Critical Thinking in Decision Making
  Critical Thinking in Problem Solving
Critical Thinking Techniques
  Question
  Interpret
  Analyze
  Conceptualize
  Compare and Contrast
  List Advantages and Disadvantages
  Synthesize
Creative Thinking Techniques
  Brainstorm
  Discover New Perceptions About Old Ideas
  Trust Your Instincts
Using Creative Thinking To Solve Problems
  Identify the Problem
  Narrow the Problem
  Develop Alternatives
  Weigh/Evaluate Alternatives
  Solve the Problem
  Evaluate the Solution

To solve a problem it is necessary to think. It is necessary to think even to decide what facts to collect.
—Robert Maynard Hutchins

It isn't news to you that the world has become very complex. You have probably observed that the older you get the more complicated life seems. Every day, you must make decisions about a variety of things ranging from the trivial— what kind of dog food you should buy for Fido, to the important— how you can find enough money to finance your college education. In the case of Fido, the answer should be simple—although just looking at the array of dog foods on the grocery shelf can almost turn this into a major decision. Nonetheless, the outcome of that decision doesn't have the same implications as the decision about financing your education or choosing a career.

Making life decisions about school and career requires thinking of the highest order. This chapter will give you skills to help you cope with important life choices. You will learn to link what you already know with new information to solve problems and to make decisions. You will learn how to apply critical thinking skills in school, on the job, and in your personal life. Mastering these skills will give you more confidence in your ability to understand complex issues and make informed choices, and you will discover how to unleash your creative thinking abilities.

You will approach new subject matter with a system for evaluating the content of what you read, see, and hear. In your daily life, you will have a logical system for making important decisions about such concerns as child care, transportation, budgeting, travel, employment, health, and fitness.

Why Critical Thinking Skills Are Important

With a little practice, every person can develop high-order thinking skills to make smart decisions, generate new ideas, and create practical solutions. Of course, you already do this automatically every day, but have you ever stopped to examine the process? By doing so, you will refine your thinking and problem solving abilities.

In college, you will apply critical thinking skills to choose courses, select instructors, determine your major area of concentration, and direct your future career plans. In your course work, these skills can improve your study skills, your test-taking ability, and your written work. Creative thinking skills will help you generate ideas for projects and reports.

Critical thinking skills can improve your personal life as well. They enable you to evaluate and judge the merit of the constant pitch from radio, television, and magazines to try, buy, or believe something. They give you the tools for making confident decisions about such things as what to read, how to spend your free time, what to purchase, where to live, and who you want for friends. Creativity adds a new dimension to your personal life by allowing you to consider new and different options for making your life more satisfying and more meaningful.

When you approach life in a purposeful manner and really think things through, you will make more intelligent, informed choices about how to achieve your education and career goals.

Decisions I Have Made

List the most important decisions you have had to make in the last two years. List the decisions in order of their importance. Make a note by each decision describing the steps you took to arrive at this decision, who helped you make the decision, and how long it took you to decide. Also, indicate how you now feel about each decision: satisfied, unsatisfied, unsure.

_____

_____

_____

_____

What Is Critical Thinking?

Sometimes the concept of **critical thinking** is called cognitive *learning, reasoning, logical thinking, thorough thinking,* or *deep thinking*. **Creative thinking** is another term often used in conjunction with critical thinking to describe the process your brain uses to generate new ideas, solve problems, and make decisions. All these terms contribute to understanding the critical thinking process described in this chapter.

Critical thinking is **active thinking**. To put it in perspective, it is almost the exact opposite of the way you think when you are watching TV. For example, when you watch a "sitcom," your brain relaxes because your mind can function at a very low level and still absorb the content of the program. The opposite is true when you need to use your brain to understand complex information, analyze data, and make sound decisions. Active thinking requires you to participate in the work of the *process of thinking*. It requires your time and energy, but it can be fun and rewarding, especially when you apply the critical thinking steps discussed in this chapter.

PART THREE   Developing Your Personal Skills

Critical Thinking in Decision Making

Selecting the college you wanted to attend is an example of how you apply critical thinking skills to making decisions without even knowing it. For example, you may have studied college catalogs, talked with students from different schools, made a list of pros and cons, talked with school counselors, consulted friends and teachers, and compared tuition and other costs. After all of this, you considered that combined information and made a decision. Of course, your ability to consider all these options may have been limited by a single factor, such as cost or location. Even then, your decision was more than a flip of the coin. In other words, you did think critically about this decision.

A more common everyday example is when you grocery shop. You are constantly making decisions; if you didn't, you would throw the first dozen items you saw into your grocery cart. That may sound silly, but the point is, you do apply a thinking process to even the most routine tasks. If you are health conscious, you read the labels and choose unprocessed, wholesome foods; if you must limit your calorie, fat, or salt intake, you read the labels and choose foods that meet your requirements. You compare and contrast prices, amounts, and brands before deciding which items to buy. So, as you place items in your shopping cart, you are applying a critical thinking skill— **compare and contrast**—without realizing it. This is just one of many critical thinking skills you already use in everyday life. By learning how to apply these skills purposely, you can become a more efficient and successful college student, a better decision maker in your personal life, and a more productive worker in your chosen career.

> We are losing our ability to manage ideas; to contemplate, to think. We are becoming a nation of electronic voyeurs, whose capacity for dialogue is a fading memory, occasionally jolted into reflective life by a one liner: "Where's the beef?" "Today is the first day of the rest of your life." "Born again." "Can we talk?
>
> Yes, we can talk; but only at the level of the lowest common denominator. We are imposing on our minds the same burdens that we have inflicted on our stomachs—precooked ideas—designed to appeal to the largest number of people at the lowest possible price: McThought.
>
> —Ted Koppel, Host, ABC News Nightline

Critical Thinking in Problem Solving

Not all problems are created equal. Some problems are easy to solve. If the problem is "How can I go to the movie on Saturday night when I don't have a baby sitter?" there are several possible solutions. Perhaps you can trade sitting services with a friend. You might consider hiring a neighborhood sitter, or maybe rent a video and stay home rather than go out. Solving problems such as this one is easy,

CHAPTER 8 Using Critical Thinking Skills

How I Make Decisions

Use this test to see how you go about making decisions

	Circle One	
1. I often have difficulty making decisions.	Agree	Disagree
2. I make decisions as quickly as possible.	Agree	Disagree
3. I put off making decisions.	Agree	Disagree
4. I rarely trust my own instincts.	Agree	Disagree
5. I am often unhappy with my decisions.	Agree	Disagree
6. I make excuses to avoid making decisions.	Agree	Disagree
7. I never change my mind after making a decision.	Agree	Disagree
8. I would rather have another person make a decision for me.	Agree	Disagree
9. I often do not feel confident of my own decisions.	Agree	Disagree
10. I delay acting on my decisions.	Agree	Disagree

Effective decision makers would disagree with all of these statements. Review the statements for which you circled "Agree." If you agreed with most of these statements, use the critical thinking skills in this chapter to improve your decision-making skills.

---

but problems that involve money, career, marriages, living arrangements, and child care require careful thought. To find the solutions that are best for you over the long term, you need to think through all the implications of each action you consider taking. This involves: 1) thorough assessment of all available information, 2) careful consideration of options, and 3) evaluation of the impact of your solution on family and friends. Consciously applying a critical thinking process to problem solving will not guarantee satisfaction with your solutions, but your rate of satisfaction will increase. You will have a clear head about why you have made certain decisions and you will make fewer decisions that you regret. And, at a minimum, you will become a better student and attain a higher level of learning. In the process, you will find that these skills make you more efficient, because you are more organized in your thinking.

Critical Thinking Techniques

Researchers have found that certain deliberate techniques sharpen your critical thinking skills. In turn, these skills make you a better student by helping you to read for understanding and retention; answer essay test questions well, and write organized, thoughtful, and coherent papers. You also can use these techniques for making important decisions in your personal life, to make better decisions in the workplace, and to solve problems on the job.

Question

Learning occurs when you search for answers. Be inquisitive! When you think critically, you use your curiosity to gain fresh insights and new knowledge. Get in the habit of preparing thoughtful questions to guide your understanding and search for new information. For example, imagine you are studying to be a physician's assistant and you are preparing a paper on the treatment of asthma. You have just read a three-page article describing a new drug for the treatment of asthma. Should you include this information in your paper? One way to deepen your understanding of the information and assess its usefulness is to make a list of questions about this new treatment.

How soon will the new medicine be available?
How does it work?
What does it cost?
Does it help all forms of asthma?
How safe is the drug?
Are there side effects? If so, what are they?
Who is the manufacturer?
How many people were included in the trials?
Where were the studies conducted?
Does the drug have FDA approval?
Is this drug expected to help everyone with asthma?
How is the drug administered?

After you ask the questions, reread the article and record the answers. If a careful rereading of the article doesn't provide enough answers, you know you need to do more research. You may be able to find additional information about this new drug in the medical reference section of your school library. Or you can ask a teacher or medical professional (pharmacist) how to learn more. The point is to be actively involved in learning—digging for information and broadening your sources until you've increased your understanding. Questioning helps you avoid the assumption that experts are always right or thorough in their presentation of information. Questioning also helps you focus your need for information so that you don't waste time with sources that are not relevant to your purpose.

Interpret

Interpreting is making sense of the material you read or hear. When you interpret, you translate and simplify concepts and data. If information is very technical, you may have to put it into your own words before you can understand it. This forces you to *think* about the words and transfer them into words that are clear to you. Think of interpreting as explaining. You can practice interpreting by using words you would use to tell a friend about the article you just read. Your explanation might look like this.

There's a new asthma drug that is very different. It makes the claim that it relieves breathing with fewer side effects. It comes in a time-release capsule that works over a three-hour period. The drug will be available within the next six months. It's more expensive, but it works.

Some of the study skills discussed earlier in this text, such as drawing diagrams and concept maps, are examples of using interpreting as a critical thinking skill when studying.

When you interpret, you filter information through your own knowledge and experience. You make connections that enable you to place the information in language and in a context that is familiar and understandable to you. This skill is particularly useful in courses where you have to understand theoretical concepts and technical information that is highly unfamiliar to you.

Interpreting makes the abstract more concrete. This activity fixes the information in your brain and prepares you for the next step in your critical thinking about this topic.

Analyze

You can aid your understanding of new or difficult information by breaking down a subject into segments for individual study. This is called *analysis*. In the case of the article on the new asthma drug, list aspects of the subject you wish to analyze on the left side of a piece of paper, and save room on the right side to note details you wish to explain in your paper.

Your list might include:

therapeutic effects	patient reactions; relief time; ease of use; age groups
costs	of research; to medical industry; to consumer
availability	timing; through prescription; over-the-counter

If you aren't able to find sufficient information for your analysis when you reread the article, you know what to search for in other sources.

Conceptualize

When you **conceptualize**, you expand specific information to a broader context. You apply ideas and information from data and events to develop new concepts or theories. For example, the article on the new asthma drug will have limited interest unless it fits into a meaningful context— you have asthma, you know an asthmatic, or you are studying in a medical field. However, even if the context doesn't fit your situation, through conceptualization you can relate this information to the wider area of new drug research. You probably know someone with a serious illness or chronic medical problem. Try to relate the information in this article to potential discoveries for curing or alleviating the symptoms of cancer, multiple sclerosis, chronic back pain, diabetes, or any other serious disease. A good way to go about this is to make a list of areas for exploration. Your list might look like this:

Steps taken by researchers to develop new drugs.
Cost of research to find new cures, treatments, and drugs.
Length of time involved in bringing new drugs to the market.
Use of clinical trials for drug approval.
Problems of public acceptance.
Information sources on drug research.

When you conceptualize, you expand your mind. You use information to stimulate your thinking in other areas. Your critical reading of the asthma drug discovery could open up the entire subject of drug research to you.

Compare and Contrast

When you look at similarities and differences between ideas, objects, or events, you are using another valuable critical thinking skill. You do this unconsciously when you buy one product instead of another, or choose one book over another. While you frequently use this technique, you probably haven't considered just what a powerful learning technique it is. For example, you can use this skill to evaluate the article you read about the new asthma medication. One way to apply this technique is to list major attributes of drugs down the left-hand side of a sheet of paper. Then make two columns with the headings *New Drug* and *Current Drugs*.

Your sheet might look like this:

CHARACTERISTICS	NEW DRUG	CURRENT DRUGS
chemical composition	similar	similar
cost	more expensive	less expensive
side effects	very few	significant for some patients
effectiveness	98%	varies from 75% to 90%
availability	not for 6 months	available now
restrictions	can't be used by diabetics or people with heart disease	none known
dosages	one time-release per day	pills three times daily
research	limited clinical trials	extensive clinical trials

List Advantages and Disadvantages

You can critically study many topics by listing the positive and negative aspects of a stated position, an event, or a discovery. In your notebook, make two headings: *advantages* and *disadvantages*. For example, as you read through the article, jot down information that fits either of these categories. Did the article on the new asthma medication clearly state how this drug helps patients, as well as discuss harmful effects? If the article is thorough, you will probably have entries in both columns. Is the cost of the new drug an advantage or disadvantage? What does the article say about availability? Does the article clearly list advantages and disadvantages, or do you have to dig these out for yourself? Were the advantages supported by data in the article?

Synthesize

To **synthesize** is to bring together the separate aspects of a topic to get "the big picture." You try to see how different elements relate to one another and how they fit together. The best way to synthesize the article on the asthma drug is to write one or more summary paragraphs recording the main points you noted when you used the previous critical thinking techniques. Once you have written this summary, you will

CHAPTER 8 Using Critical Thinking Skills

have mastery of this topic and you will be able to recall the main points. Actually, you will be surprised at what you will be able to do with this information. For example, with your knowledge about the asthma drug, you could give a brief talk on it, answer multiple-choice or true/false questions, answer an essay question with ease, or write an in-depth paper.

Creative Thinking Techniques

What is the first thing that comes to your mind when you hear the words "creative" or "creativity?" The most common association is to the world of art and the works created by artists such as painters, writers, musicians, dancers, and filmmakers. These dramatic displays of creativity are held in such high esteem in our culture that they often overshadow the more common instances of creativity that we encounter every day in ourselves as well as in others. In fact, many people, because they do not have outstanding artistic abilities, automatically assume that they lack creativity. This is not the case. Everyone has creative abilities and everyone has creative potential that can be expanded.

Do you see yourself as creative? Part of being creative is being able to generate ideas on demand. Stop for a minute and think about times when you have called on your creativity to solve problems in your life. For example, have you ever had to earn extra money? You may have considered any number of ideas such as *working overtime on your job, getting a part-time job, raking lawns,* or *babysitting.* You probably came up with a lot more ideas. The point is that you were using creative thinking, in this case **brainstorming**, to solve a problem. Brainstorming is just one of several creative thinking techniques you can *learn* to use on demand. And, when you have mastered techniques for tapping your creative potential, you will be able to direct it toward reaching academic and personal goals.

Am I a Creative Thinker?

Explain why you think that you are, or are not, a creative thinker _____
_____
_____

Describe the most creative thing that you have ever done _____
_____
_____
_____
_____

Finish these sentences: The most creative person I have ever known is _____
_____

The reason I think this person is creative is because_____
_____

This section explains how you can make creative thinking a stimulating and challenging part of your life. You will learn strategies for generating new ideas and for discovering new perceptions about old ideas.

Brainstorm

Brainstorming is a well-recognized technique for generating ideas. You can use brainstorming techniques to develop ideas for research papers, solve mathematical problems, fix your car, get a job, or plan a party. When you brainstorm, you let the ideas flow freely. You aren't critical and you aren't limited. You let your *brain do the walking*. You can brainstorm just about anyplace and about anything. However, some guidelines will make your brainstorming sessions more powerful and productive.

- Identify the issue or problem.
- Write it down.
- Set a time limit for your session. Try fifteen minutes at first.
- Get comfortable and relax.
- Focus your mind on the problem and let the ideas come.
- Write down the ideas no matter how stupid or crazy they seem.
- Review the ideas after the session.
- Consider each idea before you toss any out.
- Rank ideas using this scale: 1) very possible, 2) possible but has some problems, 3) worth investigating but lots of problems, 4) way out— not possible at this time.

Don't be discouraged if your first session doesn't produce results. Let the problem or issue simmer at the back of your mind. Then revisit it. Let your subconscious do the work for you. You'll be surprised by new ideas that develop. Your brain will be looking for solutions as you go about your normal activities.

Your ability to brainstorm on demand will improve with practice. The key to success is to RELAX. Often, this isn't easy to do. Sometimes just telling yourself to relax will make you tense. If this happens, try deep breathing and meditation techniques. Before brainstorming, sit quietly, close your eyes,

TWO FACES OF CREATIVE THINKING

Creativity is a difficult concept to define. Some researchers define creativity as thinking that results in new and innovative approaches to social and political problems, plays, novels, poems, inventions, musical compositions, and other art forms. Artists, playwrights, and inventors exhibit high levels of creativity. Some psychologists believe that creativity results from a process called **divergent thinking**. According to Guilford, 1950, divergent thinking is loosely organized, only partially directed, and unconventional. Thinking that is logical, systematic, and focused is called **convergent thinking**.

Many creative people use both convergent and divergent thinking. For example, an architect who develops a new building design that is aesthetic as well as practical exhibits both thinking processes. The architect uses creative divergent thinking to generate solutions and solve problems. However, the architect's logical, focused, and systematic convergent thinking transforms creative ideas to practical, workable solutions.[1]

What Kind of a Thinker Am I?

Do you think that you are a convergent thinker, a divergent thinker, or do you use both kinds of thinking? When you try to solve a problem, do you just naturally attack it step-by-step, or do you automatically explore a lot of solutions? Do you do a bit of both? Describe a situation where you have applied one or both of these types of thinking. Be specific.

_____
_____
_____
_____

[1] Lahey, Benjamin B. *Psychology - Fourth Edition*. Dubuque, IA: Wm. C. Brown, 1992.

CHAPTER 8 Using Critical Thinking Skills

and try to quiet your mind. If you find that your mind wanders to other subjects, don't be concerned. If other ideas or problems keep popping into your mind, get up and write them down on a piece of paper, then let go of them. Now, try again to relax for two or three minutes before bringing your problem into focus.

Sometimes people have better results brainstorming in a group. Hearing other people's ideas will often stimulate your own thinking. Seek out friends or classmates who are willing to experiment with brainstorming sessions. You can brainstorm about campus issues, such as parking problems, food, inadequate day-care facilities, campus safety, or limited open gym hours. You can brainstorm with classmates about writing term papers, using computers, scheduling practice test sessions, practicing speaking skills, or sharing lecture notes. Be sure that someone is in charge of writing down all ideas. It is very helpful if everyone can see the ideas, so try to hold your sessions in a classroom with a chalkboard or an easel and pad. If you can't meet in a classroom, get together after class, and informally brainstorm with your friends about *where you should meet, how you will conduct the session, and what materials you will need*. Be inventive.

Discover New Perceptions About Old Ideas

How often have you said to yourself, "Oh, I can't do that because…"? Of course there may be good reasons why you can't attend an event, take a job, or finish a paper on time. However, often it is much easier to make a quick excuse than to explore other options and possibilities. For example, sometimes it's just easier to take off a quarter from school rather than explore financial aid options or find a job on campus so that you can afford to stay in school. Similarly, you may find that you react out of habit when new ideas or situations arise. Sticking with old ideas and perceptions may be comfortable, but it limits your ability to learn and grow as a person. Make it a practice to examine your habits and beliefs in the light of new information and changing conditions.

> I have in mind the ability to see above and beyond the majority. I am reminded of the eagle, which has eight times as many visual cells per cubic centimeter than does a human. This translates into rather astounding abilities. For example, flying at 600 feet elevation, an eagle can spot an object the size of a dime moving through six-inch grass. The same creature can see three-inch fish jumping in a lake five miles away. Eaglelike people can envision what most would miss. Visionary people see beyond the humdrum of everyday activities into future possibilities.
>
> —*Charles Swindoll, Author*
> Living Beyond Mediocrity

Problem Solving

Describe a recent problem and what you did to solve the problem. Be specific about the problem and list the steps you took to solve it. _____

_____

_____

_____

_____

Were you satisfied with your solution? _____ If not, explain how other solutions might have been better. _____

_____

_____

Much of what we call progress in the world comes from looking at old ideas from new perspectives. If the explorers in the fifteenth century had held to the widely accepted belief that the world was flat, the new world would not have been discovered. If no one had challenged the notion that only men are smart enough to vote, women would still be without this basic right. Successful learners are those who examine information and data from all sides. They ask the questions "What if?" "How about if I tried this?" "How can that be?" and "If that works, why doesn't this?" If you had accepted the idea that you couldn't find enough money for college, you wouldn't be here. So, you may be one student who has already challenged ideas and sought alternatives.

Trust Your Instincts

Sometimes you just have a "feeling" that something is right or wrong. A feeling that seems to come from within is called your **natural instinct**. The dictionary defines instinct as a "natural aptitude." The world is far too complex to negotiate your way on natural instincts alone. However, don't turn off that "inner voice" altogether. Creativity springs from internal "hunches," combined with a solid knowledge base. For example, creative artists often generate their subject matter from within, but rely on knowledge of their chosen art form to create a work of art for others to appreciate. Similarly, great actors often rely on instinct to interpret a role, but they still follow the rules of the stage when performing. In other words, instincts, combined with intellectual knowledge and skill, is a powerful combination.

> **OBSTRUCTIONS TO CLEAR THINKING**
>
> Deeply held prejudices can cloud clear thinking. Critical thinkers set aside old prejudices and attitudes. If you are prejudiced against classmates of different gender, sexual preference, ethnic, political, or religious background, you are apt to close your mind to their contributions in class. While these students may well express opinions reflecting their own view of the world, it is important that you, as a critical thinker, listen carefully to what they say. Question and evaluate their contributions with an open mind before drawing a conclusion. You may be surprised at how much you learn. This same caution applies to reading articles, books, or speeches by people who represent different cultures. Judge the words and the facts, not the person delivering the message.

Using Creative Thinking to Solve Problems

You can learn to use creative thinking to solve problems at school and in your personal life. This section shows you how to apply creative thinking techniques to problem solving. Problems come in all sizes. Your challenge is to determine what are problems and what are mere inconveniences.

Identify the Problem

A car accident in which your vehicle is damaged is a big problem, particularly if you need it to get to work or school. Your immediate problem is how to get to school until your car is fixed. Another problem may be how to pay for the damage

CHAPTER 8   Using Critical Thinking Skills

> ## Dealing With a Problem
>
> Circle the answer that expresses how you are dealing with this problem.
>
> | | | |
> |---|---|---|
> | 1. I think about this problem a lot. | Agree | Disagree |
> | 2. I talk with my friends about this problem. | Agree | Disagree |
> | 3. I talk with my family about this problem. | Agree | Disagree |
> | 4. I don't see any solution to this problem. | Agree | Disagree |
> | 5. This problem makes me feel helpless. | Agree | Disagree |
> | 6. I need help to solve this problem. | Agree | Disagree |
>
> If you agreed with three or more of these statements, you need to work on this problem. One of the best ways to problem solve is to narrow the problem; that is, to make it manageable.

if your insurance does not cover all of the repairs. Worse yet, you may have no insurance. You can use your problem-solving skills to generate solutions to both these problems—transportation and money.

A missed bus is an inconvenience. If the missed bus results in a missed interview for a big job, then it may be a problem. The point is that many things that we call problems are one-time events. If missing a bus happened once with no serious consequence, it isn't a problem. However, if you are always missing buses, you do have a problem. In this case, you need to look at how to change your behavior to get to the bus on time. Reflect on a problem that has been nagging at you during the last few months.

Narrow the Problem

There are several steps that will help you to narrow the problem. First, you need to have a clear definition of the problem. Start by putting it in writing. Describe all sides of the issue and who is affected by or involved in the problem.

Consider this scenario: You have a vague feeling that you aren't performing very well at your part-time job. You even suspect that your boss is somewhat dissatisfied with your performance. Given this situation, you won't be able to solve the problem until you figure out why you aren't doing well at work. A little reflection leads you to realize that you are always tired when you get to work. Because you are often tired on the job, you aren't functioning at a high level. You are just getting by. Because the job is an important source of money for you, you are reluctant to face the fact that you are working too many hours and not getting enough sleep. Now that you have narrowed down the problem to a matter of sleep deprivation, you can start to solve it by looking at alternatives.

Develop Alternatives

Most problems have more than one solution. Brainstorming can help you to identify several possible workable alternatives. Remember, when you brainstorm, you list everything that comes to mind. Then you rank the alternatives and consider the most practical solutions.

For example, now that you have identified your problem clearly (lack of sleep), you are in a position to solve this problem by developing alternatives. When you brainstormed, you could have generated a list of the following alternatives.

1. find a job that pays better with fewer hours
2. take a lighter course load next semester

3. reduce hours at present job
4. reduce expenditures
5. ask family for a loan
6. seek additional financial aid from the school
7. take off one semester and save money for the next

You know that some of these alternatives are not practical. However, you list each alternative and give it consideration. You have learned that sometimes the least likely alternative can provide the solution.

Weigh/Evaluate Alternatives

Take some time to think clearly about each alternative. Consider the possibility that there is more than one solution to your problem. Sometimes talking alternatives over with friends, family members, or teachers can help you to decide which alternative will be best for you.

You may also quickly realize that some of the alternatives you brainstormed just won't work. Before you scratch any off your list, write a comment beside each one. This way, you will see clearly the problems or advantages of each. In the case of fatigue on the job, your new list might look like this:

1. find a job that pays better with fewer hours	unlikely
2. take a lighter course load next summer	look into
3. reduce hours or at job	look into
4. reduce expenditures	look into
5. ask family for a loan	already helping as much as they can
6. seek additional financial aid from the school	look into
7. take off one semester and save money for the next	no - want to finish ASAP

You have reduced your list to four viable alternatives and indicated your preferences. Since you feel uncertain about reducing your expenditures, and don't want to leave school for a semester or graduate later than planned, your first choice is to change your job situation or find another source of funds. In order to explore these alternatives, you need a plan. Your plan to solve the job problem might look like this:

Solve the Problem

Your research into these alternatives leads to the following discoveries: your employer is willing to reduce your hours (but unfortunately doesn't offer a raise), you find that you can reduce your monthly expenditures by skipping the movies each week and buying less junk food, and you discover that you are eligible for a student loan.

You evaluate each of these solutions to make your final decision. You find that, while you can reduce your monthly expenditures, the amount saved will not offset the reduction in salary from working fewer hours. If you don't decrease your hours, you may lose your job since you are unable to be more productive given your course load. Therefore, you decide to accept your employer's offer to work fewer hours and accept a student loan for next semester.

It takes work to solve problems, but most people's lives would be much better if they put the same amount of time and energy they spend worrying about

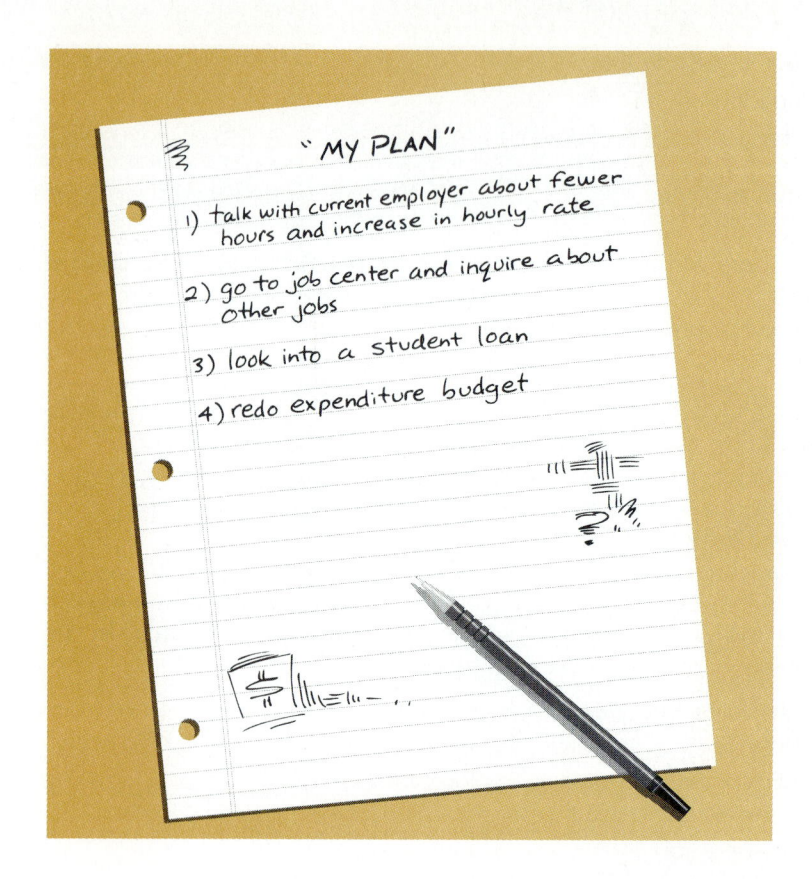

> "MY PLAN"
> 1) talk with current employer about fewer hours and increase in hourly rate
> 2) go to job center and inquire about other jobs
> 3) look into a student loan
> 4) redo expenditure budget

problems into the effort of solving them. Sometimes it takes a lot of work to find a solution that satisfies you and everyone who is affected by the problem. You will become a more successful problem solver if you use the process described in this section to attack all kinds of problems. Practice and experience in solving small problems will give you the confidence to solve bigger, more complex problems in the future. Think of problem-solving skills as a self-confidence builder. Just knowing that you have a plan for approaching problems will give you a level of comfort that you didn't previously have.

The example about the job problem shows how you can work through the process to arrive at a solution. As soon as you identify your problem, you are on the way to the solution. Obviously, all problems do not work out so neatly. However, most problems can be solved when you approach them systematically.

Follow-Up Goals

Review the critical thinking and creative thinking techniques discussed in this chapter. Describe how you could use three or more of these techniques to help you solve a problem.

_____
_____
_____
_____
_____

Evaluate the Solution

After a period of time, you should evaluate the solution you selected to make sure it is working as you envisioned. With all of the factors that may be involved in solving a problem, including its effect on your emotional state, as well as the impact on other people in your life, you want to make sure that the solution has not generated negative repercussions. Sometimes we have a tendency to select the most practical solution to a problem because practical solutions make us feel that we are "doing the right thing." We may also be afraid that others will judge us negatively if we decide on an unconventional solution to a problem. People with families tend to be drawn to solutions that "are best for everyone," even though as an individual they would prefer to do something else. Any of these factors and others can lead to solving problems in a way that makes you unhappy which, ultimately, will create a new set of problems.

Even when you are personally happy with the solution, it is still a good idea to take stock and be aware of when you need to reassess your situation. Life is about being flexible and being open to new alternatives as situations evolve and change.

> QUOTE
> People should think things out fresh and not just accept conventional terms and the conventional way of doing things.
> —Buckminster Fuller

Review and Recall

1. List four ways that critical thinking skills can help you in college and in your personal life.

    a. _____

    b. _____

    c. _____

    d. _____

2. Describe why critical thinking is important for making good decisions.

    _____
    _____

3. List six critical thinking skills.

    a. _____ d. _____

    b. _____ e. _____

    c. _____ f. _____

4. What are the benefits of brainstorming? _____
    _____

5. Describe the difference between divergent and convergent thinking. _____
    _____

CHAPTER 8 Using Critical Thinking Skills

6. List five guidelines for holding a brainstorming session.

   a. _____

   b. _____

   c. _____

   d. _____

   e. _____

7. List the recommended steps in the creative problem solving process

   a. _____

   b. _____

   c. _____

   d. _____

   e. _____

Apply Critical Thinking

Read an opinion piece from your local newspaper. Then write a short essay interpreting the opinion expressed. Evaluate how the writer used his or her critical thinking skills to arrive at the opinion.

SCANS School to Work Applications

INTERPERSONAL: *Participates as a Member of a Team*

1. You belong to an organization that must create a publicity campaign. You have over 500 members, but less than $50 to get your message out to the public. You will work with two other individuals to make it happen. Think critically about how you might tackle this campaign. What ideas can you contribute, and how might you divide the work effort with the others?

2. Work with one or more students in your class or school to solve a problem on campus. Begin by identifying the problem—is your school recycling as much as it can? Is there enough security on campus at night? Is parking or transportation a problem? Brainstorm solutions and take responsibility for one or more tasks that will help alleviate the problem. Report on your progress.

INTERPERSONAL: *Teaches Others*

3. Your friend has been told he may need surgery to relieve chronic back pain. Help your friend formulate questions to ask his physician to help him think critically about the procedure before making a decision.

4. Another friend is considering dropping out of school. She feels overworked, is tired of school, and knows she can get by—for now—on the income she makes waiting tables. Explain how you might help your friend think critically about the impact dropping out of school will have on her future.

INFORMATION: *Acquires and Evaluates Information*

5. You decide it's time to buy a personal computer. How will you decide which model to purchase? Determine the factors you must consider as you think critically about this decision. Go to a computer retailer or browse through catalogs to obtain the

information you need. What other sources can you find? Evaluate the pros and cons of various models and features. In particular, research why you might or might not purchase a Macintosh system versus an IBM-compatible machine. What's your decision? (If you already have a personal computer substitute another major purchase.)

Workplace Application

SCANS

As the human resources administrative assistant at a computer sales company, you have been asked to plan this year's holiday party. To plan the event, you must find a convenient location that will accommodate up to 150 people for a private party. List all the factors you must consider as you contact area hotels and restaurants to find an appropriate space. Then, brainstorm a theme for the party to applaud the sales staff's recent accomplishment of selling over $1 million dollar's worth of equipment during the year. How can you develop the theme with entertainment or print materials?

Personal Progress Application

SCANS

THINKING SKILLS: *THINKS CREATIVELY, MAKES DECISIONS, SOLVES PROBLEMS, VISUALIZES, KNOWS HOW TO LEARN, AND REASONS*

The SCANS report defines creative thinking as "combining ideas or information in new ways." Most creative insights come from existing knowledge used in a new way or combining information to produce something other people have not yet thought of. In fact, your brain does these things automatically, but most people are not alert to hearing the creative messages their brains are sending them.

In their book *The Einstein Factor*[2], authors Wenger and Poe describe a technique to catch consciously the flashes of insight produced by your mind and brain. While it's beyond the scope of this single exercise to present the entire process of what Wenger and Poe describe as "image streaming," there are some specific things you can do to begin priming your creativity pump and, at the same time, allowing the messages your subconscious sends you to make it into your conscious awareness. These subconscious messages are often the stuff of creativity. Get a copy of The *Einstein Factor* for more information.

Image Streaming Practice

1. Put a tape recorder next to the chair, bed or floor on which you'll do the following exercise.
2. Sit or lie comfortably and relax your muscles as much as possible. A technique called progressive relaxation, in which you tense a muscle or group of muscles for a second or two and then relax them and move on to different muscles (all the muscles in your left foot, then all the muscles in your right foot, then all the muscles between your left foot and hip, then all the muscles between your right foot and hip, and so on, until you've relaxed your way up to the top of your skull) will accomplish this if you don't already have a favorite technique.
3. When relaxed, state out loud to yourself what creative insight you'd like to achieve during your exercise.
4. Next, imagine yourself going into a big library filled with books and other resources about the things that interest you. This is your library, so design it however you want, even if that means a reggae band playing in one corner and the library full of storytellers and readers who can stop time while they tell you the information you want to hear (such a place might be an auditory learner's dream library!).
5. Mentally wander around your library. Just see what "pops up."

[2]*The Einstein Factor*, Win Wenger and Richard Poe, Prima Publishing, 1996.

CHAPTER 8 Using Critical Thinking Skills

6. When something does catch your attention, describe it out loud, even if it only appears for a split second. The important thing is to translate what you see, hear, and feel in your mental library into words on a tape recording you can refer to after you've come out of your relaxed, creative state.
7. Don't worry about trying to "program" yourself to get specific answers while you're in your library. Your subconscious knows all about the projects going on in your life. It will give you insights about those without being asked. Trying to direct your subconscious *during* this exercise may only inhibit its operation.
8. When you feel it's time to leave your library, do so. Gently bring your focus back to your physical environment.

It may take a few visits to your library before creative insights start to come. Even when they do come, they may make no sense. Don't worry about that; simply record what you experience in the library and play it back while listening consciously. This process will help get your creativity out of your subconscious where you're often unable to tap into it because you're not used to listening to your subconscious. After a while what you describe while in your library will start to trigger exciting ideas and insights.

There is brain function research to support the idea that certain brain states are the ones most often responsible for flashes of insight and intuitive leaps of understanding. Visiting your library puts you closer to those brain states. For more information on this topic, a layman's introduction is *Mega Brain Power*[3] by Michael Hutchison.

---

[3] *Mega Brain Power*, Michael Hutchison. Hyperion, 1994.

NINE

RELATIONSHIPS

CHAPTER OUTLINE

Personal Relationships
  Nurturing Good Relationships
  Handling Relationship Conflicts
  Working at Relationships
  Assertiveness
  Conflict Resolution
  Negotiation Skills
  Responsibility in Relationships

Relationships with Instructors
  Getting To Know Your Instructors
  Resolving Problems
  Accepting Criticism
  Dealing with Sexual Harassment

Other Relationships on Campus
  Valuing Diversity
  Communication Skills: A Key to Good Relationships
  Leadership Skills: A Key to Good Relationships

People come into your life for a reason, a season, or a lifetime. When you figure out which it is, you know exactly what to do.
—Michelle Ventor

One of the key advantages of education is that it leads to personal growth. As you acquire new knowledge and skills, you will see your actual thought processes and attitudes change. You may start to see the world from a new perspective, and your views of people may be altered as well. As you grow and change, your relationships will also change. In this chapter you will spend some time considering relationships as they relate to your role as a student. In order to stay focused on what you are trying to accomplish, you need to have positive relationships that are free of conflict. There are ways that you can nurture good relationships and lessen the conflict in troubled ones.

Personal growth through education should also involve forming new friendships with fellow students and instructors. Some of these relationships may be casual and transitory, while others may last through the years to come. Whether you are enrolled full time or part time, and whether you commute or live on campus, it is important to consider that involvement with people and activities on campus can broaden the dimensions of your educational experience. Statistics show that students who form relationships on campus are more likely to remain in school until finishing their degree, and they are more likely to have a positive view of their educational experiences. An instructor who becomes a mentor, a counselor who helps you find solutions to financial problems, or a classmate who shares the struggles of getting through a difficult course are all resources worth some investment of your time. Also, don't forget that fellow students go out into the world of work, and many instructors work outside of the educational setting, making them valuable resources for the career networking that will become a part of your professional life.

Personal Relationships

During this important period of your life, it is appropriate to examine your personal relationships—to consider the "good" and the "bad." The good includes relationships with people who support your goals and who are willing to help you allocate the time you need to stay focused on your studies. They are people who make you feel good about yourself and with whom you have interests in common. On the other hand, bad relationships that involve arguments, feelings of rejection, or that are lacking in support will drain your energy and distract you from your goals.

Nurturing Good Relationships

To nurture your good relationships, remember not to become so focused on your own goals that you forget about others or treat their needs as less important than yours. If you have people in your life who have made adjustments to help you have more time for school, less responsibility for household chores, or who are helping you in any way, don't ever let them feel that they are being taken for granted. Remember, "thank you," cannot be repeated too often. Little gifts and special treats are also usually welcomed. And don't forget the courtesy of a phone call to say "I'm running late," or a call in advance to reschedule something you have promised to do. Even though you are busy, notice people's moods and body language and, above all, listen to what they say. Remember, relationships will not remain positive if they are not balanced and reciprocal. As soon as someone begins to feel that they are getting "the short end," conflicts will arise.

> We mistakenly assume that if our partners love us they will react and behave in certain ways—the way we react and behave when we love someone. This attitude sets us up to be disappointed again and again, and prevents us from taking the necessary time to communicate lovingly about our differences.
>
> Men mistakenly expect women to think, communicate, and react the way men do; women mistakenly expect men to feel, communicate, and respond the way women do. We have forgotten that men and women are supposed to be different. As a result, our relationships are filled with unnecessary friction and conflict.
>
> Clearly recognizing and respecting these differences dramatically reduces confusion when dealing with the opposite sex. When you remember that men are from Mars and women are from Venus, everything can be explained.
>
> —*John Gray, Ph.D., Author*
> Men Are from Mars, Women Are from Venus

Handling Relationship Conflicts

Often when there are conflicts in relationships, the first thing we think about is how the other person needs to change. It is easy to become convinced that if only that person would change in the way you think they should change, all conflicts would disappear. In fact, it is natural to *hope* that people will change—that a friend will become more considerate, that a mate will become more generous with his or her time, or that a parent will become more supportive. It is a wonderful thing when you are able to explain to someone exactly how you wish to see them change, and then have them do it, just to make you happier. The problem is that in "real life" this rarely happens. Even when people try to change, promise to change, and really want to change, they often find it impossible to do. This is because so much of human behavior, particularly emotional feelings and reactions, is formulated in people at an early age.

When serious conflicts arise in a relationship, there are alternatives to hoping someone will change or continually telling them how you wish they would behave. In order for relationships to be positive and lasting, they need work. Often people make the mistake of thinking that if a relationship is based on mutual caring, it shouldn't require work. This attitude can get in the way of solving relationship problems because it does not take into account that conflicts are inevitable in any relationship. When you have conflicts with people who are important in your life, ending the relationship may not be a desire or an option. Sometimes distancing yourself may work—by keeping your distance you can avoid the areas of conflict altogether. In many situations, however, the best solution is to work on the relationship constructively.

Working at Relationships

Working at a relationship requires that both parties focus on themselves instead of focusing on getting the other person to change. We all fall into the trap of paying attention to what someone else is doing that makes us feel bad. A typical reaction is to become angry, express the anger, and then expect *them* to do something about it. The problem is that this reaction is unlikely to keep the problem from recurring. Thinking about what you can do to adapt to the situation is more likely to have positive results in the long run.

> **QUOTE**
> The person who seeks to change another person in a relationship basically sets the stage for a great deal of conflict.
> —Wesley Snipes

Recognize Behavior Patterns.
People's basic behavior patterns are formed very early in life and are not likely to change. This is why people who come from similar backgrounds have a better chance of having a mutually satisfying, relatively conflict-free relationship. People who are very different, and who do not share a similar frame of reference, will have more disagreements and problems in a relationship. Relationship problems that come about because of differences in attitudes, basic values, and standards of behavior are difficult to resolve. They can be improved, however, if you are willing to adapt your expectations of the other person, instead of trying to remold them in a way that suits you. If the other person is willing to do the same, you can learn from each other and, at the same time, reduce the level of conflict in the relationship.

Recognize That People Grow Apart.
Often relationships form because two people have a lot in common or share a particular vision of life at a point in time. Then, one of the people in the relationship goes through a life experience or passes through a stage of life that affects their mental outlook. This can cause conflicts, because things that you understood about the person or things that the two of you had in common are no longer valid. If you have had to rearrange your priorities to pursue your goals, you may have friends or family who feel "shut out" or that they are no longer an important part of your life. Sensitivity to other people's feelings and perceptions will help you avoid conflict and anger that can arise in this situation. If someone tells you that you seem different or that you no longer treat them the same, don't invalidate their feelings by denying it. Accept their perception, try to explain what is happening in your life, and hope they will understand. Conversely, you should recognize growth and change in others and try to adapt to it.

Set Personal Boundaries.
Boundaries are the lines we draw in relationships that help us preserve our self-respect and feelings of being in control. These include:

- *physical boundaries*—not allowing anyone to abuse your body
- *emotional boundaries*—not allowing others to do things that are hurtful to you
- *intellectual boundaries*—standing up for your ideas and opinions
- *spiritual boundaries*—standing up for the values and beliefs that define you as an individual

If you lack confidence in certain situations or have low self-esteem, you will probably have weak personal boundaries. You may allow others to exert power over you in order to feel liked or loved. When this need supersedes the need to feel equal and worthy in a relationship, people are able to take advantage of you or disrespect you. Such relationships will make you extremely unhappy over time, possibly causing depression, anxiety, distrust, or generalized anger. Phrases such as "emotionally burned," "physically or mentally abused," and "loss of faith" often are used to describe the experiences people go through when their personal boundaries are invaded.

CHAPTER 9 Relationships

Your Relationships

Make a list of the people with whom you have good relationships. What makes these relationships work? What will you do to nurture these relationships? Then list the people with whom you have relationship problems. What do you think is causing the conflict in these relationships? What will you do to work on improving these relationships?

_____
_____
_____
_____
_____
_____
_____
_____

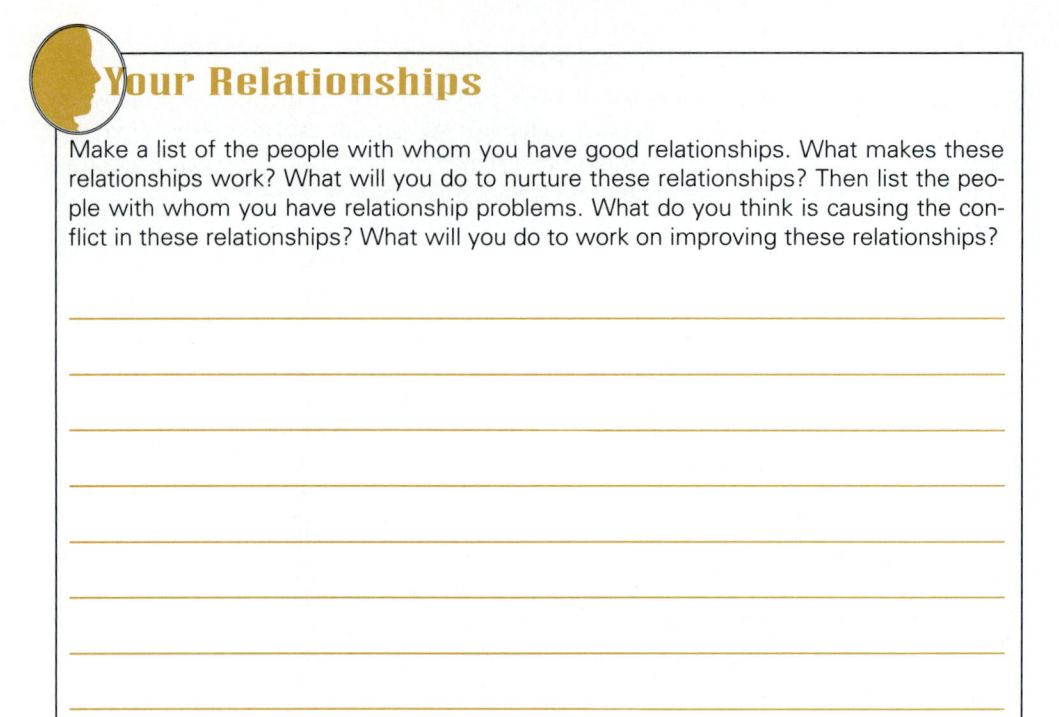

People who have weak personal boundaries may find themselves going from one unsatisfying relationship to another. They find it easier to escape than to stand up for themselves. Such persons may come across to others as someone who enjoys playing the martyr or being the victim. Often people who are weak at setting personal boundaries have a fear of conflict. These people may have experienced conflicts that got out of control in the past, or they may have been taught to avoid conflict altogether. Learning positive ways to assert yourself and resolve conflicts can help you achieve relationships that are balanced and in which you are able to have healthy personal boundaries.

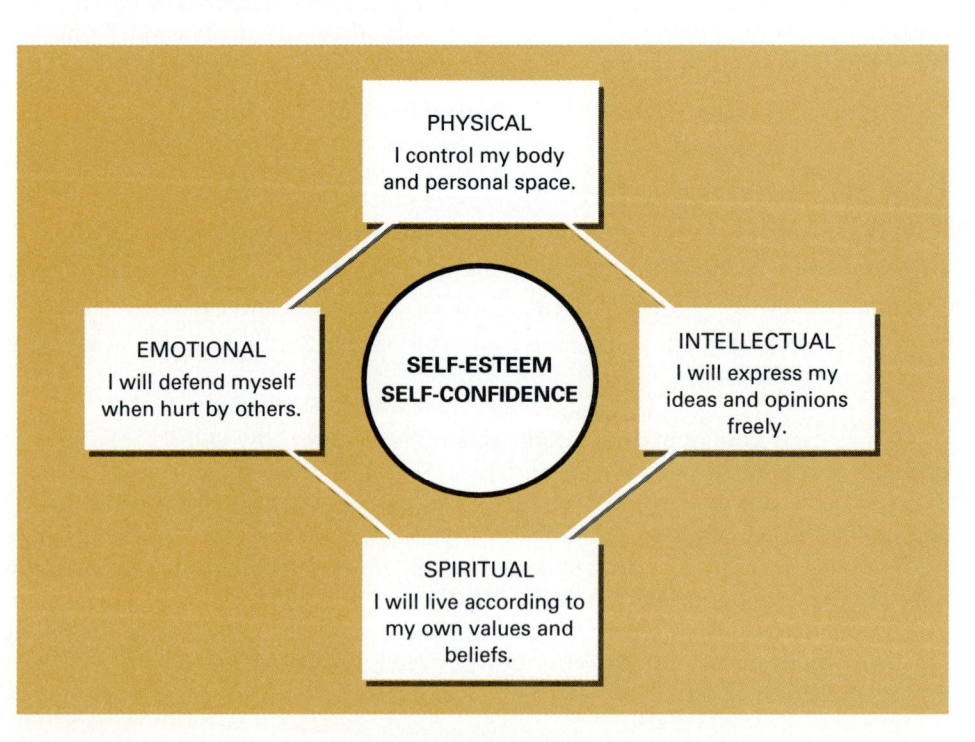

FIGURE 9-1 Personal Boundaries

PHYSICAL — I control my body and personal space.

EMOTIONAL — I will defend myself when hurt by others.

SELF-ESTEEM SELF-CONFIDENCE

INTELLECTUAL — I will express my ideas and opinions freely.

SPIRITUAL — I will live according to my own values and beliefs.

PART THREE   Developing Your Personal Skills

Assertiveness

For years experts categorized behavior associated with "getting your way" or "standing up for yourself" as either passive or aggressive. **Passive** people fail to get what they want when their needs conflict with the needs of others. They frequently have to resort to manipulation—even dishonesty—to get what they want. **Aggressive** people are those who insist on having their own way, even at the expense of others. They are the types who will "walk all over you" to impose their will. Traditionally, it was assumed that the appropriate roles for males and females were the "aggressive male" and the "passive female." As women broke out of their traditional roles of domestic partner at home and subordinate in the workplace, behaviorists began to take note of a middle ground called assertiveness.

Assertiveness is behavior that places your needs on an equal footing with others. It does not assume that your feelings are more or less important than anyone else's, but it does assume your right to have them and to express them in ways that are appropriate. Being assertive is a way of handling interactions with people that avoids leaving you feeling bad about yourself or making others feel bad about themselves. For instance, suppose someone uses something that belongs to you without your permission. This makes you angry. The passive reaction would be to say nothing; the aggressive reaction would be to launch a personal attack by saying something like, "You're always taking things that don't belong to you" or "Don't you have sense enough to know you shouldn't just take something that doesn't belong to you?" Statements like this will cause the other person to react defensively and possibly even deny that they did anything wrong. Chances are you will end up feeling less trustful of the person, and they will feel that you overreacted to something minor because you wanted a reason to attack them.

The appropriate, assertive reaction would be to express your anger by explaining your own feelings and stating in clear language exactly what you want. For example, "I was very upset when I discovered that you had worn my leather jacket without asking my permission. In the future, if you want to use something of mine, please ask me first." Or, "I make a rule of not lending my clothing to anyone, so I would prefer that you not use anything of mine in the future." This focuses the person on your feelings and what you want them to do to correct the problem. At the same time, you are not accusing them of being a bad person. This increases the chances that the incident can be treated as a misunderstanding in which both people are able to openly express their feelings and no one feels personally attacked.

In order to practice assertiveness regularly, you need to overcome any feelings that people will like you or respect you more if you just go along with what they want. Usually the opposite is true. Standing up for yourself *in an appropriate manner* will gain you the respect of most people. If you are used to holding back, you will have to practice being more open with your feelings and not worrying so much about the other person's reaction. If you tend to express your feelings in an explosive or aggressive way, you need to make an effort to focus on the other person's feelings and find ways to express yourself that do not attack or diminish them. Being able to

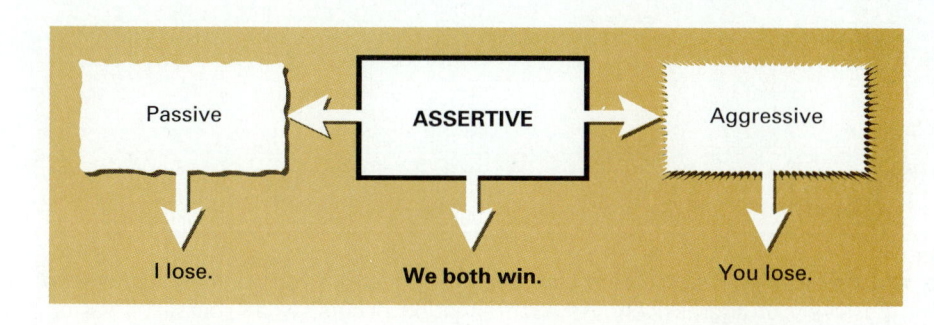

FIGURE 9-2 Passive/Assertive/Aggressive

CHAPTER 9 Relationships

express your feelings openly and to articulate them rationally helps people understand you and forces them to focus on your needs, as opposed to ignoring your feelings or having to defend themselves. This understanding increases the chance that they will like and respect you, even though they may not always agree with you.

Assertiveness Training

Check the response to each question that fits how you behave most of the time. This is only for your own use, so be honest with yourself.

	Agree	Disagree
1. I feel uncomfortable saying "no" when asked to do something I don't want to do.	_____	_____
2. I have the right to change my feelings.	_____	_____
3. When someone upsets me, I make a point of telling them off.	_____	_____
4. I frequently have trouble making my own decisions.	_____	_____
5. If I don't look out for myself, no one else will.	_____	_____
6. I offer my opinions freely and feel that I can back them up.	_____	_____
7. I understand my own needs and feel comfortable acting on them.	_____	_____
8. When someone makes me angry, I find it's usually best just to ignore it.	_____	_____
9. It upsets me when I have to admit that I've done something wrong.	_____	_____
10. I worry about upsetting others when I turn down invitations and requests for favors.	_____	_____
11. I am able to make mistakes, acknowledge them, and move on.	_____	_____
12. When I know I am right, no one can change my mind.	_____	_____
13. I expect people to respect my needs and wants.	_____	_____
14. It doesn't matter how I get what I want, as long as I get it.	_____	_____
15. It's hard for me to keep control over my time and space without feeling guilty about it.	_____	_____

Make a list of the items for which you checked "Agree." Numbers 1, 4, 8, 10, and 15 indicate passive behavior; numbers 3, 5, 9, 12, and 14 indicate aggressive behavior; numbers 2, 6, 7, 11, and 13 indicate assertive behavior. Note the category in which you had the most "Agree" answers and describe why you think this is or is not reflective of your usual behavior.

_____

_____

_____

_____

Over the next few weeks, keep notes on the situations in which you are most vulnerable to reacting passively or aggressively. As each situation occurs, write yourself a list of ideas for how you might have behaved more assertively. How might the outcome have been different?

Conflict Resolution

Assertiveness is a form of behavior that leads to flexibility, whereas passiveness and aggressiveness are rigid. The passive person is controlled and the aggressive person is controlling or attempting to be controlling. Aggressiveness and passivity each invite the opposing response, so that parties in a conflict lose site of other options. Often passive people will suddenly become aggressive when they finally get "fed up," or aggressive people will suddenly become passive during a conflict. They may say something like "Fine, you win," or "I don't want to talk about it anymore," or they may simply walk away. This is actually **passive/aggressive** behavior, though, because by ending the discussion the person has still managed to maintain control. The other party is not left with a sense that the conflict has been resolved.

When you are assertive, you are able to express yourself in a way that allows others to understand you—they know why you behave the way you do—and they can adapt accordingly. When there is conflict, and people assert themselves equally in attempting to resolve it, they are more likely to come to a mutual understanding. Even if they only agree to disagree, there is less likely to be anger or tension in the aftermath of the conflict.

To practice assertiveness in resolving conflicts, there are several key things to keep in mind; they are listed below.

Fairness. The passive person is willing to be treated unfairly and the aggressive person wants to win, whether or not the resolution is fair to anyone else. The assertive person looks for a fair resolution—one that takes into account their own feelings and those of others.

Clarity. Anger, frustration, and tension in situations is often brought about by a lack of clarity in what is wanted. Often people assume that others know, or should know, what they want. Consider that your needs may not be paramount in someone else's mind. This doesn't mean that they intend to be inconsiderate or insensitive. They may just assume that your wants are the same as theirs, unless you say they are different. How often have you been asked, when you finally got around to telling someone that you are upset about something, "Well, why didn't you say something?"

Empower Yourself. If you have a tendency to be passive, identify the areas in which you need to be more assertive. Tell yourself that you have a right to your feelings and opinions, and practice expressing them clearly. Ask for help from a friend or close relative. More than likely, someone who cares about you has seen you get pushed around by others and would be more than happy to help you change.

Listen to Others. If you have a tendency to be aggressive, consider whether you are really listening to others or simply moving ahead trying to get your own way. Do you notice how people are really responding to you? Do you look at their body language and infer meaning beyond the words they speak? How often do people agree with you and then turn around and do something different? Paying closer attention to the feedback you receive from others and reacting to what they do or say, rather than to what *you want*, will help you tone down your behavior from aggressive to assertive.

Negotiation Skills

Getting along with people, in many ways, can be summarized as a series of negotiations. **Negotiation** is an encounter or a communication in which everyone gets something they want and no one gets everything they want. Anyone who has been involved in a close relationship knows that negotiation is a key to getting along. Parents negotiate with their children all the time—"You can have one more cookie, if you promise to put your toys away when you're done." Whether you are just trying to get something you want, or are in a conflict with someone, negotiation skills can lead to a fair and satisfying outcome.

To negotiate skillfully there are some things that you need to keep in mind.

- Winning is not the goal. Everyone wins in a negotiation. If you have an *I win-you lose* attitude, you are not negotiating fairly.
- Be honest about what you want. This begins with yourself. Don't say you are willing to negotiate when, in fact, accepting less than what you want is going to make you extremely unhappy. Don't overstate what you want and then pretend to negotiate by accepting less. Most people can see through this tactic.
- Listen to what the other person wants and then look for common ground. If you cannot establish any common ground, then chances are there will be "no deal."
- If you cannot come to terms after trying to negotiate, consider a trade-off. "I will give in completely on this issue, if you will agree to give in on issue X."

Responsibility in Relationships

How far you want to go in taking responsibility for the success or failure of your relationships is up to you. There is truth in the old saying that "it takes two to tango." All of these ideas about making relationships work have more chances of success when both people are willing to do their share. But this fact only makes it all the more important that you practice focusing on your own behavior. When you find yourself in a relationship where you are doing all the work, it will be up to you to do something about it. You do not have the power to force another person to change, but you do have the power to choose not to be in the relationship. When you end a relationship after having worked constructively to make it better, you gain additional insight into yourself, as well as valuable experience that can be applied to new situations in the future.

Relationships with Instructors

You may think it impractical to suggest that you will develop an important relationship with all of your instructors, but in fact, this is the case. You will have a relationship of some kind with every instructor you have. It will be important because the two of you are engaged in a serious process of teaching and learning. Even in classes where you feel anonymous and may have no personal contact with the instructor, a relationship exists. The relationship on your side has to do with how you perceive each of your instructors—their teaching skills, their level of preparation, whether they seem interested in you as an individual, and whether they are able to ignite your interest in the subject they are teaching. When you are "turned off" by a course and can't wait for it to be over, stop to consider whether your perception of the instructor has anything to do with your attitude. If you are really unhappy with an instructor, this could cause you to view the subject matter of the course negatively. You may say, "I don't like history, it's boring" when, in fact, you could find history interesting, if your instructor didn't drone on about ancient events without ever relating them to today's world.

You can increase the chances that you will like most of your instructors. Here are ideas to consider.

- Talk to former students and get an idea of what to expect.
- If you hear things about an instructor that you feel will definitely be problematic for you, arrange to take the course with someone else.

- Once you get into a class, be open-minded and form your own opinion, even if you have heard negative things about the instructor.
- If you have a problem with an instructor's style, try to get past it and focus on the material.
- If you are not doing well in a course, try not to blame the instructor. Arrange an appointment to discuss the problems you are having and how you can improve your performance.

Your instructors gets to "know" you simply by seeing you in class continually. Whether you realize it or not, an impression is being formed before the first test or homework assignment is turned in. You can improve your chances of making a good impression on an instructor by doing the following.

- Attend class regularly and show up on time.
- Give feedback—pay attention, participate in class, and nod when the instructor makes eye contact with you.
- Do assignments and projects on time.
- Make sure that papers or any work that is turned in is neat, clean, and thorough. While most instructors will not judge form over content, they will notice form—particularly if it is exceptionally good or bad.

Instructors' Impressions

Based on your assessment of your own behavior, in terms of class attendance, your participation and demeanor in class, and the quality of your work, what kind of impression do you think you are making on your instructors? Are you satisfied with your assessment or do you need to improve? If so, what will you do to improve?

_____
_____
_____
_____
_____
_____
_____
_____
_____

Getting To Know Your Instructors

More than likely there will be some courses where you will have an opportunity to really get to know your instructors and possibly develop a relationship. While it is not wise to "pursue" a friendship with an instructor, you should be open to this possibility and take advantage of it. Instructors can be very helpful when it comes to advising you about your program of study, your major, or how to handle problems you might be having in their course or even in another course. Often instructors can act as resources. They can guide you to sources that can help supplement your learning in problem areas, or they may know a former student who can tutor you. In addition, just knowing that you are working hard to do better will usually prompt an instructor to give you a break or two where possible.

Whether you have a friendly relationship or a more formal relationship with an instructor, always remember to be courteous. Make an appointment, rather than just dropping by, when you need to see an instructor during office hours. Also, try to use only the amount of time you need. Most instructor's don't have a lot of time to spend with students and they want to see as many people as they can in addition to attending to other responsibilities. Even an instructor who has an open door policy, or one who gives you access to an off-campus phone number, will tire of a student who takes too much advantage of this.

It is best to avoid asking instructors to do special favors for you or to make exceptions to school policies for you. If you read your catalog, talk to administrators, and play by the rules, most instructors are willing to accommodate your needs when it comes to make-up exams, incomplete grades, or helping you make up for emergency absences.

Resolving Problems

If you have a problem that involves an instructor, or if a conflict arises about grades or some other issue, it is important to handle it in a constructive way. How you handle these situations will be a good test of how well you will be able to handle conflicts with supervisors and managers on the job.

Always try to resolve a problem with an instructor directly with that individual first. Before going to a higher level, consider whether the disagreement is one in which the instructor has the right to make a final decision and whether you would be better off just accepting it. For instance, if you feel that your grade on a final term paper is not reflective of the quality of your work, consider the instructor's perspective. An assignment that is evaluated on a subjective level by the instructor is subject to that individual's perceptions and value judgments. It is also subject to other criteria that may include comparison to other students' work. While you may have done your best work, you may not have done the best work in the class, something that an instructor is entitled to consider when giving you a grade.

Only after all attempts to work things out have been exhausted should you seek recourse at a higher level. Understand the procedures for taking problems to the administrative level and make sure you follow them. (If you are a recent high school graduate keep in mind that parents are not expected to be involved in resolving conflicts at the college level unless they are very serious.) Schools are bureaucracies, and complaints or problems are usually handled in a way that is most convenient for the institution. This probably will involve some structure that may or may not be suitable to your state of mind. For example, your request for a hearing may be denied if it does not meet certain established criteria for review. Keep in mind that a system exists, and try to let it work for you rather than against you.

When trying to resolve a problem, always avoid personal attacks and abusive language. This is not likely to lead to a resolution in your favor. It is more likely to make you appear to be emotional rather than rational about the situation. Stick to the facts and any supporting evidence you have for your point of view. State your case logically and clearly. When you disagree, say so without using argumentative language. No matter how sure you are that you are right, you should be prepared in case the final outcome doesn't go your way. If you are unable to resolve the conflict in a way that satisfies you, try to put the situation behind you. Rather than going over and over how unfairly you were treated, look at what you did in the situation and see if there is something you would do differently if confronted with a similar problem in the future. There is something to be learned from every problem you encounter in life. Looking at it this way gives you optimism for the future and helps you keep things in perspective.

Accepting Criticism

Our society is sometimes described in terms of "survival of the fittest." Whether or not you agree with this characterization, you have probably noticed that life is not a series of encounters with nurturing people. A good evaluation looks for strengths and weaknesses, but more often, weaknesses receive the greater emphasis. Accepting criticism is a fact of life. How you handle it is a function of your level of self-confidence and self-esteem. If you are self-confident and have a reasonably high level of self-esteem, you should be able to handle criticism well for several reasons. First, having self-confidence means that you are aware that there are some things you do well and some things in which you do not excel. If you feel good about yourself most of the time, you are able to look at yourself objectively. Often, you are aware of your faults even before someone else points them out to you. On the other hand, if you are insecure, you are more likely to stay within a range of activities in which you feel comfortable. You are less likely to venture out and take on new challenges. As a result, you will tend to avoid situations that are likely to expose you to criticism and, when faced with it, you will tend to react defensively or accept failure as being outside of your self-control.

> QUOTE
> Honest criticism is hard to take, particularly from a relative, a friend, an acquaintance, or a stranger.
> —Franklin P. Jones

Remember that a critical evaluation of your work is not (or should not be) a personal attack on you. Accept it for what it is worth and how it can help you improve your performance. Here are some tips that can help you.

- Consider the source. If the source is someone whom you respect and who is offering constructive criticism, such as an instructor, take it seriously and accept it in good faith. When criticism comes from a source, such as a friend, who thinks you are foolish to spend so much time studying for an A when a C will do, ignore it.

- If necessary, ask questions to clarify your understanding of what the problem is and solicit suggestions for improving the situation. If an instructor tells you your writing is "not clear," ask for an example of what would make it clearer. Are you using too many or too few words? Are your paragraphs disorganized? Are you misusing terminology? If you can't get an explanation from the instructor, or if you are not satisfied with the response, ask someone else to read your work and critique it.

- Explain yourself when it is in your interest to do so. Often people avoid offering an explanation when criticized for fear that they will sound "defensive." First, consider that there are times when it is in your interest to defend yourself, or at least to explain your actions. If you made a careless mistake on a test by misinterpreting the directions, it is better to explain this to the instructor than to have him or her think you were unprepared. Also, keep in mind that your tone of voice and choice of language have a lot to do with how your response is interpreted.

- Temper your reaction when you feel that criticism is unfair, particularly with people in positions of authority. Those who have authority over you are not always in a position to know the whole story, and often it is not their obligation to take your particular situation into account. Therefore, if you are criticized by an instructor for asking to postpone assignments on a regular basis, apologize and do what you can to rectify the situation. The fact that you have a job or a family, or any other good reasons for needing more time, is not the instructor's concern. While this may seem unfair to you, consider what would happen if every student expected special consideration over and over again.

CHAPTER 9 Relationships

Handling Criticism

How do you feel when you are criticized? Do you take it personally or are you able to step back and try to use the information to help yourself? Write a description of your usual reaction to criticism. What kinds of things do you say? How do you behave? After you have completed your self-analysis, get together with a group of your classmates to discuss your feelings and methods of dealing with criticism.

_____
_____
_____
_____
_____
_____
_____
_____

Dealing with Sexual Harassment

Anita Hill's accusations against Justice Clarence Thomas during his 1991 Congressional confirmation hearing was the "shot heard 'round the world" as far as the topic of sexual harassment is concerned. Since that time, sexual harassment has become a widely recognized issue, and people are more and more willing to stand up for their right not to be threatened or abused by this type of behavior.

Sexual harassment has two forms: The first, **quid pro quo,** occurs when a person in a powerful position threatens job security, promotional opportunities or— in the case of an educational setting—academic standing of a person who refuses to submit to sexual demands or tolerate innuendos. The second is creation of a **hostile environment**, which covers lewd comments or behavior, sexually explicit language or jokes, display of sexually explicit materials, or other forms of inappropriate sexual behavior that create an atmosphere of coercion to accept the behavior or suffer humiliation. This form of harassment is subject to interpretation, and the law recognizes that it is a subjective area.

While the law specifically regulates sexual harassment in the workplace, you may or may not be able to take legal action for sexual harassment in the educational setting. However, most colleges and universities have written policies that protect students and provide a process for seeking redress of harassment grievances. If you feel that you are being sexually harassed, first keep a written record detailing the incident or incidents. Whether or not you feel that you can confront the person directly and ask to have the behavior stop depends on the situation. When a person has power over you, you may feel that their ability to retaliate is too great for a direct confrontation to benefit you. Nevertheless, you owe it to yourself not to keep quiet. Talk to a counselor or administrator and, if necessary, be prepared to put your complaint in writing. On-campus resources for help may include counseling centers, health services or wellness centers, or the administrative offices of the college.

Being the victim of sexual harassment creates feelings of anger and powerlessness. Once you get involved in a process designed to resolve the situation, try to focus on being emotionally balanced, and to seek the most satisfactory resolution for yourself. Accept that this may not include a chance to exact punishment or revenge on the perpetrator. Often institutions seek to find solutions that result in the least amount of embarrassment for the institution, as well as for the parties involved. If you feel that you can live with the solution and that you have been listened to and treated fairly, there is probably no reason not to accept it. However, if you feel that your rights have been violated, or that you are being pressured to accept an unfair resolution, then you should seek legal counsel or help from an impartial entity, such as an outside organization.

Other Relationships on Campus

In Chapter 1 you considered your role as a student and where you fit in on campus. If you are living on or near the campus, or if you are a full-time commuter student, you will probably have more time than others to develop relationships with fellow students and participate in some extracurricular activities. If you can afford the time, this is an opportunity to meet people who share your interests by joining special-interest clubs, a sorority or fraternity, activist groups, or sports teams. These activities will help you develop a broad range of social skills and leadership abilities, as well as developing a network of friends that will offer social opportunities and career contacts after graduation.

If you are a returning student or an older student starting college for the first time, you are more likely to have responsibilities, such as a job and family, that detract from your ability to devote a lot of extra time to "campus life." However, this doesn't mean that you should overlook the real need to develop ties to your educational community. If you allow yourself to be isolated as a student, you are more likely to feel unfocused and alone when you have problems. Relationships with classmates and instructors, and contacts with some extracurricular activities (no matter how limited), will shore up your commitment to your education. Being able to talk with others who are in your same predicament can make the difference between finding solutions to problems and deciding to drop out of school.

> People's lives change. To keep all your old friends is like keeping all your old clothes—pretty soon your closet is so jammed and everything so crushed you can't find anything to wear. Help these friends when they need you; bless the years and happy times when you meant a lot to each other, but try not to have the guilts if new people mean more to you now.
>
> —*Helen Gurley Brown, Publisher,* Cosmopolitan

ADVANTAGES OF JOINING GROUPS

- They provide an opportunity to practice cooperation and team work—skills that are highly valued in the workplace.
- They provide an outlet for social needs and an opportunity to have fun—something to look forward to in school besides work.
- Activities related to your major or other areas of interest broaden your outlook and provide additional opportunities to sharpen your intellectual skills.
- They look good on your résumé. Although employers may act as though they expect you to live, sleep, eat, and breath your job, they like to hire people who are "well rounded."
- They provide contacts and **networking** opportunities. It is a good time to start building a network of contacts with people who can bring social and professional opportunities your way.
- They offer the opportunity to get experience interacting with different kinds of people.

Valuing Diversity

As you are developing relationships with instructors and fellow students, and as you go about deciding which extracurricular activities would be best for you, consider the value of diversity. Don't assume that the best instructor to develop a relationship with is the one who is most like you. When you go into a classroom or the cafeteria, don't automatically take a seat by the person or group of people who are most like you. Be open to developing relationships based on mutual interests, future goals, and shared needs. If you notice a student who seems to be a "whiz" in a class that gives you trouble, don't be afraid to approach him or her and ask for a joint study session, whether or not the person appears to share your same background. This includes older or younger people, men and women, and disabled people, as well as people of different races or ethnic groups.

The more you learn about things that are unfamiliar to you, the more "educated" you actually become. Companies today are spending enormous amounts of money on "diversity" training because they feel that people from different backgrounds do not understand each other well enough to work together cooperatively. Why not get a head start on working and succeeding in a diverse world by taking it upon yourself to make valuing diversity a part of your educational experience?

Communication Skills: A Key to Good Relationships

Practicing good communication skills is an important part of building successful relationships. When you meet people, they will make judgments about you, based on the way you communicate with them. Your ability to communicate also determines how well you are able to express your ideas and convince or persuade others. Solid communication skills will play an important part in your career development and may, to a great extent, determine your ability to move forward in your profession and possibly take on leadership roles. You should plan to take courses

Communication Skills Checklist

Assess your communication skills against the checklist that follows. Identify areas where you need improvement, and concentrate on building up your skills in these areas.

___ **Practice Active Listening.** Make a conscious effort to pay attention and respond directly to what people say, rather than concentrating on formulating your own response. Notice body language, facial expressions, and tone of voice, as well as the words that are spoken.

___ **Show Respect.** Acknowledge the point of view of others and show respect for their opinions, whether or not you agree with what they have to say.

___ **Be Clear.** Don't expect people to interpret the meaning behind your words. Use clear, tactful, straightforward language to express yourself. Avoid sarcasm, slang, and vulgar language. Be aware of whether your own body language is sending messages that conflict with what you are saying.

___ **Be Open.** Let down your guard and don't be self-conscious about revealing some of your personal feelings and experiences. A certain amount of appropriate self-disclosure helps people get to know you and feel comfortable being around you.

___ **Have a Sense of Humor.** Don't take yourself or others too seriously. Inject humor where appropriate and attempt to see the lighter side of situations. Try to avoid letting personal problems affect your mood and how you relate to people in general.

such as Business Communications, Oral Communications, Human Relations, and Business Management and Supervision as a part of your educational program to develop your professional communication skills.

Leadership Skills: A Key to Good Relationships

Often we hear people say, "we can't all be leaders." This idea stems from the concept of leadership as "being in charge" and the assumption that confusion results in situations where leadership is not a clearly assigned role. While this concept is applicable in many situations, there are many instances where leadership may be required of anyone at anytime. There are also circumstances where leadership resides with different people, depending on the needs of the situation. An example of this is teams in the workplace. A new product development team may be lead by an idea person, a design/development person, a production person, a packaging person, and a marketing person at different points in the life of the product. Each

---

Leadership Skills Checklist

Assess your leadership skills against the checklist that follows. Identify areas where you need improvement, and concentrate on building up your skills in these areas.

____ **Knowledge and Skills.** Master as much knowledge and as many skills as you can in your field of specialization. The more you know, the more confident you will be when called upon to assist or guide others. Continue studying your field beyond the period of your formal education. Read professional publications, attend conferences and seminars, join professional associations, and exploit all other means to keep your knowledge and skills current.

____ **Practice Critical Thinking.** Develop the ability to conceptualize, analyze, and solve problems. Even when you are forced to get caught up in details doing course work or on the job, try never to lose sight of the "big picture." Maintain an awareness of the framework in which you are operating and the long-term ramifications of your actions.

____ **Develop Human Relations Skills.** Your natural instincts and personality may or may not be adequate to getting along with the many types of people and situations you will encounter over time. Being able to understand and get along with all types of people takes effort and skill. Working at being self-aware and developing knowledge about human relations will broaden your ability to get along with all kinds of people.

____ **Take Responsibility.** Be willing to admit your mistakes to yourself and to others. If you can do something to correct the situation, do so, then move on. Don't wallow in your failures and let them hold you back. Learn from your mistakes and use them to help you do better in the future.

____ **Be Honest and Consistent.** If people trust you to be honest and consistent, they will feel comfortable abiding by your decisions and following your advice. You may change your mind from time to time, but if you have a set of core values that drive your decisions, this will be apparent to others.

____ **Be Confident.** The advice, "Never let 'em see you sweat," is not bad to follow. Confident people inspire confidence in others. If you are not naturally confident, practice behaving confidently. Try to appear calm, walk tall, meet people's eyes, offer your opinions, and behave assertively. As you see people respond positively to you, you will believe in yourself and your confidence will grow.

____ **Be Positive.** You needn't wear blinders, but at the same time, avoid the trap of becoming cynical and negative. A positive attitude and viewpoint helps you feel good more often than you feel bad, and most people prefer to be around someone who is upbeat. Being positive gives you confidence, because it helps you look for what can go right and believe that it can happen, instead of anticipating that if things can go wrong, they will.

of these persons has expertise that is paramount at different stages, and it is appropriate for each one to step forward and lead the team at those points.

When you have the most information or the most expertise among a group of people, they will look to you for leadership. Therefore, it is important to have leadership skills, whether or not you perceive yourself as a "leader type" or wish to take on the role in some formal way

Review and Recall

1. Name three reasons that conflicts may arise in personal relationships.

   a. _____

   b. _____

   c. _____

2. List and describe four areas in which personal boundaries are helpful in preserving self-respect and feelings of being in control.

   a. _____

   b. _____

   c. _____

   d. _____

3. Define the following terms :

   a. passive: _____

   b. aggressive: _____

   c. assertive: _____

4. How does assertive behavior place you on an equal footing with others?

   _____

   _____

   _____

5. Explain how these four factors work favorably in conflict resolution:

   a. fairness: _____

   _____

   b. clarity: _____

   _____

   c. self-empowerment: _____

   _____

   d. listening: _____

   _____

6. Define the term *negotiation*, and give an example of a situation in which you would use it.

   _____

   _____

188 PART THREE Developing Your Personal Skills

7. What are four things you can do to make a positive impression on an instructor with whom you have very little opportunity for personal contact?

   a. _____

   b. _____

   c. _____

   d. _____

8. Explain an appropriate procedure and attitude for resolving a problem about your grade with an instructor.

   _____
   _____
   _____
   _____

9. Name three positive things you can do when faced with handling criticism.

   a. _____

   b. _____

   c. _____

10. What are the two categories of sexual harassment and how do they differ?

    _____
    _____
    _____
    _____

11. Name four advantages of participating in groups on campus.

    a. _____

    b. _____

    c. _____

    d. _____

12. Explain how communication and leadership skills are important to good relationships.

    _____
    _____
    _____
    _____

Apply Critical Thinking

Think of a conflict that you have now or have had in the past in a personal relationship. Analyze the conflict and describe how any of the following factors affected your behavior in trying to resolve the situation:

a. Changing behavior patterns
   b. Adapting to behavior patterns
   c. Changes or stages of growth in your life
   d. Protecting or invading personal boundaries (yours or the other persons)
   e. Negotiation

SCANS School to Work Applications

INTERPERSONAL: *EXERCISES LEADERSHIP, NEGOTIATES*

1. You have become friends with a classmate, and the two of you agreed to share lecture notes when the other is absent. For the past few weeks, your classmate has been absent more often than not. You have followed through on your agreement to let him copy your notes. He is grateful, but he makes comments like, "I'm glad you're so faithful about attending class, because my schedule has been really hectic lately" and "You take such thorough notes, they're really better than what I would have learned if I had been there myself." You feel that this person intends to continue skipping class and is taking advantage of your agreement.

   Role-play this situation with a partner. Behave as you normally would, not the way you think you should. Take turns switching roles, then, on a separate sheet of paper, write down your answers to the questions that follow. After answering the questions, discuss your answers with your partner.

   a. How did you feel when you were the one taking the notes?
   b. What did you say to your classmate to communicate your feelings?
   c. How did you feel when you were the one using the notes?
   d. What did you say to your classmate to justify your actions?
   e. What was your level of satisfaction at the outcome when you played each role?
   f. Analyze your responses to items a-c in terms of: passive/aggressive/assertive behavior, conflict resolution, negotiation.

2. Write a brief statement about how you would handle each of the following situations on the job. Include specific things that you would say to the persons involved. Again, try to focus on how you normally behave, not how you think you should behave.

   a. You have an hour for lunch, and a coworker has to wait for you to return before he can take his lunch hour. Your supervisor asks you if you would mind stopping at a nearby bakery to pick up a birthday cake for her daughter because she has to lunch with a client. While the bakery is nearby, you know that the errand will take at least a half hour or more because there is always a long line of people buying carry-out lunches each day.

   b. When you were hired for your job, you were told by the human resources director that you would have a formal evaluation of your performance by your department supervisor after six months. If your evaluation is satisfactory, you will be eligible for a salary increase. When you asked how much the increase would be, you were told it will be up to the supervisor, but the amount will be discussed with you in advance. Two weeks after the end of your six-month period you notice a slight increase in your pay. It is far less than the amount others have received, based on what you've heard discussed on the office grapevine. When you ask your supervisor for an appointment to discuss your evaluation and your raise he says, "Don't worry, you're doing fine. I put through your raise. Didn't you get it? I know it's not much, but it's more than I got. Upper management has really been putting the squeeze on me lately."

   After writing down your responses, get together with a small group and discuss the issues involved in each situation and your ideas about what you would do.

Critique each others' statements to the parties involved. Then, compare the two situations. How are they alike? How are they different?

3. You have completed all of the work for a course leading up to the final examination. You expect to get an A or a B on the exam, which will earn you at least a B in the course. On the morning of the final exam, you wake up feeling awful. A stomach flu has been going around and you seem to have caught it. Your stomach feels upset, and you have a headache and a low-grade fever. You are afraid to put food in your stomach, for fear that you won't be able to keep it down. You decide to try to pull yourself together and go take the final anyway, because you don't want the instructor to think you made up an illness to get out of the exam (and besides, you want to get it over with).

    You take the test, which turns out to be more difficult than you had anticipated. When it is over you feel that you have done poorly. Before you leave class, you tell the instructor that you are ill and request that she throw the test away and let you take a makeup exam. She says, "You're such a good student, I'm sure it will be all right. Let's see how you did and then we'll discuss it." You accept this decision. You get a C on the exam. When you go to discuss it with her, she says it was your decision to take the exam. If you were ill, you should have called the school and notified her. She is sorry, but it is too late to do anything about the C on the test.

    Role-play with a partner your response to the instructor's decision. Behave as you normally would, not the way you think you should. Take turns switching roles, then, on a separate sheet of paper, write down your answers to the questions that follow. After completing your answers, discuss them with your partner.

    a. What role did the following factors play in the initial discussion between the student and instructor: fairness, clarity, empowerment, listening?
    b. What role did these factors play in the outcome of the scenario in your role-play?

SYSTEMS: *UNDERSTANDS SYSTEMS*

4. Assume that the instructor in the preceding scenario refuses to consider whatever arguments you put forth to try to get her to change her mind. You need to consider whether or not to take your problem to a higher level for resolution. Consult your college catalog or administrative personnel to clarify your understanding of your school's policies regarding the following. Make notes for future use.
    a. Emergency absences for examinations
    b. Policies for makeup examinations
    c. Policies for requests for grade changes
    d. Policies for resolving disputes at the administrative level

Workplace Application

SCANS

Your company has recently started a series of seminars aimed at getting employees to value diversity and overcome stereotypical ideas and prejudices they may be bringing into the workplace. On the first day of the seminar, the instructor talks about so many "isms" and other terms, that you wonder how you will ever get them all straightened out in your mind. Rather than cave in to feeling negative about these ideas, you decide to do some research to better understand the course terminology.

Write a definition of each of the following terms in your own words. Then, look up the definition and make any necessary corrections in yours. Select one of the terms and write an essay about your experiences with its effects, and how it affects your life.

Racism	Prejudice	Sexism
Bias	Ageism	The Glass Ceiling
Stereotype	Tolerance	Multiculturalism
Ethnocentrism	Ethnic Group	Sexual Preference

Bring your definitions and essay to class and discuss them in a group.

SCANS — Personal Progress Application

BASIC SKILLS: *READS, WRITES, LISTENS, AND SPEAKS*

PERSONAL QUALITIES: *SELF-ESTEEM; SOCIABILITY*

Read the "Speaking" section in SCANS. This section makes clear the importance of both verbal *and* nonverbal messages when communicating. Complete congruence between the messages you send verbally and the messages you send nonverbally is absolutely essential for effective, charismatic communication. (Charisma means a special magnetic charm or appeal.) Becoming a charismatic communicator is a powerful strategy for advancement in both your job and your personal life.

There are three ways for humans to communicate during interpersonal interaction: with words, with tone of voice, and with body language. Research in the early 1970s identified the relative importance of each of the three components in determining how the receiver interprets the message the sender communicates. The breakdown is:

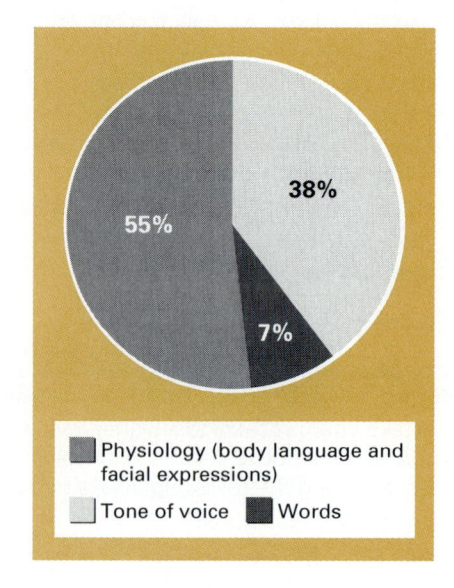

Pie chart: 55% Physiology (body language and facial expressions); 38% Tone of voice; 7% Words.

Though it may seem surprising that the words we say only account for seven percent of the meaning people ascribe to our message, you can easily prove that body language and tone of voice overpower the words used in terms of how listeners interpret your messages. Simply say the word "Yes" while meaning "No" with your tone of voice and facial expression. You've seen this happen whenever someone agrees to something while really not wanting to do it.

One key to charismatic communication is to be completely congruent with the way you communicate. In other words, say the same thing with your words, your tone of voice, and your body language. The easiest way to do this is to truly believe what you're saying, to be passionate about your message. In such circumstances, you automatically communicate congruently.

The enemy of congruent communication is doubt. To be passionate about your message you must have no doubts about its rightness. Prove to yourself that passionate, charismatic communicators are *always* congruent by doing the following exercise.

Developing Charismatic Leadership

Identify an instance in which you were emotionally moved by an actor's performance. Whether the emotion the actor evoked was excitement or fear or enthusiasm or loathing, you will find that the actor was completely congruent in his or her words, tone of voice, and actions.

Watch that performance on videotape and carefully note the actor's tone of voice and body language. Great actors are highly skilled at sending completely congruent messages.

Next, watch a performance in which an actor successfully puts across the idea that his or her character is not to be trusted. There will always be some incongruity among words, tone of voice, and body language or facial expression that the actor will manipulate to evoke mistrust in the audience.

For more detailed information on this topic and ways to practice being congruent, you can refer to *Present Yourself!*[1] by Michael Gelb.

---

[1] *Present Yourself!* by Michael Gelb, 1988, Jalmar Press

TEN

TAKING CARE OF YOURSELF

CHAPTER OUTLINE

Stress and Your Health
Recognizing the Signs of Stress
Reactions to Stress
Handling Stress—Coping Mechanisms

Nutrition and Fitness
Healthy Eating
Exercise and Fitness
Body Image

A Healthy Lifestyle
Quit Smoking
Avoiding Problems with Alcohol
Avoiding Other Harmful Drugs
Dealing with Drug Abuse
A Safe Sex Life

Health nuts are going to feel stupid someday, lying in the hospitals dying of nothing.
—Redd Foxx

We are lucky to live in a society that encourages us to take responsibility for our own health and well being. More and more the medical profession is placing emphasis on preventive health care. Toward this end, the media bombards us daily with news, feature stories, magazines, television shows, and all kinds of experts dispensing advice and ideas about preventing illness and keeping fit and healthy. You are advised to exercise regularly, eat plenty of fruits and vegetables, stay away from drugs and alcohol, protect yourself from violence, practice safe sex, lose weight, take vitamins, give up fatty foods, get enough sleep, get therapy, be positive, seek spiritual growth—oh, and by the way, don't forget—life is supposed to be fun!

Are you having fun yet? Wait! Before you decide to skip this chapter, consider that despite all the hype, you truly are concerned about being fit and healthy and there probably are some things you could be doing differently. In addition to preventing illness over the long term, maintaining your mental and physical fitness makes you feel good about yourself and helps you have more energy. As a result of feeling good, you will be more motivated and optimistic. On the other hand, striving for a healthy lifestyle that keeps you mentally and physically fit does not have to be an attempt to be "perfect." It should not produce such anxiety and guilt that your efforts and thoughts about it actually add stress to your life.

This chapter starts out with a discussion of stress because fighting it is a part of the daily struggle for good mental and physical health. This is followed by a discussion of nutrition, fitness, and lifestyle habits. All of this information will help you in designing a health maintenance program that is right for you.

Stress and Your Health

Stress is a fact of life which, unfortunately, has potentially ill effects on both physical and mental health. You can avoid these effects by becoming aware of the things that cause you stress, and making a concerted effort to eliminate as much stress from your life as possible. Even as you sit relaxing in your own home, stress can be caused by turning on the evening news and hearing the day's crime report. You are reminded that there is nothing you can do to ensure your own and your family's safety from random violence. Your mind and body are constantly responding to these types of **external stressors** that interfere with the ability to maintain a tranquil state of mind. A traffic jam, a child's failing grade, an angry boss, a missed deadline—each of these is, in isolation, a small problem. On days when a number of these kinds of stressors converge, you may experience some common effects of stress, such as an upset stomach or headache, or the desire to overeat or drink too much alcohol. You need to develop everyday coping mechanisms to handle this kind of stress. Major problems, like the loss of a job, the death of a loved one, a serious illness, or being involved in an accident stretch coping mechanisms to the limit. Over prolonged periods, this kind of stress can cause more serious reactions, such as health problems, chronic worry, or alcohol or substance abuse.

Another type of stress comes from **internal stressors**, brought on by your needs, desires, fears, attitudes, and outlook on life. When confronted with everyday stressful situations, you have a choice as to how you will react to them. People who read a book or listen to a tape while stuck in traffic will be more relaxed when they arrive at their destination than the person who looks at their watch repeatedly and lays on their horn. The parent who increases a child's study time in response to a poor report card will feel more in control and experience less stress than the parent who responds by feeling guilty for not spending more time helping the child. "I'm a bad parent or my child would be doing better in school" is the response of a person who creates high levels of internal stress. Making a conscious effort to control your internal stressors gives you a greater ability to cope with external stressors.

> You have to smile twenty-four hours a day, Momma would say. If you walk through life showing the aggravation you've gone through, people will feel sorry for you, and they'll never respect you. She taught us that [there are] two ways out in life—laughing or crying. There's more hope in laughing. A man can fall down the stairs and lie there in such pain and horror that his own wife will collapse and faint at the sight. But if he can just hold back his pain for a minute, she might be able to collect herself and call the doctor. It might mean the difference between his living to laugh again or dying there on the spot.
>
> —*Dick Gregory, Humorist*

Recognizing the Signs of Stress

A certain amount of stress is normal and necessary to being motivated. Stress can be energizing and, in fact, a complete lack of stress is unhealthy. When people are completely removed from stress they become bored and lethargic. Eventually, the lack of any tension or stimulation will, in itself, create stress on the person. Restlessness, inability to sleep, and irritability can be caused by too little stress, as well as too much. Most people, however, do not have this problem. In today's complex society, there are plenty of external stressors to go around. The hard work and pressure of trying to succeed or just stay above water create severe internal stressors for most people, as well. It is common to try to hide the effects of stress, and people will often deny that they are having difficulty handling stress—to themselves as well as to others. This reaction adds yet another layer of internal stress. It is important to be aware of your own reactions to stress so that you will recognize when you are not coping well and find ways to put yourself back in control.

Reactions to Stress

Everyone reacts to stress both physically and emotionally. The feeling of a knot in the stomach is a physical reaction to the emotional stress of fear. When an emotional stress response is severe or becomes chronic, the physical reaction is spontaneous.

CHAPTER 10 Taking Care of Yourself

People who experience a lot of internal stress are more likely to develop chronic physical symptoms than people who don't experience undue internal stress.

Obviously, you have a greater chance of gaining control over your internal stressors than over external stressors. One of the reasons that we strive so hard for success is that money gives us more control over the external world. You may have noticed how wealthy people expend huge sums trying to shield themselves from the everyday difficulties the rest of us take for granted. They hire drivers to navigate through traffic, nannies to watch their children, housekeepers to run their homes, bodyguards to protect their safety, and assistants to take care of personal needs and errands. They have secluded homes, private airplanes, their very own masseuse, and all manner of luxuries that are purchased to keep them happy and contented. And, yet, even they suffer from stress, anxiety, and depression. What, then, are "ordinary" people to do to avoid these problems?

Handling Stress—Coping Mechanisms

Each person has different levels of tolerance and different coping mechanisms. **Coping mechanisms** are the actions you take to get control over your reactions to stress. When you feel stressed, first be willing to face up to it. Don't take it as a sign of weakness that you are having trouble coping. Telling yourself that you

---

Assess Your Stress Reactions

How would you describe your usual responses to being under stress? Are you able to focus on the cause of the stress or do you try to ignore it? Do you experience physical symptoms? You should recognize when stress is taking its toll on you and devise your own personal strategies for taking control when this happens. How many items on the following list fit your reactions to stress?

Check off those that apply to you.

Emotional reactions:

___ Becoming irritable; losing temper more easily than usual
___ Crying frequently
___ Feeling worried, anxious, upset, generally fearful
___ Being self-critical, feeling guilty, low self-esteem
___ Feeling removed, disinterested, apathetic
___ Feeling generally pessimistic
___ Being unable to concentrate or focus energy for very long
___ Dreaming of escape
___ Losing interest in planning
___ Being unable to make decisions
___ Feeling unmotivated, procrastinating
___ Becoming inflexible or afraid of change
___ Feeling victimized and isolated from others

Physical reactions:

___ Having frequent headaches, stomachaches, muscle pain (especially neck and shoulders), or other minor ailments
___ Having trouble sleeping
___ Increased or decreased sex drive
___ Increased or decreased appetite
___ Becoming more accident-prone
___ Forgetting things, losing things

should be able to handle it, or comparing yourself to others who seem to be carefree despite circumstances similar to yours, will not help. Sometimes stress reactions can be caused by subconscious anxiety or delayed reactions to past events. Instead of trying to deny it, take the opportunity to understand yourself better and learn to cope with your feelings in constructive ways.

Try to focus on what is causing the stress. Many times just facing up to the existence of a problem brings relief. Instead, people often try to close the door on problems, preferring to hope they will take care of themselves. Attempting to ignore a problem does not actually relieve stress. Instead, it causes you to displace your anxiety. This is when reactions such as irritability, and lack of energy or motivation or both, will take over. Physical symptoms are highly prevalent in people who attempt to repress stress. Once you have faced the cause of your stress, then it is time to try to take control over it. Whether or not you are able to resolve the problem immediately, some relief will result in simply deciding to do something about it.

Don't Overdo.
Trying to do too many things and handle too many responsibilities at the same time is a sure way to create stress. If you are in the habit of expecting too much from yourself, and then beating yourself up when you can't deliver, you are creating unnecessary internal stress of the kind that is very likely to result in physical reactions. Don't be taken in by media hype that glorifies the perpetually busy person. Being able "to have it all" and "do it all" are unrealistic ideals for the majority of people. Use the methods suggested in Chapter 2 to identify the things that you need to do and develop a workable schedule for yourself. Setting priorities and having a plan for reaching your goals helps you avoid putting unnecessary pressure on yourself.

Balance Your Life.
No matter how much work you have to do, be sure you always include down time in your schedule. Some people need time where they can be alone to think, pursue a hobby, or just be left alone. Others prefer to spend their leisure time engaging in activities they enjoy with others. Whatever your temperament calls for, the idea is to get away from work, whether it's your studies or your job, in any way that takes your mind completely off of the things you have to get done. If you enjoy physical activity as a form of recreation, this is a great way to "burn off" stress.

Confide in Someone.
Sharing your concerns with others is also a way of relieving stress and finding solutions to problems. Some people are too good at this. There is a type known as a "stress carrier." An example is the person in the office who is always the first to hear rumors of layoffs. This kind of person talks about their own stress to anyone and everyone. They walk away relieved, and the other person is left with the anxious feeling that life must be pretty awful if this person is so upset. Don't be a stress carrier by sharing your fears, concerns, and anxieties with anyone who will listen; do find one or two people who perhaps share your situation or who are sympathetic to you and willing to listen.

Before you confide in someone, consider whether or not the person is a good listener. Typically when people talk about their problems, they want someone who will listen and understand. What they do not want is someone who has all the answers, or someone who goes on and on about what they did in a similar situation. A sympathetic listener who offers support and gives advice only when requested makes the best kind of confidante.

COPING STRATEGIES

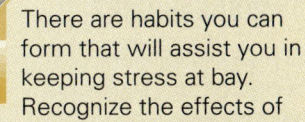

There are habits you can form that will assist you in keeping stress at bay. Recognize the effects of stress and make a concerted effort to put coping mechanisms in place—even before you need them.

- *Stress affects your memory and concentration.* Relieve yourself of this extra strain by writing things down—for example, in diaries, on wall charts, or on lists.
- *Stress makes planning and decisions difficult.* Give yourself planning time every day (first thing in the morning may be best).
- *Stress makes you tired.* Give yourself proper breaks—for meals, refreshments, exercise, and on weekends.
- *Stress slows down your speed of recovery, and lowers your resistance to illness.* Learn to stop before you are completely worn out. Take regular exercise, eat a balanced diet, and rest when you are tired or don't feel well.
- *Stress makes you feel pressured.* Think about how to take the urgency out of your life (see Chapter 2).
- *Stress tempts you to avoid difficulties or put off dealing with them, so that they do not get resolved.* Try to face them instead. It is often best to do your least favorite, or hardest task, first.
- *Stress reduces your efficiency.* Find out how you use your time—for example, by keeping a time log (see Chapter 2).

Butler, Gillian, Ph.D. and Tony Hope, M.D., *Managing Your Mind*. New York: Oxford University Press, 1995. Adapted with permission.

CHAPTER 10 Taking Care of Yourself

Look for Constructive Solutions. Constructive solutions to handling stress are those things that will give you short-term relief and long-term solutions. In the short run, you can relieve stress by getting away from the situation. If a relationship is causing you stress, go stay with a friend for a weekend. If too many responsibilities are the problem, a short vacation or a night out on the town can provide a sense of freedom—even if only temporary—that will help you put things in their proper perspective. Beware, however, of short-term solutions that can lead to further problems down the road. The use of alcohol, drugs, or caffeine may give temporary relief, but in the long run they are destructive. College students often seek other kinds of self-indulgent stress relief, such as increasing their level of social activity or sexual activity. This kind of temporary escape is very likely to lead to more problems and greater stress.

Long-term solutions may involve dealing with yourself and your ability to cope. When you are going through periods of change in your life, you confront problems and situations that you have not had to deal with before. Sometimes things seem overwhelming simply because of lack of experience. Most people still remember the pain of their first broken romance as though it was yesterday. A young person with a broken heart may feel that it will never be healed. Several broken romances later, they wonder how they ever got so worked up over a love affair. In future relationships they are more aware of warning signs, develop some coping mechanisms, and pretty soon have grown a coat of armor that protects them from being devastated by love. Hurt, yes, but not being able to get out of bed? Never again.

Practice Positive Thinking. Look at Figure 10-1 and describe the amount of liquid in the glass. Do you see it as being half-full or half-empty? This little test separates the **optimists** from the **pessimists**—the positive thinkers from the negative thinkers. The quality of your entire life can be improved if you can develop the habit of seeing the positive instead of the negative. If you are an habitual negative thinker, it is worth it to make a concerted effort to change your thinking. There are many excellent books and tapes available that can help you.

Positive thinking helps you accept that coping with problems, responsibilities, disappointments, setbacks, failures, and even tragedies is a natural part of life. As you grow older, the experience of living teaches you many of the skills you need to cope. This is called **maturity**. The fallacy, though, is that there is a "state of

ARE YOU A WORKAHOLIC?

No matter how ambitious you are, or how much you feel you have to do to uphold your responsibilities, becoming a workaholic is not a healthy response. A **workaholic** is someone who spends almost all of their time working or thinking about work. Workaholics "get high" off of losing themselves in their work, and are able to convince themselves over time that this is what they want. Often family relationships and friendships suffer, sometimes irrevocably. In addition, workaholics become one-dimensional and isolated. This can become a deterrent to the very success they are working so hard to achieve. Maintaining interests and friendships outside of work gives you a more balanced perspective on the direction you need to take to achieve your goals.

FIGURE 10-1 Half-full/half-empty Glass

PART THREE   Developing Your Personal Skills

maturity" that one reaches when one "grows up." This idea is in itself a cause of stress. It is the thing that we have been taught that makes us feel weak and causes us to beat up on ourselves when things go wrong. The fact is that very few people are mature in all areas of their lives. The majority of people are in a continuing state of learning, developing, and growing. As grown-ups, we find that just when we think we've got it all figured out, something new comes along and we are thrown off stride. The positive person sees this as reality and considers it the challenge of living life. The negative person sees this as reality and considers it a reason to stop trying. Teaching yourself to see life from the positive side, and learning to face your problems as new challenges to be met, is the best coping mechanism available to the human spirit.

> **QUOTE**
> I was going to buy a copy of *The Power of Positive Thinking*, and then I thought: What good would that do?
> —Ronnie Shaker

Talk to Yourself. Listen to things you say to yourself when you are under stress. The pressures and expectations you place on yourself cause internal stress that is heightened by **negative self-talk**. On the other hand, **positive self-talk** relieves stress, because it builds your self-confidence and makes you feel optimistic. In times of stress, it is often hard to see beyond the moment. In addition, the things you say to yourself may be based on attitudes that were formed over a period of time. If you find yourself anticipating that things are going to get worse, or feeling that you don't have any answers to help you overcome problems, give yourself a pep talk—even if you have trouble believing it at the moment. Remind yourself that no bad situation lasts forever, that you have come through similar difficult times or even worse ones, and simply say to yourself that things are going to get better. You will be surprised at how much more optimistic and hopeful you will feel after having a positive talk with yourself.

Following are some examples of self-talk that can contribute to feeling stressed, and some helpful alternatives that you might try.[1]

STRESSFUL THOUGHTS	THOUGHTS THAT RELIEVE STRESS
I have to get this done.	I will do as much as I can in the time I have.
I shouldn't ask for help.	Everyone asks for help sometimes. I would happily help someone else.
This is really important.	In five years this won't matter at all. When I'm on my deathbed, I won't be saying, "I wish I'd spent more time in the office."
I must do things well.	I can only do my best.
Others cope far better than I do.	Everyone is susceptible to stress. I am not alone in this.
There's nothing I can do.	I'll try solving the small problems first.
I'll crack up completely.	I need a break, so I'll take a break.
I can't let anyone see how I feel.	There's nothing to lose by talking to someone about my feelings.

Prolonged stress will ultimately affect your ability to function. If not alleviated, it can lead to serious depression or other medical problems. Being aware of your internal and external stressors, and developing strategies to deal with them, has to be an ongoing effort. A great part of this effort involves staying healthy and fit. Exercise helps burn off stress. Being fit makes you feel good about yourself—you feel strong and more in control when you are physically fit. Proper nutrition gives you the energy and good health you need to avoid being drained by the stresses of everyday life, as well as helping you fight off the physical effects of stress.

[1]Butler, Gillian, Ph.D., and Tony Hope, M.D., *Managing Your Mind*. New York: Oxford University Press, 1995.

CHAPTER 10   Taking Care of Yourself

Handling Stress

What are some of the things that are causing you stress at the present time? What coping mechanisms have you been using? Have you read about other strategies here that you plan to try? Make note of what you plan to do.

_____
_____
_____
_____
_____
_____
_____

Nutrition and Fitness

A healthy diet and a regular exercise program are essential to maintaining your physical and mental well being. Ironically, in the midst of the media's health and fitness blitz, surveys show growth in the number of Americans who are overweight and inactive. A large part of the problem goes back to the issue of time. Shopping and preparing balanced, nutritious meals, and exercising for 30 minutes to an hour a day just don't fit into most people's schedules. Another problem is habit. If you are in the habit of relaxing by eating snacks in front of the television, this may be one of life's pleasures that you don't want to give up.

> QUOTE
> There is no love sincerer than the love of food.
> —George Bernard Shaw

The answer involves some changes in attitude and deciding to take what is good for you and make it your own. Good nutrition does not have to mean going on a diet or never having a slab of barbecued ribs again. Exercise does not have to mean finding a way to fit an hour of sweaty torture into your already overextended schedule. Use the information available to find solutions that are right for you and that fit with how you need to live your life.

Healthy Eating

People who eat a healthy diet, maintain an appropriate weight, and still enjoy life are people who have recognized some or all of the following facts:

- No food is going to kill you, if you eat it in moderation. It is overindulgence that makes foods that are high in sugar and fat bad for you.
- "Going on a diet" does not work over the long haul. Giving up your favorite foods, drinking a gallon of water a day, and subsisting on 1000 calories will take pounds off quickly. This is a good alternative if you A) have to go to your high school reunion or B) suddenly win a free trip to the Caribbean. Under normal circumstances, dieting in this fashion will only put you in the yo-yo lifestyle. Once you let up on yourself and go back to eating what you want, there is a very good chance that you will end up weighing more than before the diet. "Sensible" diets that require that you temporarily limit yourself to certain foods in certain amounts will have the same result.
- Developing good eating habits and enjoying good foods does work, and it is not a contradiction of terms. Make a list of all the foods you like that are not fattening. Keep only those foods in the house. Treat yourself to "forbidden

fruit" when you go out to dinner, after you've "been good" all week, or when you are in a social situation such as a party. Once you develop this habit, you will be in control. You will know that you can eat those "bad" foods whenever you want and you will be able to make the choice *not* to eat them regularly.

A **balanced diet** is one that includes foods from the major food groups to balance out your intake of fiber and whole grains, vitamins, minerals, proteins, and carbohydrates. All of these nutrients are necessary to give your body the nutrition it needs so that it can maintain itself and produce the energy you need to function, as well as preventing disease and building up your immune system. As defined by the United States Department of Agriculture (USDA), which regulates the food industry, there are six major groups of food (see Figure 10-2). Note that some intake of all these food groups is necessary to maintain health, including some amount of fat. Sweets are probably the least healthy food on the pyramid. However, even sugar is a necessary nutrient. It is better to get your sugar naturally through fruits than to eat processed sugar.

Recent nutrition studies point to the benefits of not only cutting back on "bad" foods like fat and sugar, but that increasing your intake of "good" foods like fruits and vegetables builds up resistance to cancer and other diseases that are likely to occur in people as they age. These foods contain **antioxidants**, substances that inhibit the growth of disease in the body's cells.

The USDA guidelines are good to keep in mind as you select the foods you are going to eat throughout the day. It doesn't take that much discipline to eat a piece of fruit instead of a candy bar or to stop for a salad instead of a greasy hamburger. These are choices you make on a regular basis; the idea is to make the healthy choice eight or nine times out of ten. The reward is

EAT AND LOSE WEIGHT

Did you know that you can eat five times a day and not gain weight? In fact, if you eat three low-fat meals and two low-fat snacks, you are less likely to overeat because you will never get that empty-stomach, starved feeling. In order to maintain your ideal weight or to lose weight, you should eat no more than 20 to 25 grams of fat per day. Low-fat foods, especially fruits and vegetables, can be eaten as snacks and at meal times. This also helps keep your cholesterol level down, as well as providing the natural nutrients your body needs to fight the inception of diseases, like heart disease and cancer.

Fats, Oils & Sweets
Use sparingly
(only 200 calories total daily;
fats/oils, 140 or fewer daily)

Milk, Yogurt & Cheese
2 to 3 servings

Meat, Poultry, Fish, Dry Beans, Eggs & Nuts
1 to 3 servings

Vegetables
3 to 5 servings

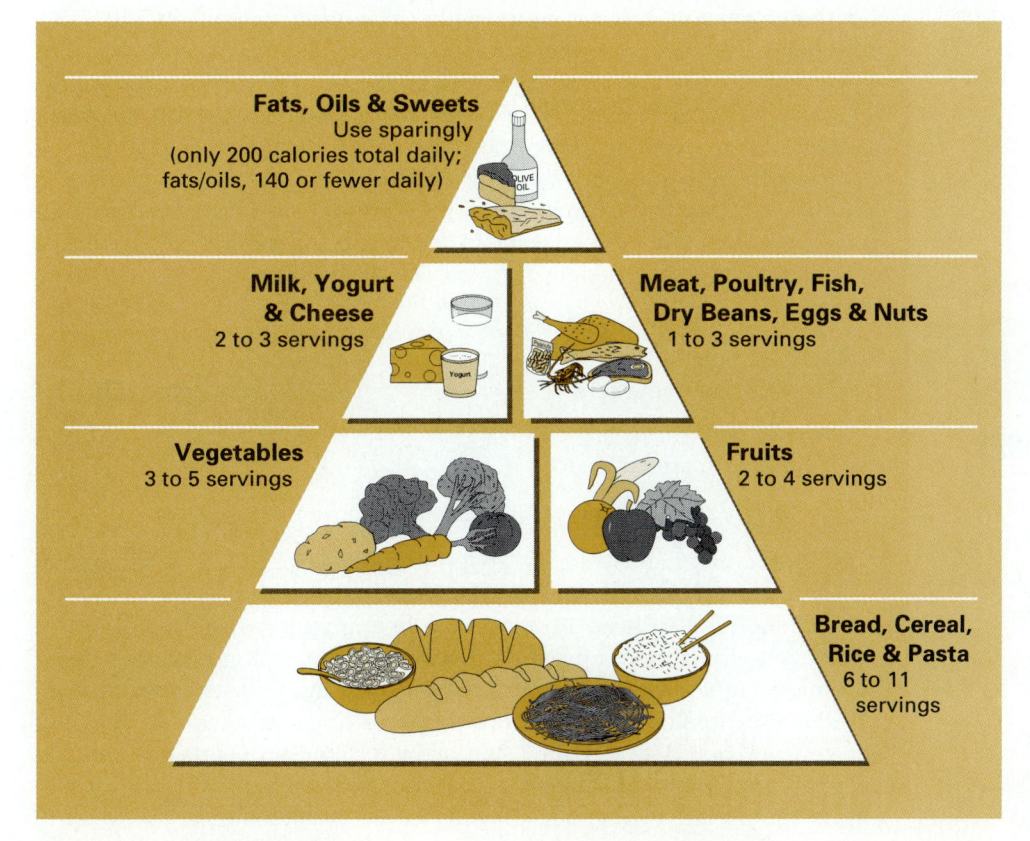

Fruits
2 to 4 servings

Bread, Cereal, Rice & Pasta
6 to 11 servings

FIGURE 10-2 USDA Food Pyramid

that you won't have to feel guilty when you do decide to have a piece of chocolate cake or a cheeseburger. When eating the wrong foods is no longer habit, the mind will quickly cease craving them, especially if you don't give it an ultimatum or a false promise of "never again."

Eating Habits

List the foods you eat for meals and snacks on a typical day. Compare your list to the chart in Figure 10-2. How would you rate your eating habits on a scale of 1 to 10? What do you plan to do to improve your eating habits?

_____

_____

_____

_____

_____

_____

CALORIE-BURNING SPORTS

Sport	Calories Burned per 20 Minutes of Activity
Karate, judo	300
Swimming	210
Racquetball	200
Squash	200
Handball	200
Water-skiing	180
Horseback riding	180
Rowing or canoeing	180
Roller or ice skating	180
Downhill skiing	180
Tennis	160
Volleyball	140
Frisbee	140
Golf	105

CALORIE-BURNING AEROBIC EXERCISES

Light weight training	315
Stair machine	260
Running	230
Jumping Rope	200
Low-impact aerobics	200
Nordic Track™ machine	165
Race walking	160
Jogging	145
Fast walking	110

Exercise and Fitness

Exercising regularly and keeping fit is a major factor in maintaining a proper diet. The two go hand-in-hand, both mentally and physically. When you exercise regularly, your metabolism speeds up, you burn fat, and therefore you can eat more without gaining weight. At the same time, being aware of keeping your body fit makes you more conscious of wanting to eat the right foods. Exercise requires effort, discipline, time, and physical energy. Who wants to make all that effort and then cancel it out by eating a whole chocolate cake?

You don't have to become a "fitness nut," but you do need to find a way to work regular exercise into your routine at least three to four times a week. Most people want to exercise. The problem is finding a form of exercise that is right for you. To accomplish this, you need to consider:

- what you enjoy doing
- what you have time to do
- what you are physically capable of doing
- what you can afford to do

Moderate expectations and knowing what is right for you—based on your temperament and your life style—are keys to a fitness program that you can sustain.

You should also keep in mind that, like anything else, boredom is a built-in factor in a fitness program. Eventually, you will get tired of doing the same routine. When you find yourself dreading your exercise routine, consider the possibility that it's not that you don't want to exercise, but that you are bored with your usual activity. Fitness experts recommend changing your physical activity at least four times a year. Walking or jogging in the spring; swimming, playing tennis, basketball, or volleyball in the summer; biking or hiking in the fall; and doing aerobics or weight training or both in the winter are some ideas for changing your mode of activity. Whatever you choose to do, just remember; when it comes to exercise, anything is better than nothing.

Body Image

Have you ever noticed that health and fitness magazines, videos, and TV programs feature hordes of young, beautifully-shaped celebrities, fitness experts, body builders, and body worshippers? No wonder so many people give up before they even begin. The fact is that the vast majority of people have never looked like that and *never will* look like that no matter what they do. Yet, the health and fitness industry continues to parade these images before us, and we continue to compare ourselves to them (and waste money on the products they sell). As a result, most Americans are dissatisfied with their weight and natural body shape—even those with "great bodies." The diet, fitness, and plastic surgery fields exist to help people, but they also make more money by playing on our lack of self-esteem and fantasies of being beautiful.

Trying to become something you are not can only lead to frustration and lower self-confidence. As you strive for a healthy lifestyle that includes proper nutrition, body weight, and exercise, remember that you have a natural body shape and weight that are right for you. Find out what these are and maintain them.

> **QUOTE**
> The waist is a terrible thing to mind.
> —Ziggy (Tom Wilson)

Fitness Plan

What kinds of exercise do you get in a typical week? How would you rate your exercise/fitness habits on a scale of 1 to 10? What do you plan to do to improve your level of fitness?

_____

_____

_____

CHAPTER 10   Taking Care of Yourself   203

NUTRITION AND FITNESS VOCABULARY

Aerobic exercise. A physical fitness activity that causes your pulse to reach 60 to 80 percent of its capacity and to stay there for twenty minutes or longer. Improves respiratory and circulatory functions.

Antioxidant. A substance contained in vitamins, particularly those naturally occurring in fruits and vegetables, that retards the deterioration of the body's healthy cells.

Calories. Units of chemical energy released to your body when food is digested. In order to sustain life, the body must consume a certain number of calories every day.

Carbohydrates. The sugar and starch found in foods, which provide the main source of energy to the body and the brain. Simple carbohydrates include foods high in refined (prepared sweets) and unrefined (fruits) sugar; complex carbohydrates include vegetables, grains, and fiber.

Cholesterol. A fat-like substance that has no calories; naturally produced by the body. It helps to form the sex and adrenal hormones, vitamin D, and bile. It is also a component of cell membranes and nerve linings and is found in the brain, liver, and blood. As cholesterol moves through the bloodstream, some of it becomes deposited on the walls of the arteries in the heart. Eventually one or more arteries can become too narrow or completely blocked, preventing the free flow of blood, which causes heart disease.

Endorphins. A group of proteins that occur naturally in the brain. Intense physical activity stimulates the production of endorphins, causing a natural feeling of euphoria (a feeling of well-being or elation).

Fat. A necessary part of the diet that serves internal body functions, such as protecting organs and absorbing calcium and vitamins.

Saturated. Fats that raise blood cholesterol level; mainly from animal products such as meat, milk, cheese, butter.

continued on next page

A Healthy Lifestyle

To focus fully on developing and maintaining positive health habits, you need to take stock of your lifestyle as a whole. Are there any unhealthy habits, addictions, or even occasional activities that you would be better off without? These may include overindulgence or abuse of alcohol, addiction to nicotine, abuse or dependence on prescription or illegal drugs, or sexual behavior that leaves you open to the risk of sexually transmitted diseases. This section will take a look at each of these potentially problematic areas from the point of view of how you can be in control, as opposed to allowing any aspect of your lifestyle to control you. Figure 10-3 shows how taking control of factors that influence your health can influence your body's resistance to serious diseases.

Quit Smoking

Smoking is both a habit and an addiction. An **addiction** is a compulsive need—one that cannot be controlled. A **habit** is a pattern of behavior that comes very close to being involuntary. Most smokers are surprised to find out that the addiction is easier to overcome than the habit. Physical addiction to nicotine can be cured in a short period of abstinence. The pleasurable habit of smoking, however, is harder to overcome.

Strong *associations* with the pleasure of smoking—behavior patterns like lighting up over a drink or with a cup of coffee after a meal, continue even when the pleasure has been replaced with a hacking cough and self-disgust. For a smoker, giving up cigarettes is like giving up a friend who was there to comfort you in moments of need. In order to quit smoking successfully, you need the resolve to end a very one-sided and destructive relationship. Kick the smoking habit, and the physical addiction will take care of itself.

There are many methods for giving up smoking and all of them work. Once you make up your mind to quit and really want to do it, you have won the hardest part of the battle. The next step is to find a strategy that will work well for you. Many people do quit "cold turkey." Others join groups, such as Smokers Anonymous, to have the support of fellow smokers and a set process to follow. Like other goals you want to accomplish, announcing it helps. Once the commitment is made out loud in front of others, you have more incentive to prove "you can do it." The support of others can also be a big help, particularly others who smoke, if they will avoid smoking around you and offering you cigarettes.

If you want to stop, but have been putting it off, recognize your excuses for not stopping, such as "I'm afraid I'll gain weight" or "As soon as exams are over." If you are saying these kinds of things, you have not yet made a decision that you really want to quit. Try keeping a "smoking log." Make a note of where you are and what you are doing each time you light a cigarette. After a few days, go over the list and see

PART THREE Developing Your Personal Skills

what triggers your smoking urge. Identify some situations and times of the day when you can cut back, even if it means changing your routine to avoid the triggering incident. An honest attempt to cut back can be a very legitimate first step to quitting. Another possibility is going on a "health kick." Devise a new diet and exercise routine and make a plan for getting yourself totally physically fit within a defined period of time. A focus on your overall health can lead to the natural desire to give up the unhealthy smoking habit.

If you are truly addicted, don't let the symptoms of physical withdrawal deter you. These will subside within days of cutting back or taking your last drag, and will be completely gone in a week or two, depending on how heavy a smoker you are. Withdrawal symptoms include:

- irritability
- headaches
- dizziness
- nausea
- skin tingling
- feeling jittery

Do not be frightened by these symptoms or use them as an excuse to smoke. Instead, think of how good you will feel when they subside and how, by not smoking, you will never have to go through this experience again. Don't try to force yourself not to eat. If you need to put something in your mouth, go ahead and do it. Any slight weight gain can be dealt with once you have conquered your immediate goal. If you are severely addicted, consult your physician about a **nicotine patch**. The patch will introduce a small amount of nicotine into your blood stream to relieve the withdrawal and help you avoid the urge to smoke. Under no circumstances should you smoke when wearing a nicotine patch. Doing so can have severe medical consequences.

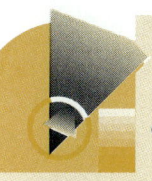

> **NUTRITION AND FITNESS VOCABULARY**
> *continued from previous page*
>
> **Unsaturated.** Fatty acids that are liquid in form and are derived from nuts, seeds, and vegetables. They do not raise blood cholesterol level, but do contribute to weight gain.
>
> **Intensity.** The degree of difficulty of an aerobic exercise program. When out of shape, begin with a low-intensity program.
>
> **Overweight.** Weight that is more than five pounds above the ideal range for your height and bone structure.
>
> **Protein.** An essential element in the production of the body's hormones; builds tissue to build and repair muscles, bones, hair, fingernails, skin, ligaments, blood immune cells, and internal organs. Available in fish, poultry, beef, egg whites, yogurt, and legumes such as lentils, split peas, or beans.

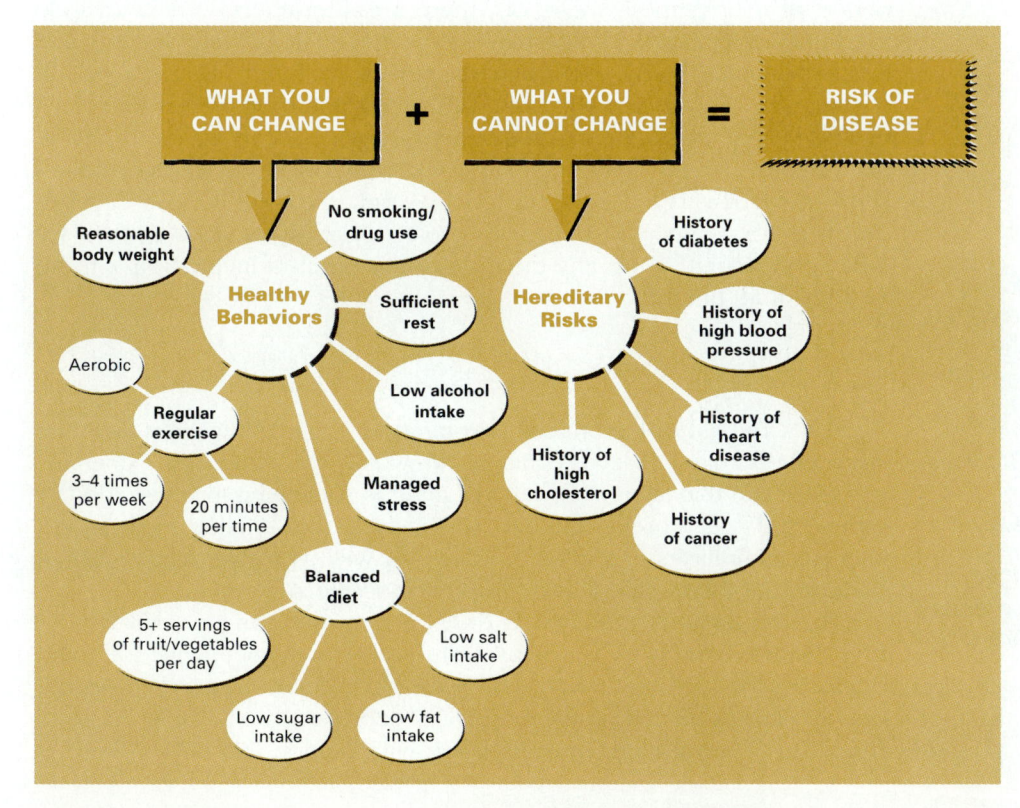

FIGURE 10-3

WHAT YOU CAN CHANGE + WHAT YOU CANNOT CHANGE = RISK OF DISEASE

Healthy Behaviors: Reasonable body weight, No smoking/drug use, Sufficient rest, Low alcohol intake, Managed stress, Balanced diet (5+ servings of fruit/vegetables per day, Low sugar intake, Low fat intake, Low salt intake), Regular exercise (Aerobic, 3–4 times per week, 20 minutes per time)

Hereditary Risks: History of diabetes, History of high blood pressure, History of heart disease, History of high cholesterol, History of cancer

CHAPTER 10 Taking Care of Yourself

TEN REASONS TO QUIT SMOKING

1. It causes serious health problems, including cancer, stroke, heart disease, chronic bronchitis, and emphysema.
2. In the home it exposes others, including children and non-smokers, to the same risks the smoker is willingly taking.
3. It smells bad, not only on your breath, but in your hair, on your clothes, in your car, and in your home. This can cause social problems, as most non-smokers are repelled, not just by inhaling smoke, but also by smelling it.
4. Smoking is no longer "glamorous" or even socially acceptable. The older you get, the more you will find this to be true within your peer group.
5. Many work sites are non-smoking areas. If you need to smoke on the job, you will be forced to go outside to smoke—rain or shine.
6. Smokers tend to have poorer general health habits when it comes to proper nutrition and exercise, which makes them generally less healthy.
7. Cigarettes are expensive.
8. Smoking causes premature wrinkling of the skin.
9. Smoking dulls the tastebuds.
10. Because of the self-destructive nature of the smoking habit, many smokers suffer from guilt, anxiety, and even self-loathing. Some become "closet" smokers—hiding their habit from others.

One more reason for men:

11. Male smokers are at risk of losing their sexual potency. Because erections are caused by blood engorging the penis, and because smoking constricts blood vessels, a high percentage of males who smoke are in danger of eventually becoming impotent. Students at the Boston University School of Medicine and University Hospital showed that men who smoked a pack a day for 20 years were 72 percent more likely to develop a blockage of the larger penile artery than were non-smokers.

One last word—never stop trying. If you don't succeed the first time you try to quit, try again. Relapses are common, just as with many other habits. Each time you try to stop and each time you find new strategies, you are getting closer to accomplishing your goal and, eventually, you will achieve it.

Avoiding Problems with Alcohol

If you are one of those people who avoid alcohol completely for personal, health, or religious reasons, you are in the minority. The fact is, most Americans do use alcohol, and most use it moderately and in appropriate situations. As long as you are in one of these categories you have nothing to worry about. There is, however, sometimes a fine line between use and abuse of alcohol. **Abuse** is the improper or excessive use of alcohol or any other potentially harmful substance. You could say the pleasures of alcohol—the taste, the feeling, the mood, the occasion—are fine, so long as you are in complete control of when, where, and how much of the substance you consume. The minute you lose control of any of these factors, such as stopping with a friend for two beers and drinking six, you have turned your use of alcohol into an abuse. If you do this on a continual basis, you could be described as having a drinking problem.

Like cigarette smoking, heavy drinking has health consequences. Some of these include liver damage, pancreatitis, high blood pressure, diabetes, heart failure, ulcers, and injury from accidents. These problems are most commonly seen in people suffering from chronic alcohol abuse. Usually before these serious health problems set in, however, heavy drinkers are subject to all kinds of problems that alcohol abuse brings into their daily lives. One reason for this is that alcohol does not only affect behavior when the actual drinking is taking place. While drinking, a person may behave obnoxiously, abusively, self-destructively, or simply stupidly. But the problem doesn't end there. When the period of drunkenness wears off, there are after-effects. These include the familiar hangover symptoms—headache, nausea, dehydration, listlessness—which pretty much leave a person dysfunctional for a period of time. After-effects are what often cause people to lose their jobs, hurt themselves or others, or start the drinking cycle all over again to relieve the pain. Eventually out-of-control drinking becomes an endless downward spiral. This is true for people who drink excessively every day, but also true for those who binge drink on weekends or during other so-called "off hours." Thus, any drinking to the point of inebriation is to be avoided at all times.

Avoiding Other Harmful Drugs

Cigarettes and alcohol are the most commonly abused drugs, but there are many others that can have equal or far worse consequences. Generally, any substance that alters your state of mind is something to be avoided or approached with extreme caution. This includes prescription medications, such as tranquilizers and amphetamines, as well as illegal drugs, such as marijuana, or the so-called hard drugs like cocaine and heroin.

The danger with prescription drugs is that they can be addictive. As with cigarettes, the body develops a physical dependency while the mind develops a need for the feelings brought on by the drug. Sometimes, when people have accidents or serious mental problems such as depression and anxiety, doctors prescribe drugs. These medications must be taken with caution and only as long as

Question Your Drinking Behavior

1. Do you "need" a drink when you feel stressed out, depressed, or lonely?
2. Are you unaware of how many drinks you can take without losing your self control?
3. Are you unable to refuse a drink, even when you're past your limit?
4. Do you drink on a regular basis, or at a regular time each day, out of habit?
5. Do you drink when you are by yourself or at night to help you sleep better?
6. Do you feel that it is okay to "get drunk" as long as you don't hurt anyone else?
7. Do you feel uncomfortable in certain situations, such as at parties, if you can't have a few drinks?

If you answered "Yes" to one or more of these questions, you need to assess your drinking behavior and make adjustments to avoid becoming a problem drinker.

absolutely necessary. Often, it is up to the patient to question whether prolonged use of the drug is justified. Many doctors will "help you" by prescribing drugs as long as you continue to ask for them.

Illegal drugs pose even greater health risks, along with grave legal consequences. Many people are tempted to try illegal drugs when they are offered them by peers at a party or some other social situation. The cost of even trying some drugs once can be too high. People have been known to have heart attacks, strokes, or seizures from smoking crack or sniffing cocaine; methamphetamines and hallucinogenic drugs like LSD have been known to cause psychotic breakdowns and violent behavior. In addition, even a one-time or infrequent use of a drug may have other negative consequences due to a lowering of your inhibitions. People are more likely to have unprotected sex or do other things that are against their self-interest when they are high on drugs.

Drugs have a powerful affect on your body. They upset the balance of chemicals in your brain and other organs. Each drug has its own signature in the way it affects the body. It also breaks down in a unique way, which allows scientists to detect the by-products of each drug in the blood or urine. This means that if a person takes a drug, within a certain time period, it can be detected by special tests of the blood or urine. Many companies screen for drug use when they hire new employees. Jobs that involve a high level of focus and concentration and responsibility for the well-being of others may require employees to submit to random drug testing during the course of their employment.

Dealing with Drug Abuse

Whether or not you ever abuse drugs, you may have someone close to you who is involved with drugs. Unfortunately today, children may be exposed to drugs at a young age in school or in their neighborhood. Giving in to the temptation to experiment or being attracted to the idea of drug use can happen to any young person from any neighborhood, economic status, or any type of family.

Parents are especially vulnerable to denial when it comes to their own children being involved in drugs. It is natural for parents to feel

> **QUOTE**
> Dreams only have a chance to live if fed the right things.
> —Grant Hill

THE POWER OF DRUGS

Different types of drugs have different effects. Understanding how drugs work will make you more aware of the power of their consequences.

Sedatives. Drugs that make you feel sleepy and less inhibited. These include alcohol, barbiturates, quaaludes and valium, and other drugs known as **tranquilizers.**

Stimulants. Drugs that make you feel more alert, energetic, and confident. These include cigarettes, caffeine, amphetamines, and cocaine.

Narcotics. Drugs that ease pain and make you feel euphoric, such as heroin, morphine, codeine, and opium.

Hallucinogens. Drugs that distort perception and provoke hallucinations and delusions, such as marijuana, LSD, methamphetamines, and PCP.

POSITIVE ALTERNATIVES

If you are using drugs or are tempted to use drugs, stop to consider the reason why. Is it peer pressure? Do you have some serious personal problems in your life that you are trying to escape? No matter what the reason, take the time to consider some positive alternatives:

- Learn how to get "high" naturally. Finding a sport that you enjoy, spending time outdoors and taking in the beauty of nature, listening to music, reading inspirational books or listening to tapes, meditating, or talking to a confidante are just some examples of ways to alleviate the pressures of problems and find peace of mind.
- Increase your energy level by eating nutritious foods, exercising, getting enough sleep, and managing your time so that you do not have to rely on stimulants to keep you going.
- Increase your confidence and self-esteem by setting realistic goals for yourself and developing your skills in areas that play to your strengths. Develop relationships with positive people and learn to practice positive thinking. Allowing yourself to experience success rather than giving in to self-destructive behavior will, over time, help you to leave past negative experiences behind you and concentrate on moving forward.

responsible for anything their children do that is wrong or harmful to themselves or others. Due to feelings of guilt and helplessness, parents will often go along with a child's denial of drug use, despite clear signs that the child is not telling the truth.

If you are a parent, or if you have a family member or friend whom you know or suspect of using drugs, reach out to organizations that specialize in helping people deal with substance abuse problems. Some of the signs of drug use include:

- withdrawal from family members and social situations
- dropping "straight" friends and taking up with "the wrong crowd"
- mood swings or changes in personality
- falling grades or work performance
- loss of interest in eating
- change in sleeping habits
- change in telephone habits, such as wanting a private line or using a pager
- change in money situation (suddenly having more or less)

A Safe Sex Life

Sex is extremely personal. Sex is also a public health issue. This may sound like a contradiction, but it is not. Society has a vested interest in controlling the spread of AIDS and other sexually transmitted diseases (STDs). Whether it is our tax dollars that are being spent on healthcare costs, our risk of contracting disease, our fear that someone in our family will suffer, or generalized fear of an epidemic we do not understand, the fact is that how you conduct your personal sex life is now a matter of concern to everyone. But, most of all, it should be of concern to you. If each and every person practices safe sex each and every time they have sex, the threat of AIDS and other STDs will be eliminated. Unprotected sex between two disease-free people in a monogamous relationship is really the only exception to practicing safe sex.

Practicing Safe Sex. If you are sexually active, you can maintain your sexual health and still enjoy sex through simple preventive measures. Have sex only with a partner who is not infected, who has sex only with you, and who does not shoot drugs or share needles and syringes. Keep in mind thatit is difficult to know these things about another person.

Always use a latex condom for any kind of sex, because it is possible you won't know if your partner is infected. Know how to correctly use condoms to ensure safety. The reservoir end of a condom should always be pinched closed as the condom is put on and unrolled, because if air becomes trapped in the reservoir, it could increase the chances of rupturing the condom due to additional pressure against the inside wall of the latex.

Latex condoms can help lower your risk of HIV infection during sex, as well as your risk of contracting other STDs. Latex condoms act as an effective barrier to diseases, but condoms are not foolproof. They don't completely eliminate the risk of becoming infected because they can break, tear, or slip off. They must be put on before any genital contact. And they must be used the right way—from start to finish—a new condom every time. Birth control pills and diaphragms will not protect you or your partner from HIV or other STDs.

Whether you have sex and whether you use condoms are decisions you can make over and over again. You can choose not to have sex, even if you have had

PART THREE   Developing Your Personal Skills

sex in the past. You can choose to use condoms even if you have not used condoms before. Make decisions about sex that are good for you and for your partner.

Review and Recall

1. Define the following terms:

   a. external stressors: _____

   _____

   b. internal stressors: _____

   _____

   c. coping mechanisms: _____

   _____

2. List five physical symptoms and five emotional symptoms of severe reaction to stress.

   a. _____ f. _____

   b. _____ g. _____

   c. _____ h. _____

   d. _____ i. _____

   e. _____ j. _____

3. Describe four coping mechanisms that can help reduce stress.

   a. _____

   b. _____

   c. _____

   d. _____

4. How can positive self-talk help you cope with stress? _____

   _____

   _____

   _____

5. List the six basic food groups as defined by the United States Department of Agriculture.

   a. _____

   b. _____

   c. _____

   d. _____

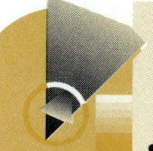

WHAT YOU SHOULD KNOW ABOUT AIDS AND AIDS PREVENTION

- About one million people in the United States are currently infected with HIV, the virus that causes AIDS. Most are between the ages of 25 and 49 and appear healthy today.

- It may take up to ten years for people who are infected with HIV to develop AIDS. They may look and feel healthy for years after becoming infected. They may not know they are infected. Even if they don't look or feel sick they can infect others.

- The most common ways in which HIV is spread are:

  Having sex with someone who is infected with HIV.

  Sharing needles or syringes with someone who is infected with HIV.

  Transmission from an infected mother to her baby during pregnancy or childbirth, or, rarely, through breast feeding.

- Unlike many other viruses, HIV is not spread through the air or water. HIV is not spread through everyday casual contact. You cannot get HIV from:

  Coughs or sneezes

  Sweat or tears

  Eating food prepared by someone with HIV

  Handshakes

  Hugs

  Mosquitoes or other insects

  Pets

  Being around an infected person

  Or from using:

  Swimming pools

  Toilet seats

  Phones or computers

  Straws, spoons, or cups

  Drinking fountains

- The chances of getting HIV from a blood transfusion in the United States are now very low. Since 1985 all donated blood is tested for antibodies to HIV. The tests are over 99 percent accurate.

- You cannot get HIV from giving blood. In the United States, every piece of equipment used to draw blood is brand new. It is used only once, then destroyed.

continued on next page

CHAPTER 10   Taking Care of Yourself

WHAT YOU SHOULD KNOW ABOUT AIDS AND AIDS PREVENTION

continued from previous page

- If you wish to be tested for HIV, you can take a blood test and get counseling both before and after being tested. Current blood tests are over 99 percent accurate. It usually takes a few weeks to a few months after infection for HIV to be detected in a blood test.
- There is no vaccine for HIV or cure for AIDS. Medicines that are now available help to treat the symptoms of AIDS patients and allow them to live more comfortably. None of these medicines can keep a person from becoming infected with HIV. None of the treatments can cure AIDS. But people can prevent HIV infection by learning the facts and acting on them.

[Source: The information in this section is based on information published by the American Red Cross.]

ORGANIZATIONS TO CONTACT FOR INFORMATION OR HELP

Alcoholics Anonymous
World Services, Inc.
P.O. Box 459
Grand Central Station
New York, NY 10163

Narcotics Anonymous World Service Office
16155 Wyandotte Street
Van Nuys, CA 91406

National Sexually Transmitted Disease Hotline
1-800-227-8922

National Institute on Drug Abuse Hotline
1-800-729-4357

Nicotine Anonymous
P.O. Box 1468
Baldwin, NY 11510

National Council on Alcoholism and Drug Dependence
12 West 21 Street
New York, NY 10010
212-206-6770

Planned Parenthood Federation of America
810 Seventh Avenue
New York, NY 10019
212-541-7800

e. _____
f. _____

6. Define the following terms:
   a. calories: _____
   b. carbohydrates: _____
   c. saturated fat: _____
   d. unsaturated fat: _____

7. Define the following terms as they relate to the use of tobacco, alcohol, and drugs:
   a. habit: _____
   b. addiction: _____
   c. abuse: _____

8. List five behavior signs that could indicate use or abuse of drugs.
   a. _____
   b. _____
   c. _____
   d. _____
   e. _____

9. Why is it dangerous to experiment with drugs, even on a "one-time" basis?
   _____
   _____

10. Why is sexual behavior no longer just a personal concern? _____
    _____
    _____

Apply Critical Thinking

Analyze each aspect of your lifestyle that has been discussed in this chapter: handling stress; nutrition habits; tobacco, alcohol, and drug use; and sexuality. Make a list in two columns: on the left side note the things you are handling well in each area and on the left side note things you would like to improve. For example "eat three meals a day"; "need to eat more fresh fruit and vegetables." Save these notes to use later for developing a set of written goals and timeframes for creating a healthier lifestyle.

School to Work Applications

SCANS

SYSTEMS: *MONITORS AND CORRECTS PERFORMANCE*

1. Select one or two of the following areas that you need to work on: Coping with Stress, Nutrition, Fitness, Smoking, Alcohol Use or Abuse, Drug Use or Abuse, Sexual Safety. Develop a plan for improving your health, avoiding a serious problem, or overcoming a problem that has already developed. Your plan may include using ideas in this chapter, getting help from a campus source for counseling or health care, getting help from an outside organization, or doing further research for information that will help you.

   Write out your plan in stages and assign timeframes to each stage. Then, develop a system for monitoring your progress. Consider keeping a diary, using your daily or weekly calendar, using a computer program to log or chart your progress, or any method that works for you and that you are motivated to pay attention to. If you feel that involving someone else in your plan or your monitoring system will help, by all means do so. Whenever you fail to meet goals you have set, develop a supplemental plan for monitoring your progress.

INTERPERSONAL: *PARTICIPATES AS A MEMBER OF A TEAM*

2. The problems of alcohol and drug abuse and sexually transmitted disease have contributed to many of the external stressors that affect our lives or our neighbors' lives. These include street crime, burglaries, neighborhood violence, family members and children at risk, and many others. Form a small group to discuss the impact of these problems on your school and community. Each person should contribute ideas about how students and individuals can get involved in helping to educate young people and improve conditions in relation to these problems. Make a decision as to something your group can do. It might be something ongoing, like a project or helping an organization, or something short-term, such as writing to your state or Congressional representatives. Select a group leader or leaders to follow up on putting your plan into action.

Workplace Application

SCANS

Employees who have alcohol and drug abuse problems cost employers millions of dollars each year. Whether it is subjecting employees to drug testing, paying for work-related problems caused by employees who abuse drugs and alcohol, firing and retraining, or implementing treatment programs, the cost to business is enormous. Do some research on one of these aspects of the problem of addiction in the workplace. You may look up information on computer databases, read articles, contact companies and interview personnel who handle these problems, or use all of these methods. Prepare a five-minute presentation to the class on a particular aspect of this problem or a particularly dramatic story that you uncover in your research.

If your instructor agrees, you may wish to work with a partner and prepare a ten-minute presentation on two compatible aspects of the problem.

Personal Progress Application

SCANS

PERSONAL QUALITIES: *DISPLAYS RESPONSIBILITY, SELF-ESTEEM, SOCIABILITY, SELF-MANAGEMENT, AND INTEGRITY AND HONESTY*

Your ability to function effectively depends on your state of health. Your mental functions depend upon the physiological processes that occur inside your brain. There is an exercise you can do to improve your health and your mental functioning and give you a wonderful sense of well-being at the same time.

CHAPTER 10 Taking Care of Yourself

The Oxygen High

Stand up (did you know your brain receives 10% more oxygen when you stand and that oxygen is one of the "fuels" of your brain?). Without moving your shoulders, take in as deep a breath as possible through your nose by allowing your stomach to expand so you can take air in all the way down to the bottom of your lungs. Fill up your lungs completely with air until you think you can't get any more air in, then hold the breath in for a second until you've relaxed a bit. Next, try to suck in through your nose one or two more tiny short breaths until you feel as though your lungs are completely expanded. Now just hold the breath for several seconds.

During this time you will be oxygenating your blood; that is, you'll be sending extra oxygen to the platelets in your bloodstream. Those red blood cells will speed the oxygen throughout your body.

Before holding your breath becomes uncomfortable, let it all out through your mouth with a "whoosh," then return to breathing normally. You'll feel a wonderful sensation wash over your body, the "sense of well-being" feeling that some people describe as a "warm fuzzy."

The sensation is simply your body's physiological response to oxygen intake. Taking such a deep breath two or three times a day is good for your body, and it carries the added benefit of making you feel wonderful, all without chemicals or the need for extensive practice.

A caution: don't do this to the point of dizziness. If the process described above does create dizziness or any other unpleasant sensation, you should check with your doctor, because a deep breath is not something that causes difficulty for healthy individuals.

ELEVEN

Managing Your Financial Resources

CHAPTER OUTLINE

Financing Your Education
   Employment
   Federal and State Loans and Grants
   Scholarships and Other Sources
Budgeting
   Identify Your Spending Habits
   Developing a Budget
Maintaining Your Financial Health
   Deal with Deficits
   Use Credit Wisely
   Beware of Cash Machines
   Pay Bills on Time
   Use Financial Services
   Read the Fine Print
   Solve Financial Problems

The abundance you desire to experience must first be an experience in your mind.
—Ernest Holmes

When you hear the words "financial security" what do you think of? For most people, this is a goal, an ideal to be achieved, in order to have a good life that is free of financial worries. Insurance companies are great at showing us how these needs affect us as they attempt to sell their products. They know feeling secure is something that hits home for everyone. For those who are not born with wealth, and whose financial life is tied to earnings from their work, achieving a satisfactory level of financial security is an individual journey. Planning, budgeting, spending, saving, investing, and managing are all aspects of a sound financial life. The degree of skill with which you are able to carry out these functions will determine your ability to achieve your personal vision of financial security.

Financial resources for the cost of your education, managing your current income or living expenses, and planning for your future are some of the financial issues that are of particular significance to you now. This chapter will explore these issues and offer ideas to help you control your financial resources.

Financing Your Education

Having already enrolled in an educational program, you have in one way or another come to terms with the financing of it, at least for the short-term. Since you are at the beginning of a long-term commitment, now is a good time to ensure that you have a solid plan that will see you through. Lack of financial resources is one of the main reasons that students drop out of college or drop in and out, taking years to complete a so-called two-year or four-year program. To make sure this doesn't happen to you, make sure you explore all the financial resources that are available to you and develop a strategy that meets your needs.

Your educational expenses include tuition, books, fees and other materials, transportation, food, housing, and clothing. This can add up to a huge expenditure and one that is unaffordable without assistance. Consider the possibilities that exist for meeting these needs; be creative in coming up with solutions that will get you the resources you need.

Employment

If you are a full-time employee, or if you plan to get a full-time job before finishing school, you may be able to take advantage of a company or labor union tuition-assistance program for employees. Some of these programs pay full or partial cost of tuition for job-related courses; others offer some reimbursement for general education programs. Companies may also offer tuition assistance or scholarships to family members of employees.

For a limited amount of financial assistance, a part-time job is an option. This must be weighed in terms of how much income it can actually generate and the extent to which it will interfere with class time, study time, and other responsibilities. If you do decide to work part-time, a job that is related to your career goals will probably be less trying than one that you take solely for the money. Working for a temporary agency is also an option to explore. Most agencies give you the option of going on a job or not when they call you, allowing you more control over your time.

> **QUOTE**
> If you think education is expensive, try ignorance.
> —Derek Bok

Another option to explore is to work for yourself instead of joining an organization. This will give you greater scheduling flexibility and could turn out to be less stressful and even more lucrative. If you think you don't have any skills you could sell on your own, you can get ideas from publications such as *Entrepreneur* and *Inc.* magazines. Also, check your local newspaper for forums, seminars, and expos on starting home-based businesses and other entrepreneurial ventures.

Federal and State Loans and Grants

Make sure you get the latest information on federal and state government financial aid programs. For information on state programs, contact your state's higher education agency, located in your state capital. For information on federal programs, contact the Federal Student Aid Information Center, P.O. Box 84, Washington, DC 20044-0084. Your school's financial aid office can provide you with detailed information on these programs and how to apply for them. Before applying for a loan, exhaust all possibilities for aid that does not have to be paid back. If you decide to apply for a loan, make sure you understand the terms and conditions of the repayment.

Grants. Grants, unlike loans, do not have to be repaid. The federal government has two programs: the Pell Grant Program, and the Federal Supplemental Educational Opportunity Grant (FSEOG). Both programs are granted on the basis of financial need. To qualify for the FSEOG program, students must have exceptional financial need. Funds for this program are available on a more limited basis than funds for Pell Grants.

These grants are only awarded to undergraduate students who have not earned a bachelor's or professional degree. Qualifications are determined by the U.S. Department of Education, which uses a standard formula, established by Congress, to evaluate the information you report when you apply. The amount of funding allocated to the grant program varies from year to year. How much you get is based on a formula that deducts the expected contribution of you and your family from your cost of attendance to determine your financial need. There may be other requirements, such as full-time attendance for a full academic year.

Loans. Low-interest federal loans are available through the Direct Loan Program, which makes loans directly to students and parents through schools. There is also a Federal Family Education Loan program that makes loans through private lenders such as banks, credit unions, and savings and loan associations. Both of these programs award subsidized loans on the basis of need, for which the federal government pays the interest, or straightforward loans, for which the borrower pays the interest.

There are also Federal Perkins loans available for both undergraduate and graduate students with exceptional financial need. These loans are made through a school's financial aid office at a very low rate of interest.

Work-Study. The Federal Work-Study Program provides jobs for undergraduate and graduate students with financial need. The program encourages community service work, and work related to your course of study. The program includes jobs both on and off campus. Students are limited to working a set number of hours per week.

National and Community Service. This program was begun during the Clinton Administration and has been open to potential disbandment because of cutbacks in the federal budget. The program provides full-time educational awards of several thousand dollars. You can work before, during, or after your postsecondary education, and you can use the funds either to pay current educational expenses or to repay federal student loans. Information on this program is available from: The Corporation for National and Community Service, 1100 Vermont Avenue, N.W., Washington, DC 20525.

Scholarships and Other Sources

Scholarships are awards based on academic achievement and other criteria, such as school activities and civic involvement. A scholarship may or may not be based on financial need. Some cover full or partial tuition only; others cover expenses as well. Most schools offer scholarship programs for qualified students. There are also many state and privately sponsored scholarships. Private foundations, religious organizations, fraternities, sororities, and organizations such as the United Negro College Fund, Elks, Kiwanis, Links, and YMCA offer educational assistance programs. Also, check out information from organizations connected with your field of interest, particularly those associated with professional degree programs. If you (or your spouse) are a veteran or the dependent of a veteran, check with your local Veterans' Affairs office to find out what benefits may be available to you. Check your local library for additional information on scholarships and other non-public educational assistance.

Another possible source of assistance is loans or gifts from relatives. Whether these are large or small, they can help defray expenses as well as giving you moral support in knowing that family members have confidence in you.

DEPENDENCY STATUS

When you apply for federal student aid, your answers to certain questions will determine whether you're considered dependent on your parent(s) (and must, therefore, report their income and assets as well as your own) or whether you're independent (and must, therefore, report only your own income and assets—and those of your spouse, if you're married).

Students are classified as dependent or independent because federal student aid programs are based on the idea that students (and their parents or spouse, if applicable) have the primary responsibility of paying for their postsecondary education. Students who have access to parental support (dependent students), should not receive need-based federal funds at the expense of independent students who do not have such access.

You're an independent student if at least one of the following applies to you:

- you were born before January 1, 1972
- you're married
- you're enrolled in a graduate or professional educational program
- you have legal dependents other than a spouse
- you're an orphan or ward of the court (or were a ward of the court until age 18)
- you're a veteran of the U.S. Armed Forces

CHAPTER 11   Managing Your Financial Resources

Financial Planning

What are your plans for financing your education? How effective will they be in seeing you through to completion of your goals? Make a list of the financial sources you plan to use and the percentage of your expenses that can be covered by each one. Are there any holes in your plan? If so, make notes on what additional research and planning you need to do.

_____
_____
_____
_____
_____
_____
_____
_____
_____

DEADLINES

When you are planning to apply for any type of financial aid, make sure you find out the deadline for submitting your application. Schools often set deadlines early in the calendar year. Students must meet these deadlines to receive certain types of funds, including FSEOG, Work-Study, and Perkins Loan program funds. For sources that do not require you to meet a deadline, you still need to submit your application far enough in advance for it to be processed before the start of the term.

Some sources take applications electronically as well as by mail, so check to see if using your computer can help speed up the process.

Budgeting

One advantage of applying for financial assistance is that it forces you to itemize your expenses and determine your exact financial needs. But, no matter how you are financing your education, once you determine how much money you have available each term, you need to develop a monthly budget and a process for monitoring your income and expenditures. This chapter has a worksheet for your use in developing your budget. However, it is important to bear in mind that keeping within your budget depends on how you *manage* your resources, not how carefully you record your income and expenses. No matter how good you are at record keeping, if your expenditures column exceeds your income column, you will have financial problems.

Identifying Your Spending Habits

An honest assessment of your attitudes toward money and your spending habits will help you identify any changes you need to make in order to live within your budget. Knowing where your money is going will lead you to make wiser spending decisions. You can decrease your expenses and stick to a budget after identifying buying habits that can be changed. The following section discusses some of the factors you should consider as you analyze your spending habits.

Spending Log

For one or two weeks keep a record in your notebook of everything you spend money on. Write down the amounts or keep receipts. Compile a list of all of your expenditures and their amounts; then go through the list and label them necessities, extras, or emergencies.

PART THREE   Developing Your Personal Skills

Habitual Shopping and Impulse Buying. We live in a consumer society where shopping and buying is considered a worthy way to pass the time and owning things is a symbol of success. We enjoy hanging out at the mall or walking the streets and "window shopping." However, there is a problem with shopping as a leisure-time activity. It leads to unplanned spending or what is called **impulse buying**. When you see a sign that says "sale" or notice something that you have been wanting for a long time, it is easy to lose your will power. Before you know it, you are convinced that you've uncovered a bargain you simply can't pass up. Habitual shoppers and impulse buyers are able to rationalize these purchases by telling themselves that the item will be gone next time, or even convincing themselves that they are saving money because they bought something on sale.

When you are trying to save money and live within a budget, it is wise to give up shopping except for those occasions when you are going to make a planned and budgeted purchase. Even when you look without buying, you risk making yourself unhappy by being reminded that you cannot afford some things you want. Too much of this feeling of being denied may backfire—you may begin to feel sorry for yourself and convince yourself that you should buy something you can't afford because, after all, "you deserve it."

Buying for Occasions. One of the ways that unplanned "extras" creep into a budget is through those special occasions that somehow must be acknowledged or celebrated. Decreasing or avoiding these kinds of expenditures can be especially difficult because they usually involve other people. Out of sensitivity to their feelings or your own sense of pride, you feel you must purchase a nice birthday gift, attend an expensive event, or chip in for a friend's birthday party. Holidays that involve gifts can be especially difficult in this regard. Pride can be a big factor here, particularly if you had more money or were able to spend more freely in the past. When faced with this situation, remind yourself that it is temporary. You can choose either to explain your situation to those who expect your generosity, or you can let your new-found frugality speak for itself. However you choose to go about it, don't allow customs and expectations to dictate your budget. Once you face up to making adjustments, it gets easier and may even become a way of life.

> Work is an essential part of being alive. Your work is your identity. It tells you who you are. It's gotten so abstract. People don't work for the sake of working. They're working for a car, a new house, or a vacation. It's not the work itself that's important to them. There's such a joy in doing work well.
>
> —Kay Stephen, Baker

Buying to Support Habits, Hobbies, and Other Indulgences.
You've probably heard about people like the woman who lost her job, but simply can't live without her weekly hairdo, massage, and manicure, or the person who used his last savings to buy a baseball card to add to his collection. Sometimes it is asking too much to get *all* of life's priorities straightened out. But that doesn't mean it's not worth trying. What are your expensive weaknesses? What do you use as life's little reward to yourself when you've had a hard day or a hard week? Do you have a hobby that burns a hole in your pocket? Do you smoke or hang out at the bar with friends? If so, consider what you could save or how you could put the money for this expense to better use.

Waste. Where can you cut down on waste? Do you buy fancy takeout food or expensive packaged food because there's no time to cook? Do you make lengthy long distance telephone calls? Do you belong to a gym, but never have time to go? Do you have magazine subscriptions for magazines you never have time to read? Do you own items, such as appliances, stereo equipment, exercise machines, or furniture that you don't need or don't use? How about clothing? Do you have good clothes that you never wear? Conduct an inventory and determine how you can make your life more efficient and less wasteful. If you can turn a profit by selling some material items you don't need, do so. A good "cleaning out" gives you a feeling of a fresh start. Also, you will be surprised to see that you truly feel freer when you eliminate waste from your life.

Savings Plan

Make a list of the ways in which you think you can cut back on your spending. Use the categories below as a guide.

- Impulse buying
- Buying for occasions
- Habits, hobbies, luxuries
- Waste
- Recreation
- Necessities (clothing, meals, transportation)
- Household expenses
- Educational expenses

Developing a Budget

Use the forms in Figures 11-1 and 11-2 to develop your own budget. Consider these to be working documents. After you have worked out a satisfactory plan, personalize the forms and make a notebook, put them on your computer, or use whatever updating and monitoring system you find comfortable.

BUDGET WORKSHEET		
Item	**Weekly Average**	**Monthly Total**
Housing		
Rent/Mortgage		
Phone		
Electric/Gas		
Food		
Groceries		
Meals Out		
Other		
Transportation		
Fare		
Gasoline		
Auto Payment		
Other		

FIGURE 11-1 Budget Worksheet

PART THREE Developing Your Personal Skills

FIGURE 11-1 Budget Worksheet (*continued*)

BUDGET WORKSHEET		
Item	Weekly Average	Monthly Total
Health		
Doctor's Visits		
Insurance Premiums		
Prescription Drugs		
Other Medication		
Dental Expenses		
Clothing		
School/Work		
Sports/Leisure		
Shoes/Accessories		
Dry Cleaning/Laundry		
Recreation		
Entertainment		
Hobbies		
Other		
Education		
Tuition		
Book/Supplies		
Fees		
Dues		
Other		
Loans		
Personal Loans		
Credit Payments		
Other Expenses		

Maintaining Your Financial Health

The term "financial health" can be interpreted to mean living within your income, being able to cover your expenses, and having funds set aside for the future or for emergencies. No matter how much you may wish you had more money (doesn't everyone?), if you can meet these criteria, you will be financially healthy, because money will not be a major source of worry and stress in your life. The value of budgeting is that it forces you to live within the confines of your income, and to confront the balance of income/expenses on a regular basis. Unusual expenses are planned and, therefore, there is less chance that you will "get in over your head."

| MONTHLY BUDGET |||||
Expense	Budgeted Allowance	Actual Expenditure	Savings	Deficit
Housing				
Food				
Transportation				
Health Care				
Clothing				
Recreation				
Education				
Loans				
Other Expenses				
TOTAL				
		Total Savings		
		Total Deficit		

Month _____

FIGURE 11-2 Monthly Budget

> It is better to have a permanent income than to be fascinating.
> —*Oscar Wilde*

People who do not budget often ignore the feeling that they are taking on too many expenses and getting in over their heads until it is too late. They do this by telling themselves that they will cut back here or there, borrow money and pay it back, use a credit card and pay it off at the end of the month, or whatever rationale makes them feel comfortable spending. This kind of thinking inevitably leads to financial problems. Remember, your goal in managing your money is always to avoid problems. Following are some suggestions for how you can maintain your financial health.

Deal with Deficits

Of course, the number one budget problem is **deficits**—spending more than your income. If a deficit occurs in your budget due to an unplanned expense, such as having to replace a major appliance or helping out a relative who has an emergency, review your upcoming expenses immediately and find places where you can cut back to compensate. If, on the other hand, your budget deficits are a recurring problem, you need to reexamine your spending pattern. There are probably some hidden expenses that need to be uncovered. For many people, this comes back to impulse shopping or supporting habits that could be changed, such as smoking, stopping off for drinks, eating out, and so on.

Use Credit Wisely

Almost any credit advisor will tell you that the only way to use a credit card or charge card is to pay off the balance each month. Of course, this advice flies in the face of the fact that using credit and charge cards to pay for material goods

220   **PART THREE**   Developing Your Personal Skills and services in installments is part of the American way of life. The reality is that, with prices being what they are, most working people simply could not afford "necessities" like a new TV set, a computer, a new winter coat, or storm windows for the house, if these things could not be purchased on credit. In addition, there are some things that you almost literally cannot do without a credit card, such as rent a car or check into a hotel. Most stores accept credit cards more readily than personal checks, and carrying large amounts of cash around is not a safe option.

Credit cards are convenient, they are safer to carry than cash, and they have a certain amount of status attached. The only problem is that they are easy to misuse. For many people, using a credit card does not feel the same as spending cash. It hurts to part with cash, but it feels good to pull out a credit card. It gives you the power to buy something you want or need whether or not you have cash to pay the entire cost of it. If you find yourself running up credit card debts, here are some ideas that can help you.

- Don't carry the cards around in your wallet. Leave them at home in a safe place and take them out only when you plan to make a budgeted purchase. Because the purchase is in your budget, you will be able to pay off the entire amount when the bill comes.
- Don't become a "collector." Customers who pay their bills on time become magnets for creditors. They seek you out with "pre-approved" credit cards and suck you in with offers of low interest rates, cash advances to pay off other creditors, PIN numbers for instant cash from automated tellers, personal checks, and cards for your whole family. No wonder people have a pocket full of plastic—how can they resist? Easy—throw away these offers and never look back.
- If you cannot pay off the entire balance, always pay more than the minimum. The only way to keep your hard-earned cash in your pocket instead of your creditor's is to ignore the minuscule minimum monthly payments. Credit experts advise that even five to ten dollars more than the minimum will greatly reduce your interest payments.

Beware of Cash Machines

For every advantage we get from technological advances, there is a down side. While Automatic Teller Machines (ATMs) are one of modern life's major conveniences, they can also offer another temptation to ignore budgetary constrictions. Say you're out with friends who suddenly decide to splurge on an expensive restaurant meal. You don't have any cash? No problem—we'll find a cash machine on the way. The temptation is too great and you cave in. Another problem that people have with using cash machines is simply forgetting to make note of the withdrawal in their checkbook. This can lead to disaster, both in terms of running out of money, and possibly overdrawing your bank account by writing checks that aren't covered.

Pay Bills on Time

A good credit rating is crucial to maintaining your financial health. If you live within your budget, you will have no problem paying your bills on time. Yet, some people simply do not understand the importance of this. It is important because creditors will report late payments and this will go on your credit record, even if you are not actually far behind in your payments. Whenever you cannot pay a bill on time, notify the creditor. This is best done by telephone, since most company records are computerized and a notation can be made on your record right away. Explain your circumstances briefly, and be prepared to offer a specific date when you will make the payment. Be honest when you do this. False promises on your record will only make the situation worse.

Use Financial Services

In order to be in full control of your money, you need to know exactly where it is and how it is working for you at all times. The first thing you need is a good bank. This means a bank that is conveniently located, offers the services you need, and does not overcharge for its services.

A checking account is essential. Compare services and make sure you understand what you are being charged for writing checks. Some banks have free checking if a minimum balance is kept; others have different criteria for whether and how much they charge for check writing. If you or someone in your family is employed by a company that has a credit union, you may find very favorable terms through this type of institution. Credit unions also offer favorable terms for major purchases (such as automobiles) and for personal loans.

It is a good idea to find a bank that offers the service of direct deposit of paychecks and other income. This will save you time and avoid the discomfort of carrying checks around until you can get to the bank. Also, check with your bank on savings and investment accounts. You need to have some funds set aside for the future or for emergencies. For this you need to find a plan that gives you access to your money when you need it, while offering interest rates that give you the best return on your account.

> **BALANCE YOUR CHECKBOOK!**
>
> Don't neglect balancing your checkbook each time you write a check, and then reconciling it with your bank statement. Banks are not infallible and neither are you—there can be an error on either side. "Bounced" checks are expensive because banks charge a fee for processing them. In addition, uncovered checks will negatively affect your credit record.

Read the Fine Print

Make sure that you understand the terms of any contract or financial agreement you enter into with a bank, creditor, or any other lending institution. Take the time to read the agreement carefully and get answers to any questions you may have. If you are signing an agreement, seek the advice of an expert if you are unsure about what any of the terms mean. Educational loans are treated just like any other creditor arrangement, which means that failure to pay or late payments will be noted on your credit record. Remember that terms for paying back loans you get for your education are probably tied to your status as a full-time or part-time student; your grade point average may also be a factor. Having a clear understanding of what your obligations are up front will help you avoid any problems or surprises at a later date.

> Money is never to be squandered or spent ostentatiously. Some of the greatest people in history have lived lives of the greatest simplicity. Remember it's the you inside that counts. Money doesn't give you any license to relax. It gives an opportunity to use all your abilities, free of financial worries, to go forward, and to use your superior advantages and talents to help others.
>
> —*Rose Fitzgerald Kennedy, Kennedy Family Matriarch*

Solve Financial Problems

If ever you do find yourself in financial trouble, don't keep your head in the sand. No matter how hard it is to postpone purchases or accept that you cannot afford to have something you want, it does not compare to the anguish you will feel if you are unable to meet your monthly expenses. If this happens to you, confront the problem and focus on finding solutions. Financial consulting services, bill consolidation loans, selling property, borrowing from friends or relatives are options that you may have to consider. Remember that waiting for a perfect solution is not the answer. A perfect solution would be winning the lottery, but the chances of that happening are slim. Look for reasonable solutions and implement them immediately, no matter how painful they are. Next to health problems, nothing causes more stress in life than financial problems.

Review and Recall

1. List five sources for financing or supplementing the financing of your educational expenses.

   a. _____

   b. _____

   c. _____

   d. _____

   e. _____

2. Define the following terms:

   a. budgeting: _____

   b. habitual shopping: _____

   c. impulse buying: _____

   d. deficit: _____

3. Explain how using credit cards can cause problems with money management?
   _____
   _____
   _____

4. What are three things you can do to avoid overspending with credit cards?

   a. _____

   b. _____

   c. _____

5. What should you do when you have to miss the due date for paying a bill?
   _____
   _____
   _____

6. List five things you can do to maintain your financial health.

   a. _____

   b. _____

   c. _____

   d. _____

   e. _____

A FINANCIAL HEALTHCARE PLAN

- Practice **delayed gratification**—put off buying today what you can do without until you have more money.

- When you have to buy, be a bargain hunter and comparison shopper.

- If you habitually shop to reward yourself or because it gives you a "thrill" to have something new, make a list of alternative things that will gratify you and keep it displayed where you can see it. Force yourself to select one of these options when you have the urge to shop. (Enlist the help of a relative or a friend, if necessary.)

- If you shop to fill the time or as a relaxing leisure activity, get involved in a hobby, do volunteer work, or make up a list of free activities (like taking a walk, exercising, playing games, fixing things, cooking) that you can do instead.

- Stay away from friends who are leisure-time shoppers, or try to get them involved in your financial healthcare plan.

- Don't make money a source of worry and irritation. Focus on what you have, not what you don't have. A positive attitude toward money frees your mind to handle it constructively and creates opportunities for financial improvement.

- Study economics and learn about investments. Assume that this information will be a necessity in your financial future.

- Have financial goals. Don't assume that you will automatically get better jobs and higher salaries or that you will "grow into" the habit of saving. Financial goals help you identify and stay focused on what you need to do to achieve them.

Apply Critical Thinking

Investment experts recommend starting an investment portfolio as soon as you begin working and saving. You may have heard or seen advertisements that say you can get started with as little as $1000. Assume you have $2000 to use to begin to accumulate your lifetime investment portfolio. How would you invest it? Choose a source of information with which you feel comfortable—books, articles, the Internet, an investment counselor—and investigate possible alternatives for your investment. Based on the information you gather, write a short description of how you would invest your money. Discuss the advantages of the investment and possible disadvantages. Explain why you think the investment is appropriate for you, and what you expect to receive as a return on your investment.

SCANS — School to Work Applications

RESOURCES: ALLOCATES MONEY

1. Project your expenses and income for the next six to twelve months, and develop a long-range budget plan. Consider possible ways that your income may increase or decrease; for example, maybe you plan to work during holidays and school vacations, or maybe you have decided to cut back on your work hours. Determine whether or not, based on what you anticipate at this time, you will be able to manage your finances for this period without running into problems.
   - If you project that your expenses may exceed your income, start now to develop plans that will improve your financial picture.
   - If you project that you will break even, analyze your expenses and look for areas where you can cut back in order to save enough to have a cushion.
   - If you project that you will have extra funds, develop plans for how you can use the extra money to make it work for you. Consider interest-earning bank account options, such as money market funds or Certificates of Deposit; purchasing additional insurance benefits; investing in retirement or annuity plans; or investing in stocks or bonds.

INFORMATION: ORGANIZES AND MAINTAINS INFORMATION.

2. Computerize your monthly budget and your six- to twelve-month budget projections. (Depending on where you are in your computer training, you may do this project now or at a future date.) You may use a spreadsheet program or one of the many financial planning software programs that are available. Consult your computer instructor or, if you wish to purchase software, talk with the service people in the store. Once you have computerized your budgets, you will find it much easier and more efficient to keep them up-to-date, and to make decisions based on "what-if" projections.

SCANS — Workplace Application

Project the salary you expect to be earning five years from now. Consider such things as your current and future work experience, your level of education, and career opportunities in the field you are planning to be working in. If you aren't sure what the salary possibilities are in your field, do some research in the library or on your computer. Trade associations, trade journals, and many career information sources track this kind of information and periodically publish surveys of different fields.

After determining a realistic projection of your salary, design a long-term financial plan for how you will utilize your income to buy the things you want, and live in a way that gives you financial security. As you plan what you will spend, don't forget to consider expenses beyond the initial purchase price for things like a home or new automobile.

After completing the first draft of your plan, share it with a partner or a small group. Try to work with people whose salary goals are in the same range as yours. Analyze each other's plans and critique them in terms of realism, accuracy, and completeness. Determine areas that need additional research. Continue working on this project until you have developed a realistic plan that reflects your goals.

Personal Progress Application

SCANS

PERSONAL QUALITIES: *DISPLAYS RESPONSIBILITY, SELF-ESTEEM, SOCIABILITY, SELF-MANAGEMENT, AND INTERGRITY AND HONESTY*

Most people are not aware of the way money accumulates in a savings plan. The cumulative effect of saving means the earlier you start the better, because you gain the advantage of having the interest on your money earn interest as well as the original principal.

For instance, someone who saves only $1000 per year for ten years, but who starts at age 21, will have $113, 000 *more* at retirement than someone who saves $1000 per year for thirty years, but who starts saving at age 35. Assuming 8% interest compounded monthly, the saver who started at age 21 and saved a total of only $10,000 would retire with a $249,000 nest egg. The saver who contributes $31,000 dollars over thirty years, but who started at age 35 would retire with only $136,000.

The Benefits of Starting Early

Say you save $1,000 every year for the next 10 years. Then say your neighbor does the same for 31 years but doesn't begin until 10 years from now. Who will end up with more money? Your neighbor, right? Not necessarily.

The trick is to start saving early. Here are the results of two hypothetical strategies. Both Katie and Matt put away $1,000 each year. Both left their money untouched until they reached age 65. Both earned the same hypothetical annual return: 8%, compounded monthly. The difference? Katie contributed for only 10 years. Matt started later and contributed for 31 years. Who wound up ahead? Take a look...

Katie
Began contributing:	age 21
Stopped contributing:	age 30
Age now:	65
Total contributed:	$10,000
Contributions or investments grew to:	$249,000

Matt
Began contributing:	age 35
Stopped contributing:	age 65
Age now:	65
Total contributed:	$31,000
Contributions or investments grew to:	$136,000

Katie: $249,000 / $10,000
Matt: $136,000 / $31,000

- Value of investment at age 65
- Amount contributed

These examples are based on annual contributions to a tax-deferred retirement plan. Your own account may earn more or less than this example, and income taxes will be due upon withdrawal from your plan account.

Source: Fidelity Investment Magazine, 1996

Start saving immediately and don't stop until you retire. When you are employed by a company that offers it, the easiest way to save is by payroll deduction—you don't even see the money before it's deposited into your savings vehicle (IRA, 401K, annuity, or other savings plan. Check out a book from the library on retirement planning to learn the differences between the various ways to save).

CHAPTER 11 Managing Your Financial Resources

PART FOUR

Looking Toward the Future

CHAPTER 12
Preparing for Your Career

TWELVE

PREPARING FOR YOUR CAREER

CHAPTER OUTLINE

Resources for Career Planning
College Courses
Career Planning Center
Student Counselors/Advisors
Assessment Instruments
Online Resources

Keeping Your Eye on the Job Market

Selecting a Major
Things to Consider Before Declaring a Major
Preparing for Your Career Outside of the Classroom
Requirements for Completing Your Major

Developing a Career Plan
Goals
Activities
Timelines

Building a Personal Portfolio in College
Transcripts
Character References

Getting Ready for the Job Search

Education today, more than ever before, must see clearly the dual objectives: education for living and educating for making a living.
—James Mason Wood

You enrolled in college at least in part because you want more than a job after graduation. You want a career. While a job is any kind of work for pay, a career is a *chosen* pursuit that appeals to you on a number of levels. It offers a chance for you to grow and excel. It is personally satisfying and should also be financially rewarding.

Just by enrolling in college, you are influencing your career path. You are doing something that will increase your marketability. A college education does not guarantee a high-paying position after graduation, but it does pave the way to careers that tend to pay more than those that do not require postsecondary education. Jacob Mincer, a Columbia University economist, estimates that college-educated employees now earn about 12% more than high-school graduates, up from the previous 7% differential. Brookings Institution economist Thomas Kane states that each year at a community college adds 5% to income, on average.[1]

This chapter provides information to help you consider career choices, select a major, and develop a career plan. With this preparation, you will be ready to go after the career you want.

[1] *Wall Street Journal,* April 29, 1995.

Resources for Career Planning

Finding a career that is right for you involves three crucial steps. The first step is to determine what you like to do and what you are good at. The second step is to determine what types of jobs align with your skills and abilities. The third step is to determine the training and experience you will need to achieve a job in your desired field. Each step of the way, tap the available career planning resources for valuable help with this important decision.

College Courses

> You create opportunity. You develop the capacities for moving toward opportunity. You turn crises into creative opportunities and defeats into successes and frustration into fulfillment. With what? With your great invisible weapons: Your good feelings about yourself, your determination to live the best life you can, and your feeling—that only you can give yourself—that you are a worthwhile, deserving person. You must fight for your right to fulfill the opportunity…to use your life well.
>
> —*Dr. Maxwell Maltz, Author*
> *The Search for Self-Respect*

The school you attend probably offers one or more courses designed to assist students with career assessment and planning. Check your course catalog. The following list of courses offered at a community college suggests the kinds of courses that you may expect to find: *Career and Personal Assessment, Career and Academic Strategies*, and *Job Seeking Skills*. In these courses you will receive guidance in choosing a career, take tests to assess your career interests and aptitudes, receive information on the job market, learn to write a polished résumé, and develop your interviewing skills.

If you plan to take a career planning course, it makes sense to enroll early in your college years. After all, the sooner you know where you are headed, the sooner you can choose classes according to a plan. Not all of your classes will relate to your major or your eventual career, but it is possible to waste valuable time and money on classes that do not move you any closer to your goals. Treat your education seriously so that your course load prepares you for the future.

Career Planning Center

Most schools and universities have a career center or career library. Here you would expect to find personalized help as you research various career fields, make career decisions, analyze job markets, and determine educational requirements for various careers. In addition to a counseling or advisory staff, most career centers have resources that may include books, pamphlets, videos, CD-ROMs, magazines, newsletters, professional journals, and online databases covering all aspects of the career search. Bulletin boards and flyers will note the dates for career workshops and seminars, job fairs, internships, financial aid, and job opportunities. Visit the career center on your school campus to find out what is available.

My Job Experiences

Complete the following sentences:

The best job I ever had was _____.

I liked this job because _____
_____.

The career that I know the most about is _____.

I know about this career because _____
_____.

I would like a career that allows me to _____
_____
_____.

PART FOUR   Looking Toward the Future

Student Counselors/Advisors

Student counselors or advisors are trained to give you guidance in your course work and career choices. If you are not required to meet with your advisor, make an appointment on your own. This is important even if you have a pretty solid career plan, since your advisor may be able to give you some shortcuts or tips to make your school experience a little easier. It is especially important to meet with an advisor if you are unsure of the route you want to take in school or where you want to end up when you're through.

Advisors have access to career assessment instruments and occupational listings. They should also be able to help you wade through course requirements and help you plan your class load so you can graduate on time, with all credits completed. Your advisor may also be able to help you if you are struggling with any aspect of your academic workload.

Assessment Instruments

Unless you are very certain about your career goals, you should plan to take an inventory of your skills and interests. Your college career center can help you with this. Staff at the career center can arrange for you to take one of the many written or computerized self-exploration assessments to help you understand your aptitudes, interests, work values, and abilities. Several of the highly respected assessment tests often used by students to help with career direction are described below. In general, assessment tests will help you identify careers that complement your interests and abilities. Talk to your advisor or a counselor in the career center to determine which tests are available and how they might help you.

> **LOST IN THE CAREER SCRABBLE? CHECK OUT THESE BOOKS!**
>
> *The Occupational Outlook Handbook (OOH)*, produced biannually by the U.S. Bureau of Labor Statistics, is considered the most comprehensive and up-to-date source of information on current occupations. The handbook describes over 250 occupations according to the following categories: nature of the work, working conditions, employment, training, job outlook, earnings, related occupations, and sources of additional information. Two other very useful books are the *Dictionary of Occupational Titles (DOT)*, which describes the functions for over 20,000 occupations, and the *Guide for Occupational Exploration (GOE)*, which arranges occupations according to interest area. These books should be available at your college career center, the college library, or the local library.

- *Career Assessment Inventory, Enhanced Version.* This tool compares occupational interests and personality preferences with those of people in over 100 careers. It does so by relating six General Occupational Themes (realistic, investigative, artistic, social, enterprising, and conventional) to specific occupational areas and non-occupational areas. You can take this test by filling out the test and mailing it to National Computer Systems for analysis. You will receive a report that relates your interests and aptitudes to occupations that require some post-secondary education. A Counselor's Summary graphically represents your individual score on each interest scale. See your instructor for this course for more information on this inventory.
- *Campbell Interest and Skill Inventory (CISS).* The CISS allows you to compare yourself to people working in various career fields. It assumes that the closer your responses are to those persons working in certain fields, the more likely it is that you would do well in those areas. The CISS orientation skills represent seven themes from the work world: influencing, organizing, helping, creating, analyzing, producing, and adventuring. The newest version of this inventory includes a parallel skill scale to estimate an individual's confidence in performing various occupational activities.
- *Holland's Self-Directed Search (SDS).* Like the CISS, this instrument can help you to see how you would fit into a work environment. It does so by categorizing individuals according to six groups: realistic, investigative, artistic, social, enterprising, and conventional.
- *Meyer Briggs Type Indicator (MBTI).* The MBTI has been used for decades to help students understand their personalities, likes, and dislikes. Take it to learn more about yourself, or to assist you with choosing your career.

If you are comfortable navigating in a computer, you can look for computerized self-assessment software programs. The only drawback is that you need to have some computer skills, and you need to locate the necessary hardware and software. The career center at your college may have one or more of the following programs available:

- *The Guidance Information System (GIS).* The GIS provides useful information about required training for many careers. It also contains information about schools and programs of study. It allows users to research independently with a key word search. The user types in a desired topic such as *location, majors,* and *school size* to investigate areas of interest.
- *Interactive Guidance and Information (SIGI).* The SIGI emphasizes individual values, current occupational data, and presents a strategy for making career choices.
- *CHOICES.* This tool focuses on adults in transition. CHOICES allows users to identify transferable skills, look at various occupations, and obtain data about financial aid and application procedures.

More computer-based assessment tools will be available soon. Check your media center or your local or state job resource center to find out what's new in career/interest testing software.

Online Resources

If you have a computer and access to the Internet, you can tap into a wealth of information about career planning and career opportunities. Your college career center or the main library may have computers tied into a major network. Staff can show you how to reach college career centers at major educational institutions. These centers offer a wide range of career planning services for their own students and anyone with online access. For example, Wesleyan University offers a computerized career information and job seeking service called *CIRRUS*, which lists career information that is found on the World Wide Web.

The World Wide Web is growing rapidly. Hundreds of home pages are now posted on the Web by schools and universities, large and small companies, and individuals. Using a key word search function, you can find information on such topics as career planning, job requirements, résumé writing, interviewing skills, placement centers, and job opportunities. America Online (AOL), an Internet service provider, has an extensive Career Center and Career Resource Library. AOL's Career Center provides the information that you would expect to find in a large university career center. Here you can receive help with résumé writing, discover the "hidden" job market, and learn how to obtain and prepare for job interviews. AOL's Career Resource Library offers assistance in areas such as career choices, goal setting, job skills, financial assistance, personality assessment, and career opportunities.

If you have chosen a career that you plan to pursue, assess how far along you are by answering the questions on the next page.

If you checked "Yes" in response to most of the statements, you have a good start in your career planning. Use the "No" statement to guide you in learning more about your chosen career path. For example, if you really don't know what the opportunities are in your chosen field, use the directories mentioned earlier in this chapter for locating information on occupations.

If you don't have a clue regarding the career you want to pursue, don't be discouraged. But don't sit idle, either. The time to start preparing for your career is now, while you are in school, not once you've received a degree and feel pres-

---

GET CREDIT WHERE CREDIT IS DUE

Are you entering school after being in the work force for five, ten, or fifteen years? If so, you may have work and/or life experiences that will translate into credits toward your degree. Talk to your academic counselor to learn whether your school awards credits for your prior experiences outside of the classroom. Also, transfer all outstanding credits from any other school you've attended, even if you obtained the credits years ago. Let the counselor know they exist, and the school will determine if they count toward your current degree program.

How Much Do I Know About My Career?

		Circle One	
1.	I have a file of information on the career I have chosen.	Yes	No
2.	I have talked to people who work in my chosen career field.	Yes	No
3.	I know what college courses I need for this career.	Yes	No
4.	I have studied the job opportunities in this field.	Yes	No
5.	I have worked full- or part-time in this field.	Yes	No
6.	I am familiar with the aptitudes needed in this field.	Yes	No
7.	Tests confirm my aptitudes for this career.	Yes	No
8.	My college courses, work, and extracurricular activities focus on this career.	Yes	No
9.	I have the time and the resources to pursue this career.	Yes	No
10.	I know the salary range and growth opportunities in this field.	Yes	No

sured to get a job. Don't panic if you don't know where you're headed yet, just get moving. Identify the resources near you and start using them.

Keeping Your Eye on the Job Market

Technology has created new careers and changed existing ones. While there are new and emerging fields directly related to technological innovations, the changes in most occupational fields relate to a modification or expansion of job duties and responsibilities. For example, computers are redefining the skill requirements for almost all jobs. At one time, a secretary was expected to type, take dictation, and to file. Today, the job is sure to require computer skills. Store clerks formerly needed only to manage a cash register; today, they must operate a computer. Typesetters used to set type by hand; today they prepare text with computers. Even doctors and nurses are expected to use the computer for monitoring patient care, ordering prescriptions, and researching new therapies.

If you have made your career choice, be sure to keep up with the changes and innovations in your field. Read professional journals, visit job sites, and talk with people working in your chosen profession. Notice how they are using technology. For example, you may be studying to become a nursing assistant, but your program does not require computer proficiency. However, when you visit the local nursing home, you observe that daily records are computerized. Even if you are hired as a nursing assistant without computer skills, promotion to a management or higher level position may well require that expertise.

> **THERE ARE MORE WAYS THAN ONE TO EARN YOUR CREDITS**
>
> When you're a working adult or a parent, it's not always possible to attend classes on a 9 to 5 schedule. Many schools realize this, and offer a variety of ways in which to complete course credits. Some offer evening or intensive weekend classes. Some offer "telecourses"— classes taught on video or through distance learning. You may be able to obtain credits for independent study. Talk to your counselor if you need to explore alternatives to daytime classes.

Selecting a Major

If you have not decided on a major, it is a good idea to take courses that cut across disciplines to help you sift through the possibilities. You have a good chance of discovering your major through these exploratory courses. If you are in a two-year school, you will need to make a decision fairly quickly or confirm that

EXPANDING JOB AREAS

The United States government continually tracks job expansion and decline. Specifically, the Bureau of Statistics in the Department of Labor publishes documents citing the number of expected job openings and the rate of growth in various occupational fields. Data shown below lists occupations that are expected to grow 25% or more between the years 1988 and 2000. Do any of these jobs appeal to you?

Occupation	%
Child Care Workers (Institutional)	27.0%
Computer System Analysts	53.3
Computer Programmers	48.1
Cooks/Chefs	27.2
Engineering Technicians	28.2
Guards	32.2
Home Health Aides	67.9
Lawyers	31.0
Licensed Practical Nurses	36.6
Nursing Aids, Orderlies, and Attendants	31.9
Physicians	76.1
Receptionists and Information Clerks	39.8
Registered Nurses	38.8
Securities and Financial Services Sales Workers	54.8
Social Workers and Human Service Workers	32.4

Source: U.S. Department of Labor, Bureau of Statistics.

---

you feel good about the decision you've already made. If you are attending a four-year school, you can usually declare your major in your second or third year. Before you declare your major, be sure you are confident of your choice. You can change midstream, but you probably will end up taking extra classes to fulfill the requirements of your new major if none of your past coursework transfers.

Remember, people tend to excel when they have a passion for their work. The current trend is to advise students to become specialists in the growing technology sector such as computer programming and design, robotics, aerospace engineering, and health specialties. If any of these careers appeal to you, talk to a career counselor about requirements for that career. Be sure that your college offers the courses and lab work required for entry-level positions in these fields. But don't pick a major only for the job possibilities if you dislike the field. That is almost sure to be a disappointment to you in the long run.

If there are two areas you want to pursue, you can go after a double major, or select a major and a minor area of study. To satisfy the course requirements of a double major, you may have to complete more courses than you normally would for a single major degree. However, a double major does demonstrate to future employers that you are willing to work a little harder than is required. A minor helps you to demonstrate a secondary area of learning that supports or enhances your primary career studies. For example, if you are interested in business and think it would be useful to understand another culture with which American businesses are expanding ties, you may want to consider a Business major and an Asian Studies minor.

Preparing For Your Career Outside of the Classroom

Prospective employers will look at more than your academic record when considering whether you are qualified for the job. You can increase your odds of being the right person by adding layers of experience to your résumé. Outside the classroom, you have the opportunity to find out if the field offers you what you want. Consider the following ways to supplement your formal education.

Get an Internship. Internships are non-paid, working positions that offer hands-on experience in your career field. Many schools require internships to fulfill a degree, and many employers look for internships to show that you are really committed to your career choice. Ask about internship possibilities through your school's career office. Be aware that internships are often very competitive and commonly require you to apply well in advance.

Volunteer. Like an internship, volunteer positions offer hands-on experience and demonstrate your career commitment. You can find out about volunteer opportunities through your local newspaper or your school's career office. If there's nothing posted that relates to what you want to do, why not call a prospective employer and volunteer your services? You can begin by saying you are interested in learning more about the field and can volunteer five hours a week (or whatever amount of time you can spare). If you do volunteer, be responsible and act as though you are in a paid position. If you are too casual about a volunteer position (and fail to show up a time or two), you probably won't be building a good recommendation when it comes time to apply for jobs.

Join an Association. Most career fields have associations that provide training and networking opportunities. Some will be limited to those who are currently employed in the field, but many are open to all interested parties. Most associations charge a fee to join, but will allow guests to attend one or two meetings free of charge. You can demonstrate your commitment to the field and form valuable professional relationships as a member of an association.

Network. To network is simply to connect with the people around you and let them know about your skills and abilities. Tell your friends, your friends' parents and your parents' friends, your neighbors, your hair dresser—just about anyone who might have use for knowing what line of work you are interested in. Make a list of all the professional people you know, and talk with them, whether or not they are in your field. You'll be surprised at how many people say, "I know so-and-so and she's a manager in the field," or something similar.

Your network is basically people who come in contact with other people—so that's just about everybody you bump into! You may learn about an opportunity or get a referral that can help you move toward your career of choice.

Stay Current in the Field. Learn as much as you can about what is happening in your career field so that your knowledge is up-to-date. If your major is political science, you should know what's going on in the major political arenas of the world. If you are in business studies, read the business section of several major newspapers weekly. Read the newspaper and any publications related to your field that can help you stay on top of trends in your field.

Stay Active. Activities such as sports, the arts, and community work are an outlet for physical energy and use of a variety of your talents and skills. In sports, you learn how to concentrate and compete. You have to work hard and demonstrate a certain amount of discipline. When you participate in a variety of activities, you learn cooperation and how to join with others to achieve a common goal. This shows prospective employers that you have the qualities that make for a successful worker.

> The...challenge that confronts us means we do not have time to waste...soaking up the trappings of an affluent society. We need to have a serious outlook most of the time, both on and off the job.
>
> What is needed is a great deal of intellectual honesty, which can only be born of knowledge, awareness, and information about what is going on in the larger world around us, as well as what is going on in our immediate communities, which are a part of that larger world and yet are apart from it. We need to keep on learning, reading, and discussing. In general, we need to take a serious view of the world in which we live.
>
> —H. Naylor Fitzhugh, Businessperson

Requirements for Completing Your Major

As you consider your choice of a major, it is important to understand the requirements for earning a degree. Your college catalog is the place to find this information. It will list the number of credits you need, and how those credits must be distributed across disciplines. In most instances about one-half to two-thirds of your total degree credits will come from your major area of study. You will be required to complete core courses and a number of electives within your major. Then you must complete an assigned number of courses and credits from other disciplines. For example, no matter what area of study you pursue, at most schools you must complete at least one or more composition classes to obtain a two- or four-year degree. Similarly, at most colleges and universities you must fulfill a second language requirement to obtain a four-year degree.

Study your course and credit requirements carefully before diving into a program. You may change your mind about a degree in computer programming after you see that your college requires you to take X amount of mathematics in fulfillment of the major. Another reason to be thoughtful about required coursework is that some required courses will only be offered at certain times, or may be difficult to get into. Plan your course schedule so that you're not stuck with a gap in your program because two required courses are scheduled at the same time, or one is not available when you want to take it.

CHAPTER 12 Preparing for Your Career

My Career Interest

Complete the following sentences.

Two areas of interest that I would like my career to relate to are _____
_____.

Two careers that I would like to know more about are _____ and
_____. These careers seem interesting to me because _____
_____
_____
_____.

Developing a Career Plan

A career plan is a set of goals, activities, and corresponding timelines to help you achieve the career of your choosing. A realistic plan is not static, but changeable. It responds to changes in your life experiences, interests, and the evolving marketplace. You can keep your career plan in your head if you like, but it's much harder to ignore when you put it in writing.

Goals

To identify your career goals, start with the general, then move to the specific. For example, you may know that you want to work with people, which is a broad goal. Perhaps you also know that you want to work with people in a helping role. That's a little more specific. You can move from determining the type of work you like to do to specifying the field in which you'd like to work. Or vice versa. If you like automobiles, you may want to help people by selling them the right car. Or by fixing people's cars. If you're interested in mental health, you may want to help people as a counselor or mental health technician. If you decide you're interested in health careers, but you're not that excited about hands-on work with people, you may want to consider a career as a laboratory technician.

Activities

Next identify career planning activities by listing those steps you must take to attain your career goals. List all activities associated with your goals, both big and small. Some examples include: apply for financial aid, complete an internship, and fulfill degree requirements. Make up a career planning file in which to keep information that you collect about your chosen career field. If you have your own computer, you may also wish to create a computerized file of information, such as names and addresses of contacts, information on organizations and trade associations you plan to contact, and conference dates for professional meetings in your area.

As you get closer to the time where you will begin to look for a job in your field or use your educational background to move up in the field in which you are currently working, your activities should become more focused on collecting information about jobs. Some activities that you will want to put in your goals include:

- Making appointments or social engagements with specific people who can give you information, job leads, or networking sources.
- Collect want ads to stay in touch with what employers are looking for.
- Investigate job opportunities in your field outside of your current location, if relocating is an option.

- Find out about salaries and benefits in the kinds of jobs that you are most qualified for.
- Consider entrepreneurial and freelance opportunities in your chosen field, should the job market become unsettled.
- Identify people who know you personally and professionally and are willing to supply references to future employers.
- Talk to your college career counselor and placement office. Keep track of campus activities such as job fairs and recruitment visits.

These activities become your checklist, helping you keep track of your progress. You will find that your list of activities will grow as you learn more about the career you want, and as the marketplace changes.

Timelines

When you attach timelines to your goals and activities, you give yourself a reason to get moving. Of course, timelines can be altered and extended (and they will be), but they help keep you on track, moving in the right direction. Timelines also force you to look at the big picture. You can make goals on several levels. First, plan what you can do today or this week. Then look at what you'd like to accomplish by the end of the month—or by the end of your school semester.

It's not hard to set timelines once you know what you want to accomplish. How many courses do you have to take each quarter? How long will it take you to complete an internship? Consider talking to someone who is where you hope to be someday, and ask that person to tell you how long it took to get there. Review the time management strategies in Chapter 2 to help manage your career preparation and job-seeking activities.

> **QUOTE**
> The worst part of success is to try to find someone who is happy for you.
> —*Bette Midler*

Building a Personal Portfolio in College

Your class work, extracurricular activities, outside jobs, and your relationships with faculty are all building blocks leading toward your post-college employment. Even if you have not chosen a specific field, your college record will be critically important to any prospective employer.

If you are majoring in a high-demand field, you may have a job offered to you at graduation time; but in most cases, you will have to conduct the job search. And even if a job is waiting, employers still expect your education and work records to be in order. You will need to supply a résumé and references, and you may have to interview with several people in the company. In every case, your transition to work will go more smoothly if you take the time to build a personal portfolio while you're in school.

Your personal portfolio will contain any and all records of your college performance, work history, and personal accomplishments to date. When it comes time to write a résumé, the information will be at your finger tips. Other important items in your portfolio are your college transcript, character references, and samples of your work.

Transcripts

Your college transcript lists your college courses, the number of credits for each course, letter grades or pass/fail, your major and minor concentrations, your GPA (grade point average), and sometimes your rank in the graduating class. Because this document is so important, you should

> **STAY ON TOP OF THE MARKETPLACE, WELL BEFORE YOU PLAN TO ENTER IT**
>
> You should know what's going on in your field of interest, long before you jump into the marketplace. How? Well, most fields have professional journals or newsletters that provide "insider" information on what's new and important. Also, your local newspaper's business section will contain articles on a broad range of businesses and their activities. You never know what type of business will be featured, so keep your eyes open. You may find a company profile useful when you're ready for interviewing. Another article may forecast job opportunities. In any event, you'll learn what kinds of businesses and jobs are really out there. Put related articles and magazine clippings about your field or industry in your career planning file. You'll be glad you did when it comes time to apply for jobs.

be sure that it is accurate. Clear up any errors regarding your courses and grades immediately. For example, if you dropped a course within the allowed timeframe, but your transcript shows a "fail" for that course, contact your instructor or advisor to correct the matter. If you wait until graduation to check on the accuracy of your records, it will be much more difficult to have corrections made.

It is not easy for the person reading a transcript to ascertain the difficulty of the courses that you take. You should not expect that the reader will give you more credit for a C in *Physics* than an A in *Business English*. High letter grades on all courses make the best impression. Thus, if you recognize early on that an elective course is over your head, drop it if you cannot earn a good grade. Obviously, if the course is required for your major, you will have to stick with it. In this case, study extra hard, get a tutor, and join a study group. Avoid taking pass/fail courses and courses that provide questionable academic benefit.

Make it a policy to meet with your advisor at least twice during the year to review your transcript for accuracy. Use this time also to review your progress toward your graduation goals. Discuss electives that you may wish to take during the next term. Focus on electives that sound academic and whose titles reflect a sense of seriousness. A course called *Comic Strip Analysis* actually may be very serious and educational as well as fun, but the title will not convey to the transcript reader the sense of academic seriousness of courses such as *Sixteenth Century Art History, Baroque Music, Statistical Methods for Business Applications*, or *Modern Architecture*.

Character References

Don't wait until graduation time to collect references. Gathering your references should be an on-going process. If you have a fine instructor with whom you are well-acquainted and you are doing exceptionally well in his or her class, ask for a letter of reference. Many professors will be happy to write a short letter on your behalf. On the other hand, some college policies may discourage this activity. In any event, it won't hurt to ask.

Professors sometimes move to other campuses, take sabbaticals, or leave for a variety of reasons. Therefore, ask for a reference as soon as the course is over. If you wait, it may be too late. Also, by waiting until graduation to ask for a reference, you may find that the great impression you made on an instructor is only a faint memory. This is no reflection on you—instructors see hundreds of students each term. It just makes sense to ask for your reference while your great scholarship is fresh in mind.

The same advice applies to references from employers. Ask for character references from your temporary or part-time employers while you are still employed or about to leave. Even though your jobs to date may not relate to your career prospects, your job history shows that you are employable, and should document important characteristics such as promptness, hard work, politeness, computer skills, and team work.

> **QUOTE**
> I long to accomplish a great and noble task, but it is my chief duty to accomplish small tasks as if they were great and noble.
> —Helen Keller

You should have at least four or five written character references, including some from people who know you well on a personal level. Provide these individuals with a copy of your résumé so that their references will tap into your strengths and interests. You should not hesitate to ask for a reference from someone you know well; nor should you be shy about suggesting the form and content. Since you will only be asking people who hold you in high regard, remind them that employers expect character references to emphasize traits of dependability, promptness, hard work, helpfulness, and so forth.

Letters of reference can be filed with the college placement office. This will enable you to have these references sent to prospective employers at any future date. Begin assembling your references early. By the time you graduate, you will have a nice set of references.

Getting Ready for the Job Search

As you approach graduation, it is time to let the world know that you are looking for a job. There are many ways to advertise yourself and to get started on the job search. Some job search activities are similar to those that were recommended when you were looking for a career direction. Begin or renew your networking activities. Tell everyone you know that you are looking for a job upon graduation. Ask employed friends to look within their own company or office for openings. While you are networking, use any or all of the resources discussed here (or earlier in this chapter) for employment opportunities.

- *College Placement Office.* Most colleges have a placement office that assists graduating students in finding employment. The office is in contact with potential employers and has listings of current job openings. They also issue announcements of company recruiting efforts on campus, invite potential employers on campus for job fairs, and assist you in finding information on employers and employment opportunities. Some offices may also offer help with résumés and development portfolios.
- *State Employment Service Offices.* These offices provide free job counseling and help in finding a job. The Employment Service Office for your state is listed in Table 12-1 (at the end of this chapter). You also can locate the Department of Labor's *Guide for Occupational Exploration* and the *Occupational Outlook Handbook* in the Employment Service Office. These books describe:
    - work duties for many different occupations
    - skills and abilities needed for different types of jobs
    - how to enter occupations
    - where jobs are located
    - training and qualifications needed
    - earnings, working conditions, and future opportunities

> **EMPLOYERS' EXPECTATIONS**
>
> Employers are looking for more than competence in the basic skills or even very specific technical skills. They place a high value on personal qualities such as integrity, self-discipline, ethics, honesty, promptness, and reliability. Be sure that you conduct yourself accordingly in your college courses and work situations so that these qualities will be noted in your character references. Extra responsibilities that you take on, such as tutoring, working with the elderly, or organizing a food drive are character-building and say a great deal about your work habits and value system.
>
> Seven Things Employers Want
>
> 1. To be responsible for yourself, your performance, and for your career.
> 2. To present yourself positively and on time every day.
> 3. To get along with others and to work in a team.
> 4. To communicate well and to understand and follow through on communications.
> 5. To solve problems, make decisions, and to learn.
> 6. To follow up, follow through, and get things done.
> 7. To accept feedback in the interest of continuous improvement.

- *Private Employment and Temporary Agencies.* Look in the yellow pages of the telephone book for a list of employment agencies. If you are placed in a job through a private agency, they will charge you or the employer a fee. Be sure that you understand clearly the fee arrangement. Even if you are looking for a full-time position, don't overlook temporary placement services. They offer three important advantages: 1) you can look at a variety of different jobs and get a *feel* for certain types of work, 2) you aren't locked into a long-term commitment, and 3) your temporary work could lead to a permanent position. It is better to be employed when looking for more permanent work. You will feel "less desperate," and it shows your willingness to do whatever it takes.
- *Newspaper Ads.* Check the "help wanted" ads in your local paper daily, or at least on Sunday when most ads appear. If you see a position that interests you, respond to it immediately. If you are looking for a job in another city, you may be able to check ads in major newspapers found in your school or public library.
- *Churches.* Sometimes churches offer employment counseling and job search help. They may even post employment openings on a bulletin board. If you attend a church or synagogue regularly, be sure to let members know of your job search.
- *Unions and Apprenticeship Programs.* Look in the yellow pages of the telephone book under "labor unions," or contact your State Apprenticeship Council. They may list job openings that fit your skills.
- *Journal and Newsletters for Professional or Trade Organizations.* You can find these journals at your local library. You may find openings listed in the journal in your occupational field.
- *Personnel Offices.* Call or visit the personnel offices of companies where you might like to work. Inquire about current job openings and ask them to send you an application. Even if you are not ready to begin working, this information will help you to understand what skills and experience the employer needs.
- *Veteran's Placement Centers.* If you are a veteran, you are entitled to services from this agency. The state employment office can tell you how to locate this agency. The veteran's placement centers often post job listings for their members.
- *Community Organizations.* Don't overlook clubs, associations, women and minority centers, or youth organizations. Some of these groups list job openings on their bulletin boards or in their newsletters.
- *Online Information Networks.* You can use your computer in your job search. O*NET provides a comprehensive database that identifies important information about occupations, worker skills, and training requirements. Check with the public library or your career center for help in linking you to this giant database.

Follow-Up Activities

Summarize how the following activities can help you prepare for a career.

Talking with a Career Counselor _____

_____

Networking _____

_____

Building a Personal Portfolio _____
_____
_____

Working for a Temporary Employment Agency _____
_____
_____

Review and Recall

1. Three steps to career planning are:

    a. _____

    b. _____

    c. _____

2. List five sources for assistance with career planning.

    a. _____

    b. _____

    c. _____

    d. _____

    e. _____

3. Describe what you can learn from a self-assessment test. _____
_____

4. Explain how the Internet can help you with career planning. _____
_____
_____

5. Name one advantage and one disadvantage of a liberal arts major.

    a. _____

    b. _____

6. Describe what you can do to prepare for your career outside of the classroom. Give specific examples that you can include in your career plan.
_____
_____

7. Where can you learn degree requirements, and what will they linclude?
_____
_____
_____

8. Explain what a career plan is and why is it useful. _____
_____
_____

CHAPTER 12 Preparing for Your Career

9. What is a personal portfolio? Why do you need one? _____
_____
_____

10. List three sources for information on job openings?

    a. _____

    b. _____

    c. _____

Apply Critical Thinking

Use the image streaming technique you practiced in Chapter 8 to do some creative thinking about your desired career. Let your mind expand as far as it can go to formulate a picture of your ideal job and career. After listening to the tape, assess your reaction to it. On a scale of 1 to 10, with 1 being reality and 10 being pure fantasy, rate your image stream career. If your rating is higher than 5, make up a list of questions to yourself that will help you discover why you feel your ideal career is in the realm of fantasy. If your rating is lower than 5 make up a list of questions to yourself that will help you discover whether you are putting unnecessary limits on your dreams.

SCANS — School to Work Applications

INFORMATION: *ACQUIRES AND INTERPRETS INFORMATION*

1. Research emerging fields. Pick one of the following fields and use the library or online sources to discover related careers.
   Aerospace
   Robotics
   Computer-aided design (CAD)
   Biotechnology
   Fiber optics

2. If you are drawing a blank on career opportunities, go to the library or get on the Internet and investigate careers. Pick three of the following careers and find out required education/training and duties.
   Real-estate appraiser
   Financial advisor
   Home economist
   CAD/CAM designer
   Systems analyst
   Insurance claims adjuster
   Network administrator/consultant
   Registered nurse
   Public safety officer
   Physical therapist
   Juvenile social worker

3. If you are unsure of your career goals, narrow your search by identifying ten things you like to do, and five careers that would allow you to do one or more of those things. What real skills and abilities would you need to obtain a position in any of the five careers you identified? Be realistic, but stretch the possibilities.

PART FOUR   Looking Toward the Future

4. List all of your recent and current hobbies and extracurricular interests. How do they relate to your career choice? If nothing seems to relate, can you make room for something else that might further your chances in your career choice? List all possible activities (other than taking a class) that might better prepare you for your future career.
5. Use the want-ads to identify four positions that interest you. Identify the education and skills required for each position. How do these requirements line up with the courses you have taken or plan to take? Will you be prepared for this type of job after graduation? Could you involve yourself in extracurricular activities or a part-time job that might prepare you for any of the positions?
6. Obtain at least one character reference for your personal portfolio. Show it to your counselor or advisor and ask him or her to assess its effectiveness. If the letter is not strong enough to help you, discuss what you can do to generate more effective letters of recommendation.

Workplace Application

SCANS

You work in the career counseling department of a small community college. Your current assignment is to forecast the job market in your area in preparation for a seminar on career opportunities, and make a pitch for the corresponding degree programs offered at the college.

To prepare for your presentation, research local career opportunities. Then create a table that contains at least six "hot jobs," starting pay scales and duties, and corresponding degree and course requirements.

Personal Progress Application

SCANS

PERSONAL QUALITIES: DISPLAYS RESPONSIBILITY, SELF-ESTEEM, SOCIABILITY, SELF-MANAGEMENT, AND INTEGRITY AND HONESTY

Read the "Manages Time" section of SCANS. The idea of goal-related activities and how to plan them across time is an important ability to develop, both as an employee and as an individual.

Creating a timeline is one way to help you plan your direction and figure out steps to help you achieve your goals. One way to construct a timeline is presented in the following exercise.

Turn a sheet of paper horizontally and draw a straight line across the paper, close to the top edge. On the left end of the line mark your birth date. On the right end of the line mark your death date (meaning, the date on which, if your life goes as you want it to, you will be satisfied with the life you've lived and will be ready to die with no regrets). Between the two points mark today's date in relative position.

Between your birth date and today's date, mark the three biggest accomplishments of your life so far in their relative positions. This will give you some perspective on where you've been.

Now, between today's date and your death date, figure out the three biggest accomplishments you want to achieve in your life. Determine a date for reaching each of those three goals, and mark them at the appropriate spots on the timeline.

Remember, for something to be a goal, as opposed to a wish or a dream, it must have a deadline, be specific, and be measurable. To say, "I want to be rich," is expressing a wish, not a goal. "I want to be rich" is not specific (you haven't defined "rich"), it doesn't have a deadline (you haven't said by what specific date you want to be rich), and it's not measurable (you haven't explained how you're going to measure your richness; will it be in terms of money, relationships, or achievements?).

Each of the three goals on your timeline must have those three characteristics.

Finally, under each goal on your timeline, list the specific steps you can think of (with the next-to-last step right under the goal and the others in order below that one) that will be necessary for you to take to reach your goal.

CHAPTER 12 Preparing for Your Career

There are several reasons for constructing this timeline:

1. It will help you figure out strategies to reach your goals.
2. It will tell you if your timeframes are realistic for achieving your goals.
3. It will solidify your goals by forcing you to think concretely about them and how, specifically, to achieve them.
4. It will send a message to your subconscious that you value your goals. Your subconscious is quite aware that most major events in your life (birth, graduations, marriages and divorces, wills, declarations of what you're worth—financial statements, prestigious awards, and so on) are legitimized by some kind of document. Your timeline is such a document, because it is probably the one written-down blueprint of your future.

STATE EMPLOYMENT SERVICE OFFICES

ALABAMA
Employment Service,
 Dept. of Ind. Rel.
649 Monroe Street
Montgomery, AL 36130
(205) 261-5364

ALASKA
Employment Service
 Empl. Sec. Div.
P.O. Box 3-7000
Juneau, AK 99802
(907) 465-2712

ARIZONA
Department of Economic
 Security
P.O. Box 6123
Site Code 730A
Phoenix, AZ 85005
(602) 542-4016

ARKANSAS
Employment Security
 Division
P.O. box 2981
Little Rock, AR 72203
(501) 371-1683

CALIFORNIA
Job Service Division
Empl. Dev. Dept.
800 Capitol Mall,
Sacramento, CA 95814
(916) 322-7318

COLORADO
Employment Programs
 Div. of Empl. & Trng.
251 East 12th Avenue
Denver, CO 80203
(303) 866-6180

CONNECTICUT
Job Service
 CT Labor Department
200 Folly Brook Blvd.
Wethersfield, CT 06109
(203) 566-8818

DELAWARE
Employment & Trng. Div.
 DE Department of Labor
P.O. Box 9029
Newark, DE 19711
(302) 368-6911

DISTRICT OF COLUMBIA
Office of Job Service
 Dept. of Empl. Services
500 C Street, NW, Rm. 317
Washington, DC 20001
(202) 639-1115

FLORDIA
Dept. of Labor & Empl. Sec.
1320 Executive Center Cir.
300 Atkins Building
Tallahassee, FL 32301
(904) 488-7228

GEORGIA
Employment Service
148 International Blvd, N
 Room 400
Atlanta, GA 30303
(404) 656-0380

HAWAII
Employment Service
 Division
 Dept. of Labor & Ind. Rel.
1347 Kapiolani Blvd.
Honolulu, HI 96814
(808) 548-6468

IDAHO
Operations Div. Emp. Svc.
 Dept of Empl.
317 Main Street
Boise, ID 83735
(208) 334-3977

ILLINOIS
Employment Services
 Employment Security
 Division
910 S. Michigan Avenue
Chicago, IL 60605
(312) 793-6074

INDIANA
E.S., Employment
 Security Div.
10 North Senate Avenue
Indianapolis, IN 46204
(317) 232-7680

IOWA
Job Service Program Bureau
Department of Job Service
1000 East Grand Avenue
Des Moines, IA 50319
(515) 281-5134

KANSAS
Div. of Employment
 & Training
 Dept. of Human Resources
401 Topeka Avenue
Topeka, KS 66603
(913) 296-5317

KENTUCKY
Dept. for Employment
 Services
275 E. Main Street, 2nd Fl
Frankfort, KY 40621
(502) 564-5331

Table 12-1 State Employment Serevice Office

LOUISIANA
Employment Service
Office of Employment
 Security
P.O. Box 94094
Baton Rouge, LA 70804-
 9094
(504) 342-3016

MAINE
Job Service Division
 Bureau of Employment
 Security
P.O. Box 309
Augusta, ME 04330
(207) 289-3431

MARYLAND
MD Department
 of Employment &
 Economic Development
1100 North Eutaw St.,
 Rm. 701
Baltimore, MD 21201
(301) 383-5353

MASSACHUSETTS
Div. of Employment Security
Charles F. Hurley Building
Government Center
Boston, MA 02114
(617) 727-6810

MICHIGAN
Bureau of Employment
 Service,
Employment Security
 Commission
7310 Woodward Avenue
Detroit, MI 48202
(313) 876-5309

MINNESOTA
Job Service & UI
 Operations
690 American Center
 Bldg.
150 East Kellogg
St. Paul, MN 55101
(612) 296-3627

MISSISSIPPI
Employment Service
 Division
Employment Service
 Commission
P.O. Box 1699
Jackson, MS 39215-1699
(601) 354-8711

MISSOURI
Employment Service
Division of Employment
 Security
P.O. Box 59
Jefferson City, MO 65104
(314) 751-3790

MONTANA
Job Service/Employment
 and Training Division
P.O. Box 1728
Helena, MT 59624
(406) 444-4524

NEBRASKA
Job Service
NE Dept. of Labor
P.O. Box 94600
Lincoln, NE 68509
(402) 475-8451

NEVADA
Employment Service
Employment Security
 Department
500 East Third Street
Carson City, NV 89713
(702) 885-4510

NEW HAMPSHIRE
Employment Service
 Bureau,
Department of Employment
 Security
32 South Main Street
Concord, NH 03301
(603) 224-3311

NEW JERSEY
NJ Department of Labor
 Labor & Industry Bldg.,
 CN 058
Trenton, NJ 08625
(609) 292-2400

NEW MEXICO
Employment Service
Employment
 Security Department
P.O. Box 1928
Albuquerque, NM 87103
(305) 841-8437

NEW YORK
Job Service Division
 NY State Department
 of Labor
State Campus
Building 12 g
Albany, NY 12240
(518) 457-2612

NORTH CAROLINA
Employment Security
 Commission of North
 Carolina
P.O. Box 27625
Raleigh, NC 27611
(919) 733-7522

NORTH DAKOTA
Employment & Training
 Division
 Job Service North Dakota
P.O. Box 1537
Bismarck, ND 58502
(701) 224-2842

OHIO
Employment Service
 Division
Bureau of Employment
 Services
145 S. Front Street, Rm. 640
Columbus, OH 43215
(614) 466-2421

OKLAHOMA
Employment Service
 Employment Security
 Commission
Will Rogers Memorial Ofc.
 Bldg.
Oklahoma City, OK 73105
(405) 521-3652

OREGON
Employment Service
 OR Employment Division
857 Union Street, N.E.
Salem, OR 97311
(503) 378-3212

PENNSYLVANIA
Bureau of Job Service
 Labor & Industry Building
Seventh & Forster Streets
Harrisburg, PA 17121
(717) 787-3354

PUERTO RICO
Employment Service
 Division
Bureau of Employment
 Security
505 Munoz Rivera Avenue
Hato Rey, PR 00918
(809) 754-5326

RHODE ISLAND
Job Service Division
 Dept. of Employment
 Security
24 Mason Street
Providence, RI 02903
(401) 277-3722

Table 12-1 State Employment Service Office *(continued)*

SOUTH CAROLINA
Employment Service
P.O. Box 995
Columbia, SC 29202
(803) 737-2400

SOUTH DAKOTA
SD Department of Labor
700 Governors Drive
Pierre, SD 57501
(605) 773-3101

TENNESSEE
Employment Service
 Dept. of Employment
 Security
503 Cordell Hull Building
Nashville, TN 37219
(615) 741-0922

TEXAS
Employment Service
 Texas Employment
 Commission
12th & Trinity, 504BT
Austin, TX 78778
(512) 463-2820

UTAH
Employment Services/Field
 Oper.
Department Employment
 Security
174 Social Hall Avenue
Salt Lake City, UT 84147
(801) 533-2201

VERMONT
Employment Service
Dept. of Employment
 and Training
P.O. Box 488
Montpelier, VT 05602
(802) 229-0311

VIRGINIA
Employment Service
 VA Employment
 Commission
P.O. Box 1258
Richmond, VA 23211
(804) 786-7097

VIRGIN ISLANDS
Employment Service
Employment Security
 Agency
P.O. Box 1090
Charlotte, Amalie, VI 00801
(809) 776-3700

WASHINGTON
Employment Security
 Department
212 Maple Park
Olympia, WA 98504
(206) 753-0747

WEST VIRGINIA
Employment Service
 Division
Dept. of Employment
 Security
112 California Avenue
Charleston, WV 25305
(304) 348-9180

WISCONSIN
Job Service
P.O. Box 7905
Madison, WI 53707
(608) 266-8561

WYOMING
Employment Service
Employment Security
 Commission
P.O. Box 2760
Casper, WY 82602
(307) 235-3611

NATIONAL OFFICE
United States Employment
 Service
200 Constitution Ave. NW
Washington, DC 20210
(202) 539-0188

INDEX

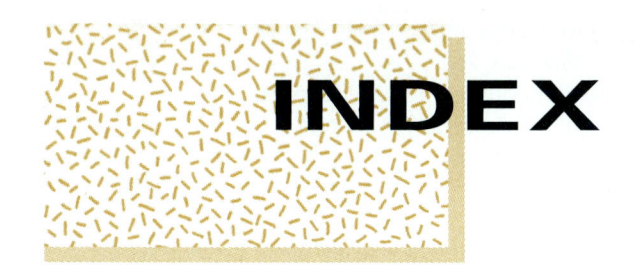

A

abstracts, 64–65
abuse, substance, 206, 207–8
academic standing, 24
active listening, 81–83, 134
active reading, 93–108
   advantages of, 93–95
   techniques of, 95–108
   tests and, 134
active thinking, 156. *see also* creative thinking; critical thinking skills
addiction, 204
adjectives, 119
adult students, 13
adverbs, 119
advisors, 23, 238
aerobic exercise, 204
aggressive behavior, 177, 179
AIDS, 208–10
alcohol, 206
America Online (AOL), 66–67, 232
analysis
   in critical thinking process, 160
   in essay test questions, 146
antioxidants, 201, 204
aptitudes, in selecting major, 19
arithmetic, in SCANS program, 20
assertiveness, 177–78
association, memory and, 141
associations, 235
assumptions, 80–81
atlases, 65
attendance, class, 81, 85
attention, in class, 82–83
automatic teller machines (ATMs), 221

B

balanced diet, 201
bar graphs, in active reading, 99–100
behavior patterns, 175
bibliographies, 126
body image, 203
books, in library, 63, 64
Books in Print, 64
boundaries, personal, 175–76
brainstorming, 162, 163–64
brochures, 65
buddy system
   learning styles and, 10
   for study, 10, 61, 85
budgeting, 216–19
   developing a budget, 218–19
   spending habits in, 216–17
burnout, as cause of procrastination, 44
Burns, David, 5–6, 8

C

calendars, 38
calories, 202
Campbell Interest and Skill Inventory (CISS), 231
campus services, 23, 24
carbohydrates, 204
Career Assessment Inventory, Enhanced Version, 231
career planning, 229–46
   developing plan for, 236–37
   job market and, 233
   job search and, 234, 239–40, 244–46
   major in college and, 233–36
   personal portfolio in, 237–39
   resources for, 230–33
career planning services, 23, 230–32, 239
cash machines, 221
CD ROMs, 66
change, as constant, 19
character references, 238–39
checking accounts, 222
CHOICES, 232
cholesterol, 204
classroom learning, 76–91
   active listening in, 81–83
   after-class review in, 86–87, 90–91
   classroom participation in, 85
   guidelines for, 79–81
   notetaking in, 83–85
   positive attitude for, 77–79
class schedules, 35–37
clear messages, 113–15
client/customer service, in SCANS program, 22

247

clippings, 65
clubs, student, 23
coffee, 142
college catalog, 22, 23
communication skills, 186–87
commuting students, 12
comparing and contrasting
   in critical thinking, 157, 160–61
   in essay test questions, 145–46
complex constructions, 115
CompuServe, 66
computer catalogs, 63, 69
computerized test banks, 145–46
computers, 126–28
   in career planning, 232–33, 240
   desktop publishing and, 127
   electronic storage and, 127
   formatting capabilities, 127–28
   laptops, 69
   literacy in using, 68
   notetaking with, 69, 105
   in research process, 69
   skills in, and SCANS program, 22
   word processing and, 127
conceptualization, in critical thinking process, 160
concise messages, 116
conflict resolution, in personal relationships, 174, 179
considerate messages, 116–17
contact hours, 23
convergent thinking, 163
coping mechanisms, 46–47, 196–200
Cornell Note-Taking System, 84
counseling services, 23
courses
   career assessment and planning, 240
   credits for, 23
   electives, 24
   finances and, 24
   grading systems for, 23–24
   in major, 19, 23
   transfer, 24
creative thinking, 162–69
   brainstorming in, 162, 163–64
   defined, 156
   image streaming in, 171–72
   problem solving in, 165–69
   in SCANS program, 20
credit cards, 220–21
credit hours, 23, 24
credit rating, 221–22
credits, 23, 232, 233
critical thinking skills, 155–72
   creative thinking, 162–69
   in decision making, 157, 158
   defined, 156
   importance of, 156
   obstructions to, 165
   in problem solving, 157–58, 165–69
   techniques to sharpen, 158–62
   tests and, 134
criticism, 183
cues, 140

D

daily planners, 39–41
dangling modifiers, 115
data collection, 68
deadlines
   financial aid, 216
   for goals, 16
   procrastination and, 44
decision making
   critical thinking in, 157, 158
   regarding college major, 19, 233–34
   in SCANS program, 20, 22
deductive paragraph construction, 114
deficits, 220
define, in essay test questions, 145
delayed gratification, 223
dependency status, 215
describe, in essay test questions, 146
desk calendars, 38
desks, 56–58
desktop publishing, 127
diagrams, in active reading, 100
dictionaries
   specialized, 65
   unabridged, 65
   word hurdles and, 106
diet, 47, 200–202
directories, 65
discuss, in essay test questions, 145
dissertation abstracts, 65
distorted thinking, 5–6, 8
divergent thinking, 163
diversity
   appreciating, 14
   defined, 11
   in SCANS program, 22
   of student population, 11–14
   valuing, 188
drafting process, 121–23
drawings, in active reading, 100–101
drug use, 204–8
   abuse, 206, 207–8
   drinking alcohol, 206
   illegal drugs, 206–8
   prescription drugs, 206–8
   smoking, 204–6

E

electives, 24
E-mail, 66
emergencies, and class attendance, 81, 85
employment
   adult students and, 13
   character references and, 239
   finances and, 214
empowerment, 179
encoding, 139, 140
encyclopedias
   general, 64
   specialized, 65
endorphins, 204
ergonomics, 57
essays, 68, 124–25
essay test questions, 144–46
exercise and fitness, 47, 143, 202–3, 204
explain, in essay test questions, 145
external stressors, 195

F

Facts on File, 65
family responsibilities, time management and, 35, 46
fat, 204–5
fear, as cause of procrastination, 43
Federal Family Education Loan, 215
Federal Perkins loans, 215
Federal Supplemental Educational Opportunity Grant (FSEOG), 214–15
finances, 24, 213–25
   budgeting and, 216–19
   employment and, 214
   financial health and, 219–22
   loans and grants in, 214–15, 216
   in SCANS program, 21
   scholarships in, 215, 216
financial aid, 24, 214–15, 216
first-generation students, 12–13
flash cards, 137, 142, 152
focus
   in classroom, 82–83
   in studying, 59–60
footnotes, 126

G

gender bias, 117
goals
   career, 236
   educational, 15–24
   setting, 15–18, 60
   study, 60
   of writing, 113
government documents, 65
grade point average (GPA), 23–24, 237–38
grading systems, 23–24
grammar, 118–19
grants, 214–15
graphics
   in active reading, 98–101
   in classroom learning, 90–91
Guidance Information System (GIS), 232

H

habit, 204
habitual shopping, 217
health care
   alcohol use and, 206
   exercise and, 47, 143, 202–3, 204
   nutrition and, 47, 200–202
   other drugs and, 206–8
   sex life and, 208–11
   sleep and, 46, 59, 79, 142
   smoking and, 204–6
   stress and, 46–47, 195–200
health services, 23
history, active reading and, 107–8
hobbies, 217
Holland's Self-Directed Search (SDS), 231
hostile environment sexual harassment, 185
human resource management, in SCANS program, 21

I

illness, and class attendance, 81, 85
image streaming, 171–72
impulse buying, 217
incomplete grades, 23
indexes, special, 64
inductive paragraph construction, 114
information skills, in SCANS program, 22
inner voice, 5, 199
instincts, 165
instructors
   focusing on, 82
   and learning style, 10–11
   and motivation for learning, 78
   talking to, 81, 85, 180–85
   and teaching style, 10, 30, 85
integrity/honesty
   in SCANS program, 21
   tests and, 144
intensity, exercise, 205

Interactive Guidance and Information (SIGI), 232
interactive tests, 146
interests, in selecting major, 19
internal stressors, 195
Internet, 66
internships, 234
interpreting, in critical thinking process, 159

J

jargon, 117
job search, 239–40
    expanding job areas, 234
    state employment service offices, 244–46
journal entries, 124

K

key words, in essay tests, 144–46
kinesthetic learning, 7, 9

L

laboratory tests, 146
language
    evolution of, 117
    grammar basics for writing, 118–19
leadership skills, 22, 187–88, 192–93
learning styles, 7–11
    nature of, 7
    self-assessment of, 9–10, 29–30
    sensory activities in, 7, 9
    tests and, 134
    working with, 10–11
learning techniques, in SCANS program, 21
librarians, 63
libraries, 23, 63–67, 126
    nonprint media, 65–66
    online information sources, 66–67, 232
    print reference materials, 64–65
    public, 64
Library of Congress Subject Headings, 63
line graphs, in active reading, 99–100
listening
    active, 81–83, 134
    critical, 84
    and learning style, 9
    in relationships, 179
    in SCANS program, 20
literature, active reading and, 107
loans, 215, 216
long-term memory, 63, 139

M

major
    choosing, 19, 233–34
    defined, 19
    grades and, 23
    requirements for completing, 19, 235
maps, 65, 101
master schedules, 38
mastery, 55
matching questions, 144
math anxiety, 107
mathematics
    active reading and, 107
    in SCANS program, 20
matriculated students, 23
maturity, 198–99
memory
    assessment of, 62
    improving, 60, 75, 138–42
    levels of, 63, 139–41
mental blocks, 106
messages, 113–19
    clear, 113–15
    concise, 116
    considerate, 116–17
Meyer Briggs Type Indicator (MBTI), 231
minority-group students, 13–14
mnemonics, 142
money management. *see* finances
motivation
    and active reading, 95
    and connecting with learning, 77–78
    procrastination and, 44
multimedia, 66
multiple-choice questions, 143

N

national and community service, 215
natural instincts, 165
needs, in selecting major, 19
negative self-talk, 199
negative thinking, 5–6, 8, 76
negotiation skills, 179–80
networking, 235
nicotine patch, 205
nonmatriculated students, 23
nonprint media, 65–66
nontraditional students, 11
    adult, 13
    minority-group, 13–14
notes and notetaking
    in active reading, 104–5

after-class review of, 86–87, 90–91
before-class review of, 80
classroom, 83–85
computers in, 69, 105
organization for, 80
in research process, 69, 126
in test preparation, 137
nutrition, 47, 200–202

O

objective tests, 143–44
online information sources, 66–67, 232
open-book tests, 146–47
optimists, 198
organization
 for classroom learning, 80
 of paper, 114
 for research, 68–69
 self-assessment of, 33–34
 of study space, 56–58
 see also time management
organizations, student, 23
outlines, 120, 121, 145
overweight, 205

P

pamphlets, 65
paragraphs, clarity of, 114
passive-aggressive behavior, 179
passive behavior, 177, 179
passive reading, 93
Pauk, Walter, 84
Pell Grant Program, 214–15
perfectionism, 5, 43–44
performance appraisal, tests and, 147–48
performance-based tests, 146
periodicals, in library, 63
pessimists, 198
photographs, in active reading, 101
physical activity
 exercise, 47, 143, 202–3, 204
 memory and, 142
pie charts, in active reading, 100
plans and planning
 career, 229–46
 daily, 39–41
 defined, 32
 project, 43, 44
 in research process, 67–69
 study, 135–36
 for taking tests, 142–43, 145
 time projections in, 32

weekly, 39–41
in writing process, 119–21
positive self-talk, 199
positive thinking
 and classroom learning, 77–79
 distorted thinking versus, 5–6, 8
 stress and, 198–99
 tests and, 139
previews
 reading assignment, 96–97
 textbook, 96
print reference materials, 64–65
priorities, in time management, 33, 37–38, 41, 45–47
prior knowledge, 97
problem solving
 creative thinking skills in, 165–69
 critical thinking skills in, 157–58
 financial, 222
 with instructors, 182–83
 in SCANS program, 20–21
 stress and, 198
procrastination, 42–45
 causes of, 43–44
 defined, 42
 reducing, 44–45
Prodigy, 66
professors. see instructors
project planning, 43, 44
pronouns, 118–19
proofreading, 122–23, 145
protein, 205
purpose, in active reading, 95–96

Q

questions
 in active reading, 97–98
 in classroom learning, 85
 in critical thinking process, 158–59
 test, 143–47
quid pro quo sexual harassment, 184–85

R

Readers' Guide to Periodical Literature, 64, 69
reading
 active, 93–108, 134
 and learning style, 9
 in SCANS program, 20
reading assignment, preview of, 96–97
reasoning
 in SCANS program, 21
 see also critical thinking skills
recall, 140–41

INDEX 251

recitation, 60
recognition, 140–41
relationships, 173–93
   with instructors, 81, 85, 180–85
   with others on campus, 185–88
   personal, 174–80
   responsibility in, 180
remembering, 139–41
reports, 68, 125–26
rereading, 101–3, 145
research papers, 68, 126
   bibliographies for, 126
   footnotes for, 126
   formatting, 127–28
research skills, 63–69
   information gathering, 69
   libraries and, 63–67
   planning and, 67–69
resource management, in SCANS program, 21
responsibility
   family, 35, 46
   in relationships, 180
   in SCANS program, 21
retrieval, 139, 140–41
review
   after class, 86–87, 90–91
   before class, 80
   of tests, 147–48
reward system, 57, 201–2
rote memorization, 141–42
run-on sentences, 114–15

S

safe sex, 208–11
saturated fat, 204
scanning, 96–97
SCANS (Secretary's Commission on Achieving Necessary Skills), 20–22
   basic skills, 20
   information skills, 22
   interpersonal skills, 21–22
   personal qualities, 21
   resources, 21
   systems skills, 22
   technology skills, 22
   thinking skills, 20–21
schedules, 35–38
   in career planning, 237
   class, 35–37
   master, 38
scholarships, 215, 216
science, active reading and, 107
seat location, 79–80

self-esteem, 4–11
   boundaries and, 175–76
   criticism and, 183
   defined, 4
   features of, 5
   learning style and, 7–11, 29–30
   positive thinking and, 5–6, 8
   in SCANS program, 21
   tests and, 139
self-fulfilling prophecies, 80–81
self-management, in SCANS program, 21
sensory activities, 7, 9
sensory register, 63, 139
sentences, clarity of, 114–15
sex life, 208–11
sexual harassment, 184–85
sexually transmitted diseases (STDs), 208–10
short answer/fill-in questions, 144
short-term memory, 63, 139
sleep habits, 46, 59, 79, 142
smoking, 204–6
sociability, in SCANS program, 21
speaking, in SCANS program, 20
special indexes, 64
staff assistants, 63
stress, 195–200
   handling, 46–47, 196–200
   reactions to, 195–96
   signs of, 195
student services/support, 23
student status, 23
study groups, 61–62, 85, 139
study partners, 10, 61
study skills, 55–62
   focus in, 59–60
   goal setting, 60
   sleep habits and, 59
   study space and, 56–58
   techniques, 60–62
   see also reading; tests; writing
subjective test questions, 144–46
subject-verb agreement, 118
substance abuse, 206, 207–8
success
   defining, 3
   happiness and, 19
summaries
   in after-class review, 86–87
   in writing process, 122
summarize, in essay test questions, 146
support systems
   buddy system in study, 10, 61, 85
   classroom, 85
   groups in, 188
   learning style and, 10–11

study groups, 61–62, 85, 139
time management and, 35
tutors in, 148
see also relationships
synthesizing, in critical thinking process, 161–62
systems
college, 22–24
defined, 22
grading, 23–24
time management, 32, 33, 34–42
systems skills, in SCANS program, 22

T

tables, in active reading, 101
talk, self, 5, 199
talking
active reading and, 103
in class participation, 85
classroom learning and, 60
to instructors, 81, 85, 180–85
learning style and, 9
teachers. *see* instructors
teaching skills, in SCANS program, 21
teaching style, 10, 30, 85
teamwork, in SCANS program, 21
technology skills, in SCANS program, 22
term papers, 68
term schedules, 38
test anxiety, 147
tests, 133–52
cheating on, 144
and classroom learning, 83
memory improvement and, 138–42
preparing for, 62, 134–37
strategies for taking, 142–48
textbooks
before-class review of, 80
breaking in, 97
highlighting, 104
margin notes in, 105
notes from, 86–87
previewing, 96
reading beyond, 105–6
in test preparation, 137
underlining, 104
see also active reading
thesaurus, 65
time management, 31–51
To Do lists in, 41–42, 44
family responsibilities and, 35, 46
organization and, 33–34
plans in, 32, 39–42, 43
priorities in, 33, 37–38, 41, 45–47

procrastination and, 42–44
in research process, 68–69
in SCANS program, 21
schedules in, 35–38, 237
stress reduction and, 35, 46–47
support systems in, 35
system for, 32, 33, 34–42
tests and, 134, 135, 143, 145
time projections in, 32
time wasters and, 47
To Do lists, 41–42, 44
trace, in essay test questions, 145
traditional students, 11–13
commuting, 12
defined, 11–12
first-generation, 12–13
transcripts, 237–38
transfer courses, 24
true-false questions, 143
tutors, 148

U

unsaturated fat, 205

V

verbs
forms of, 118
and subject-verb agreement, 118
visualization
in active reading, 98
goals in, 16
and learning style, 9
memory and, 141
in SCANS program, 21
volunteer work, 234

W

waivers, course, 23
weekly planners, 39–41
weight loss, 201
Wilson, Susan B., 16–17
word processing, 127
words
clarity of, 115
hurdles caused by, 106
respectful, 117
workaholism, 198
Work-Study Program, 215
World Wide Web, 232

worry, as cause of procrastination, 43
writing, 112–32
    computers and, 126–28
    drafting process in, 121–23
    essays, 124–25
    journal entries, 124
    and learning style, 9
    message in, 113–19
    planning in, 119–21
    proofreading in, 122–23
    reports, 125–26
    research papers, 126
    in SCANS program, 20
    in subjective and essay tests, 144–46